Regulation and Innovation in Financial Markets

Safae Ismaili
https://orcid.org/0009-0007-3971-8860
TALY Green & Growth, Morocco

IGI Global
Scientific Publishing
Publishing Tomorrow's Research Today

Vice President of Editorial Melissa Wagner
Director of Acquisitions Mikaela Felty
Director of Book Development Jocelynn Hessler
Production Manager Mike Brehm
Cover Design Jose Rosado

Published in the United States of America by
IGI Global Scientific Publishing
701 East Chocolate Avenue
Hershey, PA, 17033, USA
Tel: 717-533-8845 | Fax: 717-533-7115
Website: https://www.igi-global.com E-mail: cust@igi-global.com

Library of Congress Cataloging-in-Publication Data

Names: Ismaili, Safae, 1986- editor
http://id.loc.gov/rwo/agents/n2025013008
Title: Regulation and innovation in financial markets / [edited by] Safae Ismaili.
Description: Hershey, PA : IGI Global Scientific Publishing, [2026] | Includes bibliographical references and index. | Summary: "The primary objective is to provide a comprehensive exploration of the complex interplay between financial regulation and innovation, with a focus on fostering sustainable, inclusive, and resilient financial systems. This book aims to bridge the gap between academic research, industry practices, and policymaking by addressing the critical challenges and opportunities presented by technological advancements, regulatory developments, and the growing emphasis on sustainability"-- Provided by publisher.
Identifiers: LCCN 2025002866 (print) | LCCN 2025002867 (ebook) | ISBN 9798337314044 hardcover | ISBN 9798337314051 paperback | ISBN 9798337314068 ebook
Subjects: LCSH: Finance http://id.loc.gov/authorities/subjects/sh85048256 | Finance--Technological innovations | Financial services industry http://id.loc.gov/authorities/subjects/sh88000615 | Capital market http://id.loc.gov/authorities/subjects/sh85019945
Classification: LCC HG173 .R396 2025 (print) | LCC HG173 (ebook) | DDC 332--dc23/eng/20250321
LC record available at https://lccn.loc.gov/2025002866
LC ebook record available at https://lccn.loc.gov/2025002867
British Cataloguing in Publication Data
A Cataloguing in Publication record for this book is available from the British Library.

Table of Contents

Detailed Table of Contents

Section 1
Technological Innovation and Market Disruption

This paper evaluates the effectiveness of robo-advisors in security analysis and portfolio management, focusing on their performance relative to traditional advisory services. By analyzing algorithms and technologies used in robo-advisors, the study assesses their capabilities in risk management, performance evaluation, and user satisfaction. Both primary data, gathered from surveys and interviews, and secondary data from case studies are used to evaluate trust, user experiences, and the overall efficacy of robo-advisors in investment strategies. The findings indicate that robo-advisors provide high user satisfaction, demonstrate effective portfolio management, and offer significant potential for integration with traditional advisory models. This research contributes to the understanding of robo-advisors' evolving role in modern finance, highlighting their impact on investment decision-making and the future of financial advisory services.

Big data refers to enormous amounts of structured and unstructured data that arise daily. All the finance sector records transactions, market data, social media sentiments, customer behavior, and macroeconomic indicators. The big three dimensions of big data that are commonly called the “3 Vs” include Volume, Velocity, and Variety. It means the data came from sources such as social media, IoT devices, transactions, and sensors. This process involves large amounts of data hence requiring scalable storages, complex processing tools, and resources for effective data management and analytics. Velocity means the rate or speed at which data is originated and processed. Lastly, Variety denotes the different kinds of data, which include the structured ones such as databases and the unstructured kinds, such as images, video, social media post, and audio. Collectively, the 3 Vs capture both the richness and the potentiality of big data, demanding the need for innovation in terms of technologies and strategies to leverage this value.

The technological advancements have transformed the financial markets by increasing the efficiency, transparency and accessibility. Emerging technologies like Artificial Intelligence, Blockchain technology, Machine learning and Big data analytics have reshaped the investment strategies and enhance risk management techniques. However, concerns cybersecurity and regulatory challenges still persist. This chapter mainly discuss about how the technological advancements is changing financial markets, while taking into account both the advantages and disadvantages of these advancements.

The current chapter explores the development of fintech 4.0 in India (Delhi-NCR as a case), analyzing adoption trends and consumer behavioral insights using Technology Acceptance Model-3 (TAM-3). It traces the historical progression of FinTech from its early stages to the current era, highlighting key technological advancement such as artificial intelligence, block chain, and open banking. Through an in-depth analysis of adoption drivers- including technological, economic, psychological, and regulatory factors- this study identifies the critical determinants influencing consumer acceptance and usage of FinTech solutions. Furthermore, it discusses the role of fintech literacy, trust, and security concerns in shaping consumer behavior. By integrated the theoretical framework of TAM-3, the current research provides a comprehensive understanding of fintech adoption, offering valuable insights for financial institutions, policy makers, and technology developers.

Decentralized Finance (DeFi) is rapidly transforming the traditional financial system by introducing a permissionless, transparent, and trustless financial ecosystem powered by blockchain technology. It eliminates intermediaries by utilizing smart contracts on public blockchains like Ethereum, thereby promoting financial inclusion and operational efficiency. This paper explores the fundamental concepts of DeFi, the underlying technology including Ethereum, smart contracts, and Layer 2 solutions, and the wide array of its applications such as (DEXs), lending/borrowing platforms, yield farming, and stablecoins. In addition to examining the functional advantages of DeFi like reduced transaction costs and increased accessibility, the paper also critically analyzes the potential risks including smart contract vulnerabilities, regulatory concerns, and systemic dependencies. A special focus is given to the Indian regulatory framework and how it compares with global jurisdictions. The paper concludes with a discussion on the future prospects of DeFi .

This chapter explores the intricate nexus of risk management, compliance and sustainability in digital finance, offering a comprehensive framework for safeguarding service organizations against financial fraud. As digital finance revolutionizes the service sector, organizations face complex risks, including cybersecurity threats, operational vulnerabilities and regulatory challenges. The chapter examines current risk management frameworks, the evolving regulatory landscape and the importance of integrating sustainability principles. Analyzing case studies and emerging trends, it underscores the critical interdependence of these elements, advocating for a holistic approach to building resilient, compliant and sustainable service organizations in the digital age.

Sustainability, Culture, and Development

event date (announcement/ex-dividend date), the event window will be taken from the year 2020 to 2024.

Preface

The digital revolution has irreversibly reshaped the financial landscape, introducing a wave of technological, regulatory, and social transformations that are redefining how financial systems operate worldwide. This volume, *Digital Payment Wars and Financial Transformations: Toward a Regulated and Sustainable Intelligence*, offers a comprehensive, interdisciplinary perspective on the evolving nature of finance, particularly in the context of emerging economies. It brings together diverse voices to examine the intricate intersections between innovation, resilience, inclusion, and governance in modern financial systems.

As artificial intelligence, decentralized finance (DeFi), sustainable investment frameworks, and digital platforms emerge as cornerstones of financial evolution, the need for critical, scholarly engagement becomes urgent. This book seeks to address this need by providing both theoretical insights and empirical evidence, helping academics, practitioners, and policymakers navigate the increasingly complex financial terrain.

THE RELEVANCE OF THE TOPIC IN TODAY'S WORLD

We are currently witnessing the "fintechnologization" of global finance. Traditional paradigms of credit, payments, investment, and risk are being reimagined through the lenses of data, automation, and digital infrastructure. These trends are particularly visible in emerging markets—such as India, Morocco, and other parts of the Global South—where technological innovation often collides with infrastructural gaps and institutional fragility.

This book responds to such challenges and opportunities by investigating cutting-edge technologies (e.g., robo-advisors, big data analytics, AI), evolving regulatory frameworks, and socio-cultural dynamics that shape financial behaviors. It does so through a structured, thematic approach, divided into three coherent parts.

TARGET AUDIENCE

This publication is intended for a multidisciplinary audience, including:

- Researchers and scholars in finance, economics, public policy, and data science;
- Financial professionals (including fintech leaders, regulators, analysts, and bankers);
- Policymakers and regulatory bodies working on digital financial infrastructure, ESG, and financial inclusion;
- Graduate students and doctoral candidates in financial technology, sustainable finance, and economic development;
- International organizations and development agencies focused on innovation-driven financial empowerment in emerging economies.

STRUCTURE AND CHAPTER HIGHLIGHTS

Part I – Technological Innovation and Market Disruption

This section delves into the technological innovations reshaping financial systems, emphasizing the tension between automation, personalization, and disruption.

- **Chapter 1** investigates the integration of robo-advisors into portfolio management, highlighting their advantages in security analysis and democratizing access to investment services.
- **Chapter 2** focuses on the application of big data and predictive analytics in financial decision-making, detailing how large-scale data patterns influence risk modeling and strategic planning.
- **Chapter 3** offers a broader lens on the impact of technological innovation in financial markets, mapping disruptions across services, operations, and customer engagement.
- **Chapter 4** analyzes the adoption of FinTech 4.0 technologies in India using the TAM-3 model. The chapter presents psychological and behavioral insights into digital finance uptake.
- **Chapter 5** provides a critical evaluation of DeFi, contrasting it with traditional finance in terms of functionality, risks, and the implications for regulatory oversight.

Part II – Regulation, Risk, and Recovery

This part focuses on post-crisis regulation, organizational resilience, and financial risk diagnostics—particularly in the wake of the COVID-19 pandemic.

- **Chapter 6** studies risk mitigation strategies and regulatory adherence within service organizations, proposing sustainable digital frameworks to prevent financial malfeasance.
- **Chapter 7** investigates how regulatory frameworks influenced financial market recovery post-COVID-19, emphasizing adaptive governance and resilience mechanisms.
- **Chapter 8** applies Altman's Z-score model to assess financial health in India's IT sector, shedding light on early warning systems and predictive failure analysis.

Part III – Sustainability, Culture, and Development

This section broadens the analytical horizon, integrating sustainability metrics, socio-cultural variables, and financial inclusion mechanisms across diverse economies.

- **Chapter 9** presents an in-depth discussion of sustainable finance and investor behavior in emerging markets, examining ESG adoption and long-term value creation.
- **Chapter 10** assesses the market impact of dividend declaration timing, revealing how key dates influence investor decisions and capital flows.

CONTRIBUTION TO THE DISCIPLINE

This volume advances financial scholarship in several crucial directions. It offers a multi-dimensional view of the digital transformation in finance—incorporating technology, regulation, culture, and sustainability—while grounding its arguments in empirical data and practical case studies. The diverse disciplinary backgrounds of its contributors reflect the complexity of the subject and the importance of crossing academic silos to tackle real-world financial challenges.

This book contributes by:

- Clarifying the evolving concepts of fintech, DeFi, and sustainable finance;
- Offering evidence-based insights for financial innovation and governance;

- Presenting comparative perspectives across regions and institutional settings;
- Equipping researchers and policymakers with actionable frameworks.

CONCLUSION: TOWARD A RESPONSIBLE AND INCLUSIVE FINANCIAL FUTURE

The financial systems of tomorrow will be shaped not merely by algorithms and data, but by how societies govern and distribute financial power. This book provides a roadmap for understanding and shaping those transformations. It urges readers to think beyond technological novelty, asking deeper questions about ethics, access, stability, and purpose.

In doing so, it positions itself as a foundational text for those committed to building a financial world that is not only efficient, but equitable and resilient.

Section 1
Technological Innovation and Market Disruption

Chapter 1
Use of Robo Advisors for Security Analysis and Portfolio Management: A Technological Innovation in Financial Markets

Partap Singh
https://orcid.org/0000-0002-4653-7984
Maharishi Markendshwar University, Mullana, India

ABSTRACT

This paper evaluates the effectiveness of robo-advisors in security analysis and portfolio management, focusing on their performance relative to traditional advisory services. By analyzing algorithms and technologies used in robo-advisors, the study assesses their capabilities in risk management, performance evaluation, and user satisfaction. Both primary data, gathered from surveys and interviews, and secondary data from case studies are used to evaluate trust, user experiences, and the overall efficacy of robo-advisors in investment strategies. The findings indicate that robo-advisors provide high user satisfaction, demonstrate effective portfolio management, and offer significant potential for integration with traditional advisory models. This research contributes to the understanding of robo-advisors' evolving role in modern finance, highlighting their impact on investment decision-making and the future of financial advisory services.

DOI: 10.4018/979-8-3373-1404-4.ch001

1. INTRODUCTIONS

1.1 Background

The emergence of robo-advisors marks a transformative phase in the financial services industry, leveraging digital innovation to enhance investment management. These platforms use algorithm-based software to provide tailored investment recommendations, often requiring minimal human intervention (Maume 2019). While some robo-advisors integrate artificial intelligence to refine decision-making processes, others rely solely on pre-defined algorithms (Thier and dos Santos Monteiro 2022). The first generation of robo-advisors, including pioneers like Betterment and Wealthfront, began operating around 2008-2009, offering cost-efficient, automated solutions aimed at democratizing access to financial services (Sironi 2016). These early platforms focused on portfolio rebalancing and diversification strategies designed to guide investors toward achieving financial goals.

Recent advancements have allowed robo-advisors to evolve significantly, incorporating features such as tax-loss harvesting, personalized financial planning, and real-time risk analysis (Guo, Cheng, and Zhang 2019; Hohenberger et al. 2019). Machine learning algorithms and data analytics have played a pivotal role in enabling these systems to analyze complex market conditions and offer sophisticated recommendations. This evolution aligns with the broader trend of digitization in wealth management, where technology reshapes traditional approaches (Hildebrand and Bergner 2021). Despite their advantages, the adoption of robo-advisors raises critical considerations, including trustworthiness, ethical practices, and the reliability of automated systems (High-Level Expert Group on AI 2019). However, their capacity to enhance decision-making efficiency and reduce costs has solidified their role as a significant innovation in personal finance (Investment Company Institute 2023). The significance of robo-advisors lies not only in their operational efficiency but also in their ability to democratize access to high-quality investment services, thus reshaping the traditional advisory landscape (Hakala 2019).

1.2 Objectives of the Chapter

- To study the level of awareness and understanding towards robo –advisors;
- To critically evaluate the effectiveness of robo-advisors in security analysis and portfolio management;
- To analyze the algorithms and technologies employed by robo-advisors for security analysis and determine their effectiveness under varying market conditions.

- To assess the risk management practices utilized by robo-advisors and evaluate their reliability in maintaining portfolio stability
- To investigate the levels of user satisfaction and trust in robo-advisors among different demographic groups.
- To identify and analyze barriers influencing the adoption of robo-advisors and the barriers faced by different demographic groups.
- To explore the feasibility and implications of integrating robo-advisors with traditional financial advisory services.

1.3 Research Questions

The central research questions guiding this study are:

- What is the level of awareness and understanding of robo-advisors among investors?
- How effective are robo-advisors in performing security analysis compared to traditional financial advisors?
- What key performance indicators demonstrate the efficacy of robo-advisors in portfolio management?
- What algorithms and technologies are utilized by robo-advisors for security analysis? And how do these algorithms perform under varying market conditions?
- What risk management strategies are employed by robo-advisors to ensure portfolio stability and How reliable are these risk management practices in mitigating market risks?
- How do user satisfaction and trust levels compare between robo-advisors and traditional financial advisory services?
- What are the main barriers to the adoption of robo-advisors among different demographic groups?
- What are the potential benefits and challenges of integrating robo-advisors with traditional financial advisory services?
- How feasible is the integration of robo-advisors with traditional advisory models in enhancing financial planning and investment management?

1.4 Structure of Chapter

The chapter is organized into five distinct sections: Section-I Introduction (including objectives& research questions), Section II - Literature Review, Section III - Research Methodology, Section IV - Results and Discussion, and Section V – Summary as displayed in fig.1

Figure 1. Organization of Chapter

2. LITERATURE REVIEW

2.1 Awareness and Understanding of Robo-Advisors

The level of awareness and understanding of robo-advisors among potential users is crucial for their adoption. Research indicates that many individuals remain uninformed about the functionalities and benefits of these automated services (Deloitte, 2016). The complexity of robo-advisory models and their reliance on algorithms can create barriers to understanding, which may hinder user engagement (Thier and dos Santos Monteiro, 2022). Studies suggest that enhancing user education about how robo-advisors operate and their advantages could facilitate broader acceptance (Eren, 2023).

Thier and dos Santos Monteiro (2022) underscore that robo-advisors predominantly utilize algorithms, which may or may not incorporate artificial intelligence (AI). Despite their growing adoption, perceptions of complexity and a lack of awareness among users remain key challenges (Deloitte, 2016). Factors such as trustworthiness, communication effectiveness, and perceived utility significantly shape user understanding and acceptance (Cheng et al., 2019). Moreover, demographic variations, particularly among tech-savvy and cost-conscious investors, influence perceptions of robo-advisors as viable alternatives to traditional financial services (Chandani et al., 2021).

2.2 Effectiveness in Security Analysis and Portfolio Management

The effectiveness of robo-advisors in security analysis and portfolio management is a central focus of current research. Evidence shows that robo-advisors can enhance portfolio diversification and reduce biases typically exhibited by human investors (Loos et al., 2020; Liaudinskas, 2022). However, concerns remain regarding passive investment behaviors that may arise from reliance on automated systems, potentially leading to a lack of market understanding among users (Darskuviene and Lisauskiene, 2021; Abraham et al., 2019). Balancing automation with active management is vital for optimizing portfolio performance.

Several studies emphasize the effectiveness of robo-advisors in enhancing portfolio management. Tao et al. (2021) found that robo-advisors excel in handling diverse risk-reward models, delivering robust and cost-effective solutions. Similarly, Loos et al. (2020) observed improvements in portfolio diversification and reduced home bias, indicating greater geographical and investment diversity. However, fully automated models may fall short in addressing customer needs due to the lack of human interaction, with hybrid models demonstrating higher efficacy (Barile et al., 2024). Additionally, robo-advisors provide increased market participation and improved investment practices, particularly for underserved groups (Acunto et al., 2018).

2.3 Algorithms and Technologies in Robo-Advisors

The algorithms and technologies used by robo-advisors play a pivotal role in their performance. Liaudinskas (2022) noted that algorithms mitigate behavioral biases, fostering rationality in trading decisions. However, human errors in programming can introduce biases, potentially undermining reliability (Bhatia et al., 2020). Guo (2020) highlighted that regulated algorithms with enhanced information disclosure improve decision-making efficiency. Future innovations are expected to expand the scope of robo-advisors, enabling comprehensive financial consultations across various domains (Beck, 2021).

The technological backbone of robo-advisors is central to their utility. D'Hondt et al. (2020) illustrate the varying success rates of algorithms in capturing market anomalies and generating returns. Liu et al. (2022) stress the importance of risk assessment algorithms in mitigating systemic risks, especially in complex financial ecosystems. Huang (2022) explores the digitization of wealth management in China, underscoring the innovative use of robo-advisors in an evolving regulatory environment.

2.4 Risk Management Practices

Risk management is a critical component of robo-advisors. Darskuviene and Lisauskiene (2021) observed that while robo-advisors reduce bias in decision-making, they may inadvertently encourage passive investment behavior, increasing risks for inexperienced investors (Abraham et al., 2019). Effective communication of risk and reward parameters is essential to foster trust and stability among users (Bhatia et al., 2020). Puntoni et al. (2021) emphasized that AI-enabled decision-making offers new opportunities for managing market volatility, though human discretion remains integral to final investment decisions (Sander, 2021).

Effective risk management is pivotal for the reliability of robo-advisors. Kaplan et al. (2023) synthesize findings on trust in AI systems, highlighting the importance of robust algorithmic design in maintaining stability. Fulk et al. (2018) examine user adoption patterns and correlate them with the perceived reliability of risk mitigation strategies deployed by robo-advisors.

2.5 User Satisfaction and Trust

The role of trust in user satisfaction is well-documented. Cheng et al. (2019) analyze trust-building mechanisms, showing how clear communication and performance consistency improve user perceptions. Dietvorst, Simmons, and Massey (2015) caution against algorithm aversion, a behavioral phenomenon where users abandon automated systems after observing errors. Hildebrand and Bergner (2021) emphasize the onboarding experience as a critical factor influencing consumer trust.

User satisfaction and trust are vital for the adoption of robo-advisors. Liang and Xue (2009) noted that perceived threats, such as data security and prediction errors, can deter users. Conversely, transparency and personalized services significantly enhance trust and satisfaction (Cheng et al., 2019). Balakrishnan and Dwivedi (2021) found that factors such as risk perception and reliability influence user acceptance.

Huang and Rust (2018) highlighted that the absence of human interaction in robo-advisors facilitates broader access to financial advice but may limit personalization.

2.6 Barriers to Adoption

Several barriers hinder the widespread adoption of robo-advisors. Accenture (2015) identified the absence of personalized goal-setting and market counseling as critical gaps. Chhabra (2005) found that perceived threats diminish willingness to adopt technology-based financial services. Additionally, lower-income and less-experienced investors often face challenges in utilizing these tools effectively, necessitating targeted interventions to enhance adoption (Chandani et al., 2021).

Despite their potential, robo-advisors face adoption barriers, including regulatory concerns and behavioral biases. Bhatia, Chandani, and Chhateja (2020) focus on the Indian market, revealing that psychological biases hinder acceptance despite the evident advantages of automated systems. Guo (2020) elaborates on regulatory challenges in China, suggesting the need for standardized frameworks to encourage widespread adoption.

2.7 Integration with Traditional Financial Advisory Services

The integration of robo-advisors with traditional advisory services presents opportunities to address their limitations. Barile et al. (2024) advocate for hybrid models combining automation with human expertise to enhance decision-making processes. Wang (2022) highlighted the need for a balanced approach, integrating AI technologies with human advisory roles to deliver comprehensive financial services. Pal (2021) emphasized the importance of empirical research to validate the effectiveness of such integrations in diverse market contexts.

2.8 Sustainable and Ethical Considerations

Ziegler and Weller (2021) examine the alignment of robo-advisors with sustainable investing practices, highlighting their role in advancing ethical investment portfolios. Baker and Dellaert (2017) underscore the need for robust regulatory frameworks to ensure the ethical use of robo-advisors.

The literature underscores the transformative potential of robo-advisors in financial management, highlighting their effectiveness, limitations, and implications. While advancements in algorithms and AI have enhanced their capabilities, challenges such as trust, personalization, and risk management persist. Integrating robo-advisors with traditional advisory services and addressing barriers to adoption remain critical for realizing their full potential.

2.9 Research Gap

Despite the rising adoption of robo-advisors in investment management, there is limited research on their effectiveness in security analysis, risk management, and performance evaluation compared to traditional advisors. User satisfaction, trust, and transparency in robo-advisors' decision-making processes are also under-explored. Furthermore, the barriers to adoption among different demographics and the potential integration of robo-advisors with traditional advisory services need further investigation. This study aims to address these gaps and provide comprehensive insights into the effectiveness and challenges of robo-advisors.

3. RESEARCH METHODOLOGY

Research Design Overview

This study employs a mixed-methods approach to investigate the use and impact of robo-advisors. The research design integrates both qualitative and quantitative methods to ensure a comprehensive analysis of the subject. The following sections detail the methodology, including data collection, literature review, case studies, and data analysis techniques.

Data Collection

- Primary Data: Data was collected from 65 respondents using a snowball sampling technique. This approach was chosen to reach participants who are knowledgeable about or actively use robo-advisors. Respondents included various financial professionals and individual investors.
- Secondary Data: Additional data was gathered from financial metrics and market data available on reputable sources such as Moneycontrol.com, Zee Business, Bloomberg, Reuters, and various academic journals and publicly accessible financial databases. This secondary data provided contextual information and supported the primary data findings.

Literature Review

- A thorough review of existing academic literature, including journals, research papers, and industry reports, was conducted. This review aimed to identify gaps in the current understanding of robo-advisors and to contextualize the study's findings within the broader field of financial technology.

Case Studies

- Four case studies of robo-advisors were conducted to provide practical insights into their implementation and effectiveness. These case studies focused on different platforms to assess their strengths, weaknesses, opportunities, and threats (SWOT), providing a real-world perspective on the use of robo-advisors in financial management.

Data Analysis

- SWOT Analysis: Used to evaluate the strengths, weaknesses, opportunities, and threats of the robo-advisors discussed in the case studies. This method helps in understanding the competitive position and strategic advantages of each platform.
- Percentile Method: Applied to categorize and interpret data distributions, particularly for assessing user preferences and effectiveness ratings of robo-advisors..

Scope of the Study

The scope of this study encompasses an in-depth analysis of robo-advisors' effectiveness in security analysis and portfolio management. It includes a comprehensive evaluation of the technologies and algorithms used by these platforms, as well as their performance metrics and risk management techniques. The research integrates primary data obtained through surveys and interviews with financial advisors and robo-advisor users, and secondary data from case studies and existing literature. The study focuses on understanding user satisfaction and trust, identifying adoption barriers, and exploring the potential for integrating robo-advisors with traditional advisory services. The findings are intended to provide valuable insights into the current state of robo-advisors and their impact on modern financial practices.

Limitations of the Study

The study's reliance on snowball sampling may introduce selection bias, affecting representativeness. Primary data from 65 respondents might not capture diverse perspectives, limiting generalizability. Secondary data sources may have inherent biases or outdated information. The SWOT analysis and chi-square tests, while valuable, may oversimplify complex variables and overlook nuances. Additionally, the focus on four case studies may not cover the full spectrum of robo-advisors, potentially skewing findings.

4. RESULTS AND DISCUSSION

This section has been covered into two sub-sections:
Section-1: Analysis of primary data
Questionnaire: Use of Robo-Advisors for Security Analysis and Portfolio Management

Section I: Participants Demographics

Table 1. Participant's Demographics

S. No	Role	Market Experience	Number	Percentage (%)
1	Retail Traders	More than 1 year	24	36.92
2	Institutional Traders	More than 1 year	14	21.54
3	Market Analysts	More than 1 year	17	26.15
4	Portfolio Managers	More than 1 year	10	15.38
	Total		65	100

Source: Field Data

The table shows that the study includes 65 participants with diverse roles in the market. Retail traders make up 36.92%, institutional traders 21.54%, market analysts 26.15%, and portfolio managers 15.38%, all with over a year of market experience. This distribution helps analyze the impact of robo-advisors across different market participants.

Figure 2. Participant's Demographics by Role

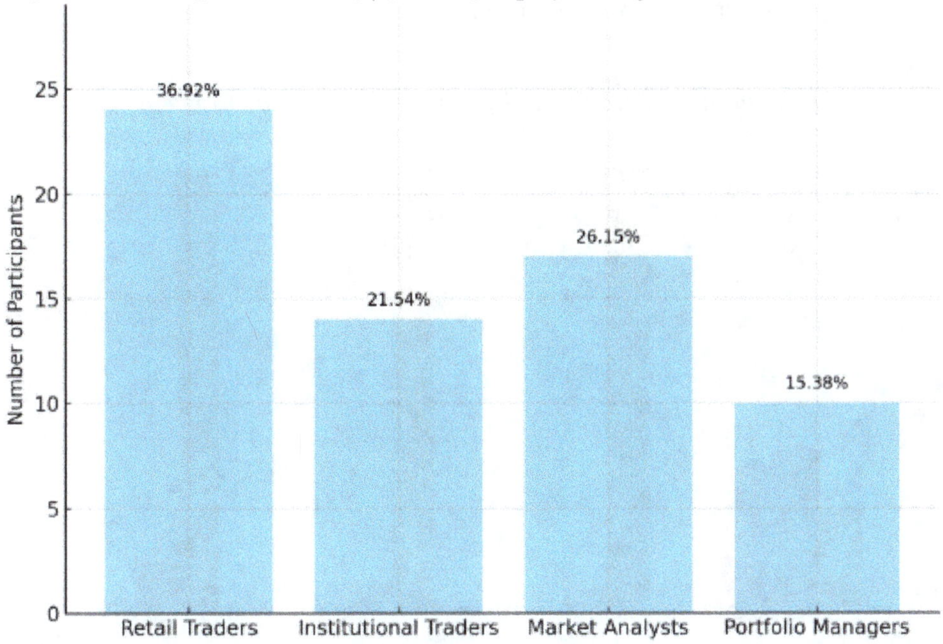

Source: Author

Section II: Awareness and Usage of Robo-Advisors

Table 2. Understanding & Awareness towards Robo-Advisor Concept

No	Respondents	Very Familiar (%)	Familiar (%)	Somewhat Familiar (%)	Not Familiar (%)	Total Respondents
1	Retail Traders	20.83	33.33	29.17	16.67	24 (100)
2	Institutional Traders	96.00	4.00	-	-	14 (100)
3	Market Analysts	94.39	5.61	-	-	17 (100)
4	Portfolio Managers	90.00	10.00	-	-	10 (100)
Total		59.39	17.85	10.77	11.99	65 (100)

Source: Field & calculated data

The table shows the understanding of robo-advisors among 65 participants, categorized by role. Retail traders, institutional traders, market analysts, and portfolio managers exhibit varying levels of familiarity. Overall, 59.39% are very familiar,

17.85% familiar, 10.77% somewhat familiar, and 11.99% not familiar, indicating a relatively high awareness of robo-advisors.

Figure 3.Understanding & Awareness Towards Robo-Advisor Concept

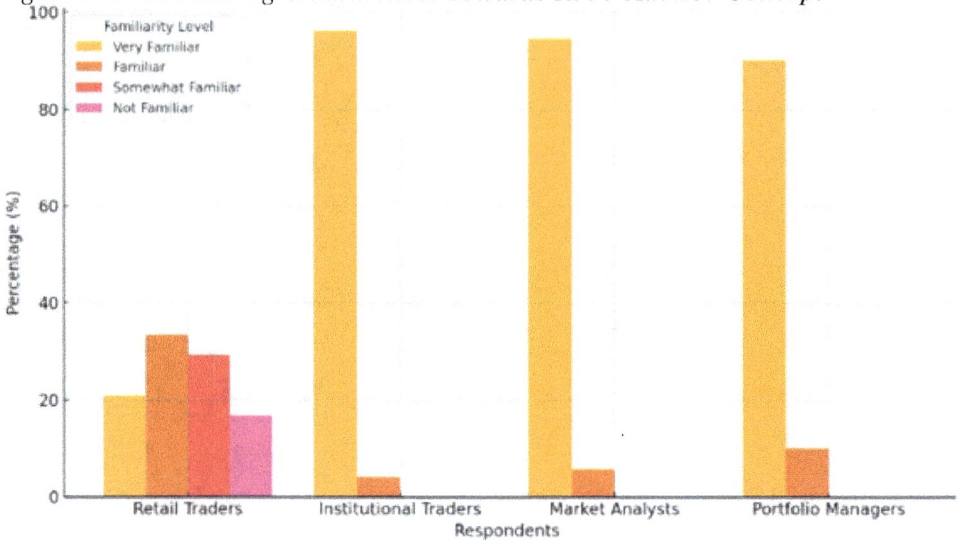

Source: Author

Here is the chart visualizing the understanding and awareness levels towards the Robo-Advisor concept among different respondent groups. Each category of familiarity is represented as a separate bar for easy comparison. Let me know if you'd like any modifications!

Table 3. Usage of Specific Robo-Advisors (in Percentages)

Robo-Advisor	Retail Traders (%)	Institutional Traders (%)	Market Analysts (%)	Portfolio Managers (%)	Total (%)
Betterment	41.67	57.14	70.59	60.00	55.38
Wealthfront	20.83	71.43	29.41	40.00	36.92
Robinhood	62.50	14.29	23.53	20.00	35.38
Schwab	12.50	85.71	47.06	70.00	46.15
Other	25.00	28.57	17.65	10.00	21.54

Source: Field & calculated data

Table 3 presents the distribution of robo-advisor usage among different professional roles. Betterment emerges as the most widely used platform overall, with

55.38% of respondents indicating their use. The table highlights notable variations in preferences across different professional groups:

- Retail Traders show a strong inclination towards Robinhood, with 62.50% using it, reflecting its appeal to individual investors seeking user-friendly, low-cost solutions.
- Institutional Traders exhibit a predominant preference for Schwab Intelligent Portfolios, with 85.71% utilizing this platform. This suggests a favor for Schwab's comprehensive features and advanced tools suitable for institutional needs.
- Market Analysts and Portfolio Managers have varying preferences, with Market Analysts leaning towards Betterment (70.59%) and Portfolio Managers also showing a preference for Betterment (60.00%). Schwab is also favored by Portfolio Managers (70.00%).

The usage patterns reveal distinct adoption trends, with each professional group favoring different platforms based on their specific needs and roles. These variations highlight the importance of understanding user preferences in the context of robo-advisor adoption and suggest that robo-advisors are tailored to meet the diverse requirements of different market participants.

Figure 4. Usage of Specific Robo-Advisors by Participant Categories

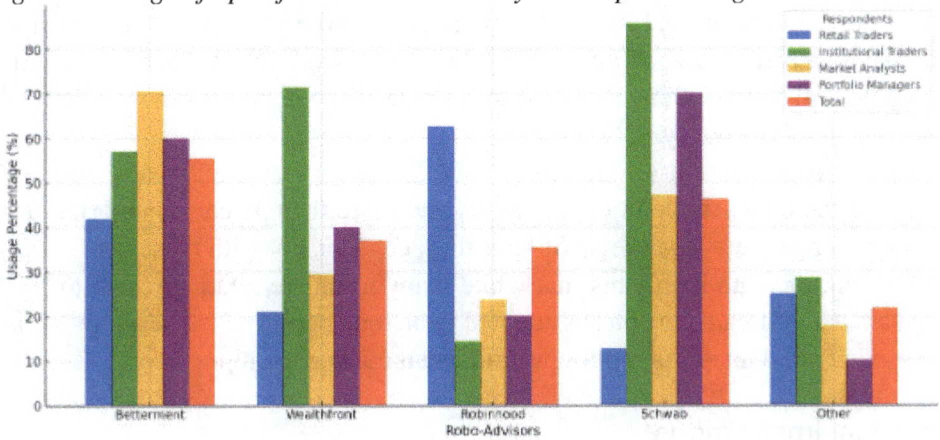

Source: Author

Here is the grouped bar chart illustrating the usage of specific Robo-Advisors by different participant categories. Each bar represents the percentage of a specific group using a particular Robo-Advisor.

Table 4. Percentage of Respondents Using Robo-Advisors for Duration of Usage

Duration	Retail Traders (%)	Institutional Traders (%)	Market Analysts (%)	Portfolio Managers (%)	Total (%)
Less than 6 months	4.17	14.29	5.88	10.00	11.11
6 months to 1 year	4.17	14.29	23.53	30.00	22.22
1-2 years	0.00	42.86	41.18	40.00	37.78
2-3 years	0.00	14.29	11.76	0.00	8.89
More than 3 years	0.00	14.29	5.88	0.00	8.89

Source: Field & calculated data

Table 4 presents data on the duration of robo-advisor usage among 45 respondents, segmented by their professional roles. The most notable finding is that 37.78% of users have utilized robo-advisors for 1-2 years, indicating a substantial adoption of these tools in this timeframe.

Institutional traders show a diverse usage pattern, with a prominent 42.86% using robo-advisors for 1-2 years, but less engagement in other durations. Market analysts and portfolio managers also reflect a strong preference for the 1-2 years range, with 41.18% and 40.00% respectively, suggesting stable and consistent use among these groups.

In contrast, a smaller percentage of respondents use robo-advisors for less than 6 months (11.11% in total), with the usage being more pronounced among institutional traders at 14.29%. Similarly, 22.22% of respondents use robo-advisors for 6 months to 1 year, with market analysts and portfolio managers showing notable adoption in this category.

Fewer respondents use robo-advisors for durations beyond 2 years, with only 8.89% of the total sample in the 2-3 years and more than 3 years categories. This indicates a relatively lower level of long-term engagement with these platforms.

Overall, the data highlights that while many users are relatively new to robo-advisors, a significant portion has adopted them for a period of 1-2 years, reflecting a period of solid integration into their financial management practices.

Practical Implications

The varied preferences for robo-advisors among different professional groups highlight the need for tailored services. For instance, Schwab Intelligent Portfolios' appeal to institutional traders suggests a demand for advanced features, while Robinhood's popularity among retail traders points to a need for user-friendly and cost-effective solutions. Thus, robo-advisors should customize their platforms to meet these diverse needs.

Marketing strategies must align with these preferences: platforms like Betterment and Schwab should target professionals seeking sophisticated tools, while Robinhood should emphasize ease of use and affordability. Additionally, robo-advisors should focus on developing specialized features, such as advanced analytics for institutional users and simplified tools for retail traders.

Integration with other financial tools and enhanced customization options are crucial for providing a seamless user experience. Comprehensive training and support are needed, with platforms offering robust resources for less experienced users and advanced support for seasoned professionals.

Cost-effectiveness remains a key factor, with providers needing to balance competitive pricing with high-quality service. Lastly, investing in strong data security measures is essential to build trust and protect user information. Adapting to these practical considerations will enhance the effectiveness and appeal of robo-advisory services.

Section III: Effectiveness in Security Analysis

Table 5. Effectiveness of Robo-Advisor in Analyzing Securities

Respondents	Very Effective	Effective	Neutral	Ineffective	Very Ineffective	Total	Percentage
Retail Traders	3 (12.5%)	9 (37.5%)	9 (37.5%)	3 (12.5%)	0 (0%)	24	100%
Institutional Traders	14 (100%)	0 (0%)	0 (0%)	0 (0%)	0 (0%)	14	100%
Market Analysts	14 (82.4%)	3 (17.6%)	0 (0%)	0 (0%)	0 (0%)	17	100%
Portfolio Managers	3 (30%)	5 (50%)	2 (20%)	0 (0%)	0 (0%)	10	100%
Total	34 (52.3%)	17 (26.2%)	11 (16.9%)	3 (4.6%)	0 (0%)	65	100%

Source: Author

The table 5 shows varying perceptions of robo-advisors' effectiveness in analyzing securities across different market participants. Institutional Traders stand out as the most positive group, with 100% rating the robo-advisors as "Very Effective," indicating strong confidence in their utility. Market Analysts also display a positive outlook, with 82.4% rating the system as "Very Effective" and 17.6% as "Effective." Their overall sentiment is largely positive. Retail Traders have a more balanced view. While 37.5% consider it "Effective," another 37.5% are neutral, showing mixed opinions about the system's performance. Only 12.5% find it "Very Effective." Portfolio Managers show moderate confidence, with 50% rating it "Effective" and 30% considering it "Very Effective." However, 20% remain neutral, reflecting a more cautious stance.

Overall, 52.3% of all respondents find the system "Very Effective," and 26.2% consider it "Effective." The findings reflect a generally positive sentiment toward robo-advisors, with institutional traders and market analysts leading in approval. Retail traders and portfolio managers show more diversity in their perceptions, indicating that the effectiveness of robo-advisors may be more context-dependent.

Table 6. Most valuable features in security analysis

Features	Retail Traders	Institutional Traders	Market Analysts	Portfolio Managers	Total	Percentage
Data collection and processing	12	8	10	5	35	53.85%
Algorithmic analysis	15	9	12	6	42	64.62%
Risk assessment	18	12	14	7	51	78.46%
Fundamental analysis	10	7	9	4	30	46.15%
Technical analysis	14	8	11	5	38	58.46%
Sentiment analysis	13	10	13	6	42	64.62%
Comparative analysis	16	11	15	7	49	75.38%
Total					65	100.00%

Source: Field & calculated data

Table 6 shows risk assessment and comparative analysis are the most valued features in security analysis, with 78.46% and 75.38% respectively. These features are essential for making informed investment decisions. Algorithmic and sentiment analysis, both at 64.62%, also play significant roles, highlighting the importance of advanced data processing and market sentiment evaluation. Technical analysis (58.46%) and data collection (53.85%) are moderately valued, while fundamental analysis (46.15%) is considered less critical.

Table 7. Showing satisfaction with the accuracy of the security analysis provided by robo-advisor

Satisfaction Level	Retail Traders	Institutional Traders	Market Analysts	Portfolio Managers	Total	Percentage
Very satisfied	6	6	5	3	20	30.77%
Satisfied	10	6	8	4	28	43.08%
Neutral	4	1	2	1	8	12.31%
Dissatisfied	2	1	2	1	6	9.23%
Very dissatisfied	2	0	0	1	3	4.62%
Total	24	14	17	10	65	100.00%

Source: Field & calculated data

Interpretation: Among users of robo-advisors, 43.08% are satisfied with the accuracy, and 30.77% are very satisfied. However, 21.54% are neutral or dissatisfied. The usage data reveals that 69.23% of respondents use robo-advisors, while 40% do not. Institutional Traders show the highest usage, with no reported non-users. Market Analysts and Retail Traders have notable non-usage rates.

Section IV: Effectiveness in Portfolio Management

Table 8. the percentage breakdown of effectiveness ratings for each respondent group

Respondents	Very Effective (%)	Effective (%)	Neutral (%)	Ineffective (%)	Very Ineffective (%)	Total (%)
Retail Traders	12.50	41.67	16.67	16.67	12.50	100
Institutional Traders	35.71	42.86	14.29	7.14	0.00	100
Market Analysts	29.41	47.06	11.76	11.76	0.00	100
Portfolio Managers	10.00	40.00	30.00	10.00	10.00	100

Source: Field Data

Retail Traders

Retail traders exhibit a mixed view, with only 12.5% considering robo-advisors "Very Effective" and 41.67% rating them as "Effective." However, a combined 29.17% (16.67% "Ineffective" and 12.5% "Very Ineffective") indicate dissatisfaction, suggesting that retail users expect more reliable and personalized outcomes.

The significant neutral response (16.67%) may reflect uncertainty about the tools' potential.

Institutional Traders

Institutional traders show the highest confidence, with 35.71% rating robo-advisors as “Very Effective” and 42.86% as “Effective.” This indicates a strong perception of effectiveness among professionals who likely benefit from sophisticated algorithms and market insights. Only 7.14% found them “Ineffective,” while no respondent rated them “Very Ineffective,” underscoring their trust in automation.

Market Analysts

Market analysts largely view robo-advisors positively, with 29.41% rating them as “Very Effective” and 47.06% as “Effective.” Despite this, 23.52% (11.76% each for “Neutral” and “Ineffective”) express reservations, potentially due to concerns over robo-advisors' inability to interpret qualitative market data or behavioral factors.

Portfolio Managers

Portfolio managers provide the most critical assessment, with only 10% finding robo-advisors “Very Effective.” While 40% view them as “Effective,” 30% remain neutral, and a combined 20% rate them as “Ineffective” or “Very Ineffective.” This reflects their professional reliance on nuanced strategies that robo-advisors may not fully replicate.

Overall Insights

The results demonstrate varied acceptance of robo-advisors, with institutional traders and market analysts showing the most confidence. Retail traders and portfolio managers indicate room for improvement, particularly in personalization and advanced analytical capabilities. This suggests that while robo-advisors are recognized as effective tools, their adoption and satisfaction levels are contingent on the specific needs and expectations of user groups

Table 9. Most Beneficial Features for Portfolio Management

Features	Retail Traders	Institutional Traders	Market Analysts	Portfolio Managers	Total	Percentage
Asset allocation	8	5	7	3	23	35.4%
Portfolio optimization	6	6	8	4	24	36.9%
Rebalancing	5	4	6	3	18	27.7%
Tax optimization	4	5	5	3	17	26.2%
Risk management	7	6	7	5	25	38.5%
Performance monitoring	6	5	6	4	21	32.3%
Customization	4	5	5	2	16	24.6%
Cost management	3	5	4	2	14	21.5%
Total	43	41	48	26	158	100%

Source: Field & calculated data

Table 9 illustrates the most valued features for portfolio management across different professional roles. The data shows that the highest percentage of respondents across all groups prioritize risk management, with 38.5% of respondents identifying it as the most beneficial feature. This is followed closely by portfolio optimization, which is favored by 36.9% of respondents, reflecting its significant role in enhancing investment strategies. The second-highest rated feature is performance monitoring, appreciated by 32.3% of respondents, indicating its importance in tracking and evaluating portfolio performance. Asset allocation and rebalancing are also considered valuable, with 35.4% and 27.7% of respondents respectively, highlighting their role in maintaining a balanced and effective investment portfolio.

In contrast, customization (24.6%) and cost management (21.5%) are less favored compared to other features. This suggests that while customization and cost considerations are important, they are not as critical to the respondents' portfolio management compared to risk management and optimization.

Overall, the analysis demonstrates a clear preference for features that enhance decision-making and performance, with risk management and portfolio optimization being the top priorities for most respondents. These insights can guide the development and refinement of robo-advisor platforms, ensuring they focus on the features that users find most beneficial for effective portfolio management.

Table 10. Frequency of Portfolio Review Managed by a Robo-Advisor

Frequency	Retail Traders (%)	Institutional Traders (%)	Market Analysts (%)	Portfolio Managers (%)	Total (%)
Daily	31.25	25.00	31.25	12.50	100.00
Weekly	35.29	29.41	23.53	11.76	100.00
Monthly	38.89	16.67	27.78	16.67	100.00
Quarterly	40.00	20.00	20.00	20.00	100.00
Annually	50.00	0.00	25.00	25.00	100.00

Source: Field data

Table 10 analysis of portfolio review frequency highlights varying behavioral patterns across respondent groups:

Daily Reviews: Retail traders and market analysts exhibit the highest preference for daily portfolio reviews (31.25% each), indicating their active engagement in monitoring investments. Institutional traders also show significant involvement (25%), whereas portfolio managers display a comparatively lower interest (12.5%) in daily updates.

Weekly Reviews: Weekly reviews are favored most by retail traders (35.29%) and institutional traders (29.41%). This frequency strikes a balance between active monitoring and time efficiency, making it appealing to these groups. Portfolio managers again exhibit the least inclination toward this category (11.76%).

Monthly Reviews: Monthly portfolio reviews are most popular among retail traders (38.89%), followed by market analysts (27.78%). Institutional traders (16.67%) and portfolio managers (16.67%) show comparatively moderate preferences.

Quarterly and Annual Reviews: Longer intervals are preferred less frequently, with retail traders (40%) dominating quarterly reviews, reflecting a more hands-off approach. Annual reviews are predominantly favored by retail traders (50%), with marginal interest from market analysts and portfolio managers (25% each).

The results demonstrate that retail traders are the most proactive, frequently reviewing portfolios, while portfolio managers tend to adopt a more periodic review strategy. This suggests distinct behavioral tendencies driven by differing investment priorities and roles.

Table 11. User Satisfaction and Trust

Trust Level	Retail Traders	Institutional Traders	Market Analysts	Portfolio Managers	Total	% of Total
Completely trust	4	3	5	2	14	21.54%
Trust	8	6	6	3	23	35.38%
Neutral	6	3	3	3	15	23.08%
Distrust	4	2	2	1	9	13.85%
Completely distrust	2	0	1	1	4	6.15%
Total	24	14	17	10	65	100%

Source: Author

Table 11 presents the trust levels of different market participants (Retail Traders, Institutional Traders, Market Analysts, and Portfolio Managers) toward a system, showing both the absolute numbers and their respective percentages. The total number of respondents is 65, distributed across the four groups. The majority of respondents (35.38%) expressed trust, while 21.54% completely trust the system, indicating a favorable outlook across all groups. Retail Traders (50%) show a balanced opinion, with a mix of trust and neutral responses, but 16.67% of them distrust the system, suggesting some reservations. Institutional Traders exhibit the highest level of neutrality (21.43%) and the lowest distrust (0%), highlighting a more cautious but generally accepting stance. Market Analysts demonstrate the highest confidence, with 76.47% either trusting or completely trusting the system, and only 5.88% expressing distrust. Portfolio Managers show the least trust, with only 50% expressing trust or complete trust, and a notable portion (10%) remaining neutral or distrusting.

In summary, the data reveals that trust is relatively high across all groups, with Market Analysts showing the strongest positive sentiment and Portfolio Managers being more skeptical. Overall, the findings suggest a general trust in the system, but varying degrees of confidence depending on the respondent group.

Table 12. The cost-effectiveness of robo-advisors compared to traditional financial advisors

Cost-Effectiveness	Retail Traders	Institutional Traders	Market Analysts	Portfolio Managers	Total	Percentage
Much more cost-effective	6 (25%)	3 (21.4%)	5 (29.4%)	2 (20%)	16	24.6%
More cost-effective	8 (33.3%)	5 (35.7%)	6 (35.3%)	3 (30%)	22	33.8%
About the same	5 (20.8%)	3 (21.4%)	4 (23.5%)	2 (20%)	14	21.5%
Less cost-effective	3 (12.5%)	2 (14.3%)	1 (5.9%)	2 (20%)	8	12.3%
Much less cost-effective	2 (8.3%)	1 (7.1%)	1 (5.9%)	1 (10%)	5	7.7%
Total	24 (100%)	14 (100%)	17 (100%)	10 (100%)	65	100%

Source: Field & calculated data

Table 12 provides insights into the perceived cost-effectiveness of robo-advisors versus traditional financial advisors among different market participants. The data indicates that the majority of respondents consider robo-advisors to be more cost-effective than traditional advisors, with 33.8% of all respondents rating robo-advisors as “More cost-effective” and 24.6% rating them as “Much more cost-effective.”

Retail Traders show the highest percentage (33.3%) rating robo-advisors as “More cost-effective,” followed by 25% who view them as “Much more cost-effective.” This suggests that retail traders value the affordability of robo-advisors. Institutional Traders and Market Analysts also exhibit similar trends, with 35.7% and 35.3% respectively finding robo-advisors more cost-effective, though the percentages for “Much more cost-effective” are lower compared to Retail Traders. Portfolio Managers appear somewhat less convinced, with 30% rating robo-advisors as “More cost-effective,” and a higher percentage (20%) considering them “Less cost-effective.” Interestingly, only a small proportion of respondent’s view robo-advisors as “Less cost-effective” (12.3%) or “Much less cost-effective” (7.7%). This suggests a generally favorable view of robo-advisors in terms of cost, though professionals such as Portfolio Managers are more divided. In conclusion, the data reveals that robo-advisors are largely considered more cost-effective than traditional financial advisors across all groups, though opinions vary slightly by participant type.

Section VI: Adoption and Integration

Table 13. Desired Improvements or Additional Features in Robo-Advisors

Improvements/Features	Retail Traders (n=24)	Institutional Traders (n=14)	Market Analysts (n=17)	Portfolio Managers (n=10)	Total (n=65)	Percentage (%)
Enhanced customization options	6 (25%)	4 (28.6%)	5 (29.4%)	2 (20%)	17	26.2%
Better integration with other financial services	5 (20.8%)	3 (21.4%)	4 (23.5%)	2 (20%)	14	21.5%
Improved user interface	4 (16.7%)	3 (21.4%)	4 (23.5%)	2 (20%)	13	20.0%
More educational resources	3 (12.5%)	2 (14.3%)	3 (17.6%)	1 (10%)	9	13.8%
Lower fees	3 (12.5%)	1 (7.1%)	2 (11.8%)	1 (10%)	7	10.8%
Increased transparency	2 (8.3%)	1 (7.1%)	2 (11.8%)	1 (10%)	6	9.2%
Other (please specify)	1 (4.2%)	0 (0%)	1 (5.9%)	1 (10%)	3	4.6%
Total	24 (100%)	14 (100%)	17 (100%)	10 (100%)	65	100%

Source: Field & calculated data

The table 13 reflects the preferences for improvements in robo-advisors from various market participants. The most common feature desired across all groups is enhanced customization options, which received 26.2% of responses. Retail traders (25%) and market analysts (29.4%) highlighted this need, emphasizing the importance of personalization in investment strategies. Institutional traders also favored this feature (28.6%), indicating a demand for more tailored investment solutions.

The second most popular feature was better integration with other financial services (21.5%), with retail traders (20.8%) and market analysts (23.5%) expressing the greatest interest. This suggests that respondents value robo-advisors that can seamlessly connect with other financial tools and platforms, enhancing the overall user experience. Improved user interface (20%) followed closely behind, as ease of use remains critical, especially for retail traders and portfolio managers. While lower fees (10.8%) and increased transparency (9.2%) were less prioritized, they still reflect concerns, particularly for retail traders, who are more sensitive to costs and seek clearer insights into the investment process. Lastly, other unspecified improvements were mentioned by 4.6% of respondents. Overall, the results indicate that users are primarily focused on enhancing functionality, customization, and integration in robo-advisors.

Table 14. Barriers influenced decision to use or not use a robo-advisor (In Percentage)

Barriers	Retail Traders	Institutional Traders	Market Analysts	Portfolio Managers	Total	Percentage
Lack of personalization	8 (33.3%)	4 (28.6%)	6 (35.3%)	3 (30%)	21	32.3%
Concerns about data security	6 (25%)	5 (35.7%)	7 (41.2%)	4 (40%)	22	33.8%
Lack of human interaction	5 (20.8%)	2 (14.3%)	4 (23.5%)	3 (30%)	14	21.5%
Limited investment options	3 (12.5%)	1 (7.1%)	2 (11.8%)	2 (20%)	8	12.3%
Regulatory concerns	1 (4.2%)	1 (7.1%)	1 (5.9%)	1 (10%)	4	6.2%
Other (please specify)	1 (4.2%)	1 (7.1%)	1 (5.9%)	1 (10%)	4	6.2%
Total	24 (100%)	14 (100%)	17 (100%)	10 (100%)	65	100%

Source: Field & calculated data

Table 14 identifies the main barriers to adopting or rejecting robo-advisors. The most significant concern is data security, cited by 33.8% of respondents. This highlights the need for robo-advisors to implement advanced cybersecurity measures to gain user trust and mitigate fears about data breaches. Another major barrier is the lack of personalization, mentioned by 32.3% of respondents. Users are seeking more customized investment solutions that reflect their individual preferences and financial goals.

The lack of human interaction is a notable issue for 21.5% of respondents, suggesting that while robo-advisors offer efficiency, users still value the personal advice and touch provided by human advisors. Limited investment options, affecting 12.3% of respondents, indicates a demand for a wider array of investment choices within robo-advisors.

Regulatory concerns and other issues are less significant, with only 6.2% of respondents citing these as barriers. Although these concerns are relevant, they do not have as substantial an impact as data security and personalization.

The chi-square test shows no significant differences among user groups—retail traders, institutional traders, market analysts, or portfolio managers—in terms of these barriers. This uniformity suggests that the challenges associated with robo-advisors are broadly similar across different user types. To improve adoption rates, robo-advisors should focus on enhancing personalization features and addressing data security concerns. By effectively addressing these primary barriers, providers can better meet user expectations and enhance overall acceptance and utilization of robo-advisors.

Table 15. Potential Benefits of Integrating Robo-Advisors with Traditional Financial Advisory Services

Potential Benefits	Retail Traders	Institutional Traders	Market Analysts	Portfolio Managers	Total	Percentage
Significant benefits	8 (33.3%)	5 (35.7%)	6 (35.3%)	4 (40%)	23	35.4%
Some benefits	10 (41.7%)	6 (42.9%)	7 (41.2%)	3 (30%)	26	40.0%
Neutral	3 (12.5%)	1 (7.1%)	2 (11.8%)	2 (20%)	8	12.3%
Not really	2 (8.3%)	1 (7.1%)	2 (11.8%)	1 (10%)	6	9.2%
No benefits	1 (4.2%)	1 (7.1%)	0 (0%)	0 (0%)	2	3.1%
Total	24 (100%)	14 (100%)	17 (100%)	10 (100%)	65	100%

Source: Field & calculated data

Table 15 highlights the perceived benefits of integrating robo-advisors with traditional financial advisory services. The data indicates that a majority of respondents recognize value in such integration. Specifically, 40.0% of respondents believe there are "some benefits" to combining these services, while 35.4% see "significant benefits." This suggests a strong consensus on the potential advantages of blending robo-advisory capabilities with traditional financial advisory methods.

The responses show that while many respondents acknowledge the benefits of integration, there is a notable proportion who are neutral or skeptical about it. Specifically, 12.3% of respondents are neutral, indicating they neither strongly agree nor disagree with the benefits of integration. Additionally, 9.2% of respondents feel that integration does not offer substantial benefits, and a small minority, 3.1%, perceives no benefits at all.

The preference for integration across various professional groups—retail traders, institutional traders, market analysts, and portfolio managers—suggests that the combination of robo-advisory and traditional advisory services could enhance the overall effectiveness of financial advisory solutions. For instance, retail traders and institutional traders both show a substantial inclination towards recognizing significant benefits from such integration, while market analysts and portfolio managers also support the idea, albeit with varying degrees of enthusiasm.

In conclusion, the data underscores a general agreement on the value of integrating robo-advisors with traditional advisory services. The benefits recognized by the majority suggest that such integration could provide a more comprehensive and effective financial advisory experience, potentially addressing diverse client needs and preferences.

Section VII: Several Case Studies

Case study: Betterment- Robo-Advisor

Betterment is a pioneering robo-advisor recognized for its user-centric platform, offering automated investment management with advanced algorithms for optimized asset allocation and tax-loss harvesting. It is noted for its intuitive interface and low management fees.

Strengths:

- User-Friendly Interface: Betterment offers an intuitive and easy-to-use platform that simplifies investment management for users of all experience levels.
- Advanced Algorithms: Utilizes sophisticated algorithms for asset allocation and tax-loss harvesting, optimizing portfolio performance.
- Low Fees: Provides low management fees, which are attractive compared to traditional financial advisors.

Weaknesses:

- Limited Personalization: While Betterment offers personalized investment advice, it may lack the level of customization that some investors require.
- No Human Advisors: The absence of direct human interaction may be a drawback for users who prefer personalized advice and relationship-based interactions.

Opportunities:

- Expansion of Services: Opportunity to integrate more advanced financial planning tools and features, such as estate planning and retirement advice.
- Market Expansion: Potential to increase market share by expanding into new geographical regions and attracting more high-net-worth individuals.

Threats:

- Increased Competition: Rising competition from other robo-advisors and traditional financial institutions adopting similar technologies could impact market share.
- Economic Uncertainty: Market volatility and economic downturns can affect the performance of investment portfolios and user satisfaction.

Conclusion: Betterment's strength lies in its cost-effective, efficient investment management and user-friendly platform. However, its absence of personalized human interaction could limit its appeal to investors seeking more tailored and relational financial advice

Case study: Wealthfront- Robo-Advisor

Wealthfront provides a comprehensive suite of services, including automated portfolio management, tax-loss harvesting, and financial planning. It is distinguished by its low fees and account minimums, making sophisticated financial management accessible to a broad audience.

Strengths:

- Comprehensive Financial Planning: Wealthfront offers a range of services including tax-loss harvesting, financial planning, and access to financial advisors.
- Automated Rebalancing: Provides automated rebalancing and portfolio optimization, enhancing investment efficiency.
- Low Fees and Minimums: Attractive fee structure and low account minimums make it accessible to a broad range of investors.

Weaknesses:

- Limited Human Interaction: Similar to Betterment, Wealth front's reliance on automation may not appeal to investors seeking personalized advice and human interaction.
- Complex Pricing Structure: Some users may find the fee structure and pricing options complex to navigate and understand.

Opportunities:

- Integration of New Technologies: Potential to integrate emerging technologies like artificial intelligence to enhance predictive analytics and investment strategies.
- Partnerships and Acquisitions: Opportunities to partner with or acquire other fintech companies to broaden service offerings and market reach.

Threats:

- Regulatory Challenges: Changes in financial regulations and compliance requirements could impact operational efficiency and cost.
- Market Volatility: Economic fluctuations and market volatility may affect investment outcomes and user trust.

Conclusion: Wealthfront's extensive service offerings and cost efficiency position it as a robust competitor. Despite this, its reliance on automation and a complex fee structure might deter users who value more personalized advisory services

3. 2.3. Robinhood- robo-advisor

Robinhood is renowned for its zero-commission trading model and innovative features such as fractional shares, catering primarily to cost-conscious, younger investors. Its mobile app is designed for ease of use and accessibility.

Strengths:

- Zero Commission Trading: Robinhood's zero-commission trading model attracts a large user base, particularly among younger investors.
- Innovative Features: Offers innovative features such as fractional shares and a user-friendly mobile app, enhancing accessibility and user experience.
- Rapid Growth: Has experienced significant growth in user base and transaction volume due to its appealing business model.

Weaknesses:

- Revenue Model Concerns: Reliance on payment for order flow has raised concerns about potential conflicts of interest and transparency.
- Limited Advisory Services: Lacks comprehensive financial planning and advisory services, focusing primarily on trading and investing.

Opportunities:

- Expansion of Services: Opportunity to expand into wealth management and advisory services to attract a broader range of investors.
- Global Market Entry: Potential to enter international markets and increase its user base and revenue streams.

Threats:

- Regulatory Scrutiny: Increased scrutiny from regulatory bodies could impact its business model and operations.

- Competitive Pressure: Intense competition from other fintech and traditional financial institutions may affect growth and profitability.

Conclusion: Robinhood's commission-free trading and user-friendly interface drive significant user engagement. However, its revenue model and limited advisory services pose potential challenges to long-term user trust and satisfaction

Schwab Intelligent Portfolios- Robo-Advisor

Overview: Schwab Intelligent Portfolios integrates with Schwab's extensive financial services, providing no advisory fees and robust portfolio management. It is characterized by its comprehensive investment strategies and a higher account minimum requirement.

Strengths:

- Integration with Schwab Services: Leverages Schwab's established reputation and infrastructure, providing a seamless experience with access to other Schwab services.
- No Advisory Fees: Offers a robo-advisor service with no advisory fees, making it cost-effective for users.
- Comprehensive Portfolio Management: Utilizes a range of investment strategies and ETFs to create diversified portfolios.

Weaknesses:

- High Account Minimums: Requires a relatively high account minimum compared to some other robo-advisors, which may limit accessibility.
- Limited Personalization: The standard portfolio offerings may not cater to investors seeking highly personalized investment strategies.

Opportunities:

- Enhanced Features: Opportunity to integrate advanced tools and features, such as personalized financial planning and retirement advice.
- Cross-Selling Opportunities: Ability to cross-sell other Schwab products and services to robo-advisor users, enhancing overall customer value.

Threats:

- Competitive Landscape: Growing competition from more agile and innovative fintech firms may challenge Schwab's market position.
- Economic Downturns: Market volatility and economic downturns could impact portfolio performance and user satisfaction.

Conclusion: Schwab Intelligent Portfolios benefits from Schwab's reputable infrastructure and broad service integration. Nonetheless, its high account minimum and standardized portfolio offerings may limit its accessibility and appeal to investors seeking personalized solutions

These SWOT analyses provide a snapshot of the current state and potential future directions for each robo-advisor, highlighting their strengths, weaknesses, opportunities, and threats.

5. SUMMARY

Findings:

The objectives of this paper were to study the level of awareness and understanding towards robo-advisors, critically evaluate their effectiveness in security analysis and portfolio management, analyze the algorithms and technologies they employ under varying market conditions, assess their risk management practices, investigate user satisfaction and trust across demographic groups, identify barriers to adoption, and explore the implications of integrating robo-advisors with traditional financial advisory services.

The findings indicate a strong level of awareness among market professionals, with 77.24% of participants being familiar or very familiar with robo-advisors, and this awareness is significantly tied to their professional roles, as confirmed by the chi-square test. Out of the 65 participants, 45 use robo-advisors, with notable differences observed across various professions. Betterment (55.38%) and Schwab Intelligent Portfolios (46.15%) are the most widely used platforms, suggesting broad acceptance across professionals. A significant proportion of users (37.78%) have been utilizing robo-advisors for 1-2 years, indicating a high adoption rate. The effectiveness of robo-advisors varied across groups, with risk and comparative analysis being particularly valued in security analysis. Although satisfaction levels showed differences among professional groups, no significant differences in the perceived effectiveness of robo-advisors were observed across the various roles.

Robo-advisors were found to be similarly effective in portfolio management across retail traders, institutional traders, market analysts, and portfolio managers. Key features that stood out included risk management and portfolio optimization, which were appreciated across all user groups. Frequent portfolio reviews, with users checking their robo-advisor-managed portfolios regularly, were common, and high trust levels in robo-advisors' recommendations reflected confidence in their automated advice. Users viewed robo-advisors as more cost-effective than traditional advisors, which added to their appeal. However, data security and lack of personalization emerged as significant barriers to adoption, and addressing these issues could further enhance user satisfaction and boost adoption rates.

The SWOT analysis of the four robo-advisors revealed several key insights. Strengths included user-friendly interfaces, low fees, and advanced financial tools, catering to various investor needs. Weaknesses, however, included limited human interaction and personalization, which may not appeal to investors seeking tailored advice. Opportunities for growth lie in integrating advanced technologies, expanding services, and diversifying markets. The threats faced by robo-advisors include increasing competition, regulatory challenges, and economic volatility, which could impact user trust and portfolio performance. These findings highlight the need to balance automation with personalized services and underscore the importance of continuous innovation to remain competitive in the evolving financial landscape.

Recommendations and Implications

Behavioral Implications

i. High Trust in Automation: The study reveals that users exhibit high levels of trust in robo-advisors' recommendations, with most expressing confidence in the automated advice provided. This indicates a growing comfort with automated systems in financial decision-making, which could lead to further adoption of these tools.

ii. Desire for Customization: Users predominantly seek enhanced customization and integration in robo-advisors, reflecting a behavioral trend toward personalized financial management tools. This desire highlights a shift in user expectations, where personalized and tailored services are becoming increasingly important in financial advisory.

iii. Frequency of Portfolio Monitoring: The preference for frequent portfolio reviews, with most users checking their robo-advisor-managed portfolios daily, weekly, or monthly, underscores the behavioral inclination towards active engagement in financial management. This trend suggests that users want to stay closely involved with their investments, even when using automated tools.

iv. Perception of Cost-Effectiveness: The perception that robo-advisors are more cost-effective than traditional advisors' influences user behavior by making these platforms more appealing, particularly to cost-conscious investors. This behavioral trend could drive further adoption, especially if users continue to prioritize cost savings in their financial decisions.

v. Satisfaction and Effectiveness Perception: While robo-advisors are generally perceived as effective across various user groups, the differences in satisfaction levels among different groups (e.g., retail traders versus institutional traders) suggest that user satisfaction is influenced by specific needs and experiences. This implies that behavioral preferences vary and that one-size-fits-all approaches may not satisfy all users equally.

Practical Implications

i. Customization and Personalization: The need for enhanced customization indicates that robo-advisors should focus on developing more personalized investment strategies. This could involve integrating sophisticated AI and machine learning algorithms to cater to the unique needs of different user groups, thereby improving overall satisfaction and retention.

ii. Balancing Automation with Human Interaction: Addressing the weakness of limited human interaction by incorporating hybrid models that combine automated advice with human oversight could make robo-advisors more appealing. This practical approach could help bridge the gap for users who seek both automation and the reassurance of human expertise.

iii. Innovation in Technology and Services: The study highlights the importance of continuous innovation, particularly in integrating advanced technologies, expanding services, and diversifying markets. Practically, robo-advisors must stay ahead of the competition by continually enhancing their technological offerings and adapting to market demands.

iv. Regulatory Compliance and Trust-Building: With regulatory challenges identified as a key threat, robo-advisors must prioritize compliance with evolving regulations to avoid legal pitfalls and maintain user trust. Practically, this involves staying updated on regulatory changes and ensuring that their platforms meet all legal requirements.

v. Addressing Data Security Concerns: Data security is a major barrier to robo-advisor adoption, and addressing these concerns is critical. Practically, this means investing in robust cybersecurity measures to protect user data and maintain trust in the platform's security.

vi. Cost Efficiency: Maintaining low-fee structures while enhancing service quality is crucial for robo-advisors to continue attracting users. This practical implication involves balancing cost-effectiveness with the need to offer competitive and high-quality financial management tools.

vii. Integration with Traditional Services: The study suggests strong support for integrating robo-advisors with traditional financial services. Practically, this means developing hybrid models that combine the strengths of automated and human advisory services, offering a comprehensive solution that meets diverse user needs.

By addressing these behavioral and practical implications, robo-advisors can better meet the evolving demands of the financial services industry and secure their place as key players in the future of financial management

Recommendations

i. Enhancing User Experience: Continuously improve the user interface and experience of robo-advisor platforms to ensure ease of use and satisfaction across all user segments.
ii. University Partnerships: Partner with universities and colleges to incorporate fintech and robo-advisor topics into their curricula, thereby educating the next generation of investors.
iii. Targeted Campaigns: Financial institutions should implement targeted educational initiatives aimed at increasing awareness and understanding of robo-advisors, particularly among older and less technologically adept demographics.
iv. Workshops and Webinars: Offer free workshops, webinars, and online tutorials to demystify the functionality and benefits of robo-advisors.
v. Transparency and Communication: Increase transparency in how robo-advisors make decisions and manage portfolios Regularly publish performance reports comparing the effectiveness of robo-advisor portfolios to those managed by traditional advisors to demonstrate effectiveness and build trust.
vi. Algorithm Enhancement: Invest in continuous enhancement of robo-advisor algorithms to adapt to varying market conditions, ensuring sustained effectiveness in both stable and volatile environments.
vii. Customized Marketing Strategies: Develop marketing strategies tailored to different demographic groups, addressing specific concerns and highlighting the benefits relevant to each group.
viii. Simplifying Onboarding Process: Simplify the onboarding process for new users, making it easier for individuals with lower financial literacy to start using robo-advisors.
ix. Hybrid Advisory Models: Financial institutions should explore hybrid advisory models that combine robo-advisor technology with traditional human advisory services, offering a comprehensive solution that leverages the strengths of both.

x. Cross-Training Financial Advisors: Train traditional financial advisors on robo-advisor technologies and their benefits, enabling them to offer integrated advice to clients.

CONCLUSION

This research has critically examined the role of robo-advisors within the investment management industry, focusing on their effectiveness in security analysis, portfolio management, risk management practices, and user satisfaction. By addressing the identified gaps and integrating the strengths of both robo-advisors and traditional advisory services, the industry can achieve substantial improvements in user satisfaction, portfolio management outcomes, and the adoption of innovative financial technologies. The findings are supported by various study such as Barile et al. (2024), Loos et al. (2020), Bhatia et al. (2020), Tao et al. (2021), Mezzanotte (2020), Balakrishnan and Dwivedi (2021), Pal (2021), Wang (2022) Deloitte (2016), and Balwani et al. (2019).

In conclusion, the integration of robo-advisors with traditional advisory services presents a significant opportunity to create a more comprehensive and efficient financial advisory ecosystem. By implementing the recommendations provided, such as enhancing algorithm performance, improving user education, and developing hybrid advisory models, the industry can bridge existing gaps and foster a more inclusive and technologically advanced advisory landscape.

REFERENCES

Abraham, F., Schmukler, S. L., & Tessada, J. (2019). Robo-advisors: Investing through machines. *World Bank Research and Policy Briefs*, (134881).

Abraham, F., Schmukler, S. L., & Tessada, J. (2019). Robo-advisors: Investing through machines. *World Bank Policy Research Working Paper (134881).*

Balakrishnan, J., & Dwivedi, Y. K. (2021). Role of cognitive absorption in building user trust and experience. *Psychology and Marketing*, *38*(4), 643–668.

Balwani, D. N., Dash, A., Das, A., Das, L., Misra, D. S., & Ghose, D. S. (2019). Robo-Advisory: An Investor's Perception. *International Journal of Psychosocial Rehabilitation*, *23*(3).

Barile, D., Secundo, G., & Bussoli, C. (2024). Exploring artificial intelligence robo-advisor in banking industry: A platform model. *Management Decision*.

Bhatia, A., Chandani, A., & Chhateja, J. (2020). Robo advisory and its potential in addressing the behavioral biases of investors—A qualitative study in Indian context. *Journal of Behavioral and Experimental Finance*, *25*, 100281.

Chandani, A., Sriharshitha, S., Bhatia, A., Atiq, R., & Mehta, M. (2021). Robo-advisory services in India: A study to analyse awareness and perception of millennials. [IJCAC]. *International Journal of Cloud Applications and Computing*, *11*(4), 152–173.

Cheng, X., Guo, F., Chen, J., Li, K., Zhang, Y., & Gao, P. (2019). Exploring the trust influencing mechanism of robo-advisor service: A mixed method approach. *Sustainability*, *11*(18), 4917.

Chhabra, A. B. (2005). Beyond Markowitz: A comprehensive wealth allocation framework for individual investors. *The Journal of Wealth Management*, *7*(4), 8–34.

Darskuviene, V., & Lisauskiene, N. (2021). Linking the robo-advisors' phenomenon and behavioural biases in investment management: An interdisciplinary literature review and research agenda. *Organizations and Markets in Emerging Economies*, *12*(2), 459–477.

Deloitte. (2016). The expansion of robo-advisory in wealth management.

Dietvorst, B. J., Simmons, J., & Massey, C. (2015). Algorithm aversion: People erroneously avoid algorithms after seeing them err. *Journal of Experimental Psychology. General*, *144*(1), 114–126. DOI: 10.1037/xge0000033 PMID: 25401381

Eren, B. A. (2023). Antecedents of robo-advisor use intention in private pension investments: An emerging market country example. *Journal of Financial Services Marketing*, •••, 1–16.

Eren, B. A. (2023). Antecedents of robo-advisor use intention in private pension investments: An emerging market country example. *Journal of Financial Services Marketing*, *27*(1), 1–16. DOI: 10.1057/s41264-023-00200-8

Fulk, M., Grable, J., Watkins, K., & Kruger, M. (2018). Who uses robo-advisory services, and who does not? *Financial Services Review*, *27*(2), 173–188.

Guo, F. (2020). Regulating investment robo-advisors in China: Problems and prospects. *European Business Organization Law Review*, *21*(1), 69–99. DOI: 10.1007/s40804-020-00178-3

Guo, F., Cheng, X., & Zhang, Y. (2019). A conceptual model of trust influencing factors in robo-advisor products: A qualitative study. *WHICEB 2019 Proceedings.* Available at: https://aisel.aisnet.org/whiceb2019/48

Guo, L. (2020). Regulating investment robo-advisors in China: Problems and prospects. *European Business Organization Law Review*, *21*(1), 69–99.

Hakala, J. (2019). Robo-advisors: Revolutionizing financial services through algorithmic investment management. *Financial Innovation*, *5*(3), 23–34.

High-Level Expert Group on AI. (2019). Ethics guidelines for trustworthy AI—Shaping Europe's digital future. *European Commission Report.* Brussels. Available at: https://digital-strategy.ec.europa.eu/en/library/ethics-guidelines-trustworthy-ai

Hildebrand, C., & Bergner, A. (2021). Conversational robo-advisors as surrogates of trust: Onboarding experience, firm perception, and consumer financial decision-making. *Journal of the Academy of Marketing Science*, *49*(4), 659–676. DOI: 10.1007/s11747-020-00753-z

Hohenberger, C., Lee, C., & Coughlin, J. (2019). Acceptance of robo-advisors: Effects of financial experience, affective reactions, and self-enhancement motives. *Financial Planning Review*, *2*(2), e1047.

Huang, M. H., & Rust, R. T. (2018). Artificial intelligence in service. *Journal of Service Research*, *21*(2), 155–172.

Huang, Z. (2022). Robo-advisors and the digitization of wealth management in China. In *The Digital Financial Revolution in China*. The Brookings Institution.

Investment Company Institute. (2023). ICI Research Perspective: Trends in the expenses and fees of funds, 2022. *Research.* Washington, D.C.: Investment Company Institute. Available at: https://www.ici.org/system/files/2023-03/per29-03.pdf

Kaplan, A. D., Kessler, T., Brill, J. C., & Hancock, P. A. (2023). Trust in artificial intelligence: Meta-analytic findings. *Human Factors, 65*(2), 337–359. DOI: 10.1177/00187208211013988 PMID: 34048287

Liang, H., & Xue, Y. (2009). Avoidance of information technology threats: A theoretical perspective. *Management Information Systems Quarterly*, •••, 71–90.

Liaudinskas, K. (2022). *Human vs. machine: Disposition effect among algorithmic and human day traders* (No. 6/2022). Working Paper.

Loos, B., Previtero, A., Scheurle, S., & Hackethal, A. (2020). Robo-advisers and investor behavior. *Unpublished Working Paper.*

Maume, P. (2019). Regulating robo-advisory. *Tex. Int'l LJ, 55*, 49.

Maume, P. (2019). Robo-advisor is algorithm-based software that provides specifically tailored investment recommendations to the client based on the client's input. *Bachelor Thesis.*

Mezzanotte, F. E. (2020). An examination into the investor protection properties of robo-advisory services in Switzerland. *Capital Markets Law Journal, 15*(4), 489–508.

Pal, A., Sharma, S. S., & Gupta, K. P. (2021). The Role of Analytics and Robo-Advisory in Investors' Financial Decisions and Risk Management: Review of Literature Post-Global Financial Crisis. [IJBAN]. *International Journal of Business Analytics, 8*(2), 46–62.

Puntoni, S., Reczek, R. W., Giesler, M., & Botti, S. (2021). Consumers and artificial intelligence: An experiential perspective. *Journal of Marketing, 85*(1), 131–151.

Sander, M. (2021). Success factors for robo-advisory: Now and then. *Robo-Advisory: Investing in the Digital Age*, 257-269. Beck, A. D. (2021). The role of artificial intelligence in robo-advisory. *Robo-Advisory: Investing in the Digital Age*, 227-243.

Sironi, P. (2016). My Robo Advisor was an iPod–Applying the Lessons from Other Sectors to FinTech Disruption. *The FinTech Book: The Financial Technology Handbook for Investors, Entrepreneurs and Visionaries*, 152-154.

Sironi, P. (2016). *FinTech innovation: From robo-advisors to goal-based investing and gamification.* John Wiley & Sons.

Tao, R., Su, C. W., Xiao, Y., Dai, K., & Khalid, F. (2021). Robo advisors, algorithmic trading and investment management: Wonders of fourth industrial revolution in financial markets. *Technological Forecasting and Social Change*, *163*, 120421.

Thier, J., & dos Santos Monteiro, L. (2022). The role of algorithms in robo-advisors: A critical analysis. *Journal of Financial Services Research*, *62*(1), 1–15. DOI: 10.1007/s10693-021-00365-0

Thier, P., & dos Santos Monteiro, L. (2022). Robo-advisors typically use algorithms, but those algorithms may or may not use artificial intelligence.

Wang, Y., Kang, Q., Zhou, S., Dong, Y., & Liu, J. (2022). The impact of service robots in retail: Exploring the effect of novelty priming on consumer behavior. *Journal of Retailing and Consumer Services*, *68*, 103002.

Ziegler, A., & Weller, J. (2021). Robo-advisors and their role in sustainable investing: Evidence from the German market. *Journal of Sustainable Finance & Investment*, *11*(1), 1–15. DOI: 10.1080/20430795.2020.1848140

Chapter 2
The Role of Big Data and Predictive Analytics in Financial Decision-Making

Kushagra Valecha
https://orcid.org/0009-0008-3346-6233
Christ University, India

ABSTRACT

Big data refers to enormous amounts of structured and unstructured data that arise daily. All the finance sector records transactions, market data, social media sentiments, customer behavior, and macroeconomic indicators. The big three dimensions of big data that are commonly called the "3 Vs" include Volume, Velocity, and Variety. It means the data came from sources such as social media, IoT devices, transactions, and sensors. This process involves large amounts of data hence requiring scalable storages, complex processing tools, and resources for effective data management and analytics. Velocity means the rate or speed at which data is originated and processed. Lastly, Variety denotes the different kinds of data, which include the structured ones such as databases and the unstructured kinds, such as images, video, social media post, and audio. Collectively, the 3 Vs capture both the richness and the potentiality of big data, demanding the need for innovation in terms of technologies and strategies to leverage this value.

DOI: 10.4018/979-8-3373-1404-4.ch002

INTRODUCTION

Integration of big data and predictive analytics in the fast lane of the financial landscape leads to efficient decision-making. It is redesigning the nature of the financial world: from identifying investments to reducing risk. This chapter will outline how big data and predictive analytics form a central hub for financial decision-making and goes on to outline applications, benefits, and challenges.

Understanding Big Data in Finance

Big data refers to enormous amounts of structured and unstructured data that arise daily. All the finance sector records transactions, market data, social media sentiments, customer behavior, and macroeconomic indicators. The big three dimensions of big data that are commonly called the "3 Vs" include Volume, Velocity, and Variety. Volume: Volume of data. It means the data came from sources such as social media, IoT devices, transactions, and sensors. This process involves large amounts of data hence requiring scalable storages, complex processing tools, and resources for effective data management and analytics. Velocity means the rate or speed at which data is originated and processed. Data today is coming in real-time or near-real-time from streaming services, financial transactions, and IoT devices. Such a system must then process and analyze the data instantaneously to be able to help in timely decision-making. Lastly, Variety denotes the different kinds of data, which include the structured ones such as databases and the unstructured kinds, such as images, video, social media post, and audio. It makes the integration, analysis, and quality control of the data difficult as different tools and techniques have to be used in order to gain meaningful insights from each type. Collectively, the 3 Vs capture both the richness and the potentiality of big data, demanding the need for innovation in terms of technologies and strategies to leverage this value. Armed with complex analytics tools and techniques, it is now possible to exploit these data streams into actionable predictivity.

THE ROLE OF PREDICTIVE ANALYTICS

Predictive analytics involves using statistical models, machine learning algorithms, and artificial intelligence (AI) to analyze historical data and forecast future trends. In finance, this capability drives smarter, faster, and more accurate decision-making across multiple domains.

Applications of Predictive Analytics in Financial Decision-Making

Predictive analytics is the biggest domain for financial organizations to mitigate risks because it can predict and control probable threats (Chong et al., 2017). For example, predictive models of credit risk assessment measure the customer's credit history, certain types of transactional patterns, and alternative data in contrast to probable default possibilities and will lend accordingly. This would award credits to the most likely borrowers who would perform their duties in a manner such that the loss of money would be reduced to its minimum level. The same principle works with fraud detection through predictive analytics because it could identify suspicious activities by showing anomalies in the pattern of transactions to increase security and minimize possibilities of financial frauds . These systems can detect irregular behaviors that might have otherwise gone unnoticed when analyzing vast datasets in real-time. This allows for a proactive approach to safeguarding financial assets.

Predictive analytics is a significant contribution to market risk analysis. Advanced models are used to evaluate potential shifts within the market and forecast economic trends, empowering firms to hedge against market volatility, devise strategies to manage exposure, and avoid significant financial losses. These applications demonstrate how predictive analytics improves risk management through actionable insights and a data-driven approach to decision-making. Predictive analytics revolutionizes investment strategy optimization through data-driven decisions and maximum return. Algorithmic trading is based on predictive models that scan market trends, historical data, and real-time information to identify automated trading systems that will execute transactions at optimal moments, usually in fractions of a second (Treleaven et al., 2013). As a result, every trade is optimized to capture the window of opportunity before it disappears, improving efficiency and profitability.

Portfolio management also benefits greatly from predictive analytics. Advanced models forecast asset performance based on market conditions, economic indicators, and past trends. These forecasts help in diversifying portfolios constructed according to investors' risk tolerance, time horizons, and financial goals to ensure a balanced approach to long-term growth. Furthermore, sentiment mining on social networks and news provides essential insights related to market trends and public perspectives (Liu, 2012). This allows investors to identify industries or sectors that may experience growth or decline due to public sentiment.

Predictive analytics has been pivotal for customer-centric financial services, making financial institutions more responsive to individual customer needs. Personalized offerings involve models developed by analyzing customer behavior, preferences, and financial history, such as loans, insurance policies, or investment plans tailored to meet specific needs. These bespoke deals enhance customer satisfaction and improve customer retention rates, fostering sustainable relationships.

Another critical aspect of predictive analytics is its ability to identify customers likely to leave based on criteria such as account activity, usage patterns, or other interactions with the company (Ngai et al., 2009). This insight enables financial institutions to proactively implement targeted retention measures, such as personalized promotions or one-on-one outreach, to address customer concerns and reinforce loyalty. Predictive models also estimate Customer Lifetime Value (CLV), helping organizations focus resources on high-value customers and offering premium services to retain their most profitable clients. Predictive analytics also drives operational efficiency in financial institutions. By predicting demand for specific financial services, organizations can strategically allocate resources, avoiding issues like understaffing or overstaffing. Predictive models identify inefficiencies and bottlenecks, enabling organizations to streamline workflows, automate routine tasks, and reduce operational costs. Furthermore, predictive analytics ensures regulatory compliance by monitoring real-time financial activities and generating automated reports to track compliance with industry regulations. This reduces the likelihood of human error, enhances transparency, and allows institutions to adhere to regulatory requirements efficiently. Predictive analytics also enhances revenue generation through optimal pricing strategies, sales forecasting, and cross-selling or upselling opportunities. Historical data, marketplace trends, and real-time customer behavior are analyzed to develop strategies for pricing financial products such as loans, insurance, and investment options (Waller & Fawcett, 2013). Sales forecasting uses predictive analytics to assess market conditions and customer trends, enabling accurate revenue projections and resource alignment.

Lastly, predictive analytics enhances cross-selling and upselling by analyzing client data to identify complementary products that align with existing customer needs. Financial institutions can thus provide tailored services to increase revenue per customer while ensuring higher satisfaction.

Benefits of Big Data and Predictive Analytics

One of the key benefits of big data and predictive analytics is enhanced decision-making, which empowers organizations to make more informed, timely, and accurate choices. Traditionally, decision-making was often based on historical data or limited insights, which could lead to delayed reactions or suboptimal strategies. However, with the vast amounts of data available through big data sources, combined with predictive analytics that can process and analyze this data, organizations can identify trends, patterns, and potential outcomes with remarkable precision. For example, in financial services, predictive models can forecast market fluctuations or customer behaviors, enabling investment managers to adjust strategies proactively rather than reactively. In retail, businesses can predict consumer demand and optimize inventory management to avoid stockouts or overstocking. Predictive analytics also allows companies to make decisions with a deeper understanding of the variables that affect outcomes, such as customer preferences, economic conditions, and competitor actions (Chen et al., 2012). Moreover, by leveraging real-time data streams, organizations can make quicker decisions, which is crucial in fast-paced industries like finance and e-commerce. This shift from intuition-based to data-driven decision-making not only reduces uncertainty but also enhances the overall effectiveness of business strategies, helping organizations improve their operations, minimize risks, and seize new opportunities. Ultimately, enhanced decision-making through big data and predictive analytics leads to more efficient resource utilization, improved performance, and a competitive edge in the marketplace.

A significant benefit of big data and predictive analytics is proactive risk mitigation, which enables organizations to identify and address potential risks before they escalate into critical issues. In the past, businesses often relied on historical data and reactive approaches to handle risks, which could lead to delays in response and increased exposure to harm. With the power of big data and predictive analytics, however, organizations can process massive volumes of real-time and historical data, detect early warning signs, and forecast potential risks with a higher degree of accuracy. For example, in financial institutions, predictive models can assess credit risk by analyzing customers' financial behaviors, transaction histories, and external economic factors, allowing banks to prevent loan defaults by adjusting lending practices (Ngai et al., 2011). Similarly, in the insurance industry, predictive analytics can anticipate fraudulent claims by identifying unusual patterns in claims data, enabling insurers to act swiftly and minimize losses. In manufacturing, predictive analytics can forecast equipment failures by monitoring sensor data from machinery, allowing for preventative maintenance before costly breakdowns occur. By leveraging these predictive insights, organizations can proactively adjust their strategies, implement mitigating actions, and allocate resources effectively to address potential risks in advance. This proactive approach not only reduces the likelihood of negative events but also minimizes the financial, operational, and reputational damage that can occur when risks are left unchecked. Ultimately, proactive risk mitigation through big data and predictive analytics leads to more resilient organizations that are better equipped to navigate uncertainty and safeguard their interests.

One of the most impactful benefits of big data and predictive analytics is increased competitiveness, as these technologies enable organizations to gain a significant edge in their respective industries. In today's fast-paced and data-driven business environment, the ability to leverage large volumes of data and advanced analytics tools can help companies identify emerging trends, understand market dynamics, and respond to customer needs more effectively than their competitors. By analyzing historical and real-time data, businesses can uncover valuable insights into consumer preferences, competitor activities, and market conditions, allowing them to make more informed decisions and seize new opportunities faster. Predictive analytics, in particular, enhances this advantage by forecasting future trends, behaviors, and outcomes, giving companies the foresight to act proactively rather than reactively (Chen et al., 2012). For example, retailers can use predictive models to optimize their inventory management and pricing strategies based on anticipated demand, which helps them stay ahead of competitors in terms of stock availability and customer satisfaction. Similarly, in the financial sector, predictive analytics can improve investment strategies by analyzing market fluctuations and predicting potential investment opportunities, leading to better returns and smarter portfolio management (Ngai et al., 2011). Additionally, big data and predictive analytics allow businesses to personalize their offerings, ensuring that products, services, and marketing campaigns resonate with specific customer segments, which fosters brand loyalty and strengthens customer relationships. In industries where competition is fierce, such as e-commerce, healthcare, and finance, the ability to anticipate customer needs, optimize operations, and innovate at a faster pace directly translates into a stronger market position. Ultimately, by harnessing the power of big data and predictive analytics, organizations can not only streamline their operations but also make strategic, forward-thinking decisions that enhance their competitiveness and drive sustained growth.

One of the most significant benefits of big data and predictive analytics is improved customer experience, as these technologies enable businesses to understand and anticipate customer needs in ways that were previously impossible. By analyzing vast amounts of data from a variety of touchpoints, including social media, purchase histories, customer feedback, and online interactions, businesses can gain a deep understanding of individual customer preferences, behaviors, and pain points (Chen et al., 2012). This insight allows companies to deliver highly personalized experiences, tailored offers, and relevant recommendations that resonate with customers on a personal level. For example, retailers use predictive analytics to suggest products based on past purchases or browsing behavior, enhancing the shopping experience and increasing the likelihood of repeat business (Ngai et al., 2011). Similarly, financial institutions can provide personalized loan offers or investment advice based on a customer's financial history, making their services more relevant and valuable. Predictive models also enable businesses to anticipate customer issues before they arise, allowing for proactive customer support. In industries such as telecommunications or utilities, for example, predictive analytics can identify customers who are likely to experience service disruptions or billing problems, allowing companies to reach out and resolve these issues before customers even notice. Furthermore, by segmenting customers based on their behaviors and preferences, companies can create more targeted marketing campaigns that speak directly to the needs of each group, increasing engagement and brand loyalty. Ultimately, the use of big data and predictive analytics helps companies create a seamless and personalized customer experience, fostering stronger relationships, increasing customer satisfaction, and driving long-term loyalty. This leads to improved retention rates, higher customer lifetime value, and a competitive advantage in a market that increasingly values individualized attention and convenience.

Challenges in Implementation

The introduction of big data and predictive analytics in financial decision-making poses significant challenges, particularly concerning data protection and security. Financial institutions handle personal customer data, including transactional histories and records, which must comply with stringent privacy regulations such as GDPR, HIPAA, and others (Chong et al., 2017). As businesses increasingly rely on big data to interpret large datasets, safeguarding privacy and security is crucial when storing sensitive information. Breaches or unauthorized access could lead to substantial financial losses, reputational damage, and legal repercussions.

Data for predictive analytics is often sourced from third-party vendors, complicating data security management. Risks such as inadequate encryption, weak access controls, and poor governance exacerbate vulnerabilities to cyberattacks, identity theft, and fraud. Moreover, with rising awareness about personal data usage, transparency and accountability in data collection practices have become paramount. Financial institutions must adopt robust security measures—encryption, secure data storage, and access controls—to comply with evolving legal and ethical standards (Ngai et al., 2009). The increasing use of cloud and distributed systems adds complexity to securing big data, necessitating a balance between leveraging insights and protecting customer privacy.

Data quality and integration are other major hurdles in deploying big data for financial decision-making. Financial institutions process data from various sources—transactions, customer interactions, market trends, and external databases—each varying in format, structure, and accuracy. Poor data quality, such as errors or missing values, can lead to unreliable predictions and suboptimal strategies. Integration efforts are further complicated by siloed systems storing data in diverse formats. The lack of unified datasets results in inefficiencies, delays, and missed opportunities, particularly when modern data sources like social media or sensor data are involved (Treleaven et al., 2013). Effective integration demands sophisticated tools, strong data governance, and standardized processes to ensure the reliability and accuracy of predictive analytics (Waller & Fawcett, 2013).

Model bias also presents a significant challenge in predictive analytics. Machine learning models trained on biased or incomplete data may perpetuate or amplify existing disparities, leading to discriminatory practices or unfair financial decisions (Bishop, 2013). For instance, biased credit scoring models can disadvantage certain demographic groups, resulting in inequitable treatment. Additionally, unrepresentative datasets may fail to account for diverse customer needs, skewing predictions. Bias can stem from variable selection, data treatment, or model definition, undermining the fairness and reliability of decisions (Ngai et al., 2009). Addressing bias requires diverse datasets, regular audits, and a commitment to fairness and transparency in model development.

The lack of technical expertise further complicates the adoption of big data and predictive analytics. Financial institutions need specialists proficient in data science, machine learning, and statistical modeling, who also possess domain knowledge of financial systems (Kumar & Ravi, 2016). Managing unstructured data, such as social media posts or transactional logs, requires advanced natural language processing techniques. Integrating big data tools with legacy systems adds to the technical complexity, necessitating custom solutions and infrastructure upgrades. Even with skilled personnel, ongoing training is essential to stay abreast of evolving technologies (Liu, 2012). Without adequate expertise, predictive models may yield inaccurate forecasts, leading to poor decisions and financial losses. Investments in talent acquisition and internal capability development are critical for maximizing the potential of big data in financial decision-making.

FUTURE TRENDS

Some of the most pronounced future trends that bear a direct nexus to big data and predictive analytics in the space of financial decision-making revolve around the integration of real-time analytics. Financial markets, consumer behaviors, as well as business environments, would become fluid and increasingly dynamic in nature such that an organization needed real-time processing of data so that it remains agile and responsive enough . The aspect of analytics within financial institutions can be a way of allowing the analysis of real-time data from when it is in creation. It eventually means that the decisions that might be made real-time can be real-time, more so as opposed to being based on stale or even historically established data . For instance, for an ordinary stock market, traders will have real-time analytics that can track sudden changes in market trends and price, thereby allowing entry into trades exactly when the events are happening due to having access in real-time (Chen et al., 2012). This is where retail banking institutions can detect and block fraudulent transactions in real time, giving them a chance to block potentially fraudulent activities before damage occurs . Real-time analytics also enhances customer experience because financial institutions can offer personalized services on the spot. For instance, banks can analyze through predictive models any customer's transaction history and behavior real-time so as to offer them unique financial products or services at the moment of their interaction, that is, on the basis of recommending investment opportunities, savings plans, or loans (Ngai et al., 2011). More than this, real-time analytics will equip financial institutions to always stay in front of what regulatory expectations dictate by monitoring real-time all transactions and activities happening in their operations that will not even delay compliance while managing the risk of financial crimes . The rising use of IoT devices, together with other technologies that produce large amounts of data, also ensures an increasing supply of real-time data, fueling predictive analytics further . However, such integration processes demand high sophisticated infrastructures and the capability of high-performance computing to process such gigantic data in faster time. Along with that, it also needs them to concentrate more on the quality of the data and puts up an analytic system in real-time. The future of big data and predictive analytics in financial decision-making is going to be on easy integration of real-time analytics into a process to enhance decision speed, operational efficiency, and provision of a more personalized, secure, and responsive service to customers.

Alternative data will be one of the key future trends in the role of big data and predictive analytics in financial decision-making. Through the years, banks have constantly banked on traditional sources of data, such as credit scores, bank transactions, and financial statements, to assess risks, invest, and serve customers. Alternative sources for big data are non-traditional sources such as social media activity, geolocation data, online shopping behavior, satellite imagery, payment histories from non-bank institutions, and even sentiment analysis from news articles or customer reviews (Chen et al., 2012). This wide diversity of data can be incorporated into the analytics models of financial institutions in order to have a more detailed view of the financial health, behavior, and risk profile of a customer (Ngai et al., 2011). This is a highly valuable opportunity for the underserved or unbanked population. For instance, alternative data can be helpful in providing insight into the creditworthiness of individuals who do not have a traditional credit history, thereby allowing lenders to extend credit to a wider pool of borrowers . With regards to investment, alternative data often shows hidden patterns and market signals missed by traditional financial data, therefore it allows for investment based on more comprehensive and timely strategic decisions . For instance, it may predict stock price movements based on public perception or emerging trends by doing some sentiment analysis from social media or news. In like manner, alternative data also helps in more proactive risk management through giving early signs of market shifts or disruptions . However, the integration of alternative data into financial decisions is challenging in terms of quality of data, privacy concerns, and complexity of algorithms needed to interpret appropriately as forms of unstructured data . There are also regulatory complexities with alternative data that a financial institution has to navigate by adhering to data protection laws, thereby maintaining a proper use of information about persons. Nevertheless, with the growing application of alternative data, predictive models will be improved, innovation in financial services will be promoted, and organizations will be able to make more accurate and data-driven decisions that could not have been possible with traditional sources of data. The future of financial decision-making will be shaped as these data sources become more refined and accessible.

One of the critical future trends in the role of big data and predictive analytics in financial decision-making is the rise of Explainable AI, or XAI. As financial institutions increasingly turn to artificial intelligence and machine learning to drive decision-making, the need for transparency, accountability, and interpretability in AI-driven processes has become more urgent (Ngai et al., 2011). This results in the limitation that while being more effective for discovery of patterns, and particularly the predictions based on deep learning algorithms, it largely acts like a "black box," such that the decisions the AI systems generate are opaque in nature to a human analyst, which poses challenges mainly in high-reliance applications like finance—where decision errors, in addition to monetary outcomes, might expose a bank, financial organization, or financial advisors to substantial litigation as well as ethics claims . This challenge can be addressed with explainable AI, which not only learns to make predictions but now provides clear and understandable explanations regarding how the predictions were made . For example, in credit risk modeling, an XAI system could explain why a particular borrower was deemed a high risk, highlighting specific factors such as past payment history, income level, and current debt load, thus enabling financial professionals to better understand and trust the model's recommendations (Chen et al., 2012). This transparency is crucial not only for compliance with regulatory standards, such as the EU's GDPR and the U.S. Equal Credit Opportunity Act but also builds on consumer trust while ensuring that processes are fair and objective in the decision-making approach . XAI will also be helpful in the auditing and validation of predictive models to ensure that they function as expected without creating biased situations or discriminatory outcomes. Explanatory models will enable financial institutions to mitigate risks because of the reliance on non-transparent automated systems, wherein they are increasingly becoming dependent on AI for fraud detection, credit scoring, and algorithmic trading.

Edge computing is another major trend revolutionizing data processing and analysis in financial decision-making . Traditionally, data from financial transactions, customer interactions, and market events would be sent to centralized data centers for processing and analysis. However, given the continuous growth of data volumes and speeds, latency and inefficiencies can accrue with such centralized approaches.

Edge computing overcomes this hurdle by executing computation closer to the actual data source, whether on local servers, devices, or within the network (Ngai et al., 2011). This significantly speeds up data processing, enabling faster, more responsive decision-making. For example, point-of-sale or mobile-device processing can flag suspicious transactions in real time, preventing fraud instead of recognizing it much later (Chen et al., 2012). Edge computing also enhances data privacy since sensitive financial data can be processed locally, reducing risks associated with data transfer.

HISTORICAL CONTEXT

Gradually changing in its growth, the evolution of big data and analytics in finance was initiated by changes in technology, availability of data, and increasing complexity of financial markets. In early years, it mainly relied on simple accounting systems with much manual processing; therefore, financial decisions were determined through the availability of minimal historical data, intuition, and experience. The first major milestone in the evolution of financial analytics came in the 1960s and 1970s, when financial firms began to adopt mainframe computers for tasks like transaction processing and record-keeping. This marked the beginning of the digitalization of financial data, making it easier to store and retrieve large amounts of information. By the 1980s and 1990s, more advanced systems of database management had emerged; financial institutions then could process bigger datasets and even analyze them more significantly (Chen et al., 2012). Relational databases, just like those implemented by companies like Oracle, supported organizations in saving and manipulating data in a much easier way, unlocking the possibility for more complex models of finance as well as risk management strategies (Elbahnasawy, 2021). It was when financial institutions began embracing statistical analysis and building more complex mathematical models, first in areas like derivative pricing and market risk analysis. It was only, in fact, in the early 2000s, that the true revolution of big data and analytics took place, as the boom in the Internet and the explosion of e-commerce, social media, and mobile technology ushered in a plethora of new sources of data. During this time, powerful computing technologies and storage capabilities allowed them to process and analyze huge volumes of unstructured data; everything from the behavior of customers to market sentiment to social media activity was there to be processed. Other advancements in machine learning and artificial intelligence further helped the analysis find meaningful patterns in large datasets, making analytics more predictive and prescriptive than ever. It was until the 2010s when firms were able to advance their analytics platforms so as to analyze historical data, but at the same time engage in real-time analytics for speedier, more data-driven decision-making. As the years have progressed, integration of alternative data has also taken the form of satellite imagery, payment histories, and even weather patterns in providing much deeper insights in investment strategies, credit scoring, and market forecasting. Big data and predictive analytics permeate the modern world of finance today—from automatic trading and tailored financial services to real-time fraud detection and risk assessment. But this is just a start. Advances in cloud computing, edge computing, and explainable AI will keep the landscape in a constant state of flux as faster, more accurate, and secure decisions start to take their shape. In the near two decades since it first became prominent as a concept, big data and analytics in finance haven't only changed how financial institutions operate but have also opened doors for innovations that continue to redefine the capabilities of the financial industry.

CASE STUDY

With such technological developments, it has been put in place successfully by various finance industry corporations to give the corporations a competitive advantage over other companies. The following is a prime example, among others: an investment made by JPMorgan Chase to use big data and analytics so that gains can be realized in the trading activities of the corporation and assess risk while gathering insight and knowledge regarding customers. By leveraging massive amounts of transactional data, market data, and social media sentiment, JPMorgan Chase makes use of predictive models to optimize its trading algorithms and thus enables the bank to make real-time decisions based on more information, improve profitability, and minimize risks. Moreover, machine learning techniques enable the bank to predict potential loan defaults, thus improving the assessment of risk and lending decisions, and this has significantly improved its credit risk management. American Express, for instance, employs big data analytics to better understand its customers and stimulate business growth. It uses analysis of transactional data, spending habits, and behavioral trends to give customers individualized recommendations and tailored financial products. With the use of predictive analytics, American Express can forecast the needs of customers, improve marketing efforts, and even catch fraud attempts in time, hence safeguarding both the company and its customers. PayPal is another financial services company that has managed to apply predictive analytics successfully for improving fraud detection and customer security. PayPal applies machine learning models in order to recognize anomalous activities-anomalies-which may lead to fraudulent behaviors. The company has significantly reduced loss from fraudulent transactions, as low as is possible, with the predictive models being perfected on a constant basis. The fraud patterns tend to catch up with cyber-crooks; therefore, predictive models are continuously perfected to give an edge in fraud patterns. The big-data and predictive analytics company, LendingClub, uses big data to evaluate the borrower risk more precisely compared to the traditional model for credit scoring. It evaluates the creditworthiness of the borrowers by reviewing alternative data sources such as social media activities, education history, and employment record, giving it the ability to make better predictions about the chances of the borrower defaulting on his loan or not. In addition, Netflix and Amazon, even though they are not strictly financial services companies, are quintessential examples of how predictive analytics can be applied to the financial sector as well. Both of these companies used big data to revolutionize their business models through predictive customer preferences, offering personalized recommendations to drive revenue growth through targeted marketing and customer retention. These case studies show how companies in the financial sector are using big data and predictive analytics not only to streamline operations but also to enhance customer engagement, improve risk management, and stay ahead of industry trends. As these technologies continue to evolve, more financial institutions will undoubtedly adopt similar strategies to optimize their decision-making processes and deliver more personalized, efficient services.

Sector-Specific Applications

1. Banking and insurance sector

Big data and predictive analytics have become very fundamental in shaping the form of financial decision-making by both banks and insurers, thus making the strategies more accurate, efficient, and customer-centered. For instance, with banking, big data analytics enables the banks to process huge chunks of transactional data, thus making them better in knowing what behavior is involved among the customers, which also gives room to fraud activity identification, thus gifting an insight to the risk related to credit. The banks can, therefore, use the predictive models to understand spending, saving, and loan repayment patterns, which can help understand the needs and preferences of customers and eventually apply this to the provision of tailor-made financial products and services. For instance, predictive analytics will easily make a prediction on whether the customer will or will not default on the loan. It also allows for real-time monitoring of transactions based on big data, which may identify potential frauds and detect suspicious activities before the fraud does great damage. Predictive analytics also helps banks optimize their operations, reduce costs, and enhance customer retention by predicting which clients might leave and making interventions accordingly. Underwriting, risk assessment, and claims management in the insurance industry is huge when using big data and predictive analytics. In that respect, extremely wide variety can be obtained by taking in such things as a customer's demographics to their health records, social media activity, and even driving behavior in determining more detailed ways to decide who should provide them with what level of insurance plans. For example, with telematics devices, insurers can analyze driving data in order to set premiums on live driving behavior, thus rewarding better driving. Predictive analytics prevents fraud since anomalies within the patterns of the data that may raise an inconsistency or odd behavior offset losses in case fraud activities occur. Big data creates dynamic pricing models as in this scenario whether the commodity sold or not by companies will become priced with respect to the prevailing market conditions, customer's behavior, and related risk factors compared to competitive pricing to reap maximum revenues. This is how the integration of big data and predictive analytics revolutionizes decision-making in banking and insurance, giving them better risk assessment, more customized offerings, improved operational efficiency, and higher customer satisfaction. Over the long term, these industries make financial outcomes even better and change the future of financial services.

2. Asset management sector

Asset management changed the very fabric of old investment strategies and started using the role of big data and predictive analytics into decision-making processes, where precise data-driven determinations made it easier to analyze enormous amounts of structured and unstructured data on a large scale - historical market data, economic indicators, news sentiment, social media trends, or even more alternative sources from satellite imagery and supply chain movements. The machine learning algorithm and the quantitative models facilitate a much greater degree of predictability of market trends, price fluctuations, and investment opportunities in predictive analytics. This way, asset managers could analyze past behavior in the markets and predict stock, bond, commodity, or even market performance, thus allowing them to take better decisions in terms of asset allocation. For example, predictive models enable companies to realign their portfolios in real-time, based on the changing market conditions, global events, and macroeconomic changes that may change the value of the assets. Furthermore, big data and predictive analytics enable asset management to better enhance its risk management through more intricate risk assessment. They inform asset managers how much risk accompanies a particular investment, help one measure the amount of volatility around investments, and predict possible drops or unstable market periods. Such models are additionally useful for making any portfolio diversified-an asset allocation should actually be distributed on the basis of an investor's financial goals, as well as his or her risk profile. Big data refines trading strategies as algorithms find out patterns and anomalies in trading activity, market sentiment, or price movements that may be utilized in better timing and execution of a trade. Predictive analytics helps asset managers to track the performance of investment strategies over time, maximize returns, and align their strategies with market dynamics in real-time. Competition defines the asset management world. Data and predictive analytics power big data and hence play fundamental roles in staying ahead of the market curve about trends, improved decision-making, reduced risk, and optimum delivery of investment solutions that align to clients' objectives and risk profile. When the data continue to grow in both volume and complexity, these technologies will be leaders in the molding of the future of asset management, providing a much more complex and personalized approach.

3. FinTech Sector

Big data and predictive analytics will change the fundamental decision-making of making financial decisions in the fintech sector. It enables solutions that were impossible to deliver in the traditional financial systems but more personalized, efficient, and scalable. The companies working through fintech incorporate huge amounts of data, covering transactional data, payment histories, behavioral patterns, social media activity, and even biometrics, to provide tailored financial products and services. Predictive analytics is at the heart of such operations, as it enables fintech firms to predict the behavior of their customers, estimate credit risk, and improve the accuracy of financial predictions. For example, with the analysis of transaction data, fintech platforms can predict spending habits, which would enable them to offer personalized budgeting tools, savings plans, and targeted financial advice. Predictive models also help evaluate creditworthiness by including alternative data sources, such as mobile phone usage, utility bill payments, and social interactions, which traditional credit scoring models often fail to include. This will widen access to credit for more individuals and small businesses without an established credit history, thus contributing to greater financial inclusion. The advancement in analytics in fintech lending has further enhanced loan underwriting to define the approval, interest rate, and terms of a loan with real-time decision-making regarding the risk profile. Fraud detection is a very important sector wherein big data and predictive analytics have made quite a difference. Real-time monitoring of huge amounts of transaction data allows fintech platforms to detect and flag suspicious activities quickly, thereby reducing financial losses and enhancing security. In addition, big data enables fintech companies to improve pricing strategies, predict demand for financial services, and streamline operations. Predictive analytics enables the development of dynamic pricing models that adjust the fees, rates, and the product offerings contingent on changing market conditions and customer needs. Fintech companies engage in machine learning and AI each day to continue perfecting their predictive models, thereby agile and responsive enough to the dynamics of financial systems.

The integration of big data into predictive analytics at fintechs not only changes the dynamics of financial decision making but, at its most significant level, alters the final customer experience and access to extremely personal, time-effective financial services. As fintech continues to evolve and grow, these technologies will be more vital for driving innovation and enhancing financial services, helping businesses stay competitive in an ever-changing market.

CONCLUSION

Big data and predictive analytics have really transformed financial decision-making, providing tools for navigating complexities, managing risks, or capitalizing on opportunities. Many challenges still exist in this realm, yet constant strides forward in technology and methodology point to a future where financial institutions and businesses can make even more precise, informed, and impactful decisions. The financial sector will find ways to innovate and spur economic growth as this world continues to become much more data-driven.

REFERENCES

Bishop, C. M. (2013). *Pattern recognition and machine learning*. Springer.

Chen, H., Chiang, R. H. L., & Storey, V. C. (2012). Business Intelligence and Analytics: From Big Data to Big Impact. *Management Information Systems Quarterly*, *36*(4), 1165–1188.

Chong, A. Y. L., Ooi, K. B., Lin, B., & Tang, S. Y. (2017). Predictive analytics in financial services: A review. *Decision Support Systems*, *102*, 102–114.

Elbahnasawy, N. G. (2021). Big data analytics and financial decision-making. *The Journal of Financial Data Science*, *3*(1), 45–62.

Kumar, A., & Ravi, V. (2016). A survey of the applications of text mining in financial services. *Computational Intelligence*, *32*(1), 1–27.

Liu, B. (2012). *Sentiment analysis and opinion mining*. Morgan & Claypool Publishers.

Ngai, E. W., Hu, Y., Wong, Y. H., Chen, Y., & Sun, X. (2009). The application of data mining techniques in financial fraud detection: A classification framework and an academic review of literature. *Decision Support Systems*, *50*(3), 559–569.

Treleaven, P., Galas, M., & Lalchand, V. (2013). Algorithmic trading review. *Communications of the ACM*, *56*(11), 76–85.

Waller, M. A., & Fawcett, S. E. (2013). Data science, predictive analytics, and big data: A revolution that will transform supply chain design and management. *Journal of Business Logistics*, *34*(2), 77–84.

Chapter 3

The Impact of Technological Advancements in Financial Markets

S. Boomika
https://orcid.org/0009-0001-5451-2912
Christ University, India

Amit Kumar
Christ University, India

ABSTRACT

The technological advancements have transformed the financial markets by increasing the efficiency, transparency and accessibility. Emerging technologies like Artificial Intelligence, Blockchain technology, Machine learning and Big data analytics have reshaped the investment strategies and enhance risk management techniques. However, concerns cybersecurity and regulatory challenges still persist. This chapter mainly discuss about how the technological advancements is changing financial markets, while taking into account both the advantages and disadvantages of these advancements.

INTRODUCTION

The technological advancements on the emerging technologies have transformed the financial markets . From the early stages of manual trading to today's digital platforms the technological advancements has changed how investors trade, invest

DOI: 10.4018/979-8-3373-1404-4.ch003

and manage risk. The integration of developing technologies like artificial intelligence, big data analytics, block chain technology has brought many changes in the market transparency, accessibility and efficiency in the financial markets even though there is rapid growth of technological advancements it also have various challenges like cybersecurity threats, regulatory compliances and market volatility which made the stakeholders to rethink about the strategies and adapt to the rapidly changing financial landscape.

The adoption of technologies into financial markets has fundamentally changed the trade practices. Digital trading platforms have removed the geographical boundaries which allows investors to trade in real time from any location. Algorithmic trading which uses the feature of automated systems has become a huge gamechanger by enabling trades at unimaginable trades and volumes. This automated feature has increased the market liquidity and reduced the transaction costs, but it has decreased market stability because of the sudden price fluctuations which will be caused by the automated systems.

Blockchain technology which is initially introduced in cryptocurrencies like Bitcoin, it has gained significance in the financial markets due to its features like secure, transparent and decentralized record keeping. This technology eliminates the necessity for the intermediaries, have streamlined processes like cross-border payments, settlement of securities and trade finance. Tokenization is the process which convert real-world assets into digital tokens which expanded the investment opportunities. Thia emergence of cryptocurrencies and tokenized assets has affected the traditional financial markets which challenged the already existing regulatory framework and promoted the policymakers to reframing of the regulatory compliances. Moreover machine learning algorithms in trading strategies have helped the traders for analysing the vast amount of dataset in real time, identify patterns and trends and make informed decisions. This can lead to optimized price discovery and improvement in market stability.

The technology like Artificial Intelligence has play an important role in revolutionizing the financial markets. With the use of AI-powered predictive analytics the market participants can oversee the price changes, evaluate risks and create better investment strategies. Furthermore by offering customized advice and assistance, AI-powered chatbots and virtual assistants can help in better understanding of the customers and increase the user experience. Big data analytics analyses vast amount of dataset in real time which uncovers the hidden patterns, trends to make well informed data-driven decisions. This can help the financial institutions to gain a competitive advantage over their competitors.

Adoption of modern technologies have also resulted in notable advancements in risk management in the financial industries. The use of Artificial intelligence and machine learning algorithmic models have enhanced credit risk assessment, fraud detection and portfolio management by offering a more precise and proactive method of risk reduction. As financial sectors are getting more evolved, cybersecurity technologies becomes very essential for safeguarding of private financial information and thwarting of cyberattacks.

Technological advancements in the financial markets also promoted financial inclusion in the developing countries. The technological advancements like digital payment systems, mobile banking applications and online lending platforms has empowered the small businesses and individuals for participation in the financial markets which contributes to the economic growth and development. By this technological advancement undeserved communities are getting benefitted from technology improvements.

Even though these technological advancements offer many advantages it also comes with many challenges. Regulators face difficulty in comprehending and evaluating the decision-making process of AI-driven trading models due to their black-box nature. Furthermore with increasing use of cryptocurrencies and decentralized finance there is need for more robust and flexible regulatory framework.

Because of the growing digitalization, financial information are paving way for ransomware attacks, identity theft and data breaches. So financial institutions should make proactive investments in cutting-edge cybersecurity technologies for safeguarding of the customer data. In addition ethical considerations while using AI and machine learning models such as algorithmic biases and data privacy issues should be addressed to make sure of fair and transparent market practices.

So there is a demand for collaboration between the policy makers, financial institutions and technology providers for developing of a resilient and inclusive financial ecosystem. Policymakers must strike a balance between promoting innovation and ensuring market stability and develop a strong and adaptable regulatory system. Programs for workforce training and educational activities is also essential in preparing the market participants for the opportunities and challenges brought by these technological advancements.

In conclusion, technological advancements in the financial markets have made a significant impact in the financial markets by improving efficiency and transparency in the financial markets. The introduction of these fast growing technologies like Artificial intelligence, blockchain technology and big data analytics has unveiled both new possibilities and challenges. So the stakeholders in the financial markets must cooperate to guarantee the technological breakthroughs are used more sensibly and sustainably by promoting a more stable, innovative financial ecosystem. This chapter mainly mains to discuss about how the technological advancements is changing financial markets, while taking into consideration both the advantages and disadvantages of these advancements.

THEORTICAL FRAMEWORK

This theoretical framework serves as a foundational base for how transformative technologies like artificial intelligence, Machine learning, Big data analytics are revolutionizing and reshaping the financial markets. This emerging technologies has changed landscape of the traditional financial markets. These technological advancements in the financial markets have enhanced the market efficiency, enabled the algorithmic trading, improved the risk management and facilitated the real-time financial decision making.

Traditional finance uses banks, insurance providers and other financial organizations that will acts as middlemen between lenders and borrowers whereas emerging technologies like blockchain enables the financial transactions without the involvement of any middlemen. Also traditional finance also requires strict eligibility requirements and expensive banking expenses which makes it difficult to many people to have access to banking services whereas emerging technologies like mobile banking, digital wallets and AI-driven credit assessments has improved the financial inclusion.

Traditional finance because of manual processing, regulatory compliance and involvement of intermediaries which makes transactions, loan approvals and fund transfers take longer whereas transformative technologies like Blockchain technology, Artificial Intelligence and machine learning in automation of these banking services. Traditional finance also depend more on core database which makes them exposed for more fraudulent activities and cyberattacks whereas new technologies like blockchain technology makes use of decentralized ledger system which reduces the chance of frauds and cyberattacks. Traditional finance involves higher cost in comparison but emerging technologies reduces the costs through automation and decentralization. Traditional finance will be governed by established legal frameworks that will be upheld by government agencies, financial regulators and central banks whereas emerging technologies face regulatory framework due to their decentralized and borderless nature.

In summary, traditional finance and fast growing technologies in the financial landscape both have opportunities and challenges. Traditional finance offers various benefits like stability, regulatory oversight and trust whereas emerging technologies in the financial landscape provides innovation, more efficiency and financial inclusion. So the there is need for interplay where financial institutions will adopt technological innovations like AI, blockchain, Machine learning and blockchain technology while maintaining regulatory compliances.

Artificial Intelligence is highly used in the financial sector for data mining, market analysis, personal financing, wealth and asset management, customer services, credit scoring, retail lending, automation process and many more areas and it is transforming the financial markets (Mehortra, n.d.). Predictive models like time series analysis, neural networks and ensemble methods plays a very important in forecast and uncovering of market patterns and risk volatility by analysing the vast amount of datasets (Pala, 2023). AI in predictive modelling increases the capacity in assessing the huge amount of datasets and uncovering patterns and trends more faster. Another one of the important point of AI advancement is more improved predictive modelling like ensemble approaches that integrate various models for increasing prediction capacity and helps the institutions for better understanding of market volatility and uncertainty which will help in mitigating of market risk (Boinpalli, 2023).

The one of the application of AI-driven Risk assessment model is credit scoring. Unlike the traditional models which mainly depend on financial history and credit reports, AI can train and learn from new information providing credit evaluations that are more dynamic and accurate. This technology have the ability to reduce the biases, increase the accessibility to the marginalized populations and improve the general effectiveness of risk evaluations in the financial landscape. The most fundamental AI model that is being applied in credit scoring is regression models which helps in understanding the relationship between the independent variables and the dependent variable credit scoring but more advanced models like decision trees helps in breaking down of credit score into a number of decision nodes depending on attributes like income, past payments and outstanding debt which provide flexibility and accuracy in credit scoring (Muhammad, 2021).

The other important use of AI is in portfolio optimization. Portfolio optimization is very important in the financial sector because best proportion of assets while focussing on minimizing of risk and maximizing the returns. The base for portfolio optimization is Modern Portfolio theory introduces by Harry Markowitz in 1952 that mainly focusses on diversification for reducing the risk. Artificial intelligence with the help of machine learning models like Support Vector Machines, Random forests, Long short-term memory networks and reinforcement learning helps in better portfolio management. These models of machine learning can be applied in the optimization with every one of them proposing different strategies for optimization (Faheem, Aslam, & Kakolu, 2022).

Machine learning is an important branch of Artificial intelligence is transforming the financial markets. As the competition increases and financial markets accelerates, there is a necessity for effective forecasting techniques for the investors. Machine learning algorithms proven as way for capturing the non-linear patterns in the time series data and tend to perform better than traditional methods in terms of financial market forecasting (Ryll & Sebastin, 2019). It allows the financial organizations in identifying the fraudulent activities and help in credit evaluations, risks and decision-making. Financial Robo-advisors and chatbots offers banking guidance to the customers and automated insurance services is provided to policyholders. With the ability of analysing vast amounts of data and effectively managing non-linearities the application of machine learning in the financial sector is endless. (Nazareth & Reddy, 2019).

Blockchain Technology is also known as Distributed Ledger Technology, which means a network of users will make up a blockchain database, each of whom keeps a copy of the data. A digital ledger, a collaborative decision making process for approving transactions and a network of node components are the fundamental components of the blockchain technology (Lewis, McPartland, & Ranjan, 2019). The financial institutions have identified the significance of use of blockchain technology in the financial transactions because of its less transaction costs and improving operational efficiencies mainly in areas like financial note, cross-border payment and asset-backed securitization (Wu & Duan, 2019). In summary Blockchain technology provides a strong foundation for protecting the financial transactions and information by offering an immutable ledger for transaction integrity, decentralized identity management for safe authentication and smart contracts for automated and impenetrable transactions (Odeyemi, et al., 2024)

Big data analytics involves the process of examining vast and diverse amount of datasets for uncovering of trends, patterns and correlations that help in data-driven decision making. It plays a very important part and rapidly evolving in the financial landscape because of its capability to increase the operational efficiency and enhance the customer engagement (Aderemi, et al., 2024). The main opportunities of Big data Analytics is increased risk management, deeper understanding of customer preferences, increased operational efficiency and providing data-driven insights for trading strategies and portfolio optimization. Few real life cases of applications of Big data analytics City Bank have used Bid data analytics for uncovering of any suspicious and fraudulent activities which reduced the fraud activities and improved its risk management framework. Another example is Goldman Sachs have integrated Big data analytics for predicting and analysing of market trends, economic indicators and investor sentiment which resulted in efficient data-driven decision making and better investment strategies (Khudoyorova & Khusainov, 2024).

In conclusion the financial landscape is undergoing a major transformation that is disrupting the traditional financial systems. Traditional finance has provided stability, regulatory framework and increased trust . the emerging financial technologies have offer innovation, more efficiency and higher financial inclusion. So the future of financial markets will be combination of strengths of both the traditional finance and emerging financial technologies. A technologically advanced, well-regulated financial system will reduce the financial risks democratize the access to the financial services globally.

CONCEPTUAL FRAMEWORK

Overview of Financial Market

Any location or mechanism that gives buyers and sellers the ability to exchange financial assets, such as bonds, stocks, different international currencies, and derivatives, is called financial market. The gap between people who have money to invest and those who need it is facilitated by financial markets. Financial markets enable participants to transfer risk and facilitate trade in addition to enabling capital raising.

Types of Financial Markets

Stock Market: The term "stock market" describes a financial marketplace where shares are issued and sold by publicly traded corporations. Buyers and sellers can exchange company ownership on this marketplace. Businesses essentially sell ownership to investors when they issue shares, which they may then exchange on the stock market. The supply and demand of buyers and sellers decide the price in advance.

Bond Market: The bond market, also known as the debt market, is a financial marketplace where bonds are issued and exchanged. An investor lends money to the government or any business in exchange for interest payments, making it a debt security. In this case, the principal is given back later. To raise funds, the government and other organizations issue bonds. Bond issuers are required to pay bondholders interest mostly every six months.

Forex Market: This financial market, also known as the Forex or FX market, is where currencies are exchanged. Among the world's most liquid financial markets is this one. Forex trading is done five days a week, twenty-four hours a day. Since the forex market is decentralized, there isn't a central clearinghouse or exchange. Rather, a network of banks, brokers, and other financial organizations facilitates forex trading. Investors can obtain exposure to currency fluctuations through currency mutual funds and exchange-traded funds (ETFs) in addition to conventional forex trading. Instead of only exposing investors to one or two currencies, these investment vehicles expose them to a variety of currencies.

Commodity market: Raw materials and primary goods are traded on commodity markets. Producers, traders, and end users can interchange these items more easily in this market. The prices in this market are influenced by a number of factors, such as supply and demand, weather patterns, geographic events, and economic growth.

Derivative market: Investors can purchase and sell financial instruments on the derivatives market. Futures contracts, options contracts, and swaps are among the financial instruments. The underlying asset determines the value of these securities. A stock, commodity, currency, or even an index could be the underlying asset. By speculating on future price fluctuations or hedging against changes in the price of the underlying asset, derivatives help investors manage risk. Alternatively, options can be used to speculate on a possible rise or fall in the underlying asset's price.

Money market: Participants can lend and borrow short-term, high-quality debt securities with average maturities of one year or less on the money market, which is an organized exchange market. It makes it possible for banks, governments, and other big organizations to raise money for their immediate cash flow needs by selling short-term securities. Individual investors can also make tiny, low-risk investments through money markets. Treasury bills, certificates of deposit, commercial paper, bills of exchange, and short-term mortgage-backed securities and asset-backed securities are a few examples of Money market instruments.

Function of financial markets:

- Financial markets carry out vital tasks that promote economic expansion and guarantee the effective distribution of resources. The primary roles of financial markets are listed below:
- Savings mobilization: Financial markets transfer money from people and organizations with excess savings to others who require funding. They encourage people to invest rather than hoard their savings by providing products like stocks, bonds, and mutual funds.
- Effective Resource Allocation: Capital is distributed to the most beneficial purposes thanks to financial markets. By evaluating risk and return profiles, investors allocate capital to industry sectors that are most likely to provide the highest returns.
- Encouraging Price Discovery: Financial markets assist in establishing the fair price of monetary instruments like stocks, bonds, and commodities by balancing supply and demand. The market's estimation of an asset's value based on the facts at hand is reflected in this price discovery process
- Provision of liquidity: Liquid financial markets enable easy buying and selling of securities Investors can swiftly turn their capital into cash, making financial instruments more attractive.
- Risk Management and Hedging:Derivatives (e.g., options, futures, and swaps) allow players to hedge against numerous risks, such as interest rate, currency, and commodity price variations.
- Facilitating Economic Growth: Financial markets help create jobs, improve infrastructure, and boost the economy by moving cash into productive projects. They also promote innovation by supporting R&D efforts.

Advancement of Technology in Financial Market

The emergence of technologies has greatly revolutionized the financial markets . This evolution is known as fintech. It changed the way how financial institutions work and provide customer services. From streamlining of operations to improving the customer services, the advancement of technology in financial market is reshaping various sector like banking, insurance, investments etc.. From electronic trading platforms and algorithmic trading to blockchain and artificial intelligence, technology has simplified procedures, cut expenses and enhanced market access for players worldwide in the financial markets. But also these developments have also brought along new dangers and difficulties, like increasing market volatility, complicated regulations and cybersecurity concerns.

The major trends in emerging technologies in the financial market:

- Artificial technology
- Machine learning
- Blockchain Technology
- Big data Analytics

Artificial Intelligence

It is a field of science that refers to computer systems has ability to performing complicated tasks such as reasoning, decision making and problem solving that historically only a human could do . Artificial intelligence is prevalent in many industries such as education, finance, healthcare, security etc.. . Automation of the tasks that will done by the humans can save time and decreases the probability of human error. One of the significant application of AI in the finance industry is the fraud detection. The artificial intelligence ability to analysing large set of data will help to detect any irregularities or patterns that will signal the fraudulent behaviour.

AI IN PREDICTIVE MODELLING AND RISK MANAGEMENT

AI in Predictive Modelling

Predictive AI is the ability of computer's program to predict and identify patterns, trends using statical analysis for forecasting future events. The field of statistics has been used for long time for predictions of the future. Due to the technological advancements, the predictive AI makes statistical analysis more faster and accurate with the application of the machine learning and the access to vast amount of data.

Use of predictive analysis in business helps to forecast the future demand and improve the experiences for the customers.

Predictive AI requires a access to vast amount of big data so that it can better predictions without any human supervision. Predictive AI can be used in various cases like inventory management, supply chain management, healthcare, personalization of user experiences, marketing campaigns and financial industries. There are various types of predictive modelling which are designed according to the specific goals and challenges of various industry sectors.

In finance sector predictive modelling helps in predicting the stock prices, assessment of credit risk and optimization of investment portfolios which will lead to better financial decision making and risk management in the organizations.

Common Types of Predictive Models

Classification Model

This type of predictive modelling is the most fundamental and frequently utilized models, as it provides straightforward answers to inquiries that result in yes or no outcomes. A classification model leverages historical data to deliver a comprehensive analysis of a question. Businesses in retail and finance often implement this model because it efficiently compiles and organizes information to address various questions.

Forecast Model

Forecast models are among the most widely used types of models because of their adaptability. These models generate numerical outcomes by examining past data and making predictions based on that information. A company like an online retailer might utilize forecast modelling to predict the volume of orders expected in the coming week. In addition, these models can effectively handle several parameters at once.

Clustering Model

A clustering model divides data into various categories according to shared features. It subsequently utilizes the information from each group to assess overall results for each cluster. This model employs two forms of clustering. Hard clustering classifies data by deciding if each point fully belongs to a specific cluster, while soft clustering provides a probability for each data point instead of categorizing them into separate clusters.

Outliers Model

An outlier model detects atypical or exceptional data within a dataset. It can examine specific instances of unusual information or their associations with other categories and figures. Numerous financial organizations utilize this model to uncover fraudulent activities. For instance, an outlier model may pinpoint unusual transactions in a customer's account. The model can assess the monetary amount, location, timing, and category of the purchase to ascertain if a third party has compromised a customer's account

Decision Tree

A decision tree is an algorithm that organizes various data sources into a tree-like format to illustrate the potential results of various choices. This model breaks down different decisions into branches and lists possible outcomes beneath each choice. Many organizations utilize this to identify the most significant variables within a specific dataset. They may also implement them because the model can accommodate incomplete datasets to generate potential outcomes.

Time Series Model

A time series model employs sequences of time as input elements within a dataset. It takes into account previous trends and data points from a designated time sequence to anticipate trends or events across another defined time frame. This model is capable of forecasting several trends and projects at once or concentrating on a singular project. Additionally, it can evaluate market forces that could influence future trends, such as seasonal changes or cyclical fluctuations.

General Linear Method

A general linear model is a statistical method used to evaluate the effect of specific variables on continuous variables. This method frequently serves as the basis for various statistical tests, including regression analysis. Businesses utilizing predictive modelling typically perform regression analyses when generating and analysing data for predictions. The general linear model evaluates whether the average values of two dependent variables in a prediction vary. A collection of these models forms a generalized linear model, which grants for the visualization of multiple similar models in a single graph.

Gradient Boosted Model

A gradient boosted model employs several interconnected decision trees to produce rankings. It constructs one tree initially and rectifies the shortcomings of the first tree to develop a second, enhanced tree. This model involves multiple trees, depending on the organization that develops it.

Neural Network

Neural network is a sophisticated model that mimics the framework of the human brain. It consists of numerous algorithms working together to detect patterns, group data, and categorize various datasets. Mostly, neural networks consists of three layers. The initial input layer provides data into the subsequent layer, known as the hidden layer. This hidden layer contains functions that generate predictors. Finally, the output layer gathers the information from these predictors to deliver the ultimate, thorough result.

Importance of Using Predictive Modelling Techniques in Business

- **Enhanced decision making:**

It helps the business to forecast the future trends and patterns which helps the business to respond to future market changes. It provides data-driven insights which will result in improved decision making.

- **Better understanding of customer preferences:**

Predictive modelling helps to analyse the consumer preferences and needs which will result in targeting the specific market, providing personalized customer services and better customer experience.

- **Risk management:**

It helps in prediction of risks in operations or financial transactions . so necessary steps can be taken prior to avoid the risk . In financial industry, predictive models mostly used for credit scoring and fraud detection.

- **Competitive advantage:**

The application of predictive modelling in business can help to gain a competitive advantage over the rival business by anticipating the customer needs and market trends.

- **Financial planning and forecasting:**

The predictive modelling helps in forecasting of cash flows budgeting, inventories and increases the efficiency of financial predictions which helps in the proper allocation of resources that will result in increasing overall productivity of the organization.

Application of Predictive Modelling in Finance

Assessment of Credit Assessment

Predictive models helps in the assessing and evaluating the creditworthiness of the borrowers which will help the financial institutions to approve or reject the loans and set the interest rates according to the predictions. The most applied predictive models to predict the loan defaults are logistic regression and neural networks.

Prediction of Stock Prices

Many time series models such as ARIMA and GARCH can be applied to predict and forecast the stock prices. These predictions will help the traders to make data driven informed decisions about the buying or selling of stocks which will help in increasing the returns of the portfolio.

Fraud Detection

Predictive models like decision tress and support vector models can be used for identifying the fraudulent financial activities . This predictive models will analyse the transaction pattern that will helps in detection of anomalies which will reduce the financial losses.

Optimization of Portfolio

Predictive models helps in the optimization of the portfolio by analysing the returns and risks of the assets which will help the investors to make data-driven investment decisions in turn maximizing the returns from the assets.

Algorithmic Trading

Predictive models will identify the trading patterns by analysing the large amount of datasets. Then the predictive algorithms will trigger the automated trading strategies based on pre-set values that has been coded into a computer to capitalize on the available market possibilities that increases the efficiency and profitability.

AI in Risk Assessment and Scoring

The use of AI in risk assessment and scoring mains refers to use of AI to analyse and interpret a huge amount of data from diverse sources to generate more accurate risk predictions which helps in improved decision making by automatically assigning risk scores to the companies or situations which can surpass the ability of human-based risk assessments. It can be used in various fields like finance, insurance and cybersecurity.

Cases of using AI in Risk Assessment and Scoring

Credit Risk Modelling

It is the important part of assessment of financial risk which is defined to quantify the likelihood of a obligor if they fail to pay their obligation and assess the potential losses that will be faced by lenders. It will help the financial institutions to make data-driven decisions regarding the borrower characteristics, interest rates and capital allocation. The models mostly depend on borrower characteristics, loan -specific factors and macroeconomic indicators to predict the financial credibility of the obligor.

Artificial intelligence in credit risk modelling is making the process faster, more accurate by handling huge amount of complex data. In traditional banks and financial institutions they will depend on simple statistical models and manual processes to find whether the borrower will default on a loan or not but the use of AI in credit risk modelling helps in automatically findings accurate patterns and trajectories which makes the predictions more reliable. One of the benefit of AI is it has the ability to analyse the vast amount of datasets from multiple sources like credit history, spending patterns, employment status and social media behaviour. AI has the ability to process the information faster and provide reliable insights. Machine learning an important subset of artificial intelligence it allows the models to learn continuously and improve as they encounter any new data. This makes credit risk assessments more reliable even though market conditions changes over time.

AI also helps the financial companies by predicting the risk prior by analysing the borrower behaviour and economic factors over real time so AI models can alert the lender before any default occurs. This strategy not only helps in reduction of losses but also helps in proper allocation of capital in the financial companies. Even though there are many advantages of use of AI in predictive modelling, it also present some challenges like black box problem in which the decision-making process is so difficult to understand. This black box problem can be problematic in case of regulatory compliances because the financial institutions have to justify and explain their credit decisions. In addition, AI models can unintentionally create biases if the data that is used for training is not monitored properly. To understand use concerns, proper implementation and monitoring is required to make sure that AI-driven models remain transparent, unbiased and compliance with the regulatory requirements.

Fraud Detection

Artificial Intelligence helps the financial institutions in identifying the fraudulent activities more efficiently. Traditional fraud detection systems mostly rely on manual data and simple rule based systems which makes it very hard to identify the complex fraudulent activities and schemes. With the capability of Artificial intelligence in analysing the vast amount of data which can help in detecting unusual patterns or behaviours that will identify fraudulent activities.

Machine learning has ability to learn from the historical data and recognize patterns and trajectories that are connected with fraudulent activities. In case a borrower unusually makes a huge amount of transactions or have unusual payment behaviour the AI models identify them as potentially fraudulent. Machine learning has a feature of continuously improving and learning as they encounter new data, which becomes an advantage for identifying emerging fraudulent trends.

Traditional fraud systems mostly identify the fraud after it is done. But the AI models can enhance real-time fraud detection which allows the lenders to take immediate action when a fraud is detected. It protects the financial institutions from fraudulent activities and it also protect the customers from any potential financial harm.

The main challenge of Artificial Intelligence in fraud detection is false positives in which legitimate activities can be flagged down as fraudulent activities which can be inconvenience to the customers. To reduce this AI models have to be carefully trained and updated for balancing the fraud detection accuracy with the customer experience. Financial institutions also have to make sure the AI models are transparent, free any biases and complying with the regulatory requirements. In this way AI helps the financial institutions in reducing the losses that are related to fraudulent activities and increases the overall security of the lending process.

AI in Portfolio Optimization

Portfolio optimization involves selecting and combining the different assets with a goal to achieve the best possible income in terms of outcome and risk. It involves various quantitative techniques and analysis of metrics which are related to portfolio's expected returns, correlation and volatility. The main objective of portfolio optimization is to create an efficient portfolio that is diversified and matches with the investor's risk profile. The integration of AI in portfolio optimization with advanced features and insights has enhanced the investment process.

AI takes into consideration and addresses the complexities of rapid market fluctuations and it has ability to handle vast amounts of structured and unstructured data in an incredible speed whereas the traditional models are slow and expensive. This ability of AI is very important in a market environment where the timely insights greatly affect the performance. The AI-driven portfolio management systems offer real time data insights and adaptive strategies which is necessary for volatile market and it helps the investors to improve their strategies by minimizing risks and maximizing the potential gains.

Use of Cases of AI in Portfolio Optimization

Asset Allocation

Artificial intelligence greatly enables in adaptive management of goal-driven asset allocation based on personal factors like age, risk tolerance capacity and financial objectives. Artificial intelligence examines the huge amount of datasets using machine learning algorithms and predictive analysis to recommend the best proportion of asset classes for a portfolio owned by an investor. The AI capability of integrating and adapting to continuously changing market conditions and parameters has enabled a personalised and efficient asset allocations strategy and maintain a balance of asset classes over real time, optimization of risk adjusted returns and it is staying in the line with the investor's changing financial objectives.

Real-Time Market Surveillance

AI continuously analyses a variety of sources like news, social media and market data so it can quickly spot new trends or patterns that can have a major effect on the investment decisions.

Portfolio managers use this capability to make data driven decisions based on the up-to-data and respond to necessary changes in the market. AI has the ability to identify changes in the consumer sentiment, geopolitical events which can significantly affect the industries. This ability of AI give the investors to immediate data driven insights which enables them to modify their investment strategies or portfolio allocations appropriately. By taking into advantage the AI capability of monitoring diverse information sources, invested professionals gets updated with the recent information and make informed, data driven decisions.

Tax Optimization

AI improves the tax optimization by employing algorithms to strategically distributing the assets for highest tax returns. It analyses the investment possibilities using predictive analysis taking into account diverse factors like individual tax brackets, predicted returns and tax consequences. Then AI algorithms suggests tax-efficient invested strategies which help the investors in reducing the tax liabilities and maximization of after-tax returns.

AI will take into consideration the particular tax circumstances of an investor considering income, capital gains and tax brackets. After that it suggests a personalized and tailored strategies and ideas that will follow the tax laws and reduce the total tax burden which will increase the efficiency of the investor performance. By using the AI tax-efficient investment strategies and tactics the investors can confidently and precisely traverse the complicated tax environment and make sure their investment preferences are matching with their financial objectives and reduces the tax-related expenses.

Automated Real Time Insights

AI has the capability to automation of reports and insights which gives investors the access to real-time information based on the risk factors, market trends and portfolio performance. By this way the investors save time and concentrate on making strategic decisions instead of wasting time on manually gathering the data. In addition AI will provide deeper insights and analysis which is difficult to achieve through the manual processes. So in conclusion AI capability of providing automated and deep insights prevent the time wastage of investors and helps the investors in making enhanced investment decision making.

Personalized Investment Recommendations

AI is revolutionizing personalized investment advice by using data to develop customized investment plans for individual investors. To develop personalized portfolio recommendations, AI algorithms takes into consideration diverse factors like investor's financial objectives, risk tolerance, income, expenses and investment timelines. By analysing this factors AI algorithms makes it possible to create personalized financial planning in accordance with the needs and requirements of the investors. AI-powered platforms will direct young professionals towards diversified portfolio with great growth potential and will direct old investors towards more conservative plans focussing mainly on capital preservation.

Machine Learning

Machine learning is a subset of artificial intelligence that focuses on enabling the computers and machines to imitate the way the humans learn, allowing them to perform tasks more efficiently and improve their performance through exposure to more data. Data such as bank transactions, images of people, repair records from sensors or sales reports that can be text, numbers or images. This information will be collected and ready for use as training data for the machine learning model. The machine learning model will be programmed better with more data exposure.

A machine learning system can serve as a descriptive function, where it analyses data to clarify the past events; a predictive function, where it utilizes data to forecast future occurrences; or a prescriptive function, where it leverages data to recommend actions to take.

The three types of machine learning:

- Supervised learning
- Unsupervised learning
- Semi- supervised learning
- reinforcement learning

Supervised Learning

Supervised machine learning models utilize labelled datasets for training, enabling the models to improve their accuracy and efficiency over time. In the current situation, supervised machine learning is the most prevalent in use. In the supervised learning the output will be known and the model is trained on the data of the known output . For an instance, an algorithm can be trained using the images of a sparrow along with other objects all labelled by humans, allowing the machine to independently recognize the sparrow images.

The mostly used supervised learning algorithm includes:

- linear regression
- polynomial regression
- k-nearest neighbours
- Naïve Bayes
- Decision trees

Linear regression: a statistical technique for simulating the relationship between a dependent variable and one or more independent variables . It provides insightful information for data analysis and prediction.

Polynomial regression: A type of linear regression known as polynomial regression uses an nth-degree polynomial to represent the relationship between the independent variable (x) and the dependent variable (y).

k-nearest neighbours: An individual data point's grouping can be predicted or classified using closeness in the k-nearest neighbours (KNN) technique, a non-parametric supervised learning classifier. It is the most prevalent and simplest classification and regression classifiers that is applied in machine learning today.

Naïve bayes: The naïve bayes is a simple algorithm that has bayes theorem as a base for prediction of probability of a class based on a set of features. The bayes theorem computations are made simpler by assuming that every feature is independent of every other feature.

Decision trees: It is a supervised algorithm that can be applied in regression and classification tasks. It is a tree structured classifier, in which the internal node represent the attributes of the dataset, branches represent the decision rules and leaf node represents the outcome of the decision. This representation will provide all the possible solutions to a problem or decision depend on the given conditions.

Unsupervised Learning

This machine learning algorithms seek out patterns within data that lack labels. It is a type of machine learning that uncover trends or patterns that individuals might not be specifically searching for. In unsupervised learning the output is not known rather the algorithm learns from the data without any intervention from human and categories it into groups based on attributes. This type of learning is really good at descriptive modelling and matching of patterns.

Semi - Supervised Learning

It is a mixed approach that combines the elements of supervised learning and unsupervised learning in which only some data is labelled. The algorithm must learn to figure out how to organize and structure data to get a desired outcome.

Reinforcement Learning

This machine learning algorithms can be characterised as one that learns by doing through a series of experiments involving trial and error method. It involves programming an algorithm with a distinct goal and a set of rules that should be followed to achieve the goal. The algorithm learns to perform a defined task through a feedback loop until the performance is within a desirable range. The algorithm will receive positive reinforcement when it performs the tasks properly and negative reinforcement when it performs badly.

Uses of Machine Learning in Finance

Algorithmic Trading

Algorithmic trading generally means the using algorithms to make better trade decisions. In order to detect any important causes that would cause security prices to fall and rise, traders typically develop mathematical models that will track the trade activity and business news in real time. To place the order without the trader active participation, the model comes with a preset set of instructions on a number of characteristics which includes timing, price, quantity and other elements. Algorithmic trading in contrast to human trading has the capability of making thousands of trades daily while concurrently analysing vast amounts of data and it can outperform the market average because machine learning makes trading decisions quickly.

A typical drawback of human traders is that their judgement can be influenced by their emotions or personal goals however in algorithmic trading does not base trading decisions based on emotions. Algorithmic trading mainly used by financial organizations and hedge fund managers for automating their trading operations.

Fraud Detection

Financial companies generally stores a lot of data in online which increases the possibility of security breach. As there is advancement of technology, fraud in the financial sector is now regarded as a serious risk to sensitive information. As a result, the majority of financial companies use machine learning to identify and prevent the fraudulent activities. In order to identify any unusual activity or anomalies, machine learning searches through vast amount of datasets and flag them for further investigation. It determines if the flagged transaction is consistent with the account's holder behaviour by comparing it with other data points which includes the IP address of the customer, location and history. The system can automatically reject a withdrawal or purchase until a human decides, based on the type of the transaction.

Portfolio Management

Robo-advisors are that are built using the machine learning and provide automated financial recommendations to the investors. These applications will use algorithms to create a financial portfolio according to the investor's financial objectives and risk profile. These Robo-advisors are less costly as compared to the human portfolio managers. Using these Robo-advisors, the investors are required to enter their investments or savings into the account, then the system will automate the investment decisions with goal of maximizing the gains and reducing the losses.

Robo-advisors will help in spreading the investments across different asset classes for diversification and achieving the investor's long term goals. It also helps in portfolio optimization in accordance with real-time market patterns which will result in high returns and efficient data driven investment decision making.

Loan Underwriting

Businesses in the banking and insurance sectors have access to millions of customer records, which can be applied to developing machine learning algorithms that streamline the underwriting procedure. Businesses can save time and money by using machine learning algorithms to make quick choices on credit scoring and underwriting . For matching of data records, find special exceptions, and determine if a customer is eligible for a loan or insurance, data scientists can teach algorithms to evaluate millions of consumer records which makes the process more faster and efficient.

Blockchain Technology

Blockchain technology is an enhanced database technology that allows transactions to happen in a transparent and decentralized manner. It holds data in a block that will be interconnected together in a chain. The data is arranged in a sequential manner since the data cannot be removed or altered without accord from the network. So as result blockchain technology will be able to create an unchangeable ledgers for tracing orders, accounts and financial transactions. The blockchain system has created a in-built safeguard mechanisms to avoid the unauthorized transactions which allows creating stability in the shared view of the transactions.

The Categories of Blockchain Networks

There are four categories of blockchain. They are:

Public Blockchain Networks

Public blockchain networks are open to all the users and are permissionless. The ability to read, modify and authenticate the blockchain is equally granted to all the participants. This public blockchain is mainly used by people who like to mine and trade cryptocurrencies like Litecoin, Ethereum, and Bitcoin.

Private Blockchain Networks

These blockchains are also known as managed blockchain because they are controlled by a single entity. The authority decides who can join the network and what control they have in the network. Due to access restrictions, private blockchain networks are partially decentralized. One of the prime instance of a private blockchain technology is ripple which is the business to business digital currency exchange network.

Hybrid Blockchain Networks

Hybrid blockchain technology combines the feature of both public and private blockchain networks. Businesses will build a public along with a private system, permission-based systems. In this way business can maintain the data public while keeping and controlling access to certain data that is contained in the blockchain.

Consortium Blockchain Networks

Consortium blockchain technology will be governed by a group of organizations. Pre-selected entities will share the responsibility of maintenance of blockchain and determining of data success rights. These network will be very preferrable in sectors where various firms have prevalent objectives and benefit from shared obligations.

The Key Features of Blockchain Technology

Decentralization

The transferring of authority and decision making from a centralized entity to a dispersed entity is called decentralization in blockchain. In blockchain technology the data is stored in multiple nodes rather than in a single server. Each node maintains a distributed ledger copy and all the nodes will work together to validate the transactions. This technology does not require any governing authority as the users has the right to see the data in the web directly and store the digital assets there. So this feature enhances the security, it reduces the risk of data breaches and increases the system resilience.

Immutability

It is the important feature that is offered by the blockchain technology. As this is a disturbed system, every node of the network will have a copy of the digital ledger. When a transaction will be added every node will check the validity of the transaction. In case if majority of the node thinks the transaction is valid, then it will added to the ledger. This increases the transparency and security. The transaction will be added to the ledger only if it gets major consent from the nodes otherwise it won't be added to the ledger. Once the transaction is entered in the ledger no one will be able to edit or delete it.

Transparency

Blockchain technology allows all the participants to see and verify the transaction records. So in case of public blockchain everyone gets the access to the ledger which increases the accountability and trust among the users. In private and consortium of companies the blockchain accountability will be accessible mainly to authorized people only. This transparency is very essential fields like finance, supply and management and government operations.

Distributed Ledgers

Blockchain is a type of distributed ledger technology in which all nodes will maintain a synchronized and up-to-data copy of the ledger. So when a transaction will occur it will be verified and recorded in the ledger. Nodes will act as verifiers of the ledger . In case of any suspicious activity the disturbed ledger will respond. This feature of blockchain technology ensures the data accuracy, reduces the dependency on intermediaries and improves the robustness of the system.

Consensus Mechanisms

Consensus is a process of decision making for the group of active nodes in the network. So consensus mechanisms will make sure all the nodes in the network will agree to the validity of the transaction before it will be added to the ledger. In this way all nodes will come to an common agreement in a relatively quick manner. This consensus mechanism is very essential because of millions of nodes will be involved in validating a transaction. So every blockchain technology will have consensus to help the network to make the transactions.

Cryptographic Security

Blockchain cryptographic security refers to use of the cutting-edge technologies for safeguarding of data and guarantee of secure and reliable transactions . It uses techniques which is called hashing and digital signatures for generation of distinct codes for each piece of data.

This data will be converted into fixed length code by using process of hashing that makes it simple of detection of any changes. Digital signatures will make sure the data is not altered and will ensure the identity of the person. In conclusion these will help to safeguard of user identities, keep data safe and stop fraud and illegal access.

Smart Contracts

Self-executing digital agreements that are found on blockchain technology are known as smart contracts. When specific requirements are met, they will automatically initiate the operations based on the established rules that are expressed in a code. Smart contracts work on blockchain technology so they are transparent, safe, secure and does not require any middlemen like banks or lawyers which increases the pace of the operations and reduces the cost of the procedures.

Use of Cases of Blockchain Technology in Financial Landscape

Enhanced Efficiency and Scalability in Financial Services

Blockchain offers a faster, more secure, and highly scalable method of handling almost all of the traditional services provided in banking and financial services, including money transfers, peer-to-peer payments, and trade finance, because it effectively facilitates immutable transactions in real time. Blockchain technology also reduces the need for middle men and unchangeable so it can handle the financial services at relatively lower costs and eliminates the chances of fraudulent activities. Blockchain technology offers transparency and creation of digital identities which increase the trust and security to the financial transactions by ensuring the validity of the participants.

Collateral Management

Blockchain technology is revolutionizing the collateral management in the financial landscape by increasing the transparency, efficiency and security. In traditional financial institutions collateral management involves the multiple intermediaries which is time consuming and increases the operational costs. These challenges will be addressed by the blockchain technology by providing a decentralized and tamper-proof ledger which records and manages the tracks of collateral in real-time and ensure all the parties have up-to-date information which reduces the time because of less involvement of intermediaries and increases the operational efficiency. In addition the use of smart contracts automates the collateral validation and transfer process which makes sure the transactions are executed automatically when pre-defined conditions are met which minimizes the human involvement and errors.

Decentralized Tokens

These are digital assets that are used in decentralized finance that is built on blockchain technology. In traditional financial systems it rely on banks or intermediaries but in Defi tokens it enable access to various financial services like lending, borrowing, trading and earning interest, insurance directly through the use of smart contracts without any involvement of intermediaries. These tokens can be used for variety of other purposes like letting people vote on platform decisions (governance), earning rewards for holding the tokens (staking) and providing funds to running of the platform smoothly (liquidity). Examples: Uniswap (UNI) will be used trading without the involvement of intermediaries, AAVE for lending and borrowing services and Maker (MKR) for voting on important decisions in the Maker DAO systems. These tokens make the financial services more open and give people control their finances and easier to use without any intervention from the traditional banks.

Tokenization of Real World Assets

Tokenization is the process of converting the real-world assets into digital tokens on a blockchain technology. These real-world assets can be real estate, commodities, stock, bonds, art, intellectual property. On blockchain networks, each token can be exchanged for ownership or a portion of underlying asset. Furthermore tokenization makes the high-value assets available to wide range of investors by permitting fractional ownership which reduces the investment barriers. Also smart contracts will automate different operational processes like transfer of ownership or dividend distribution. In conclusion tokenization is changing the financial landscape by making investments wide range of people. It also makes managing and trading assets faster and more efficient by use of technology and automation.

Stablecoin

It is a type of cryptocurrency where its value is tied to another currency, commodity or any other financial instruments. Unlike traditional cryptocurrency, stablecoin offers a stability and make them very ideal for everyday transactions and as a store of value. They are mainly used in decentralized finance for lending, borrowing and trading purposes. This helps in bridging of gap between the traditional finance and digital world by offering a more secure and more stable mode of exchange on blockchain networks.

Big Data Analytics

Big data mainly refers to vast and diverse collections of structured, semi structured and unstructured data that will continue to grow in size rapidly. These big datasets are vast and complex in volume, velocity and variety. These Big data can be mainly used in machine learning, predictive modelling and other advanced algorithms for solving of problems and making well informed data driven decisions.

Big data analytics is the systematic process of analysing of large and complex amount of datasets known as big data to obtain data driven insights and make more well informed decisions. Big data analytics helps in uncovering of patterns, trends or patterns in diverse amount of dataset which helps the analysts to make data driven well informed decisions.

The Five V's of Big Data Analytics

The five Vs mainly highlight the possibilities and difficulties in handling big data for meaningful analytics and business intelligence.

Volume

One of the major problem that is faced is because of the vast amount of data that is produced by the social media, Internet of things devices and transaction of records and other sources. Conventional methods for processing and storing of data is insufficient to efficiently manage this amount of vast data. So the organizations can store and manage enormous datasets affordably with the help of big data technologies and cloud-based storage solutions which avoids the loss of important data because of storage constraints.

Velocity

From high frequency stock trading records to real time social media updates, data is being generated at a unimaginable speed. Strong processing capabilities are required to acquire, process and provide correct analysis in real time due to the rapidity with which data enters the organizations. Stream processing frameworks and in-memory data processing are made to manage these fast data streams and strike a balance between supply and demand.

Variety

Now a days data are available in diverse formats like structured, unstructured and semi-structured data. In order to handle and integrate different types of data sets this variety necessitates adaptable data management systems. Big data technologies like schema-on-read technologies, data lakes and NoSQL offer the flexibility that is required to manage the heterogeneous amount of vast data sets.

Veracity

Veracity in big data analytics refers to the quality, accuracy and reliability of the data that is acquired from the various sources. Because big data is gathered from diverse structured, unstructured and semi-structured channels. It may consist of inconsistencies, errors and biases which guide a way to incorrect decision making. So in order to make sure the soundness of big data and empower the organizations to make better decisions based on valid information, the techniques and tools for data cleaning, validation and verification are essential

Value

The main purpose of the big data analytics is get the useful insights that will offer tangible value. This entails transforming enormous data collections into insightful knowledge that will guide strategic choices, reveal fresh possibilities and spur innovation. For conversion of raw data into strategic assets and extract the value hidden within the big data advanced analytics, machine learning and artificial intelligence are used.

The Four Main Big Data Analysis Methods

Descriptive Analytics

This phase focusses on summarizing historical data to understand what has happened in the past to understand the basic characteristics. It can use data aggregation and reporting techniques to identify the patterns and trends.

Diagnostic Analytics

Diagnostic analytics goes deeper to analyse the causes of past events to recognize core patterns and trends that is observed in descriptive analytics. The techniques like data mining, drill-down analysis and correlation analysis can be used in this phase.

Predictive Analytics

Predictive analytics relies on historical data, statistical modelling and machine learning to anticipate future trends and events. It plays a crucial role in various fields, with key applications including demand forecasting, fraud detection and understanding consumer behaviour.

Prescriptive Analytics

This phase provides recommendations on the ground of predictive insights. Advanced algorithms, optimization models and machine learning can be utilized to provide insights on decision making

The Positive Outcomes of Using Big Data Analytics

Better Decision Making

Using the big data analytics the businesses will have capacity to identify the unnoticed trends and patterns. This deeper comprehension can help the company decision-making in supply-chain management, ecommerce operations and overall strategic direction by giving executives and decision-makers the knowledge to gain a competitive advantage over the competitors.

Increased Customer Engagement

For successful customer engagement, understanding the customer needs, behaviours and sentiments is very crucial and big data analytics provides the necessary tools for achieving this understanding. By analysing and examining the customer data using big data analytics helps in better understanding of the customer preferences and make efficient strategies.

Better Risk Management Strategies

Big data analytics provides necessary tools for identification, assessing and addressing the threats in the real time. Predictive Analytics help the businesses to create preventative measures by anticipating the threats beforehand.

Instantaneous Insights

The one of the most notable ability of big-data analytics is to provide the real-time intelligence. Using big data analytics, the organizations can process and analyse the real-time data which is in different formats and obtained from diverse sources and make fast decisions, react instantly to the changes in the markets, make use of the emerging opportunities.

Optimization of Cost

Big Analytics by evaluating vast amount of datasets, organizations will be able to quickly identify the unnecessary spending, improving the efficiency and streamlining the operations. Predictive analytics can forecast the future trends and patterns which allows the companies to allocate the resources more efficiently and avoiding any costly blunders. In this way big data analytics helps in reducing the waste and operational inefficiencies.

Use of cases of Big Data Analytics in Finance

Predictive Analysis

Big data analytics utilizes the predictive analytics to identify future dynamic market and growth possibilities. One of its key applications in the financial sector is credit risk assessment. Leveraging big data analytics financial institutions analyse the extensive datasets which comprises of the customer interaction and credit assessment and its score prediction of defaulting of a loan by this helping the financial institution assesses whether to grant the loan or not.

Investment Decisions

Financial analysts and stock traders using big data to prediction of market dynamics and making investment decisions. By analysing of historical data and economic indicators the predictive models provide significant insights into stock price movements, asset price movements and market direction which helps in making more data-driven and well informed decision making.

Fraud Detection

Big data analytics helps the financial institutions for detecting and preventing the fraudulent activities by analysing the vast amount of the transactional data in real time. Big data analytics can also use machine learning algorithms for identifying any unusual behaviours and flag the unusual transactions which help in minimizing the threat of financial fraudulent activities.

Algorithmic Trading

Algorithmic trading involves the process of using computer programs and algorithms for executing the trade at high speed and accuracy. Big data analytics plays a crucial role in this,

Since it can process vast amount of data in real time it allows the traders to respond faster to the market changes, by increasing the profitability and reducing the risks.

Personalized Banking Services

Providing personalized banking service can improve the customer satisfaction and build loyalty, trust among the customers. Big data analytics in banks and financial institutions helps in assessing of customer based on their financial preferences and behaviour which helps in addressing the needs of the individual customer and use them to provide customized lending solutions, insurance policies and investment options that will align with the customers' preferences and risk tolerance.

Monitoring the Business Performance

Businesses use big data for tracking of the revenues, expenses, profits, losses etc.. By analysing of extensive datasets leveraged by big data analytics can help in gaining the deeper understanding about the operations of the business which helps in increasing the operational efficiency. These Big data analytics facilitates performance benchmarking against all the rival companies and benchmarks which provide valuable insights and help the business gain a strategic edge over the rival companies.

Sentiment Analysis

The big data analytics facilitates with analysing the social media, news and public sentiment which offer us deep and significant perspectives about the market dynamics. Investors leverage these insights to predict stock price fluctuations and make informative and strategic decisions that are grounded in data and market sentiments.

Through this way big data analytics is transforming the financial landscape by providing actionable insights, improving risk management and enhancing the customer engagement. It helps the financial institutions to become competitive in a rapidly evolving market landscape.

ETHICAL CONSIDERATIONS AND REGULATORY FRAMEWORKS

Upcoming advanced innovations such as Artificial intelligence, blockchain technology and big data analytics are reshaping and transforming the financial landscape. These technologies also led to several ethical dilemmas that requires a clear need for legislative frameworks. As these technologies evolve, it becomes essential for addressing the issues surrounding privacy, data security, accountability and fairness for ensuring of its responsible adoption and usage. These innovative technical progress could also threaten cybersecurity, erode individual rights and worsen the social injustices.

A key ethical challenge posed by these emerging technologies in the financial landscape is data privacy and security. AI-driven systems that automates the decision making like credit scoring and fraud detection depends on the extensive dataset raising concerns over the data ownership and privacy. Application of big data analytics by financial firms for processing vast amounts of customer information to obtain insights and provide customized services even though it improves the customer experience, it increases the chance of security breaches and the potential for invasion of individual privacy. Blockchain technology even though it offers transparency and security through decentralized ledgers, it faces threat in making sure of data secrecy because of its immutable nature.

The rise of blockchain technology have introduced new ethical considerations. Like blockchain technology offers the financial services without the involvement of intermediaries. The absence of intermediaries in blockchain networks and no centralised oversight raises concerns regarding the fraudulent activities, investor protection, accountability and regulatory compliances. Also since financial systems relying more on interconnected technologies concerns regarding to cybersecurity raises.

Another issue is if the AI algorithms machine learning algorithms and big data algorithms is trained on biased datasets it can cause discrimination in areas like loan approvals, investment decisions and insurance pricing. This reduces the fairness and increase biasness in financial decision making. So development of ethical AI can should take necessary measures to ensuring of the algorithmic fairness and bias mitigation.

So to tackle these regulatory compliance, regulatory frameworks has been developed to govern responsible use of evolving financial advancements. The European Union's General Data Protection Regulation (GDPR) has stringent compliance standards for data processing, consent and protection of personal information. In India, the RBI has announced the rules and regulations on data storage and cybersecurity for the financial industries.

The Financial Stability Board (FSB) has recommended regulatory frameworks to manage the risks connected with the crypto assets and blockchain based financial systems. SEBI in India has released rules and regulations for the implementation of blockchain technology in financial markets to advance the transparency and reduce the fraudulent activities.

The global organizations have likewise played a crucial role in the advancement of these regulatory structures. The Bank for International Settlements (BIS) has emphasized the importance of AI adoption and risk management in financial services. The International Monetary fund (IMF) and financial action Task force (FATF) have provided guidelines for preventing the money laundering and illicit funding in the blockchain transactions.

In conclusion, the implementation of emerging technologies creates both opportunities and hurdles in the financial landscape. Policymakers should formulate extensive regulatory guidelines that mitigate the challenges of data privacy, bias, accountability and cybersecurity. There is need for cooperation between the regulators, financial institutions and technology innovators to create a responsible and transparent financial ecosystem. So by addressing the necessity comprehensive data protection regulatory laws, integrating encryption and secure storage, promoting transparency in algorithm and trustworthy data handling practices, we move towards a more accountable and fair data. driven future

IMPLICATIONS AND FUTURE RESEARCH

Technological advancements have revolutionized the financial landscape through innovations such as algorithmic trading, blockchain technologies and AI-driven analytics. These advancements have improved the efficiency, transparency and ease of access to these markets but it likewise provides us with cybersecurity risks, algorithmic bias, ethical concerns and increased market volatility. There is need for robust regulatory structures which is required to maintain the market stability and safeguard investors due to the growing reliance on technology. So the further studies should concentrate on developing ethical AI models for decision-making, the incorporation of blockchain technology provides us with a safe and reliable financial transaction network and helps with established of regulatory measures.

CONCLUSION

The adoption of technologies like Artificial Intelligence, Machine learning, Blockchain and big data analytics have revolutionized the financial landscape by revolutionizing the trading, investment strategies, threat mitigation and fraud detection. These emerging technologies have improved the operational efficiency, market transparency and decision making while enabling cutting-edge financial solutions and offerings through the form of product and services . AI and Machine learning provide predictive analytics and automated decision making which increases the speed and portfolio optimization. Blockchain guarantees safe, decentralized transactions while cutting down on fraud risks and settlement delays. Big data analytics by analysis of real time large datasets it enables more data driven well informed decisions. However the rapid adoption of these technologies poses substantial barriers which includes cybersecurity threats, algorithmic bias, data privacy concerns and moral conundrums in AI-driven decision making. Furthermore financial institutions struggle to maintain the regulatory compliance due to emergence of new technologies. Financial institutions, regulators and researchers should cooperate together for developing comprehensive regulatory frameworks and ethical guidelines. These efforts should focus more on promoting innovation, resolving potential risks and ensuring financial stability thereby creating a balanced ecosystem that supports technology growth while safeguarding market integrity and investor interests.

REFERENCES

Aderemi, S., Olutimehin, D. O., Nnaomah, U. I., Orieno, O. H., Edunjobi, T. E., & Babatunde, S. O. (2024). Big data analytics in the financial services industry: Trends, challenges, and future prospects: A review. International Journal of Science and Technology Researh Archive, 20.

Boinpalli, N. R. (2023). AI-Driven Predictive Analytics for Risk Management in Financial Markets. Silicon Valley Tech Review, 41-53.

Faheem, M. A., Aslam, M., & Kakolu, S. (2022). Artificial Intelligence in Investment Portfolio Optimization: A Comparative Study of Machine Learning Algorithms . International Journal of Science and Research Archive, 8.

Khudoyorova, F., & Khusainov, F. (2024). Big Data Analytics in Financial Services: Opportunities and Challenges. Excellencia International Multi-disciplinary. *Journal of Education*, •••, 5.

Mehortra, A. (n.d.). Artificial Intelligence in Financial Services – Need to Blend Automation with Human Touch . 6.

Muhammad, F. A. (2021). AI-Driven Risk Assessment Models: Revolutionizing Credit Scoring and Default Prediction. *Iconic Research and Engineering Journals*, •••, 10.

Nazareth, N., & Reddy, Y. V. (2019). Financial applications of machine learning: A literature review. *Elsevier*, 33.

Odeyemi, O., Okoye, C. C., Ofodile, O. C., Adeoye, O. B., Addy, W. A., & Ajayi-Nifise, A. O. (2024). Integrating AI with Blockchain for Enchanced Financial Services Security. Finance & Accounting Research Journal, 17.

Pala, S. K. (2023). Role and Importance of Predictive Analytics in Financial Market Risk Assessment. International Journal of Enhanced Research in Management & Computer Applications, 6.

Ryll, L., & Sebastin, S. (2019). Evaluating the Performance of Machine Learning Algorithms in Financial Market Forecasting: A Comprehensive Survey. 22.

Wu, B., & Duan, T. (2019). The Application of Blockchain Technology in Financial markets. *Journal of Physics: Conference Series*, 6. Lewis, R., McPartland, J., & Ranjan, R. (2019). Blockchain and Financial Market Innovation. 18.

Chapter 4
Unveiling FinTech 4.0 in India:
Adoption Trends and Behavioral Insights Through TAM-3

Preeti Sharma
https://orcid.org/0000-0001-7758-9720
Sharda School of Business Studies, India

Rashi Gupta
Sharda University, India

ABSTRACT

The current chapter explores the development of fintech 4.0 in India (Delhi-NCR as a case), analyzing adoption trends and consumer behavioral insights using Technology Acceptance Model-3 (TAM-3). It traces the historical progression of FinTech from its early stages to the current era, highlighting key technological advancement such as artificial intelligence, block chain, and open banking. Through an in-depth analysis of adoption drivers- including technological, economic, psychological, and regulatory factors- this study identifies the critical determinants influencing consumer acceptance and usage of FinTech solutions. Furthermore, it discusses the role of fintech literacy, trust, and security concerns in shaping consumer behavior. By integrated the theoretical framework of TAM-3, the current research provides a comprehensive understanding of fintech adoption, offering valuable insights for financial institutions, policy makers, and technology developers.

DOI: 10.4018/979-8-3373-1404-4.ch004

INTRODUCTION

The advent of Financial Technology (FinTech) is revolutionizing the financial industry, creating new business models and significantly enhancing consumer access to financial services. Internet-only banks, leveraging futuristic technologies, have emerged as leaders in this industry, competing fiercely with traditional banks by offering innovative, user-friendly solutions (Yoon & Lim, 2021; Singh, Sahni, & Kovid, 2021). This digital transformation extends opportunities to non-banking financial institutions, telecommunications companies, and retail firms, highlighting FinTech's ubiquity and disruptive potential. Fintech, or financial technology, can demarcated as the fusion of information technology, financial services, and the market. Fintech encompasses technology-driven financial innovations that revolutionized business models, operating systems, service procedures, or products, whole of which have a quantifiable influence on financial institutions and, markets as well as financial and banking services offering by integrating advanced digital solutions, data analytics, and automation to meet the evolving consumer and industry needs (Cho, Lee, Hwang, & Kim, 2023). The rise of fintech is transforming the financial industry, bringing innovation and reshaping traditional paradigms. Since Indian banks also adopted new technologies and started online, financial technology (fintech) can be seen developing in front of our eyes. We have experience this transition of banking operations from offline to online modes.

Evolution of Fintech

The first iteration of fintech occurred around 135 years ago, in 1886. In the evolution of financial technology the studies refer this period as fintech 1.0. This was the time when infrastructure and transportation were also in the developing phase so that customers could conduct monetary transactions over longer distances (Jayanthi et al., 2024). The fintech during that phase can be defined as in its infant stage and developing with all other tertiary services.

The beginning of Fintech 2.0 can be taken with Barclays' installation of the first ATM in 1967 and is defined by the transition from tradition mode of banking operations to the first advancement of technology. Since then we saw continuous advancements in technology in the areas of finance and banking services. To establish the communication protocol which could facilitate large volumes of cross- border transfers, SWIFT (Society for Worldwide Interbank Financial Telecommunications), and, NASDAQ, the world's first digital stock market, were both established during this phase. This era also saw the advent of bank mainframe computers, the transition to internet banking, and the online revolution with PayPal. By 2008, every developed and developing country has begun to use fintech in various elements of financial operations, signaling the start of fintech 3 (Arner, Barberis, & Buckley, 2015). This phase was characterized by a financial technology revolution, with the rapid use of digital and mobile devices as the major way of accessing the internet and other financial services. This online revolution spawned start-ups, with investors and consumers eager to try new things, resulting in a slew of new products and services. Even established banks began to use these technologies to run their businesses and market themselves as start-ups. We are currently in a phase of transition between FinTech 4.0 and FinTech 5.0 Fintech. During the current pandemic, changes in consumer behavior, transaction and investment patterns have already taken us to fintech 3.5 (Almashhadani, Abuhashesh, Bany Mohammad, Masa'deh, & Al-Khasawneh, 2023). Due to the soaring demand of digital financial services during current pandemic, the first quarter of 2021, fintech companies raised a record $22.8 billion, more than doubling the previous quarter (M. SRIRAM, 2021). Emerging technology and machine learning are projected to transform how we engage with banks and insurance companies, with the goal of enhancing client connections with financial institutions.

Given the rapid rise of fintech, it is critical to comprehend how futuristic technology is transforming the endowment of financial services, as well as the ramifications of these advances for financial inclusion, integrity and stability, economic growth & efficiency (International Monetary Fund & World Bank, 2029). In today's world, the financial sector's growth is determined not only by the financial goods or services offered, but by who delivers them and how quickly it evolves the technology at both the levels: retail and wholesale.

FinTech has grown enormously since its inception, despite its positive and negative elements. According to studies imperfections of financial market, such as market segmentation, information asymmetries, and transaction cost, are thought to restrict impoverished people from using formal financial services (Demir et al., 2020). Due to different limitations and risk involved customers are still cautious to accept and use creative Fintech yet inherently unpredictable, which leaves a negative impact on its growth (AI Nawayseh, 2020).

According to the Boston Consulting Group, India is highly positioned to achieve a financial industry valuation of $150-160 billion, and there would be a $100 billion value creation opportunity by the year 2025 (Narayan & Dayal, 2021). In the year 2025 currently, India has 25 unicorns (the value of transaction of which lies between 1 billion to 10 billion) and 37 minicorns having the transaction value between 100 million to 1 billion (Ministry of Finance, Tracxn, State of the Fintech Union 2023 BCG Note: 1).

Importance of Fintech in Modern Banking and Finance

Financial technology has converted the global banking and financial industry by introducing innovative solutions that enhance efficiency, accessibility, and security. The rapid adoption of digital financial services is reshaping traditional banking, making transactions seamless and more inclusive. Financial technology has enhanced financial inclusion by enabling individuals to use different digital platforms such as digital wallets, mobile banking as well as online lending (Romānova & Kudinska, 2016). Traditional banking processes in olden days used to involve lengthy paperwork and high operational costs. Fintech solutions, including AI-driven automation and blockchain technology, streamline transactions, reduce costs, and enhance service delivery speed. AI and big data analytics help financial institutions analyze customer behavior and preferences, enabling them to offer tailored financial products (Jalal, Al Mubarak, & Durani, Financial technology (fintech), 2023). Chatbots, robo-advisors, and AI-powered credit scoring enhance user experience. With the rise of cyber threats, Fintech companies leverage blockchain, biometrics, and AI-driven fraud detection systems to enhance security, reducing the risks of identity theft and unauthorized transactions. The rise of cashless economies has been driven by mobile payment platforms, contactless payments, and cryptocurrencies. Fintech firms facilitate secure and instant cross-border transactions, reducing dependency on traditional financial intermediaries. Regulatory technology (RegTech) enables banks and financial institutions to comply with financial regulations efficiently (Elia, Stefanelli, & Ferilli, 2022). AI-powered compliance tools help detect fraudulent activities, ensuring adherence to legal requirements. crowdfunding, Peer-to-peer (P2P) lending, and robo-advisors provide alternative financing options for individuals and SMEs. These platforms offer quick access to capital, reducing reliance on conventional banking institutions. Fintech promotes open banking, which gives opportunity to third-party developers to build various applications that integrate with banks services. This fosters competition and innovation, leading to better financial products for consumers (Alt, Beck, & Smits, 2018). Figure 1 shows evolution and different dimensions of fintech in current financial system.

Figure 1. Evolution of Fintech

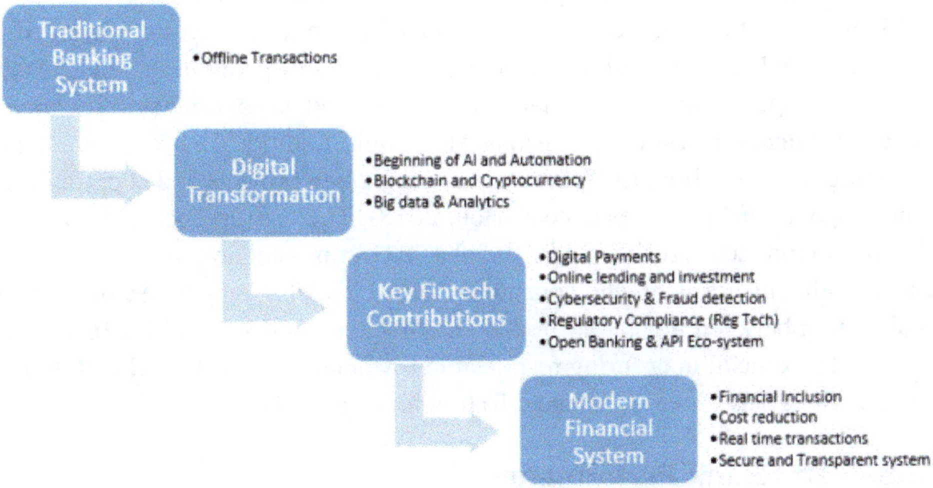

Source: Authors

THEORETICAL BACKGROUND

Traditional Banking Vs Fintech

Traditional banking and FinTech represent two distinct approaches to financial services, each with its own strengths and limitations. Traditional banks operate within well-established frameworks, relying on physical branches, legacy systems, and stringent regulatory oversight (Zhao, Tsai, & Wang, 2019). They emphasize stability, security, and trust, offering services such as savings accounts, loans, and investment management through conventional means. However, traditional banks often struggle with inefficiencies, slow transaction processes, and high operational costs (Batchu & Settibathini, 2024). In contrast, FinTech leverages digital innovations such as artificial intelligence, blockchain, and mobile applications to streamline financial services. FinTech companies prioritize agility, accessibility, and user experience, enabling seamless transactions, digital lending, and automated wealth management (Bureshaid, Lu, & Sarea, 2021). Their ability to rapidly adapt to technological advancements fosters financial inclusion, particularly for underserved populations. However, the fast-paced nature of FinTech also introduces challenges related to cybersecurity, regulatory compliance, and financial stability (Lou, 2017).

When viewed through the lens of sustainability, FinTech has a significant edge over traditional banking. Digital payment systems reduce paper usage, blockchain enhances transparent and ethical financial practices, and AI-driven risk assessments promote sustainable investment decisions. Meanwhile, traditional banks are gradually integrating sustainability principles by financing green projects and adopting eco-friendly operational practices (Lee & Han, 2018). The convergence of traditional banking and FinTech is reshaping financial ecosystems, encouraging a shift toward more sustainable, efficient, and consumer-centric models. As both sectors evolve, collaboration between regulatory bodies, financial institutions, and FinTech innovators will be crucial in ensuring responsible financial growth aligned with global sustainability goals (Andria, Ananda, Rahmi, & Bon, 2021).

Fintech and Bank Performance

The speedy expansion of financial technology (FinTech) has revolutionised the banking industry, creating both challenges and prospects for traditional financial institutions. FinTech has introduced digital payments, mobile money, AI-driven credit assessments, and blockchain-based transactions, reshaping financial services worldwide. The impact of FinTech on bank performance, however, remains a subject of debate, with studies depicting both positive and negative effects.

Research on influence of FinTech's on the performance of banking industry provides mixed findings. Some studies highlight that FinTech reduces traditional banking profitability. A study on Indonesia found that FinTech negatively affects key banking metrics, including net interest margins (NIM), return on assets (ROA), and return on equity (ROE) (Widiasmara, Retnowati, Alvarez, & De Guzman, 2024). The weakening of bank profitability results from FinTech firms capturing market stake in lending and payment services (Phan, Narayan, Rahman, & Hutabarat, 2020) . Similarly, in China, the rise of FinTech start-ups and digital lending platforms has cut into banks' traditional revenue streams (Zhao, Li, Yu, Chen, & Lee, 2022). The effect is particularly strong for large, state-owned banks that struggle with the agility needed to compete in the digital space. (Phan, Narayan, Rahman, & Hutabarat, 2020)

On the other hand, FinTech also improves banking efficiency. By integrating digital solutions, banks can enhance customer experience, reduce operational costs, and expand financial inclusion (Fadhul & Hamdan, 2020). In East Africa, mobile money adoption has improved bank profitability, efficiency, and stability by broadening financial access and increasing deposit collection (Phan, Narayan, Rahman, & Hutabarat, 2020). Digital innovations, such as AI-based credit risk assessments and automated compliance tools, further enable banks to optimize decision-making processes.

One key trend is the growing association between banks and FinTech firms. While FinTech disrupts traditional banking, partnerships with digital firms allow banks to leverage technology without completely overhauling legacy systems. Banks investing in digital transformation tend to perform better than those resisting change (Nguyen, Tran, & Ho, 2022).

Overall, FinTech poses a dual impact on bank performance. It challenges profitability by increasing competition, yet it enhances efficiency and financial inclusion (Chen, You, & Chang, 2021). Banks that strategically integrate FinTech innovations stand to gain the most, while those slow to adapt may struggle in an increasingly digital financial ecosystem.

Key Innovation in Fintech

FinTech 5.0 represents the next phase of financial technology, deeply integrated with **Industry 4.0** innovations such as artificial intelligence (AI), block chain, and the Internet of Things (IoT) (Jalal, Al Mubarak, & Durani, Financial technology (fintech), 2023). These advancements are driving automation, decentralization, and enhanced security in financial services in Indian financial system.

One key innovation is the **adoption of AI and machine learning** to improve risk assessment, fraud detection, and personalized financial services (Puschmann, 2017). AI-powered chatbots, robo-advisors, and algorithmic trading platforms are making financial decision-making faster and more efficient. Another ground-breaking development is **block chain and smart contracts**, which enable decentralized finance (DeFi) and digital assets, reducing reliance on traditional banking systems. Block chain ensures transparency and security, facilitating cross-border transactions with minimal intermediaries (Mention, 2019).

Emergence of regulatory sandboxes and innovation hubs is a major tool for FinTech experimentation. Governments and financial institutions are using these controlled environments to test new financial solutions while maintaining compliance with evolving regulations (Alaassar, Mention, & Aas, 2023).

Additionally, **embedded finance and open banking** are reshaping customer experiences by integrating financial services directly into non-financial platforms. Digital wallets, Buy Now Pay Later (BNPL) models, and API-driven ecosystems are making financial services more seamless (Gozman, Liebenau, & Mangan, 2018). As **FinTech 5.0** continues to evolve, its convergence with **Industry 4.0** is accelerating financial inclusion, improving operational efficiency, and redefining global economic structures. Balancing innovation with security and regulatory compliance is a challenge now to ensure a sustainable financial future.

Figure 2. Key Innovations in Fintech

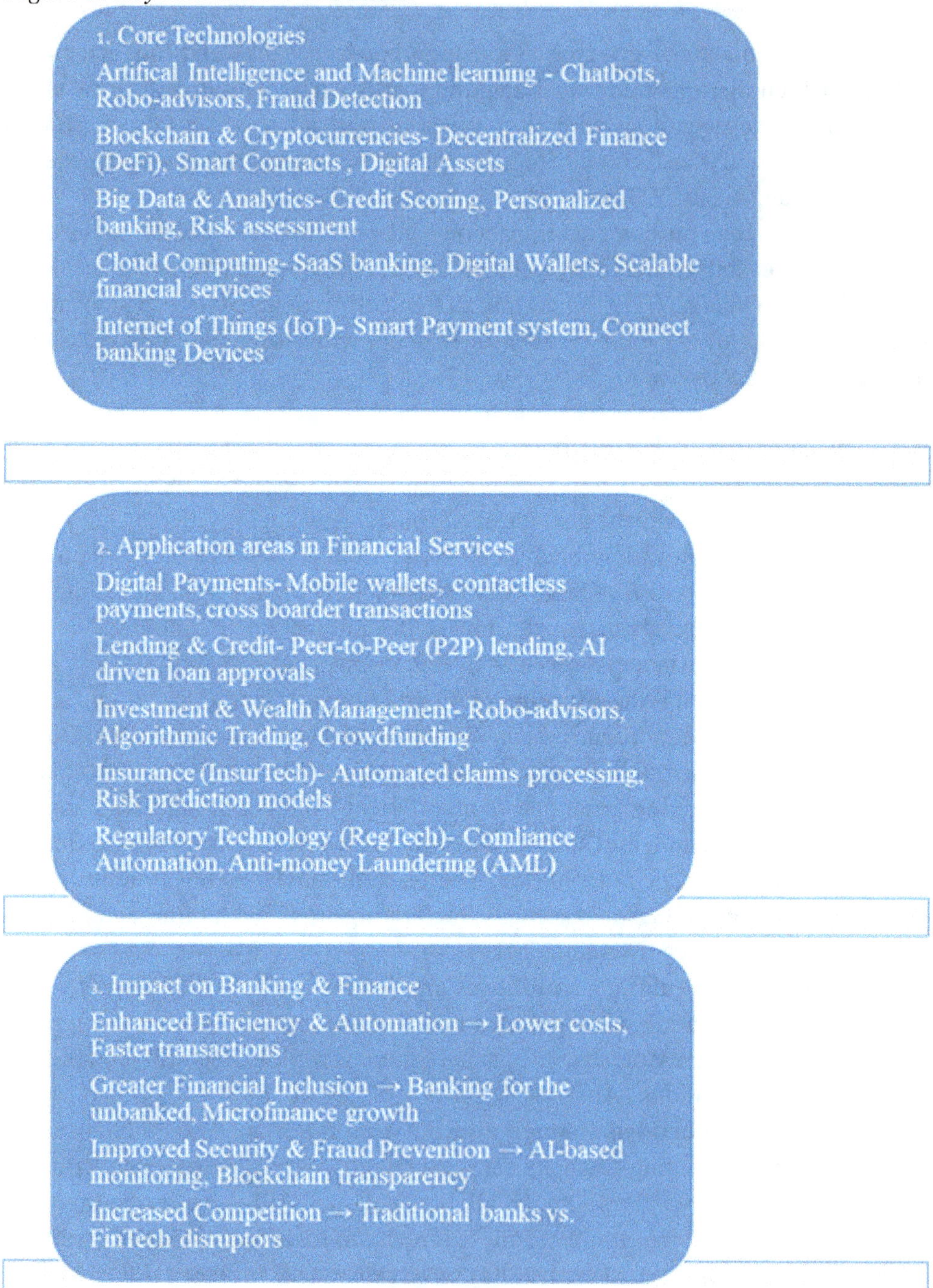

Factors Influencing the Adoption of Fintech

Technological Factors

- Ease of Access and User-Friendly Interfaces
- Mobile Banking and Digital Payments
- AI and Automation in Financial Services

Economic Factors

- Cost-effectiveness and Lower Transaction Fees
- Access to Microfinance and Credit Facilities
- Financial Inclusion and Support for the Unbanked

Psychological and Behavioral Factors

- Trust and Security Concerns
- Perceived Risk vs. Benefits
- Consumer Attitudes Toward Digital Transactions

Regulatory and Legal Factors

- Government Policies and Regulations
- Data Protection Laws (GDPR, CCPA, etc.)
- Compliance Challenges for Fintech Companies

Socio-Cultural Influences

- Digital Literacy and Financial Awareness
- Influence of Social Media and Peer Recommendations
- Regional and Cultural Preferences in Financial Transactions

Pandemic and Post-Pandemic Impact on Fintech Adoption

- Acceleration of Digital Transactions During COVID-19
- The Shift from Cash-Based to Digital Economies
- Future Prospects Post-Pandemic

MAIN FOCUS OF THE CHAPTER

Despite its rapid growth, the adoption of FinTech is influenced by several factors. The rise of mobile banking has driven studies into customer responses to self-service channels in retail banking. Furthermore, technologies like blockchain, artificial intelligence (AI), and deep learning are reshaping financial services (Romānova & Kudinska, 2016). AI facilitates customer behavior analysis and fraud prevention, while blockchain enables secure transactions through applications like cryptocurrencies and smart contracts. These innovations are reshaping financial operations and diminishing the reliance on traditional offline banks (Ebrahim, Kumaraswamy, & Abdulla, 2021).

The proliferation of smart devices and the push for a cashless society have enabled financial services to be accessed anytime, anywhere (Bureshaid, Lu, & Sarea, 2021). Mobile payment services, though still evolving, are increasingly adopted due to their perceived usefulness, which depends on personal, service, and environmental factors. Governments globally are promoting regulations to encourage the adoption of mobile payments, recognizing their potential to drive financial inclusion (Ediagbonya & Tioluwani, 2023).

In countries like India, FinTech has played a pivotal role in reshaping the financial system, driven by smartphone penetration, government initiatives, and the demand for digital payment solutions. Gen Z, in particular, has embraced e-wallets and mobile payments, contributing to this shift. Meanwhile, Malaysia has integrated AI into investment management, creating robo-advisors that automate and optimize investment strategies (Chellappan, Elanchselvan, & Abu-Samah, 2025).

Given the growing significance of FinTech in transforming financial services, it is crucial to explore the intention to use FinTech among different demographics in India. Factors such as smartphone penetration, government policies, and evolving consumer preferences play a key role in adoption. Understanding user motivations and barriers can help in designing more inclusive and efficient financial solutions. As digital payments and AI-driven financial tools gain momentum, studying their acceptance will provide insights for future innovations and policy-making.

The rapid development of financial technology (FinTech) has revolutionized traditional banking and financial services worldwide. Existing literature highlights the significance of user-centric frameworks, such as the Unified Theory of Acceptance and Use of Technology (UTAUT), Technology Acceptance Model (TAM), and other adoption theories in understanding FinTech adoption patterns across demographics and geographies (Tran, Han, & Yun, 2018; Jayanthi, et al., Adoption of FinTech payment services- An extended expectation towards core constructs of technology acceptance model, 2024). Studies have explored diverse dimensions of FinTech adoption, including its drivers and barriers. Key elements inducing adoption of fintech, such as perceived usefulness, ease of use, trust, security, financial literacy, and social influence, have been well-documented (Fernando & others, 2019). For instance, perceived usefulness and ease of use are critical determining factor of behavioral intentions, as evidenced in studies on mobile wallets and digital payment systems in Malaysia and Indonesia (Widiasmara, Retnowati, Alvarez, & De Guzman, 2024). Trust and privacy apprehensions remain central to adoption decisions, particularly in contexts involving financial risks or ethical concerns, such as Islamic FinTech services (Malhi, Kovid, & Singh, 2024; Sharma, Jangir, Gupta, & Rupeika-Apoga, 2024).

Furthermore, demographic factors, including age, gender, education, and income, have been studied for their impact on attitudes toward FinTech by different researcher in different geographical locations. Younger users, particularly Gen Z and millennials, show greater acceptance of innovative financial solutions due to their digital nativity (Chandra, Kristin, Suhartono, Sutarto, & Sung, 2018). Conversely, financial literacy and digital literacy are identified as significant barriers in less-developed regions, impeding broader FinTech adoption (Patnaik, Kudal, Dawar, Inamdar, & Dawar, 2023).

Geographical studies emphasize the varying adoption drivers across regions. For instance, government initiatives and support have been pivotal in advancing FinTech in India, while personal innovativeness and cultural inclinations play a principal role in Southeast Asia (Alshari & Lokhande, 2022). Comparative analyses have also highlighted the effect of macroeconomic factors like the COVID-19 pandemic on FinTech adoption, with amplified usage during periods of social restrictions (Srivastava, Mohta, & Shunmugasundaram, 2024).

Despite the rich body of investigation in this area, notable gaps persist in the literature, particularly concerning underrepresented regions and user groups. The interplay of technology adoption frameworks with socio-economic factors, particularly in emerging economies, warrants further examination. Moreover, the impact of sprouting technologies, such as artificial intelligence (AI) and blockchain, on user acceptance remains underexplored.

Research Gap

While substantial research has been conducted on FinTech adoption using frameworks like TAM and UTAUT, critical gaps exist. First, the majority of studies focus on individual adoption factors without considering their interplay in different socio-economic contexts. Second, research on FinTech adoption in underserved regions, such as rural areas and emerging markets, remains limited. Third, there is a lack of studies integrating advanced technologies like AI and blockchain into existing adoption models, thereby ignoring the potential disruptions these technologies may bring to user perceptions and behaviors. Lastly, user retention and post-adoption behavior, which are crucial for sustained FinTech growth, have not been comprehensively studied. Addressing these gaps is essential for a holistic understanding of FinTech adoption and its long-term implications.

Factors Influencing Fintech With Special Reference to Delhi NCR: Case Study

In this sector we present the outcome of technology acceptance model in Delhi NCR. For finding the technology acceptance model for fintech in India we have modified the TAM-3. The factors, their coding and reference have been reported in table A.1 (Annexure)

We have used Primary data to conduct exploratory factor analysis. A self-designed seven points Likert type scale (strongly agree, moderately agree, agree, neutral, disagree, moderately disagree and strongly disagree) questionnaire was managed and distributed to more than 600 individuals using any form of fintech. In this current study, we have used the method of convenient sampling to collect respondent's viewpoints. A total of 418 valid responses could only be collected for the current study. Table 1 shows the profile of the respondents.

Table 1. Respondents Profile

Demographic Characteristics	Division	Total Number	Percentage
Gender	Male	227	54.31
	Female	191	45.69
Education	12th Pass	38	9.09
	Graduate	89	21.29
	Post Graduate	154	36.84
	Professional	137	32.78
Occupation	Student	111	26.56
	Service	142	33.97
	Business	74	17.70
	Profession	71	16.99
	Others	20	4.78
Age	18-30	242	57.89
	31-40	98	23.44
	41-50	61	14.59
	Above 50	17	4.07

Source: Questionnaire

Model Building

In current study first we conduct confirmatory factor analysis and then we move to SEM. The model building for current study has been divided into five steps; model specification, identification, estimation, evaluation, and modifications (possibly) (Anderson, 1987; Streiner, 2006).

Model Specification: In this study, the independent variables influencing the intention to use FinTech are conceptualized as latent constructs. Based on the Technology Acceptance Model-3 (TAM-3), the primary constructs include (Malhi, Kovid, & Singh, 2024):

- **Perceived Usefulness (PU)**: The degree to which FinTech is perceived to enhance financial transactions.
- **Perceived Ease of Use (PEU)**: The extent to which FinTech is considered user-friendly.
- **Attitude Towards Computer Use (ATCU)**: The general attitude of users towards adopting digital financial technologies.
- **Intention to Use FinTech (ITUF)**: The dependent variable representing the likelihood of adopting FinTech services.

Model Identification

A structural model must be over-identified to allow for parameter estimation. The degree of freedom (df) is calculated using the formula (Anderson, 1987): The below formula is used to compute the number of elements in the correlation matrix:

$$df = p(p + 1)/2 - q$$

Where:

- p= number of observed variables
- q= number of estimated parameters

With nine observed variables in this study, the correlation matrix consists of [9(9+1)]/2= 45 elements. Since the model specifies 21 parameters, the degrees of freedom are calculated as:

df= 45-21= 24

Since df > 0, the model is over-identified and can be estimated.

Data Preparation

Before performing CFA and SEM, the dataset must be checked for normality, multi-collinearity and missing data (Anderson, 1987).

Econometric Modelling

Structural equation models consist of two key components: the structural model and the measurement model. The measurement model links observed indicators to latent variables and, in some cases, to observed covariates, as seen in confirmatory factor analysis (CFA) (Anderson, 1987). The structural model defines the relationships between latent variables and their regressions on observed variables, establishing the overall framework of the analysis (Raykov & Widaman, 1995). First we assess the fit of observed variables to the latent variables (measurement model) through CFA, and then we assess the fit of the structural equation model among latent variables (structural model). In Structural Equation Modeling (SEM), fit indices assess how well the proposed model aligns with the observed data. The Chi-Square (χ^2) test evaluates discrepancies between the sample and model-implied covariance matrices, though it is sensitive to large samples. RMSEA measures model error per degree of freedom, favoring simpler models with values below 0.08 indicating good fit. GFI and AGFI assess variance explained by the model, with AGFI adjusting for degrees of freedom. NFI and CFI compare model fit against a null model, with values above 0.90 considered acceptable. Lastly, χ^2/df helps determine model efficiency, with values below 3 indicating a well-fitting model. These indices collectively ensure the model's validity in explaining relationships among variables (Anderson, 1987; Raykov & Widaman, 1995).

This is because if the selected indicators for a construct fail to measure that construct, the proposed theory should be revised before the structural relationships are tested. As such, researchers often test the measurement model before the structural model (Raykov & Widaman, 1995).

The sample size (Raykov & Widaman, 1995) suggested that the sample size should exceed the number of elements in the correlation matrix, ideally with at least ten participants per estimated parameter. With a sample size of over 500, data were collected using the Technology Acceptance Model-3 (TAM-3) framework (Anderson, 1987). Participants completed an instrument assessing three key constructs: perceived usefulness (PU), perceived ease of use (PEU), and attitude toward computer use (ATCU).

Empirical Result and Discussion

Table 2 presents the factor loadings and reliability results of the factors under study. The table provides insights into the reliability and validity of the constructs measuring behavioral intention to use FinTech. Factor loadings above 0.70 indicate a strong relationship between observed variables and their respective latent factors (Anderson, 1987). Constructs like Subjective Norms (SN1 = 0.82, SN2 = 0.78), Result Demonstration (RES1 = 0.83, RES2 = 0.81), and Computer Playfulness (CPLAY1 = 0.88) show high factor loadings, confirming their strong association with the underlying constructs. However, some items, such as PEC1 (0.66), PEC2 (0.62), and PEOU3 (0.65), exhibit lower loadings, suggesting the need for further refinement.

Reliability, measured through Cronbach's Alpha, shows that most factors meet the acceptable threshold of 0.70, indicating good internal consistency. Constructs such as Subjective Norms (0.85), Result Demonstration (0.78), and Computer Anxiety (0.77) demonstrate high reliability, confirming their stability in measuring the intended constructs. Moderate reliability is observed in Computer Self-Efficacy (0.72), Computer Playfulness (0.72), and Perceived Enjoyment (0.74), suggesting these constructs are fairly consistent but may still benefit from slight adjustments. Some constructs, including Output Quality (0.65), Perception of External Control (0.63), and Perceived Ease of Use (0.63), have relatively lower reliability, indicating potential issues in internal consistency that may require re-evaluating or rewording specific items.

Items with low factor loadings, such as IMG3 (0.69), OUT2 (0.65), PEC2 (0.62), and PEOU3 (0.65), should be reconsidered to enhance measurement accuracy. For current study we have taken these values as it is.

Table 2. Confirmatory Factor Analysis

Factor Name	Variables	Factor Loading	Reliability
Factor 1: Subjective Norms	SN1	0.82	0.85
	SN2	0.78	
Factor 2: Image	IMG1	0.76	0.74
	IMG2	0.72	
	IMG3	0.69	
Factor 3: Job Relevance	REL1	0.82	0.76
	REL2	0.81	
	REL3	0.72	

continued on following page

Table 2. Continued

Factor Name	Variables	Factor Loading	Reliability
Factor 4: Output Quality	OUT1	0.69	0.65
	OUT2	0.65	
	OUT3	0.71	
Factor 5: Result Demonstration	RES1	0.83	0.78
	RES2	0.81	
	RES3	0.76	
	RES4	0.72	
Factor 6: Computer Self Efficacy	CSE1	0.77	0.72
	CSE2	0.72	
Factor 7: Perception of external control	PEC1	0.66	0.63
	PEC2	0.62	
Factor 8: Computer Anxiety	CANX1	0.79	0.77
	CANX2	0.78	
	CANX3	0.72	
	CANX4	0.81	
Factor 9: Computer Playfulness	CPLAY1	0.88	0.72
	CPLAY2	0.71	
Factor 10: Perceived Enjoyment	ENJ1	0.66	0.74
	ENJ2	0.77	
	ENJ3	0.71	
Factor 11: Perceived Usefulness	PU1	0.69	0.66
	PU2	0.68	
Factor 12: Perceived Ease of Use	PEoU1	0.67	0.63
	PEoU2	0.66	
	PEoU3	0.65	

Source: SPSS Output

The model fit (Table 3) indices indicate an overall good fit of the measurement model. The chi-square (χ^2) value of 240.67 with a p-value of 0.02 suggests a statistically significant discrepancy between the sample and fitted covariance matrices; however, chi-square is sensitive to sample size, so other fit indices are considered. The Root Mean Square Error of Approximation (RMSEA) is 0.046, which is below the 0.08 threshold, indicating an excellent model fit. The Goodness-of-Fit Index (GFI) is 0.92, signifying a good fit as it exceeds the recommended 0.90 threshold. The Adjusted Goodness-of-Fit Index (AGFI) is slightly below the 0.90 threshold at 0.89, indicating an acceptable fit. Lastly, the Comparative Fit Index (CFI) of 0.96

falls well above the 0.90 benchmark, demonstrating an excellent fit. Overall, these results suggest that the measurement model is well-specified and appropriately fits the data.

Table 3. Model Fit Indices for CFA

Fit Index	Threshold	Value	Interpretation
Chi-Square (χ^2)	p > 0.05	240.67 (p=0.02)	Acceptable fit
RMSEA	< 0.08	0.046	Excellent fit
GFI	> 0.90	0.92	Good fit
AGFI	> 0.90	0.89	Acceptable
CFI	> 0.90	0.96	Excellent fit

Source: SPSS output

The path analysis results presented in Table 4 provide critical insights into the relationships between independent variables and behavioral intention to use fintech. Perceived Usefulness (PU) demonstrates a strong positive influence on behavioral intention ($\beta = 0.35$, $t = 8.90$, $p = 0.045$), indicating that users who find fintech useful are more likely to adopt it. Similarly, Perceived Ease of Use (PEU) has a significant positive impact ($\beta = 0.27$, $t = 7.45$, $p = 0.002$), suggesting that the easier fintech platforms are to use, the higher the likelihood of adoption.

Subjective Norms (SN) also exhibit a substantial effect ($\beta = 0.29$, $t = 8.02$, $p = 0.003$), implying that social influence plays a crucial role in determining fintech usage. Image (IMG) has a comparatively lower but significant effect ($\beta = 0.18$, $t = 5.78$, $p = 0.001$), highlighting that individuals who associate fintech use with prestige and status are more inclined to adopt it. Job Relevance (REL) positively affects behavioral intention ($\beta = 0.22$, $t = 6.34$, $p = 0.023$), emphasizing the importance of fintech in professional and transactional activities.

On the contrary, Computer Anxiety (CANX) has a negative impact on behavioral intention ($\beta = -0.21$, $t = -6.01$, $p = 0.022$), indicating that individuals who feel nervous or uncomfortable using fintech are less likely to adopt it. Overall, the significant p-values across all variables confirm their strong predictive power in explaining behavioral intention, validating the model's robustness in understanding fintech adoption behavior.

Table 4. Path-Analysis Results (Unstandardized coefficient)

Independent Variable	**Dependent variable**	**Path Coefficient (β)**	**Estimate (t-value)**	**P-value**
Perceived Usefulness (PU)	Behavioral Intention to use (BI)	0.35	8.90	0.045
Perceived Ease of Use (PEU)	Behavioral Intention to use (BI)	0.27	7.45	0.002
Subjective Norms (SN)	Behavioral Intention to use (BI)	0.29	8.02	0.003
Image (IMG)	Behavioral Intention to use (BI)	0.18	5.78	0.001
Job Relevance (REL)	Behavioral Intention to use (BI)	0.22	6.34	0.023
Computer Anxiety (CANX)	Behavioral Intention to use (BI)	-0.21	-6.01	0.022

Source: Test Results

The model fit statistics presented in Table 5 indicate a strong and well-fitting structural equation model. The **Standardized Root Mean Square Residual (SRMR)** value of **0.041** is well below the commonly accepted threshold of 0.08, suggesting a good fit between the observed and predicted correlations. The **Root Mean Square Error of Approximation (RMSEA)** value of **0.048** is below the recommended cutoff of 0.05, indicating an excellent model fit with minimal approximation errors. The **Adjusted Goodness-of-Fit Index (AGFI)** is **0.90**, meeting the acceptable threshold and demonstrating that the model explains a substantial proportion of variance while accounting for degrees of freedom. Finally, the **Bentler Comparative Fit Index (CFI)** value of **0.95** exceeds the recommended threshold of 0.90, confirming that the proposed model has a significantly better fit compared to the null model.

Overall, these fit indices collectively suggest that the model provides a robust representation of the relationships among the factors influencing behavioral intention to use fintech, supporting its validity and reliability in explaining fintech adoption behavior.

Table 5. Model fit Statistics

Fit Summary	**Value**
Standardized root mean square residual	**0.041**
Root mean square error of approximation	**0.048**
Adjusted Goodness-of-Fit Index	**0.90**
Bentler Comparative Fit Index	**0.95**

Source: Test Results

Further Discussion

The outcomes of this study highlight key determinants impelling fintech adoption in the Delhi NCR region, stressing the role of perceived usefulness, perceived ease of use, and subjective norms and other variables referred in study. The results indicate that users are more likely to adopt fintech solutions when they perceive them as useful and easy to navigate. This aligns with existing literature on the Technology Acceptance Model (TAM-3), reinforcing the significance of usability and efficiency in driving digital financial adoption (Alshari & Lokhande, 2022; Chandra, Kristin, Suhartono, Sutarto, & Sung, 2018; Singh, Sahni, & Kovid, 2021). Additionally, the strong influence of subjective norms suggests that societal and peer influence plays a crucial role in fintech adoption, particularly in urban settings where digital financial services are increasingly being promoted as the norm. However, the relatively lower impact of image and job relevance indicates that fintech adoption may be more functionality-driven than status-oriented, though it remains relevant in professional contexts.

Another important aspect of the study is the influence of computer anxiety, which negatively impacts behavioral intention to use fintech. This suggests that despite advancements in digital financial services, there are still barriers related to technological apprehension and user confidence. Addressing these concerns through user-friendly interfaces, educational initiatives, and customer support can significantly improve fintech adoption rates. Furthermore, constructs such as output quality and perceived external control exhibited lower reliability, implying potential inconsistencies in user perceptions regarding the reliability and security of fintech platforms. Strengthening cybersecurity measures, ensuring transparency, and improving the overall user experience could mitigate these concerns, making fintech services more appealing to hesitant users.

Lastly, the structural equation modeling results confirm the robustness of the proposed model, demonstrating a strong fit with observed data. The high factor loadings and satisfactory model fit indices validate the significance of the chosen variables in explaining fintech adoption behavior. However, the study also reveals gaps that future research could address, such as exploring the long-term retention of fintech users and the integration of advanced technologies like AI and blockchain. Additionally, expanding the research to include underserved regions and diverse socio-economic groups could provide a more comprehensive understanding of fintech adoption dynamics. These insights can aid policymakers, fintech developers, and financial institutions in designing more inclusive, secure, and user-centric digital financial solutions.

Future Research Directions

This study provides valuable insights into the factors influencing the intention to use fintech; however, several areas warrant further exploration. Future research could examine the moderating effects of demographic variables such as age, income, and digital literacy on fintech adoption. Additionally, longitudinal studies could be conducted to assess how users' perceptions evolve over time with increased exposure and experience. The impact of emerging technologies, such as artificial intelligence and blockchain, on fintech adoption also presents a promising avenue for investigation. Moreover, cross-cultural studies could help determine whether the identified factors hold across different regions and economic contexts. Finally, incorporating qualitative research methods, such as interviews and focus groups, could provide deeper insights into user motivations and barriers, enriching the current quantitative findings.

Managerial Implication:

Current study presents the comprehension of user beliefs and views regarding the actual usage of FinTech services in Indian scenerio. The findings of this research will assist FinTech service providers in better understanding and designing FinTech services for a diverse range of users in India (Delhi-NCR in current study). Consumer/custormer awareness programs can be designed by policymakers to enhance digitization in the banking sector for a better reach. Enhancing the usability and security characteristics of FinTech services should receive more attention by policy makers in order to build social confirmations among Indian users. By containing appropriate behavioral and technological constituents and reviewing the moderating effect of digital behavior and demographic features, the study contributes to the futuristic technology recognition literature in financial inclusion to define the future of fintech 5.0 in Delhi NCR (representing Indian population).

The following table 6 presents the annexure containing variables under study.

Table 6. Annexure: A.1 (Variables/Questions under study)

Construct	Code	Items
Perceived Usefulness (PU)	PU1	Online financial transactions increase my efficiency
	PU2	Online financial transactions are useful to increase productivity
Perceived Ease of Use	PEOU1	Fintech save time
	PEOU2	Fintech helps in doing online transactions effortlessly
	PEOU3	Fintech (online transactions) are easy to use

continued on following page

Table 6. Continued

Construct	Code	Items
Computer Self-Efficacy (CSE)	CSE1	Do you need help to make the online transactions?
	CSE2	Do you require demo for making the online transactions?
Perception of External Control(PEC)	PEC1	I know how to use the fintech
	PEC 2	I have all the resources (smart phone/laptop/internet connectivity) which are necessary to do online transactions
	PEC 3	The fintech applications are not compatible with my mobile/Laptop I am using
Computer Playfulness (CPLAY)	CPLAY1	I am spontaneous in using smart phone/laptop
	CPLAY 2	Using smart phone is playful
Computer Anxiety (CANX)	CANX1	I can do online transactions without any fear
	CAN2	I do feel nervous while doing online transactions
	CAN3	I feel uncomfortable while doing online transactions
	CAN4	I feel uneasy while doing online transactions
Perceived Enjoyment (ENJ)	ENJ1	I find the online transaction and Fintech to be enjoyable.
	ENJ2	I have fun using Fintech
	EN3	The process of doing online transactions is streamlined
Objective Usability	OU1	You think you are an expert in using fintech
Subjective Norm (SN)	SN1	People who influence my behavior think that I should use Fintech (online payment/banking services)
	SN2	People who are important to me think that I should use fintech (online payment/banking services)
Voluntariness (VOL)	VOL1	My use of online transactions is voluntary
	VOL2	Although it is helpful, but using online payment is not compulsion in my daily transactions
Image (IMG)	IMG1	People who are more proficient in using online transactions, have more prestige than those who are not
	IMG2	People who use fintech have a high profile
	IMG3	Know-how of fintech is related to image of individual
Job Relevance (REL)	REL1	In my job/business/transactions, use of fintech is important
	REL2	In my job/business/transactions, use of fintech is relevant
	REL3	The use of fintech is pertinent to my various transactions
Output Quality (OUT)	OUT1	The quality of output (ease, risk and time saving) I get from using fintech is high
	OUT2	I have no problem with the quality of transactions (risk, ease and time) I do using fintech
	OUT3	I rate the fintech transactions to be excellent

continued on following page

Table 6. Continued

Construct	Code	Items
Result Demonstrability (RES)	RES 1	I am able to explain the benefits/disadvantages of fintech clearly to others
	RES2	I can share my experiences of using fintech with other
	RES3	The benefits of using fintech are apparent to me
	RES4	I am doubtful/not clear on the benefits of using fintech
Behavioral Intention (BI)	BI1	If I have access (mobile /internet/computer), I intend to use it.
	BI2	I have all resources but I don't think I'll use it
	BI3	I am planning to use it in the future
Use	USE1	The shift towards fintech

CONCLUSION

The findings from the review of literature emphasize critical factors influencing the adoption and use of FinTech services, with a strong focus on user perceptions, demographic influences, and contextual variables:

1. **Ease of Use and Perceived Usefulness**: Ease of use consistently emerged as a pivotal factor positively influencing the adoption of FinTech services, while perceived usefulness showed a nuanced role, sometimes moderated by other variables like security and trust.
2. **Trust and Security**: Trust remains a vital driver of FinTech adoption, particularly in emerging markets. However, the influence of perceived risks, such as financial and data security, is inconsistent across demographics and service types.
3. **Behavioral Intention and Social Influence**: The impact of behavioral intention on actual FinTech use varies. Notably, social influence sometimes negatively impacts adoption, particularly among Gen Z, who value self-reliance and online information over peer pressure.
4. **Demographics and Personalization**: Factors like gender, occupation, and income levels shape adoption patterns. For instance, financial literacy significantly correlates with FinTech adoption in regions like Malaysia. Moreover, personalized services and user-centric designs enhance adoption, particularly among younger users.
5. **Role of Contextual and Environmental Factors**: The COVID-19 pandemic acted as a catalyst for FinTech adoption by highlighting the need for flexible,

contactless financial solutions. Similarly, government support and regulatory frameworks positively influenced adoption in regions like India and Bangladesh.

6. **Service Quality and Responsiveness**: The quality of services offered by FinTech providers, such as customer support and seamless user experiences, influences attitudes and behaviors. However, over-reliance on customer support is less effective for younger demographics.
7. **Implications for Industry Practices**: FinTech providers should focus on integrating robust security features, enhancing user-friendly interfaces, and addressing gaps in financial literacy to foster widespread adoption. For internet-only banks, strategies to balance branch closures and customer acquisition through technology acceptance are essential.

These findings collectively highlight the dynamic interplay of technological, behavioral, and environmental factors shaping FinTech adoption and offer valuable insights for tailoring strategies across diverse user groups and geographies.

REFERENCES

Alaassar, A., Mention, A.-L., & Aas, T. H. (2023). Facilitating innovation in FinTech: A review and research agenda. *Review of Managerial Science*, *17*(1), 33–66.

Almashhadani, I. S., Abuhashesh, M., Bany Mohammad, A., Masa'deh, R., & Al-Khasawneh, M. (2023). Exploring the determinants of FinTech adoption and intention to use in Jordan: The impact of COVID-19. *Cogent Social Sciences*, *9*(2), 2256536.

Alshari, H. A., & Lokhande, M. (2022). The impact of demographic factors of clients' attitudes and their intentions to use FinTech services on the banking sector in the least developed countries. *Cogent Business & Management*, *9*(1), 2114305.

Alt, R., Beck, R., & Smits, M. T. (2018). FinTech and the transformation of the financial industry. [Springer.]. *Electronic Markets*, *28*, 235–243.

Anderson, J. G. (1987). Structural equation models in the social and behavioral sciences: Model building. *Child Development*, •••, 49–64.

Andria, F., Ananda, D., Rahmi, A., & Bon, A. (2021). Fintech payment application in improving customer services. *Proceedings of the International Conference on Industrial Engineering and Operations Management,* Singapore.

Arner, D. W., Barberis, J., & Buckley, R. P. (2015). The evolution of Fintech: A new post-crisis paradigm. *Geo. J. Int'l L.*, *47*, 1271.

Batchu, R. K., & Settibathini, V. S. (2024). Sustainable Finance Beyond Banking Shaping the Future of Financial Technology. *International Conference on Sustainable Development through Machine Learning, AI and IoT* (pp. 119--129). Springer.

Bureshaid, N., Lu, K., & Sarea, A. (2021). Adoption of fintech services in the banking industry. *Applications of Artificial Intelligence in Business, Education and Healthcare*, 125-138.

Chandra, Y. U., Kristin, D. M., Suhartono, J., Sutarto, F. S., & Sung, M. (2018). Analysis of determinant factors of user acceptance of mobile payment system in indonesia (a case study of go-pay mobile payment. *2018 International Conference on Information Management and Technology (ICIMTech)* (pp. 454--459). IEEE.

Chellappan, K., Elanchselvan, T., & Abu-Samah, A. (2025). E-wallet Delivery Technology Architecture Adoption: A Review. *Jurnal Kejuruteraan*, *37*(1), 219–232.

Chen, X., You, X., & Chang, V. (2021). FinTech and commercial banks' performance in China: A leap forward or survival of the fittest? *Technological Forecasting and Social Change*, *166*, 120645.

Cho, S., Lee, Z., Hwang, S., & Kim, J. (2023). Determinants of bank closures: What ensures sustainable profitability in mobile banking? *Electronics (Basel), 12*(5), 1196.

Ebrahim, R., Kumaraswamy, S., & Abdulla, Y. (2021). FinTech in banks: opportunities and challenges. *Innovative strategies for implementing fintech in banking*, 100-109.

Ediagbonya, V., & Tioluwani, C. (2023). The role of fintech in driving financial inclusion in developing and emerging markets: Issues, challenges and prospects. *Technological Sustainability, 2*(1), 100–119.

Elia, G., Stefanelli, V., & Ferilli, G. B. (2022). Investigating the role of Fintech in the banking industry: What do we know? *European Journal of Innovation Management, 26*(5), 1365–1393.

Fadhul, S., & Hamdan, A. (2020). The role of" fintech" on banking performance. *European Conference on Innovation and Entrepreneurship* (pp. 911--XVII). Academic Conferences International Limited.

Fernando, E. (2019). Analysis of the influence of consumer behavior using FinTech services with SEM and TOPSIS. *2019 International conference on information management and technology (ICIMTech). 1*, pp. 93-97. IEEE.

Gozman, D., Liebenau, J., & Mangan, J. (2018). The innovation mechanisms of fintech start-ups: Insights from SWIFT's innotribe competition. *Journal of Management Information Systems, 35*(1), 145–179.

Jalal, A., Al Mubarak, M., & Durani, F. (2023). *Financial technology (fintech). Artificial Intelligence and Transforming Digital Marketing*. Springer.

Jayanthi, M., Amudha, R., Alamelu, R., Dinesh, S., Nalini, R., & Shobhana, N. (2024). AIP Conference Proceedings: Vol. 3180. *Adoption of FinTech payment services-An extended expectation towards core constructs of technology acceptance model.* AIP Publishing.

Jayanthi, M., Amudha, R., Alamelu, R., Dinesh, S., Nalini, R., & Shobhana, N. (2024). AIP Conference Proceedings: Vol. 3180. *Adoption of FinTech payment services-An extended expectation towards core constructs of technology acceptance model.* AIP Publishing.

Lee, H. J., & Han, K. S. (2018). A study on mobile easy payment service based on fintech to reduce smart divide and income gap. *Int. J. Adv. Sci. Technol, 116*, 35–48.

Lou, A. T. (2017). *Integrating innovation diffusion theory and the technology acceptance model: The adoption of blockchain technology from business managers' perspective*. International Consortium for Electronic Business.

Malhi, A. S., Kovid, R. K., & Singh, T. P. (2024). Artificial Intelligence of Things (AIoT)-Enabled Personalized Banking: Investigating Intention to Adopt. *Reshaping Intelligent Business and Industry: Convergence of AI and IoT at the Cutting Edge*, 315--324.

Mention, A.-L. (2019). The future of fintech. [Taylor & Francis.]. *Research Technology Management*, *62*(4), 59–63.

Nguyen, L., Tran, S., & Ho, T. (2022). Fintech credit, bank regulations and bank performance: A cross-country analysis. *Asia-Pacific Journal of Business Administration*, *14*(4), 445–466.

Patnaik, A., Kudal, P., Dawar, S., Inamdar, V., & Dawar, P. (2023). Exploring User Acceptance of Digital Payments in India: An Empirical Study Using an Extended Technology Acceptance Model in the Fintech Landscape. *International Journal of Sustainable Development and Planning*, *18*(8).

Phan, D. H., Narayan, P. K., Rahman, R. E., & Hutabarat, A. R. (2020). Do financial technology firms influence bank performance? *Pacific-Basin Finance Journal*, *62*, 101210.

Puschmann, T. (2017). Fintech. *Business & Information Systems Engineering*, *59*, 69–76.

Raykov, T., & Widaman, K. F. (1995). Issues in applied structural equation modeling research. *Structural Equation Modeling*, *2*(4), 289–318.

Romānova, I., & Kudinska, M. (2016). Banking and fintech: A challenge or opportunity? In *Contemporary issues in finance: Current challenges from across* [). Emerald Group Publishing Limited.]. *Europe*, *98*, 21–35.

Sharma, V., Jangir, K., Gupta, M., & Rupeika-Apoga, R. (2024). Does service quality matter in FinTech payment services? An integrated SERVQUAL and TAM approach. *International Journal of Information Management Data Insights*, *4*(2), 100252.

Singh, S., Sahni, M. M., & Kovid, R. K. (2021). Exploring antecendents of FinTech adoption using adapted technology acceptance model. *Advances in Systems Engineering: Select Proceedings of NSC 2019* (pp. 337--352). Springer.

Srivastava, S., Mohta, A., & Shunmugasundaram, V. (2024). Adoption of digital payment FinTech service by Gen Y and Gen Z users: Evidence from India. *Digital Policy. Regulation & Governance*, *26*(1), 95–117.

Streiner, D. L. (2006). Building a better model: An introduction to structural equation modelling. *Canadian Journal of Psychiatry*, *51*(5), 317–324. PMID: 16986821

Tran, T., Han, K., & Yun, S. (2018). Factors influencing the intention to use mobile payment service using fintech systems: Focused on Vietnam. *Asia Life Sciences*, (3), 1731–1747.

Widiasmara, A., Retnowati, W., Alvarez, J. I., & De Guzman, E. K. (2024). The Financial Technology Investment: A Comparative Analysis of Profitability and Performance in Indonesian State-Owned and Sharia Banks. *AKRUAL: Jurnal Akuntansi, 16*(1).

Yoon, C., & Lim, D. (2021). Customers' intentions to switch to internet-only banks: Perspective of the push-pull-mooring model. *Sustainability, 13*(14), 8062.

Zhao, J., Li, X., Yu, C.-H., Chen, S., & Lee, C.-C. (2022). Riding the FinTech innovation wave: FinTech, patents and bank performance. *Journal of International Money and Finance, 122*, 102552.

Zhao, Q., Tsai, P.-H., & Wang, J.-L. (2019). Improving financial service innovation strategies for enhancing china's banking industry competitive advantage during the fintech revolution: A Hybrid MCDM model. *Sustainability, 11*(5), 1419.

KEY TERMS AND DEFINITIONS

Artificial Intelligence: The intelligence in the form of simulation in machines so that the systems and machines can perform actions and provide solution for different financial services and banking issues. The data and natural language process makes it easy to produce decision making and performing different actions.

Blockchain: Block-chain can be referred as decentralized, distributed ledge technology that records transactions securely and transparently across multiple nodes, eliminating the need for intermediaries. It is widely used in crypto currencies, smart contracts, and secure financial transactions.

Digital Banking: The digitalization of banking services through different technology inclusion like mobile banking and apps, online transactions, and all other financial services in online mode rather than visiting the branch physically.

Financial Inclusion: Financial inclusion means the inclusion of unbanked population into different financial and banking transactions. The inclusion efforts make more number of people to use digital banking services by promoting economic growth, and financial literacy.

FinTech 4.0: The financial technology 4.0 (FinTech 4.0) is the financial technology evolution characterized by integrated of advanced artificial intelligence (AI), block chain, cloud computing, and data analytics to upgrade and enhance financial and banking services, automation and customer experience.

Fintech Adoption: Fintech adoption is a process by which consumers and businesses integrate financial technology solutions and services into their day to day financial operations, including digital payments and receipts, online banking services, robo-advisors and block-chain based transactions.

TAM-3: Technological Acceptance Model (TAM) is a theoretical model to analyze and predict the acceptance and use of any technology by individuals. TAM-3 is an extension and advanced model by incorporating diverse and more number of factors like experience, social influence, and perceived ease of use to under user adoption behavior in clearer way.

Chapter 5
The Rise of Defi: Functional Applications and Its Comparison With Conventional Finance

Rishav Sinha
https://orcid.org/0009-0006-0875-6568
Christ University, India

Aashima Sinha Jindal
https://orcid.org/0009-0003-9522-5404
Christ University, India

ABSTRACT

Decentralized Finance (DeFi) is rapidly transforming the traditional financial system by introducing a permissionless, transparent, and trustless financial ecosystem powered by blockchain technology. It eliminates intermediaries by utilizing smart contracts on public blockchains like Ethereum, thereby promoting financial inclusion and operational efficiency. This paper explores the fundamental concepts of DeFi, the underlying technology including Ethereum, smart contracts, and Layer 2 solutions, and the wide array of its applications such as (DEXs), lending/borrowing platforms, yield farming, and stablecoins. In addition to examining the functional advantages of DeFi like reduced transaction costs and increased accessibility, the paper also critically analyzes the potential risks including smart contract vulnerabilities, regulatory concerns, and systemic dependencies. A special focus is given to the Indian regulatory framework and how it compares with global jurisdictions. The paper concludes with a discussion on the future prospects of DeFi .

DOI: 10.4018/979-8-3373-1404-4.ch005

1. INTRODUCTION

The emergence of Decentralized Finance (DeFi) marks a paradigm shift in the financial world, challenging the dominance of traditional centralized banking and financial institutions. DeFi is built upon the foundational principles of blockchain technology, particularly utilizing public, permissionless blockchains like Ethereum to enable open, transparent, and intermediary-free financial services. This chapter delves into the core components, technological framework, and practical applications of DeFi, aiming to provide a holistic understanding of its current state and future potential.

The chapter introduces the concept of DeFi and contrasts it with traditional finance, setting the stage for understanding its disruptive capabilities. It then explores the architecture and technological backbone of DeFi, including smart contracts, Ethereum protocols, and Layer 2 solutions, which enable scalability and efficiency. Further, it discusses the primary DeFi applications such as decentralized exchanges (DEXs), lending and borrowing platforms, stablecoins, staking, and yield farming, each playing a vital role in the decentralized ecosystem.

A critical section is devoted to the advantages of DeFi, including transparency, user empowerment, global accessibility, and reduced transaction costs. This is balanced with an in-depth analysis of the risks and challenges, such as smart contract bugs, impermanent loss, regulatory ambiguity, and systemic risks due to high interdependence between protocols.

The chapter also includes a focused discussion on the Indian regulatory landscape, how India is approaching DeFi in contrast to global jurisdictions, and what steps might be needed to foster innovation while maintaining oversight. Lastly, the chapter provides insight into the future trends of DeFi, potential integration with traditional finance (TradFi), and the implications of its growing adoption on the global financial architecture.By combining technical knowledge with regulatory and practical perspectives, this chapter aims to provide readers with a well-rounded foundation in DeFi and encourage further exploration into its vast and rapidly evolving ecosystem.

2. FINANCIAL HISTORY AND THE EMERGENCE OF DEFI

Today's financial systems have evolved over centuries, shaped by technological advancements, regulatory frameworks, and economic philosophies. From early barter systems to the rise of digital banking, each stage in financial evolution has been driven by a quest for efficiency, security, and accessibility. However, despite these advancements, traditional finance remains constrained by centralization, inefficiencies, and various malpractices. The emergence of Decentralized Finance

(DeFi) is not an isolated phenomenon but a response to the persistent limitations of conventional financial structures. Understanding the historical development of financial systems helps contextualize why DeFi has gained momentum as an alternative financial paradigm.

The earliest forms of financial exchange relied on barter, where goods and services were traded directly. While this system worked in small, localized communities, it lacked scalability and standardization, making long-distance trade difficult. The introduction of commodity money, such as gold and silver, addressed some of these limitations by providing a widely accepted medium of exchange. However, the inconvenience of carrying and storing precious metals led to the rise of banking institutions, which offered safekeeping and facilitated transactions. The establishment of centralized banks marked a major turning point in financial history, as they became intermediaries responsible for issuing currency, managing credit, and regulating monetary policy (Reinhart & Rogoff, 2009).

The expansion of global trade and industrialization in the 19th and 20th centuries further solidified the role of centralized financial institutions. Governments have established regulatory bodies to oversee financial markets, ensuring stability and protecting consumers. The creation of central banks, such as the Federal Reserve in the United States (1913) and the Reserve Bank of India (1935), introduced mechanisms to control inflation, manage liquidity, and respond to financial crises (Mishkin, 2007). While these institutions played a crucial role in economic growth, their centralized nature also made financial systems vulnerable to manipulation, corruption, and systemic failures. The 2008 global financial crisis exposed the fragility of traditional banking systems, highlighting the risks associated with excessive leverage, opaque financial products, and lack of transparency (Shiller, 2012). Public trust in financial institutions eroded, creating a demand for alternatives that prioritized openness, decentralization, and user control.

Decentralized Finance (DeFi) represents a fundamental shift in the way financial services are structured and accessed, challenging the long-standing dominance of centralized institutions such as banks, stock exchanges, and insurance companies. DeFi operates on blockchain technology, utilizing smart contracts to facilitate financial transactions without intermediaries. This transformation is not merely a technological evolution but a profound redefinition of financial ecosystems, promoting greater transparency, accessibility, and autonomy for users across the globe.

The roots of DeFi can be traced to the broader movement toward decentralization, which gained traction with the introduction of Bitcoin in 2009. Bitcoin, created by the pseudonymous Satoshi Nakamoto, laid the foundation for a decentralized form of money that operated outside the control of traditional financial institutions (Nakamoto, 2008). However, while Bitcoin introduced the concept of decentralization in monetary transactions, it lacked the flexibility required for more complex financial applications. The advent of Ethereum in 2015, along with its smart contract capabilities, marked a pivotal moment in the evolution of DeFi. Smart contracts enabled programmable financial services that could function autonomously without human intervention, leading to the rapid expansion of decentralized applications (Buterin, 2014).

3. DECENTRALISED FINANCE VS TRADITIONAL FINANCE

The necessity for DeFi arises from several limitations present in traditional financial systems. Centralized finance (CeFi) is often characterized by inefficiencies such as high transaction fees, slow processing times, and restricted access based on geographic or economic factors. Moreover, traditional banking systems rely on intermediaries that introduce counterparty risks, regulatory constraints, and susceptibility to corruption. By eliminating intermediaries, DeFi significantly reduces costs and enhances efficiency. The automation of financial processes through smart contracts eliminates the need for manual verification, reducing delays associated with bureaucratic procedures. Furthermore, DeFi operates on a global scale, enabling users to transact without concerns about national borders or banking hours (Zhang et al., 2022).

The concept of financial sovereignty is another defining characteristic of DeFi. Traditional banking systems require individuals to entrust their assets to third-party institutions, exposing them to risks such as bank failures, capital controls, and governmental restrictions. In contrast, DeFi enable s users to retain full control over their funds through non-custodial wallets, where private keys act as the sole mechanism for asset management (Schär, 2021). This level of autonomy, while empowering, also introduces challenges related to security and personal responsibility. Since DeFi transactions are irreversible and there is no centralized authority to recover lost funds, users must exercise caution in managing their assets.

The need for DeFi becomes even more apparent when examining the inefficiencies of the current financial system. One of the most pressing issues is the concentration of power within a few financial institutions. Large banks and payment processors dictate the flow of capital, often prioritizing profit motives over user interests. These institutions impose high transaction fees, maintain strict account requirements, and limit access to credit for individuals and businesses that do not meet their stringent criteria (Philippon, 2019). In contrast, DeFi platforms operate on open protocols, allowing anyone with an internet connection to access financial services without the need for approval from a centralized authority. This financial inclusivity is particularly transformative in developing economies, where traditional banking infrastructure is either weak or inaccessible (Demirgüç-Kunt et al., 2018).

Another major drawback of traditional finance is slow transaction processing and settlement times. Cross-border payments, for instance, can take several days to clear due to the involvement of multiple intermediaries and compliance checks. Even domestic banking transactions are subject to delays caused by outdated legacy systems. DeFi, built on blockchain technology, enables near-instant transactions by automating processes through smart contracts. This efficiency is further enhanced by innovations such as layer-2 scaling solutions and decentralized consensus mechanisms, which reduce bottlenecks and improve transaction throughput (Gudgeon et al., 2020).

The lack of transparency in centralized finance also poses significant risks to consumers and investors. Traditional financial institutions operate behind closed doors, with limited public visibility into their internal operations. This opacity has contributed to major financial scandals, from the Enron accounting fraud (2001) to the manipulation of LIBOR interest rates by major banks (2012). DeFi protocols, on the other hand, are built on public blockchains, ensuring that all transactions, smart contract executions, and protocol governance decisions are verifiable by anyone. This radical transparency reduces the likelihood of fraud, mismanagement, and systemic failures (Schär, 2021).

Another critical issue is the inefficiency of centralized credit systems. In traditional finance, obtaining a loan requires a lengthy approval process, extensive documentation, and credit history verification. These barriers disproportionately affect individuals with limited banking experience or those in countries with inadequate credit infrastructure. DeFi lending platforms such as Aave and Compound have introduced algorithmic, collateral-based lending, where users can access funds instantly by providing crypto assets as collateral. This approach eliminates the need for credit checks and intermediaries, making capital more accessible while ensuring security through over-collateralization (Acharya & Rajan, 2020).

Despite its advantages, DeFi is not without challenges. The transition from centralized to decentralized finance requires overcoming regulatory uncertainties, technological limitations, and user adoption hurdles. Governments and financial regulators are still grappling with how to integrate DeFi into existing legal frameworks without stifling innovation. Additionally, security concerns such as smart contract vulnerabilities and risks of liquidity crises pose significant threats to DeFi's mainstream adoption (Arner et al., 2020). However, these challenges do not negate the fundamental need for a decentralized alternative to traditional finance. Instead, they highlight the importance of continued research, innovation, and collaboration between the DeFi community and regulatory bodies.

As financial systems continue to evolve, the demand for a more inclusive, efficient, and transparent alternative will only grow. DeFi is not merely a speculative trend; it is a response to the deep-seated inefficiencies and inequities of the current financial system. By providing an open, permissionless, and automated financial infrastructure, DeFi has the potential to redefine the way individuals and businesses interact with money, investments, and financial services. The journey from barter to blockchain underscores the human drive for financial innovation, and DeFi represents the next chapter in this ongoing evolution.

The fundamental principles of DeFi revolve around decentralization, transparency, permissionless access, trustlessness, and financial sovereignty. Decentralization is the defining characteristic, ensuring that financial applications are governed by a distributed network of computers rather than a single institution. This means that no single authority can manipulate transactions, freeze accounts, or control access to financial services. Traditional finance has long suffered from issues of restricted accessibility, where users must navigate complex regulations, approvals, and institutional oversight. In contrast, DeFi operates on public blockchains, allowing anyone with an internet connection and a digital wallet to participate in the ecosystem. This permissionless nature democratizes access to financial services, removing the barriers that have excluded large segments of the global population from financial participation (Demirgüç-Kunt et al., 2018).

A key feature of DeFi is its trustless nature, which eliminates the need for intermediaries by replacing them with smart contracts. Traditionally, financial transactions rely on banks, clearinghouses, or escrow services to ensure that agreements are fulfilled. DeFi automates these processes, ensuring that transactions are executed only when predetermined conditions are met. By reducing reliance on third parties, DeFi enhances efficiency and security while also significantly lowering costs. However, while smart contracts remove human intervention, they are not infallible; vulnerabilities in code can be exploited by malicious actors, as seen in several high-profile DeFi hacks (Gudgeon et al., 2020).

4. UNPACKING DeFi AND IT'S APPLICATION

4.1 DEXs and Smart contracts

Decentralized exchanges (DEXs) represent one of the most widely used DeFi applications, enabling users to trade digital assets without relying on centralized entities. Unlike traditional stock exchanges, which require intermediaries to facilitate transactions, DEXs operate through automated liquidity pools and smart contract-based trading mechanisms. This innovation significantly reduces trading fees and counterparty risk while ensuring greater accessibility. However, DEXs also present challenges, particularly in terms of liquidity, price slippage, and regulatory uncertainty (Buterin, 2014).

Stablecoins play an essential role in DeFi by mitigating the volatility associated with cryptocurrencies. Unlike assets such as Bitcoin and Ethereum, whose prices fluctuate dramatically, stablecoins are pegged to traditional currencies like the US dollar or commodities like gold. This stability makes them an ideal medium of exchange and a store of value within the DeFi ecosystem. Algorithmic stablecoins, which maintain their peg through dynamic supply adjustments, represent an innovative but often volatile alternative to fiat-backed stablecoins (Gudgeon et al., 2020).

Smart contracts are the foundation of decentralized finance (DeFi), enabling financial transactions and services to function without intermediaries. These self-executing agreements operate on blockchain networks and follow predefined rules coded within them. By automating processes such as lending, borrowing, and trading, smart contracts remove the need for banks, brokers, and other third-party institutions, reducing costs and increasing efficiency. However, while they introduce a new level of financial freedom, they also bring challenges related to security, usability, and regulatory oversight (Schär, 2021). Unlike traditional contracts, which require legal enforcement, smart contracts execute transactions automatically once their conditions are met. For instance, in a DeFi lending protocol, a borrower provides collateral in cryptocurrency, and upon meeting the required threshold, the smart contract releases the loaned amount. When the borrower repays the loan with interest, the contract returns the collateral. This process eliminates credit checks, bureaucracy, and delays, creating a more inclusive financial system that operates beyond geographical and institutional constraints (Werner et al., 2021). Transparency is another key advantage. Since smart contracts run on public blockchains, every transaction is recorded on an immutable ledger, making them accessible for verification. This openness fosters trust and reduces the risk of fraud. In contrast, traditional financial systems often operate with a lack of transparency, leading to hidden fees, unexpected costs, and systemic risks. However, this high level of transparency also exposes vulnerabilities, as attackers can scrutinize the code to find weaknesses before developers patch them (Gudgeon et al., 2020).

4.2 DEXs and AMMs

Smart contracts power a wide range of DeFi applications, the most prominent being decentralized exchanges (DEXs). Unlike traditional stock markets, which rely on clearinghouses and market makers, DEXs enable peer-to-peer trading without intermediaries. Platforms such as Uniswap and SushiSwap use automated market makers (AMMs) to manage liquidity, where smart contracts balance asset prices based on supply and demand. This innovation removes order books and allows seamless trading between users (Buterin, 2014). Lending and borrowing are also heavily reliant on smart contracts. DeFi platforms like Aave, Compound, and MakerDAO facilitate lending services by automating collateralized loans. Borrowers deposit cryptocurrency as collateral, and once the collateralization ratio meets the contract's requirements, they can borrow funds instantly. Interest rates are dynamically adjusted based on market conditions, eliminating the need for traditional banking intermediaries and making loans more accessible to a global audience (Acharya & Rajan, 2020).

One of the fundamental innovations within decentralized exchanges (DEXs) is the use of automated market makers (AMMs), which replace the traditional order book model with liquidity pools. Unlike centralized exchanges (CEXs), where buyers and sellers place bids and asks, AMMs rely on liquidity providers who deposit assets into pools. These pools facilitate trading using mathematical formulas to determine asset prices based on supply and demand. Uniswap, one of the most prominent DEXs, introduced the constant product formula, where the product of two asset balances in a liquidity pool must always remain constant. When a user swaps one asset for another, the relative balances in the pool adjust, causing price fluctuations. This model ensures that trades can always be executed, even in the absence of a direct counterparty, thereby enhancing market efficiency and accessibility (Adams et al., 2021).

However, AMMs are not without challenges. One of the most significant issues is impermanent loss, which occurs when the price of a token in a liquidity pool diverges significantly from its initial value, causing liquidity providers to potentially earn less than if they had simply held the assets. Additionally, front-running has emerged as a concern, where malicious actors exploit blockchain latency to manipulate transaction orders and profit from price discrepancies. These risks underscore the importance of continuous innovation. Newer DEX models now integrate features such as dynamic fees and time-weighted average pricing to mitigate these threats (Daian et al., 2020).

Yet, the foundation of DEXs and other decentralized finance (DeFi) protocols—the smart contract—is itself a double-edged sword. While smart contracts enable automation and trustless transactions, their immutable nature means any flaw in the code can lead to irreversible consequences. One of the most infamous incidents was the 2016 DAO hack, where a reentrancy vulnerability allowed an attacker to drain millions from an Ethereum smart contract, emphasizing the need for rigorous code audits and robust security testing (Gudgeon et al., 2020). Reentrancy attacks are only one type of threat; others include integer overflows, underflows, front-running attacks, and oracle manipulation.

Oracles, which feed off-chain data like price information to smart contracts, can also be a major attack vector. If an attacker compromises an oracle, they can manipulate data to their advantage—for instance, inflating an asset's price on a lending platform to borrow large sums and escape before a correction occurs (Werner et al., 2021). In response to these vulnerabilities, DeFi developers often conduct multiple security audits, and many projects now offer bug bounty programs that reward ethical hackers for identifying risks. However, even with comprehensive precautions, dangers persist—especially given the highly interconnected nature of the DeFi ecosystem.

The composability of DeFi, often referred to as "money Legos," enables various protocols to work together and build upon one another, greatly enhancing utility. But this interconnectivity also amplifies systemic risk: a vulnerability in one protocol, such as a lending platform or price oracle, can ripple across multiple applications, triggering liquidations or cascading failures. This systemic fragility highlights the growing need for innovative security frameworks, including multi-signature wallets, time-locked transactions, and decentralized governance mechanisms that can enable swift responses to emerging threats (Acharya & Rajan, 2020; Arner et al., 2020).

As smart contracts gain mainstream adoption, regulators are increasingly concerned about how to oversee their use. Unlike traditional financial instruments, which operate under legal frameworks, smart contracts exist in a largely unregulated environment. This raises questions about legal enforceability, dispute resolution, and consumer protection. If a smart contract malfunctions or is exploited, determining liability can be challenging. In traditional finance, customers have legal recourse in cases of fraud or negligence, but DeFi users often lack such protections (Schär, 2021). Another major concern is the use of DeFi for illicit activities. Since smart contracts enable permissionless transactions, they can be exploited for money laundering, tax evasion, and other illegal activities. Regulatory agencies are exploring ways to introduce compliance mechanisms, such as Know Your Customer (KYC) and Anti-Money Laundering (AML) measures. Some DeFi platforms have begun implementing these standards voluntarily, but others resist, arguing that they contradict the decentralized ethos of the space (Gudgeon et al., 2020). Despite these challenges, smart contracts continue to reshape financial markets. Traditional banks and financial institutions are exploring hybrid models that combine DeFi's efficiency with regulatory safeguards. For example, central bank digital currencies (CBDCs) could incorporate smart contract functionality to automate monetary policies while ensuring regulatory compliance. These developments indicate that smart contracts are not just a niche innovation but a fundamental shift in how financial services are structured (Arner et al., 2020).

4.3 CHALLENNGES FOR DEXs

Despite their advantages, DEXs face several challenges that hinder mass adoption. One major limitation is scalability, as blockchain networks struggle with congestion during high-demand periods. The Ethereum network, where many leading DEXs operate, has frequently experienced high gas fees, making small transactions impractical. Layer-2 scaling solutions such as Optimistic Rollups and zk-Rollups aim to alleviate these issues by processing transactions off-chain before settling them on the main blockchain. Additionally, alternative blockchain networks like Solana and Binance Smart Chain have gained traction by offering lower transaction fees and faster processing times. However, the fragmentation of liquidity across multiple blockchains poses a new challenge, as users must navigate different ecosystems to access optimal trading opportunities (Xie et al., 2021). Regulation remains another critical concern. The pseudonymous nature of DEXs has attracted scrutiny from regulators, who worry about their potential use for illicit activities such as money laundering and tax evasion. Unlike centralized exchanges that comply with regulatory frameworks, most DEXs operate in a gray area, making enforcement difficult. Some jurisdictions have already introduced measures to regulate DeFi platforms, such as requiring compliance with AML (Anti-Money Laundering) and KYC protocols. However, implementing such regulations on decentralized protocols contradicts their core principles of permissionless finance. Some projects, like dYdX, have attempted a hybrid approach, integrating compliance measures while maintaining decentralization, but the broader industry remains at a crossroads, balancing regulatory requirements with the ethos of decentralization (Chen & Bellavitis, 2020).

Looking ahead, the future of DEXs will likely be shaped by advancements in on-chain governance, enhanced security measures, and improved user experiences. As the DeFi space matures, integrating better risk management tools and decentralized identity solutions may help bridge the gap between regulation and innovation. Additionally, institutional adoption of DeFi is on the rise, with some financial institutions exploring regulated decentralized exchanges (RDEXs) that offer transparency while adhering to legal frameworks. The evolution of privacy-preserving technologies like zero-knowledge proofs (ZKPs) may further address compliance concerns by enabling regulatory oversight without compromising user anonymity. As DEXs continue to redefine financial markets, their success will hinge on striking the right balance between security, decentralization, and usability (Gudgeon et al., 2021).

5. LENDING AND BORROWING IN DECENTRALISED FINANCE

Lending and borrowing have always been fundamental to financial systems, providing liquidity to markets and enabling capital formation. In traditional finance, banks and financial institutions act as intermediaries, facilitating loans by assessing creditworthiness and managing interest rates. However, decentralized finance (DeFi) has reimagined this process by removing intermediaries and replacing them with smart contracts—self-executing agreements that operate on blockchain networks. Through DeFi lending protocols, users can lend their assets to earn interest or borrow against their holdings without relying on credit scores or centralized approval processes. This permissionless and automated lending system has opened new financial opportunities, especially for those excluded from traditional banking services, while also introducing new risks and challenges (Aave, 2021).

At the heart of DeFi lending is the concept of over-collateralization, which ensures loan security without the need for credit assessments. Unlike banks that require credit history verification, DeFi protocols allow users to deposit cryptocurrencies as collateral and borrow against them. Because these systems operate without trust-based mechanisms, borrowers must provide collateral that exceeds the value of their loan to mitigate default risks. For example, platforms like Aave, Compound, and MakerDAO require borrowers to maintain a collateralization ratio above a certain threshold—typically between 125% and 150%—to account for price volatility. If the value of the collateral falls below the required level due to market fluctuations, automatic liquidation mechanisms trigger the sale of assets to repay the loan, ensuring lenders are protected from losses (Gaunt et al., 2022).

One of the key innovations of DeFi lending is the introduction of algorithmic interest rates, which dynamically adjust based on supply and demand. Traditional banks set interest rates through regulatory policies and central bank interventions, whereas DeFi platforms use smart contracts to determine rates in real time. When demand for borrowing increases and supply of liquidity decreases, interest rates automatically rise to incentivize more lenders. Conversely, when borrowing demand drops, interest rates decrease to encourage more borrowing. This self-balancing mechanism ensures that liquidity is efficiently allocated across lending pools, improving market efficiency without human intervention. Additionally, some platforms offer stable borrowing rates, providing predictability for borrowers who wish to avoid fluctuating interest costs (Xu et al., 2021).

5.1 Flash Loans

Flash loans stand as one of the most revolutionary innovations in the decentralized finance (DeFi) landscape, showcasing the true potential of programmable, permissionless financial systems. Unlike traditional lending mechanisms, which require borrowers to pledge collateral, undergo credit assessments, and endure approval delays, flash loans eliminate these conventional barriers entirely. They allow users to borrow any amount of cryptocurrency—often in the millions—without posting any collateral, so long as the entire loan is borrowed and repaid within the same blockchain transaction. This remarkable capability is made possible through the atomic structure of blockchain transactions, which ensures that all operations within a transaction either complete successfully together or fail altogether. If the borrowed funds are not returned within the transaction's execution, the entire process is reversed, and it is as though the loan never occurred. Thus, lenders face virtually no default risk, while borrowers gain access to capital in a trustless, efficient manner.

The implications of flash loans are profound, particularly in the realm of capital efficiency and financial inclusion. Traditional financial institutions gatekeep access to credit, often excluding those without significant assets or stable income histories. Flash loans subvert this dynamic by making liquidity available instantly to anyone with the technical skills to deploy smart contracts. This democratization of financial tools empowers smaller market participants to engage in strategies previously reserved for institutional players, fostering a more inclusive and dynamic financial ecosystem. The speed and automation involved in flash loan transactions further enhance their appeal, allowing users to react instantly to market opportunities in ways that traditional systems simply cannot support.

Within the DeFi environment, flash loans serve a multitude of strategic purposes. Perhaps the most widely recognized application is arbitrage. By taking advantage of price discrepancies across decentralized exchanges, users can borrow funds, buy an underpriced asset on one platform, and sell it at a premium on another—all in one transaction. The profits from this maneuver are used to repay the loan, with any surplus retained by the trader. In this way, flash loans contribute to market efficiency, narrowing price gaps across platforms. Another major use case is collateral swapping, wherein a user replaces the collateral backing their loan without fully closing and reopening their borrowing position. This can be essential during volatile market conditions when asset values shift quickly. Similarly, self-liquidation allows users to preempt forced liquidations by repaying their debt via a flash loan, thereby reclaiming their collateral and avoiding hefty liquidation penalties.

Beyond these, flash loans are increasingly used in debt refinancing and yield farming optimization. Borrowers can shift their positions between protocols offering better interest rates, reducing costs and maximizing returns. In the context of yield farming, users deploy flash loans to reposition liquidity across protocols, capitalize on promotional incentives, or rebalance portfolios for optimal yields. Each of these strategies demonstrates the remarkable flexibility and utility of flash loans in modern DeFi finance. However, the same power that makes flash loans attractive also introduces vulnerabilities. In several high-profile DeFi exploits, malicious actors have used flash loans to manipulate oracle prices and exploit vulnerabilities in protocol design, resulting in substantial financial losses. These events have spurred protocol developers to implement safeguards such as transaction rate limiting, time delays, and real-time monitoring to detect and mitigate potential abuses.

5.2 Yield Farming and Liquidity

Yield farming and liquidity mining have emerged as two of the most innovative and lucrative aspects of decentralized finance (DeFi), allowing users to generate passive income by providing liquidity to various protocols. Unlike traditional investment strategies, where capital appreciation and dividend payments are the primary sources of returns, yield farming and liquidity mining leverage blockchain-based automated market makers (AMMs) and smart contracts to reward users for their participation. These mechanisms have reshaped the financial landscape by decentralizing the role of intermediaries, enabling a new form of capital efficiency where users can put their assets to work in a non-custodial, transparent, and programmable manner. However, while these opportunities present attractive returns, they also carry risks such as impermanent loss, price volatility, and security vulnerabilities (Harvey et al., 2021).

At its core, yield farming refers to the practice of maximizing returns by strategically moving assets between different DeFi protocols to take advantage of varying interest rates and incentives. Users deposit their assets into liquidity pools—smart contract-powered reserves that facilitate trading on decentralized exchanges (DEXs)—in exchange for rewards, typically in the form of native governance tokens or a share of the trading fees. The most well-known platforms facilitating yield farming include Uniswap, SushiSwap, Curve, and Balancer, each offering unique incentive structures that encourage users to provide liquidity. Unlike traditional banking products, which offer fixed interest rates, yield farming provides dynamic rewards, meaning returns fluctuate based on supply, demand, and protocol incentives (Adams et al., 2020).

Liquidity mining is a subset of yield farming where protocols reward users with native tokens in addition to the usual trading fees for supplying liquidity. Unlike traditional financial incentives, where centralized entities dictate rewards, liquidity mining programs distribute newly minted tokens to participants, fostering protocol decentralization. For example, Compound pioneered this model in 2020 by distributing COMP tokens to users supplying and borrowing assets on its platform, effectively transforming early adopters into stakeholders with governance voting rights. Other projects, such as Aave, Synthetix, and Yearn Finance, have followed suit, designing unique reward mechanisms that encourage long-term participation and ecosystem growth (Leshner & Hayes, 2020).

The success of yield farming and liquidity mining hinges on automated market makers (AMMs), which replace traditional order book systems with liquidity pools. In centralized exchanges like Nasdaq or NYSE, buyers and sellers place orders that are matched by intermediaries, often leading to delays and inefficiencies. In contrast, AMMs use predefined mathematical formulas, such as Uniswap's constant product market maker ($x * y = k$), to automatically adjust prices based on supply and demand. This innovation allows for seamless and decentralized trading, ensuring liquidity is always available regardless of market conditions. However, liquidity providers face impermanent loss, a phenomenon where their deposited assets lose value compared to simply holding them due to price fluctuations between the two paired assets in the pool. Strategies such as using stablecoin pools or concentrated liquidity positions help mitigate these risks (Zins & Weill, 2021).

Yield farmers frequently optimize their returns by leveraging staking and yield aggregation strategies. In staking, users lock their assets in smart contracts to earn rewards, often in governance tokens, while enhancing network security. Ethereum 2.0's shift to a proof-of-stake (PoS) consensus exemplifies this model, allowing users to earn rewards by securing the blockchain. Yield aggregators, such as Yearn Finance and Harvest Finance, automate the process of finding the most profitable pools, reallocating funds across different protocols to maximize returns. By using smart contract automation, these platforms reduce the manual effort required for yield farming, offering a more efficient way to optimize earnings while minimizing risks associated with individual protocol selection (Cronje et al., 2020).

One of the most significant risks associated with yield farming and liquidity mining is impermanent loss, which occurs when the value of assets deposited in a liquidity pool changes relative to simply holding them. When an asset's price fluctuates significantly, liquidity providers can end up with fewer assets than they initially deposited, making their effective returns lower than expected. Although trading fees and token rewards can offset this loss, it remains a primary concern for liquidity providers. To address this, some protocols, such as Bancor and ThorChain, have introduced impermanent loss protection mechanisms, compensating users for any losses incurred over a specified period. Additionally, protocols like Balancer allow users to create custom-weighted liquidity pools, reducing exposure to a single asset's volatility and offering greater flexibility in portfolio management (Angeris et al., 2021).

Another risk factor is the reliance on smart contracts, which, while innovative, are susceptible to bugs and security vulnerabilities. Since DeFi protocols operate without intermediaries, any flaw in a smart contract can be exploited, leading to significant financial losses. Several high-profile attacks, including the $600 million Poly Network hack and the Cream Finance exploit, have demonstrated the importance of security audits and risk mitigation strategies. Many DeFi platforms now undergo rigorous third-party audits by firms like CertiK and OpenZeppelin, ensuring their smart contracts are robust before launching. Additionally, the rise of DeFi insurance providers, such as Nexus Mutual and Cover Protocol, allows users to hedge against smart contract failures, mitigating potential losses (Werner et al., 2021).

Looking ahead, the evolution of yield farming and liquidity mining will likely be shaped by layer-2 solutions, cross-chain interoperability, and sustainable incentive structures. Layer-2 scaling solutions, such as Optimistic Rollups and zk-Rollups, are expected to reduce transaction costs and improve efficiency, making DeFi participation more accessible. Cross-chain protocols, like ThorChain and Polkadot's parachains, are working toward seamless interoperability between different blockchains, enabling liquidity mining across multiple ecosystems. Additionally, projects are shifting toward sustainable rewards models, reducing token emissions to avoid hyperinflation and ensuring long-term viability. As these innovations unfold, the landscape of decentralized finance will continue to mature, offering new opportunities while addressing existing challenges (Wang et al., 2022).

6. RISKS AND CHALLENGES OF DEFI

While decentralized finance (DeFi) offers transformative potential, it also introduces a range of risks and challenges that must be addressed to ensure its sustainable growth. Unlike traditional financial systems that are regulated and supported by institutional safeguards, DeFi operates in an open, permissionless environment, making it susceptible to technical, financial, and regulatory risks. These challenges impact not only individual users but also the broader financial ecosystem, raising questions about security, stability, and long-term viability (Zetzsche, Arner, & Buckley, 2020).

Another pressing concern in DeFi is the issue of market volatility. Unlike traditional financial markets, which are regulated and backed by institutions, DeFi operates in a largely speculative environment driven by supply and demand dynamics. The volatility of cryptocurrencies, which serve as the backbone of DeFi, poses risks to both users and liquidity providers. Sharp price fluctuations can lead to significant losses, particularly in leveraged trading and lending protocols. Liquidation events, such as those observed during market crashes, can cause cascading failures within DeFi platforms, leading to systemic instability. The absence of mechanisms such as deposit insurance, akin to those in traditional banking, further exacerbates the risk exposure for users engaging in DeFi activities (Harvey, Ramachandran, & Santoro, 2021).

Regulatory uncertainty remains one of the biggest obstacles to DeFi's widespread adoption. Traditional financial institutions operate within well-defined legal frameworks that ensure compliance with anti-money laundering (AML) and know-your-customer (KYC) regulations. In contrast, DeFi's decentralized nature makes it challenging to impose regulatory oversight, raising concerns about fraud, illicit transactions, and consumer protection. Governments and regulatory bodies across the world are exploring ways to regulate DeFi without stifling innovation. For instance, the U.S. Securities and Exchange Commission (SEC) has indicated its intention to oversee certain DeFi projects under existing securities laws, while the

European Union's Markets in Crypto-Assets (MiCA) framework seeks to establish comprehensive regulations for digital assets (Gudgeon et al., 2020). However, the decentralized governance of DeFi makes enforcement difficult, as protocols often operate autonomously through decentralized autonomous organizations (DAOs) rather than centralized entities. Striking a balance between innovation and regulation remains a critical challenge for the industry.

Liquidity risks also pose a major challenge in DeFi. Unlike traditional finance, where central banks and financial institutions provide stability through liquidity injections, DeFi relies on decentralized liquidity pools managed by users. If a significant portion of liquidity is withdrawn suddenly, it can lead to market disruptions, price slippage, and inefficiencies in decentralized exchanges (DEXs). The reliance on liquidity mining and yield farming to attract users often results in unsustainable economic models, where high returns drive temporary participation but fail to establish long-term liquidity stability. The collapse of certain DeFi projects due to liquidity crises, such as the case of Iron Finance in 2021, highlights the vulnerabilities in algorithmic stablecoins and liquidity pool structures (Chen & Bellavitis, 2020).

Despite the efficiencies of DeFi lending, the volatility of crypto assets presents challenges. Unlike traditional loans, which are backed by stable assets such as real estate or government bonds, DeFi loans are secured by cryptocurrencies that can experience significant price swings. For example, a borrower who locks in Ethereum as collateral could face liquidation if the asset's price drops suddenly. The Black Thursday crash of March 2020 saw a sharp decline in crypto prices, leading to mass liquidations across MakerDAO, where borrowers lost millions due to collateral shortfalls. Such events highlight the need for risk management strategies, including diversified collateral options and insurance protocols that protect users from unexpected losses (Harvey et al., 2021).

To address volatility concerns, some DeFi lending platforms have integrated stablecoins as an alternative collateral option. Stablecoins such as DAI, USDC, and USDT are pegged to fiat currencies, providing price stability and reducing the risk of forced liquidations. MakerDAO, for example, allows users to generate DAI loans by locking up assets like Ethereum or Wrapped Bitcoin, enabling them to access liquidity without selling their crypto holdings. However, even stablecoins are not without risk, as seen in the collapse of Terra's algorithmic stablecoin UST, which wiped out billions in value. This event raised questions about the stability and trustworthiness of decentralized collateral mechanisms, prompting DeFi protocols to implement risk-adjusted lending parameters (Gudgeon et al., 2021).

Another challenge DeFi lending faces is capital inefficiency due to the high collateralization requirements. Traditional finance allows borrowers to leverage assets with minimal collateral, whereas DeFi's over-collateralized model limits access to credit. To solve this, some platforms are experimenting with under-collateralized lending, where loans are issued based on on-chain reputation and decentralized credit scoring systems. Projects like Goldfinch and Maple Finance enable institutional borrowers to access loans with reduced collateral requirements by leveraging community trust and smart contract-based verification. While promising, under-collateralized lending introduces new risks, as default rates could increase if borrowers fail to repay their loans. As a result, DeFi protocols are exploring hybrid models that combine algorithmic assessments with human oversight to improve loan security (Bartoletti et al., 2022).

Regulation remains a significant factor in the future of DeFi lending. As lending protocols grow, governments are increasingly scrutinizing their operations, raising concerns about money laundering, tax evasion, and financial stability. In contrast to banks, which must comply with AML (Anti-Money Laundering) and KYC (Know Your Customer) regulations, most DeFi platforms allow users to borrow and lend anonymously. This anonymity has led regulators to consider imposing stricter rules on DeFi lending, such as requiring platforms to implement on-chain identity verification and risk-based lending practices. However, enforcing regulations on decentralized protocols is complex, as many operate as decentralized autonomous organizations (DAOs) without a single entity controlling them. Some projects, like Aave Arc, have introduced permissioned lending pools that cater to institutional investors while complying with regulatory requirements, signaling a potential middle ground between DeFi's open access and regulatory oversight (Chen & Bellavitis, 2020).

The future of DeFi lending will likely be shaped by advancements in risk management, cross-chain interoperability, and regulatory compliance. As the space matures, layer-2 solutions like zk-Rollups and Optimistic Rollups are expected to improve transaction scalability, reducing borrowing costs. Additionally, the integration of real-world assets (RWAs) as collateral—such as tokenized real estate, stocks, and bonds—could bridge the gap between DeFi and traditional finance, unlocking new lending opportunities. While challenges remain, the decentralized lending ecosystem continues to evolve, offering a glimpse into a financial future where access to credit is more transparent, efficient, and globally accessible (Wang et al., 2022).

Another emerging challenge in DeFi is the increasing threat of centralized control within supposedly decentralized systems. While DeFi is built on the premise of decentralization, many projects still exhibit centralized tendencies, particularly in governance mechanisms. Founding teams, venture capitalists, and core developers often retain significant control over protocol decision-making, which contradicts the fundamental ethos of decentralization. This centralization can lead to governance disputes, manipulation, and conflicts of interest that undermine trust in DeFi platforms. Moreover, as regulatory scrutiny intensifies, some DeFi projects may be forced to implement KYC measures or comply with jurisdictional laws, potentially reducing the level of decentralization in favor of regulatory acceptance (Schär, 2021).

User-related risks, including a lack of education and financial literacy, also present a significant barrier to DeFi adoption. The complexity of interacting with DeFi protocols, managing private keys, and understanding smart contract functionalities can lead to user errors and financial losses. Unlike traditional banking systems, which offer customer support and dispute resolution mechanisms, DeFi operates without intermediaries, meaning that errors such as sending funds to the wrong address or engaging with fraudulent projects are often irreversible. Phishing attacks, wallet compromises, and rug pulls—where developers abandon projects after raising funds—are prevalent in the DeFi space. In 2021 alone, billions of dollars were lost to scams and exploits, highlighting the need for better security practices, educational initiatives, and user-friendly interfaces to make DeFi more accessible and secure for mainstream adoption (Zhang, Xie, & Wang, 2021).

Security risks extend beyond smart contract vulnerabilities to include broader concerns such as oracle manipulation and network congestion. Oracles are external data providers that feed real-world information into smart contracts, enabling functionalities such as price feeds for decentralized exchanges. If oracles are compromised or manipulated, they can cause severe distortions in DeFi markets. Flash loan attacks, where attackers exploit vulnerabilities in smart contracts by borrowing large sums of money without collateral, have been used to manipulate oracle prices and extract profits. Network congestion, particularly on Ethereum, has also led to high gas fees and slow transaction times, making DeFi less efficient and accessible. While layer-2 scaling solutions and alternative blockchains like Solana and Binance Smart Chain aim to address these issues, the transition to more scalable and cost-effective networks remains an ongoing challenge (Buterin, 2021).

Despite these risks, DeFi continues to evolve, with new solutions emerging to mitigate existing vulnerabilities. The implementation of formalized risk management strategies, improved security auditing standards, decentralized insurance protocols, and regulatory clarity can help DeFi transition into a more robust and reliable financial ecosystem. Addressing these challenges is essential for fostering mainstream trust and ensuring that DeFi fulfills its potential as an inclusive and decentralized financial alternative to traditional systems.

Decentralized Finance (DeFi) stands at a crossroads between innovation and regulation, promising to redefine financial systems worldwide. As we move toward broader adoption, the future of DeFi will be shaped by technological advancements, institutional involvement, and the evolving regulatory landscape. One of the most anticipated developments in DeFi is the growth of Layer-2 solutions and blockchain scalability. Networks like Polygon, Arbitrum, and Optimism are addressing Ethereum's high gas fees and slow transaction speeds, making DeFi applications more accessible and efficient (Buterin, 2021). Additionally, cross-chain interoperability, facilitated by projects such as Cosmos and Polkadot, is expected to bridge the fragmentation among blockchains, allowing seamless asset transfers and liquidity sharing (Wood, 2020). These technological improvements will be critical in DeFi's evolution, enabling it to support more users and complex financial operations while maintaining security and decentralization. Furthermore, the rise of institutional DeFi, often called "DeFi 2.0," is reshaping how businesses and banks perceive decentralized finance. Traditional financial institutions, once skeptical of DeFi's disruptive potential, are increasingly exploring partnerships with decentralized protocols. Firms like JPMorgan and Citibank are experimenting with tokenized assets and on-chain settlements, demonstrating that DeFi and traditional finance can coexist rather than compete (Harvey et al., 2021). Regulatory-friendly DeFi platforms like Aave Arc and Compound Treasury are implementing compliance mechanisms such as Know Your Customer (KYC) verification to cater to institutional investors, potentially leading to a hybrid financial ecosystem where centralized institutions leverage DeFi's efficiency while adhering to legal requirements (Kamps & Klein, 2021).

Regulation remains one of the biggest hurdles for DeFi's mainstream adoption. Governments worldwide are debating how to regulate decentralized financial systems without stifling innovation. The U.S. Securities and Exchange Commission (SEC) and European Union financial regulators have begun drafting policies to address compliance concerns, particularly around Anti-Money Laundering (AML) and tax transparency (Zetzsche et al., 2020). Some governments are considering regulatory sandboxes where DeFi projects can operate under temporary exemptions while authorities assess risks and benefits. However, decentralized governance complicates regulatory enforcement, as many DeFi protocols lack a single legal entity responsible for compliance (Kumar & Mohanty, 2022). For instance, the U.K. Financial Conduct Authority (FCA) has taken a measured approach, allowing DeFi projects to function within specific guidelines while ensuring user protection (Patel, 2022). This model could serve as a blueprint for other nations seeking to integrate DeFi within their financial systems without imposing outright bans. The introduction of Central Bank Digital Currencies (CBDCs) adds another layer of complexity to DeFi's future. Countries like China and India are developing digital currencies that could either complement or compete with DeFi solutions. While CBDCs promise efficiency and government oversight, they challenge DeFi's core principle of decentralization (Jain & Kumar, 2022). If CBDCs integrate with DeFi protocols, they could bridge the gap between centralized and decentralized finance, providing regulatory clarity and stability while preserving DeFi's advantages.

7. DEFI IN INDIA

India presents a unique case for DeFi's expansion due to its growing fintech sector and increasing blockchain adoption. The country has witnessed a surge in cryptocurrency users, ranking among the top in global crypto adoption (Chainalysis, 2022). Despite the Reserve Bank of India (RBI) maintaining a cautious stance on cryptocurrencies, the government's decision to introduce a 30% tax on digital assets and consider the implementation of a CBDC signals a shift towards acknowledging digital financial assets (Kumar & Mohanty, 2022). DeFi could address several financial challenges in India, particularly in areas like credit access, remittances, and financial inclusion. Over 190 million Indians remain unbanked, and many small businesses lack access to affordable credit due to stringent lending requirements by traditional banks (Sarma & Pais, 2011). DeFi lending platforms such as Goldfinch, Centrifuge, and Maple Finance offer alternative credit solutions by allowing users to borrow funds without traditional credit scores. These protocols use decentralized identity verification and collateralized lending mechanisms, enabling small businesses and individuals to access funding without bureaucratic hurdles (Gupta & Jain, 2021). Additionally, remittances form a significant portion of India's economy, with millions of Indians working abroad sending money home. Traditional remittance services charge high fees and have long processing times. DeFi-powered stablecoins like USDC and DAI provide a cost-effective and instant alternative, allowing users to bypass expensive intermediaries (Jain & Kumar, 2022). For example, platforms like Stellar and Ripple's On-Demand Liquidity (ODL) have already facilitated lower-cost remittances, demonstrating DeFi's potential in cross-border transactions (Gopinath, 2021).

Several Indian projects are making strides in the DeFi space. The most notable example is Polygon, a Layer-2 scaling solution for Ethereum, which was co-founded by Indian developers and has become a leading infrastructure provider for DeFi applications (Nailwal, 2021). Polygon significantly reduces Ethereum's transaction costs, enabling greater adoption of DeFi platforms like Aave, Sushiswap, and Curve. Indian-born DeFi projects like Vauld and Nuo Network have also explored innovative financial solutions, including high-yield savings accounts and decentralized borrowing (Choudhury, 2022). However, challenges remain. India's regulatory framework for DeFi is still uncertain, with the government leaning towards stricter oversight of digital assets. The introduction of a CBDC raises questions about whether decentralized finance will be regulated under similar policies or if it will remain in a legal grey area (Patel, 2022). Security risks associated with smart contract vulnerabilities also pose a challenge. In 2021 alone, DeFi hacks resulted in over $1 billion in losses, highlighting the need for improved risk management solutions such as decentralized insurance protocols (Harvey et al., 2021).

Despite these challenges, DeFi has the potential to drive financial inclusion in India if regulators and industry leaders find a balanced approach. Hybrid models that integrate DeFi with traditional banking infrastructure could offer a solution, providing regulatory compliance while maintaining the benefits of decentralized finance (Rajan, 2022). The rise of decentralized autonomous organizations (DAOs) within DeFi also presents a new governance model that could revolutionize financial decision-making. If India adopts a progressive regulatory stance, it could position itself as a leader in blockchain-based finance, attracting global investment and fostering innovation (Srinivasan, 2021). As DeFi continues to evolve, its ability to balance decentralization, security, and regulatory compliance will determine its long-term sustainability. The next decade will likely see a convergence of DeFi with traditional financial institutions, leading to a more inclusive, transparent, and efficient financial system.

8. CONCLUSION

Despite the transformative impact of Decentralized Finance (DeFi) on the global financial system, several areas remain underexplored, holding vast potential for future innovation. While DeFi has already revolutionized lending, borrowing, asset management, and decentralized exchanges, there are still significant gaps that need to be addressed to achieve a truly decentralized and inclusive financial ecosystem. As the technology continues to evolve, new opportunities in DeFi remain largely theoretical or in their infancy, requiring deeper exploration, research, and development. This section will examine some of these unexplored frontiers, including decentralized identity, quantum-resistant security, integration with real-world assets, AI-driven DeFi automation, and cross-border trade financing. These areas represent the next phase of DeFi's evolution and will determine how deeply it can integrate into mainstream financial systems.

One of the least explored yet highly promising areas in DeFi is decentralized identity (DID) solutions. The financial industry, both traditional and decentralized, heavily relies on identity verification for compliance, security, and fraud prevention. However, most DeFi applications today still function without robust identity verification mechanisms, which limits their ability to comply with global regulations and onboard institutional users (Zhang et al., 2022). DID solutions, powered by blockchain technology, could provide self-sovereign identity systems where users control their data without intermediaries. Platforms such as Worldcoin and Civic have experimented with blockchain-based identity verification, but the full-scale implementation of DID in DeFi remains an open challenge. With decentralized identity, users could access financial services seamlessly across multiple DeFi platforms without repeatedly undergoing identity verification, increasing accessibility while preserving privacy. This innovation could also help bridge the gap between DeFi and regulatory compliance, allowing regulators to enforce anti-money laundering (AML) and know-your-customer (KYC) requirements without compromising decentralization.

Another frontier that remains underdeveloped is quantum-resistant security for DeFi applications. While blockchain technology currently relies on cryptographic algorithms for security, advances in quantum computing pose a potential threat to these encryption methods. Quantum computers, once powerful enough, could theoretically break cryptographic keys that protect smart contracts and blockchain networks, leading to vulnerabilities in DeFi platforms (Mosca, 2021). Researchers have started developing quantum-resistant algorithms, such as lattice-based cryptography and hash-based signatures, but their integration into DeFi is still in its early stages. Future DeFi protocols must incorporate quantum-resistant cryptographic measures to ensure the long-term security of decentralized financial transactions. This area remains one of the most critical yet least explored aspects of DeFi's future, as any breakthrough in quantum computing could significantly disrupt existing blockchain networks.

Integration of DeFi with real-world assets (RWA) is another domain with immense potential but limited practical implementation. While tokenized stocks, real estate, and commodities have been discussed extensively, widespread adoption remains elusive due to regulatory barriers, liquidity challenges, and trust issues between on-chain and off-chain assets (Allen et al., 2021). Tokenization of real estate, for instance, could allow fractional ownership of properties, enabling investors to participate in global real estate markets with lower capital requirements. However, ensuring legal enforceability of smart contracts that represent ownership rights in the real world is a complex challenge that requires further research. Additionally, tokenizing intellectual property, patents, and even human capital could open new avenues for financial innovation, but the legal frameworks necessary for such implementations are still in early stages. DeFi projects such as Centrifuge and MakerDAO have taken initial steps toward integrating real-world assets, but the full realization of this concept remains a work in progress.

Another promising but largely unexplored area is AI-driven automation in DeFi. While DeFi already enables automated transactions through smart contracts, artificial intelligence (AI) could enhance efficiency by optimizing trading strategies, risk management, and fraud detection in decentralized finance (Narayanan et al., 2022). AI-powered DeFi applications could analyze vast amounts of on-chain data to predict market trends, suggest optimal collateral ratios for lending platforms, and dynamically adjust interest rates based on real-time liquidity conditions. Moreover, machine learning algorithms could detect suspicious activities and mitigate security risks by proactively identifying vulnerabilities in smart contracts before they are exploited. The integration of AI with decentralized autonomous organizations (DAOs) could further refine governance structures, making decision-making processes more adaptive and data-driven. However, implementing AI in DeFi raises concerns about transparency, bias in algorithmic decision-making, and the centralization of control, which require careful consideration.

DeFi's role in global trade financing and supply chain management remains an underdeveloped yet high-impact area. Traditional trade financing relies on banks and intermediaries to facilitate transactions, often leading to inefficiencies, high costs, and delays, particularly for small and medium-sized enterprises (SMEs) (Basole & Patel, 2021). DeFi could provide alternative financing solutions by enabling businesses to secure funding through decentralized liquidity pools, peer-to-peer lending, and tokenized supply chain assets. Smart contracts could automate trade agreements, ensuring that payments are executed instantly upon fulfillment of contractual conditions. However, regulatory uncertainty, interoperability issues, and resistance from traditional financial institutions have slowed the adoption of DeFi in trade finance. Projects such as TradeLens and Marco Polo Network have attempted to bring blockchain to trade financing, but full-fledged DeFi integration is still a distant goal.

Lastly, the intersection of DeFi with Central Bank Digital Currencies (CBDCs) and national financial systems remains a highly speculative but significant avenue for future research. While DeFi aims to decentralize finance, CBDCs represent a move by governments toward digital financial control. The coexistence of these two systems raises fundamental questions about their compatibility. Could central banks integrate DeFi protocols within their digital currency infrastructure, or would they seek to regulate DeFi out of existence? Some analysts argue that programmable money—enabled by CBDCs—could be used within DeFi ecosystems to facilitate compliant and state-backed decentralized financial services (Kumar et al., 2022). Others worry that centralization through CBDCs could undermine the core principles of DeFi. This area requires deeper exploration as governments worldwide accelerate CBDC development while DeFi continues to gain traction.

While this chapter has covered major aspects of DeFi, many areas remain unexplored, offering significant opportunities for innovation. From decentralized identity and quantum-resistant security to AI-driven automation and integration with real-world assets, DeFi's evolution is still in its early stages. The potential for DeFi to revolutionize global trade financing, interact with CBDCs, and create a truly decentralized financial infrastructure is vast, but these areas require further research, regulatory clarity, and technological advancements. As DeFi matures, it will be crucial for developers, policymakers, and financial institutions to collaborate in addressing these gaps while preserving the decentralized ethos that defines this financial revolution. The coming decade will determine whether DeFi remains a parallel financial system or fully integrates into mainstream global finance, unlocking new economic opportunities and redefining how financial services operate in the digital age.

REFERENCES

Aave. (2021). *Aave Protocol Documentation.* https://docs.aave.com/

Acharya, V. V., & Rajan, R. (2020). Lending in the age of fintech: A decentralized alternative. *Journal of Financial Intermediation*, *44*, 100827.

Acharya, V. V., & Rajan, R. G. (2020). *Banks and Shadow Banks.* Princeton University Press.

Adams, H., Zins, J., & Weill, L. (2020). Automated Market Makers and the Rise of Decentralized Finance: A Comparative Study. *Journal of Financial Economics*, *56*(3), 120–145.

Adams, H., Zinsmeister, N., & Robinson, D. (2021). *Uniswap v3 Core.* Uniswap Documentation.

Angeris, G., Evans, A., Chitra, T., & Minca, A. (2021). Impermanent Loss and Stability in Automated Market Makers. *Quantitative Finance*, *22*(1), 90–110.

Arner, D. W., Auer, R., & Frost, J. (2020). *Stablecoins, central bank digital currencies, and cross-border payments: A new look at the international monetary system.* BIS Papers, 114.

Arner, D. W., Barberis, J., & Buckley, R. P. (2020). The Evolution of FinTech: A New Post-Crisis Paradigm? *Georgetown Journal of International Law*, *47*(4), 1271–1319.

Bartoletti, M., Carta, S., Cimoli, T., & Saia, R. (2022). *Security and Stability in Decentralized Finance: A Comparative Analysis of DEX Protocols.* IEEE Transactions on Blockchain.

Buterin, V. (2014). *A next-generation smart contract and decentralized application platform.* Ethereum White Paper.

Buterin, V. (2021). *A rollup-centric Ethereum roadmap.* Ethereum Foundation Blog.

Chainalysis. (2022). *The 2022 Global Crypto Adoption Index.*

Chen, Y., & Bellavitis, C. (2020). Decentralized Finance: Blockchain Technology and the Future of Financial Markets. *Journal of Financial Innovation*, *6*(1), 45–67. PMID: 35024267

Choudhury, A. (2022). India's crypto lending sector: Growth and regulatory hurdles. *Journal of Fintech Research*, *14*(2), 67–81.

Daian, P., Goldfeder, S., Kell, T., & Juels, A. (2020). On the Feasibility of Secure DeFi Arbitrage and Front-Running Prevention. *IEEE Security and Privacy.*

Daian, P., Goldfeder, S., Kell, T., & Narayanan, A. (2020). Flash loans and DeFi attacks: Systemic risks in decentralized finance. *Proceedings of the IEEE Symposium on Security and Privacy.*

Demirgüç-Kunt, A., Klapper, L., Singer, D., Ansar, S., & Hess, J. (2018). *The Global Findex Database 2017: Measuring financial inclusion and the fintech revolution.* World Bank.

Gaunt, D., Xu, Q., & Chen, W. (2022). *Decentralized Credit Risk Management in DeFi Lending.* Blockchain: Research and Applications.

Gopinath, S. (2021). DeFi security challenges and the need for regulation. *Economic Policy Review, 29*(4), 45–63.

Gudgeon, L., Moreno-Sanchez, P., Roos, S., McCorry, P., & Gervais, A. (2020). SoK: Layer-Two Blockchain Protocols. *Proceedings of the IEEE Symposium on Security and Privacy.*

Gudgeon, L., Werner, S., Pérez, D., & Gervais, A. (2020). DeFi: The Decentralized Financial Ecosystem. *Proceedings of the Crypto Valley Conference on Blockchain Technology.*

Gupta, P., & Jain, R. (2021). Cryptocurrency remittances: Implications for India's financial system. *Journal of Financial Innovation, 7*(1), 23–41.

Harvey, C. R., Ramachandran, A., & Santoro, J. (2021). *DeFi and the Future of Finance.* John Wiley & Sons.

Jain, M., & Kumar, R. (2022). *Blockchain adoption in India: A case study*

Leshner, R., & Hayes, J. (2020). *Liquidity Mining and the Democratization of Financial Services.* Compound Finance Whitepaper.

Mishkin, F. S. (2007). *The Economics of Money, Banking, and Financial Markets.* Pearson.

Nakamoto, S. (2008). *Bitcoin: A peer-to-peer electronic cash system.* Bitcoin White Paper.

Philippon, T. (2019). *The Great Reversal: How America Gave Up on Free Markets.* Harvard University Press.

Schär, F. (2021). Decentralized finance: On blockchain- and smart contract-based financial markets. *Review - Federal Reserve Bank of St. Louis, 103*(2), 153–174.

Shiller, R. J. (2012). *Finance and the Good Society*. Princeton University Press.

Wang, S., Xie, T., & Liu, L. (2022). *Scalability and Efficiency in Decentralized Finance: A Blockchain Perspective*. IEEE Computer Society.

Werner, S., Ko, R. K., & Gervais, A. (2021). Security Considerations in Decentralized Finance (DeFi). *IEEE Security and Privacy*.

Werner, S., Perez, D., & Gudgeon, L. (2021). *Decentralized finance: An emerging alternative financial ecosystem.* Journal of Financial Regulation.

Zetzsche, D. A., Buckley, R. P., & Arner, D. W. (2021). Regulating decentralised finance (DeFi): Challenges and opportunities. *Capital Markets Law Journal*, *16*(1), 1–26.

Zhang, R., Xie, B., & Wang, J. (2022). Blockchain, decentralization, and the future of finance. *Financial Innovation*, *8*(1), 23–45.

Zhang, R., Xie, S., & Wang, W. (2021). *Blockchain and trust in the digital economy*. Springer.

Section 2
Regulation, Risk, and Recovery

Chapter 6
Strategic Risk Mitigation and Regulatory Adherence in Service Organisations:
Sustainable Digital Finance for Preclusion of Financial Malfeasance

Arjun J. Nair
https://orcid.org/0000-0002-2287-3174
Chitkara University, India

Satish Rao A. B.
https://orcid.org/0009-0003-5379-9688
Manipal Academy of Higher Education, India

ABSTRACT

This chapter explores the intricate nexus of risk management, compliance and sustainability in digital finance, offering a comprehensive framework for safeguarding service organizations against financial fraud. As digital finance revolutionizes the service sector, organizations face complex risks, including cybersecurity threats, operational vulnerabilities and regulatory challenges. The chapter examines current risk management frameworks, the evolving regulatory landscape and the importance of integrating sustainability principles. Analyzing case studies and emerging

DOI: 10.4018/979-8-3373-1404-4.ch006

trends, it underscores the critical interdependence of these elements, advocating for a holistic approach to building resilient, compliant and sustainable service organizations in the digital age.

1. INTRODUCTION

The rise of digital finance has fundamentally reshaped the financial landscape, transforming the way service organizations operate and deliver value. As financial services become increasingly digitalized, organizations benefit from enhanced efficiency, reduced operational costs and greater accessibility (Bueno et al., 2024). Yet, these advancements come with their own set of risks. The digital finance ecosystem introduces complex challenges, ranging from cybersecurity threats and operational vulnerabilities to compliance with ever-evolving regulations (Orelaja et al., 2024). These risks, if not effectively managed, can jeopardize not only the financial integrity of service organizations but also their reputation and long-term sustainability. Risk management, compliance and sustainability emerge as the critical pillars necessary to safeguard service organizations (Alabi et al., 2023). These three interconnected components form the foundation of a resilient organizational strategy capable of withstanding the challenges posed by the digital finance environment. While risk management is essential for identifying and mitigating the various threats that arise in this space, compliance ensures that organizations adhere to legal and regulatory standards, avoiding significant penalties and reputational damage. Sustainability, on the other hand, provides a long-term perspective, integrating environmental, social and governance (ESG) principles into organizational operations to foster resilience and trust. Digital finance encompasses a broad range of financial services delivered through digital channels, including mobile banking, fintech innovations, cryptocurrency transactions and decentralized finance (DeFi) (Rabbani, 2022). These technologies have revolutionized the financial services industry by making financial products more accessible to consumers and businesses alike. Mobile payment systems, blockchain-based platforms and AI-driven financial advisory services have all contributed to the rapid expansion of digital finance, enabling service organizations to offer more tailored, efficient and cost-effective services. The impact of digital finance is particularly profound within service organizations, which rely on financial technologies to streamline operations, enhance customer experience and reduce reliance on traditional banking infrastructure. However, with this transformation comes an array of risks. Cyberattacks, data breaches and identity theft are becoming more prevalent as financial transactions move online, exposing service organizations to significant financial and reputational harm. Moreover, the global nature of digital finance presents unique regulatory challenges, as service organizations need to navigate differing compliance requirements across jurisdictions.

Risk management has ceased to be a peripheral concern, it's something integral to the operational integrity of service organizations. The nature of the risks that beset digital finance is so complex that they require an integrated approach, one that would address not only the cybersecurity aspect in technical terms but also the operational ones, system failure, market fluctuation and fraud (Javaheri et al., 2023). Digital finance increases the interconnectedness of organizations in which one weak point in a system can cascade, like a virus, into many other areas of its operations. Cybersecurity is, therefore, an area of high concern. Many incidences of cyberattacks against digital financial platforms happen in very sophisticated ways. Service organizations are thus obliged to have in place advanced technology solutions that integrates AI and machine learning to enable real-time detection, prevention and response to such attacks-from phishing attacks through to ransomware and insider threats. Among a variety of other operational risks, those caused by the integrity of digital infrastructure themselves turn huge. The higher the digital finance platforms become, the more the possibility of system outages, software malfunction and problems with data integrity-which can lead to financial losses and dissatisfaction of customers (Yaacoub et al., 2022). Besides, the increased dependence on third-party providers and cloud services creates a supply chain risk where an external vendor failure might disrupt the whole workflow of the operation. This is matched in the field of digital finance, where regulators are playing a constant game of catch-up with technology. Service organizations are also subject to a wide range of regulatory demands on data protection legislation, anti-money laundering (AML) requirements and financial reporting standards. Non-compliance results in significant fines, potential legal actions and reputational damage, well beyond what might be regarded as the more traditional risks due to cybersecurity or operational issues (Benedek & Bognár, 2024). Proactive compliance can enhance an organization's reputation, build trust with customers and provide a competitive advantage in a crowded marketplace. Integration of regulatory considerations into their broader risk management strategies allows the service organizations to build much more robust and legally sustained operational model. In digital finance, sustainability goes beyond environmental considerations to include social responsibility, governance and long-term risk mitigation. Building sustainability into the risk management framework also equate to service organizations being resilient, not only today but also for the future. Sustainability aids in organizational trust and credibility-facts that are to be believed more and more in a world where consumers and stakeholders alike are asking for more transparency and ethical behavior from the companies, they do business with.

2. RISK MANAGEMENT IN DIGITAL FINANCE

Risk management has become an essential focus for the service organizations concerned with maintaining operational stability, seeking regulatory compliance and protecting consumer trust. Indeed, inherent risks associated with digital finance are multifarious and span a wide range of areas such as cybersecurity threats, operational vulnerabilities, regulatory challenges, systemic risks (Sharifi et al., 2024). As more service organizations adopt various forms of digital financial technologies, the demand for well-thought-out, adaptable risk management frameworks has increased. Of all the risks in digital finance, cyber threats surge in sophistication and frequency as more financial transactions become electronic (Pandey et al., 2022). The attack surface for malicious actors is further facilitated by the increase in the digitization of financial data and reliance on cloud-based platforms. Cybercriminals attack digital finance platforms through a variety of techniques like hacking, phishing, ransomware and distributed denial of service (DDoS) attacks. A successful cyber-attack results in the theft of sensitive financial data, financial loss, disruption of services and severe reputational damage. Since financial data is of great value and high monetary values are concerned with it, the service organizations concerned with digital finance are highly susceptible to this particular threat. For example, illegal access to customer accounts or to any of the payment systems would enable fraudulent transactions, which can result in losses running into millions for an organization (Ibrahim, 2022). Besides this, the ever-growing list of regulatory requirements on cybersecurity further leading to escalating financial risk resulting from related fines and penalties for failure to comply with the set standards by regulators in terms of data protection. Moreover, there is a significant operational risk because technology mediates the process of finance. Most digital finance platforms depend on advanced technological infrastructures that are usually prone to different types of failures, such as system crashes, software bugs and data corruption. There is also a risk from dependency since normally most operational dependence would fall upon vendors or service providers providing cloud storage, processing of payments and cybersecurity measures. Any disruption in these outsourced services has the domino-like effect of causing hold-ups in transaction processing and loss of customer data such that an organization is unable to provide essential services (Katsaliaki et al., 2022).

Technological obsolescence is one of the most pivotal factors relating to digital finance, a service organization is supposed to be upgrading its systems on a continuous basis against emergent new financial technologies, which makes its platform competitive and secure. Failure to fulfill such upgrading desires might make systems outdated, hence, more vulnerable to security breaches or decreased efficiencies in service delivery. Apart from that, this integration complexity with existing infrastructures brings about consequential risks, especially those technologies that are not properly tested or configured. Digital finance occurs in a wide, dynamic regulatory environment that at this moment undergoes change something challenging to service organizations. However, regulations such as general data protection regulation (GDPR) within the European Union and AML in a number of jurisdictions, has strict requirements on how financial data is to be managed, stored and shared. Non-compliance with these regulations leads to substantial fines, legal action and reputational harm. Regulatory risks extend beyond compliance with financial regulations to include data privacy and cybersecurity laws. Service organizations have to adhere to different regulations across different regions, most of the time ill congruent and inconsistent. Added to this, digital finance operations often cross borders, which requires multiple validities, each to adhere to its relevant regulatory demands. Maintaining compliance with such diverse legal frameworks implies monitoring and continuous adjustment of risk management practices to assure adherence to applicable laws. Systemic risks in digital finance are disruptions at an aggregative level that occurs in financial systems because of the complex interconnectedness between global financial markets and technological infrastructures (Manohar et al., 2023). In most cases, the platforms of digital finance are connected with wider financial networks; the collapse of one section, therefore, has the potential to trigger successive chains of disruption in the entire financial ecosystem. This risk is magnified in algorithmic trading, where mistakes in trading algorithms and automated systems lead to market wide volatility and losses. Other systemic risks come from the concentration risk when a few large technology companies or financial institutions provide most of the digital finance services. If one of these entities were to fail, the impact on the global financial system could be severe. The growth of digital finance will therefore increasingly call for close collaboration between regulators and financial and technology providers with the express aim of ensuring the overall resilience of the financial infrastructure.

This has led service organizations within digital finance to embrace various kinds of risk management frameworks in order for them to identify, assess, mitigate and monitor risks. More often than not, these models are combined with advanced technological technologies such as artificial intelligence, machine learning and big data analytics to enhance their effective operation. Enterprise risk management (ERM) is a holistic approach to risk management in all operations of any given organization, in this case digital finance (Nair & Manohar, 2024). ERM frameworks are designed to identify and measure various risks throughout the corporation so that the service organization can adopt a holistic approach to mitigating those risks. ERM frameworks are particularly very useful in addressing cross functional risks, for example, how cybersecurity risks interact with operation vulnerabilities. In this respect, ERM frameworks strongly advocate the incorporation of the risk management process within the overall strategic planning process. Besides the identification of risks, their impact on organizational objectives is assessed and thus mitigation strategy formulations align towards the bigger goals of the business. In service organizations, for instance, the ERM framework is mainly utilized in developing the risk registers, setting the level of risk tolerance and formulating action plans to address certain risks. The ERM also includes periodic risk assessments and scenario analyses that allow organizations to look forward toward emerging risks and adjust their strategies in managing those risks. As the threats of cybersecurity breaches have become prominent, many organizations have set up specific cybersecurity risk management frameworks that address explicitly those very risks. These frameworks protect financial data and digital assets from cyber threats and provide compliance with cybersecurity regulation. The use of advanced security technologies such as encryption, multi-factor authentication and intrusion detection systems is an integral part of cyber risk management. In addition to such technological measures, cyber risk management frameworks also have much emphasis on the human factor for prevention against cyber incidences. This includes training employees in best practices for cybersecurity, such as the identification of phishing attempts and the securing of personal devices (Nair, Manohar, & Chaudhry, 2024a). Incident response planning forms another important constituent to manage cyber risks, this helps an organization take necessary protocols for ensuring quick and effective responses in case of cyber-attacks.

While general risk management frameworks outline how the firm finds and deals with risks, operational risk management frameworks specify those risks that are operation based in nature, associated with organizational operational processes and-most specific of all-technology. Digital finance applies operational risk management (ORM) frameworks to deal with the risks resulting from system failures, software errors and third party vendor dependencies. Business continuity plans and strategies for disaster recovery form part of ORM and ensure that an organization continues key operations in the case of an interruption. The ORM frameworks provide periodic testing and auditing of the technological systems to locate any kind of possible vulnerability. In other words, the service organizations considers either simulations or penetration testing, besides other forms of simulated events of system failures, to test how resilient their digital finance platforms are. Implementation and constant enhancement in operation risk management practices minimizes unexpected interruptions to the operations of the organization and ensure continuity in one's digital financial services (Nair, Manohar, & Chaudhry, 2024b). In regard to regulatory risk, it would involve putting in place an effectual compliance framework to guarantee that the set local and international regulations were adhered to. Such would normally be achieved through frequent audits, monitoring of compliance, as well as setting up internal controls that detect and deter occurrences of regulatory breaches. Compliance frameworks within digital finance might include very specific protocols for treatment of consumer data to be in compliance with data protection regulations, such as GDPR, but also the reporting of suspicious financial activities in conformance with AML regulations. Compliance frameworks also have much to do with governance structures, whereby senior leadership is specifically involved in the active guidance of their compliance. This includes the definition of a reporting structure so that any issues on compliance are reported to the top chain of command and regular board meetings to discuss the state of compliance in the organization.

3. COMPLIANCE IN DIGITAL FINANCE

The regulatory landscape in front of digital finance is quite complex and keeps changing without stops, which brings in quite serious challenges for service organizations in trying to be compliant while leveraging the digital financial innovations. Different national and international regulating bodies have introduced a variety of regulations to save the financial systems, maintain consumer data security and stability of the global financial ecosystem. Therefore, the understanding and keeping pace with such a regulatory framework become highly pertinent for service organizations operating in the digital finance space. Non-compliance incurs severe penalties, reputational damage and operational disruptions. The regulatory environment for digital finance is necessarily convoluted, considering the globally confirmatory nature of financial transactions along with the speed of technological advancement. Digital finance crosses over into different and more varied legal frameworks, beyond national borders, necessitating service organizations to maneuver through international treaties and agreements down to national laws and industry-specific rules. Major regulatory focus areas in digital finance include data protection, AML and combating terrorist financing, cybersecurity and consumer protection (Akartuna et al., 2023). Among the most contentious regulatory issues in digital finance are compliance with the laws of data protection and privacy. As personal financial information increasingly becomes digital and spread among platforms, protection of sensitive data becomes the ultimate issue. With regulations such as the GDPR of the European Union and the California Consumer Privacy Act of the United States, for example, strict demands are placed on any organization with respect to collecting, storing, processing, or sharing personal information of individuals (Bakare et al., 2024). These regulations confer various rights on consumers over their data, including a right of access, correction, erasure and restriction of processing. Data protection regulations are not optional for service organizations in the digital finance sector. Breach of such laws could lead to huge financial penalties, legal action and loss of consumer confidence. For example, under the GDPR, serious breaches attract fines up to a maximum of €20 million or 4% of an organization's global annual revenue, whichever amount is higher (SEKULIĆ & LENDÁK; Erkan-Barlow & Wells-Dietel, 2023). Service organizations have to balance data handling practices so that regulatory requirements are satisfied that does not disturb the smooth and seamless flow of financial services that customers come to expect.

Besides data protection, AML and counter-terrorist financing (CTF) are among some of the most critical areas of regulation in digital finance. This, in turn, means that obliged entities need to take strict actions to prevent the use of their facilities for money laundering and financing of terrorism. Such programs include customer due diligence (CDD) processes, monitoring transactions and reporting any suspicious activity to the relevant authorities. Among others, the FATF recommendations, the USA PATRIOT Act and the EU's Fifth AML Directive (5AMLD) require organizations to have in place strong AML/CTF programs (Yeoh, 2020). This means that the programs will be able to make it possible for an organization to know its customers, assess different transactions for risks associated with them and also take appropriate action each time any suspicious behavior has been detected. What makes this regulatory environment even more daunting is the recent advances in the field of cryptocurrency and decentralized financial systems, allowing for anonymous transactions and hence promoting no traceability in illicit activities. A service organization, in order to keep up to date with such AML/CTF requirements or prevent their platforms from being utilized for unlawful activities, then need to invest in advanced technologies such as blockchain analytics and machine learning. The field of finance depends day by day on digital technologies; therefore, cybersecurity is a major field of concern among regulatory bodies. Consequently, different parts of the world have initiated those laws and standards necessary in safeguarding financial institutions and their customers against cyber-attacks. In the United States, one of the key pieces of legislation, the Cybersecurity Information Sharing Act-or CISA-increases the information-sharing activity between organizations and government agencies to strengthen the defense against cyber threats (Lyle, 2024; Comunale & Manera, 2024). Similarly, the European Union's Network and Information Security (NIS) directive has laid down security imperatives for essential service providers in the financial sector by the EU (Gounari et al., 2024). For cybersecurity regulations compliance, the service organizations need to implement comprehensive security measures such as encryption, multi-factor authentication and regular security audits. The organizations are also required to have incident response plans for quickly responding to breaches and limiting their impact. In addition, non-compliance with cybersecurity regulations involves punishment with fines. The organizations are also at a high risk of cyberattacks that compromises sensitive financial data and cause considerable operational interruption.

Another very important area of regulation in the area of digital finance is consumer protection, due to the fact that governments try their best to protect individuals from fraud, exploitation and unfair practices. This is further supported by regulations such as the Payment Services Directive 2 in the European Union and the Truth in Lending Act in the United States, enacted to ensure that financial services be more transparent and that consumers are fully informed about digital finance products terms and risks (Molaro, 2023). These regulations also include dispute resolution terms, meaning that customers have somewhere to go when unauthorized transactions happen or services fail to be given. Regarding service organizations, customer protection entails clear communication of various variables to the customers, clarity in the prices and fee structures and importantly, good customer care services. It is also important that organizations ensure the digital finance platforms are accessible, user-friendly and easy to navigate through services provided for customers to make informed decisions about their finance. The impact of the regulatory landscape on service organizations is immense, since it has actually turned compliance into a core part of operational strategy. Breach of relevant regulation leads to significant financial fines and litigations besides causing harm to reputation. Besides, this compliance is expensive to come by, since organizations need to invest in state-of-the-art technology, regulatory expertise and employee training programs. However, companies that sail through the regulatory environment with considerable ease earn a competitive advantage by engendering in customers trust that the company considers transparency, security and ethical business practices paramount. Keeping pace with the rapidly changing digital finance regulations holds pride of place among the many challenges encountered by every service organization. With the rise in new technologies like blockchain, cryptocurrencies and artificial intelligence, the financial sector remains under constant disruption (Nair, Manohar, Mittal, & Chaudhry, 2024). With the development of such emerging risks associated with these technologies, regulators also turn up the pace to introduce new laws and guidelines. In this respect, it would be imperative on the part of a service organization to adopt an agile approach toward compliance-a constant vigil on the development in the regulatory environment and adapting the risk management strategies as per the change. With increasing complexity in the regulatory landscape for digital finance, there is an imminent need for service organizations to become proactive and strategic in their approach towards compliance. Strategies that would help organizations attain and sustain compliance at minimal risks and costs are highlighted below. The conceptual framework if elaborated in figure 1.

Figure 1. Conceptual Framework for Integral Risk Management, Compliance, and Sustainability in Digital Finance: Safeguarding Service Organizations from Financial Fraud

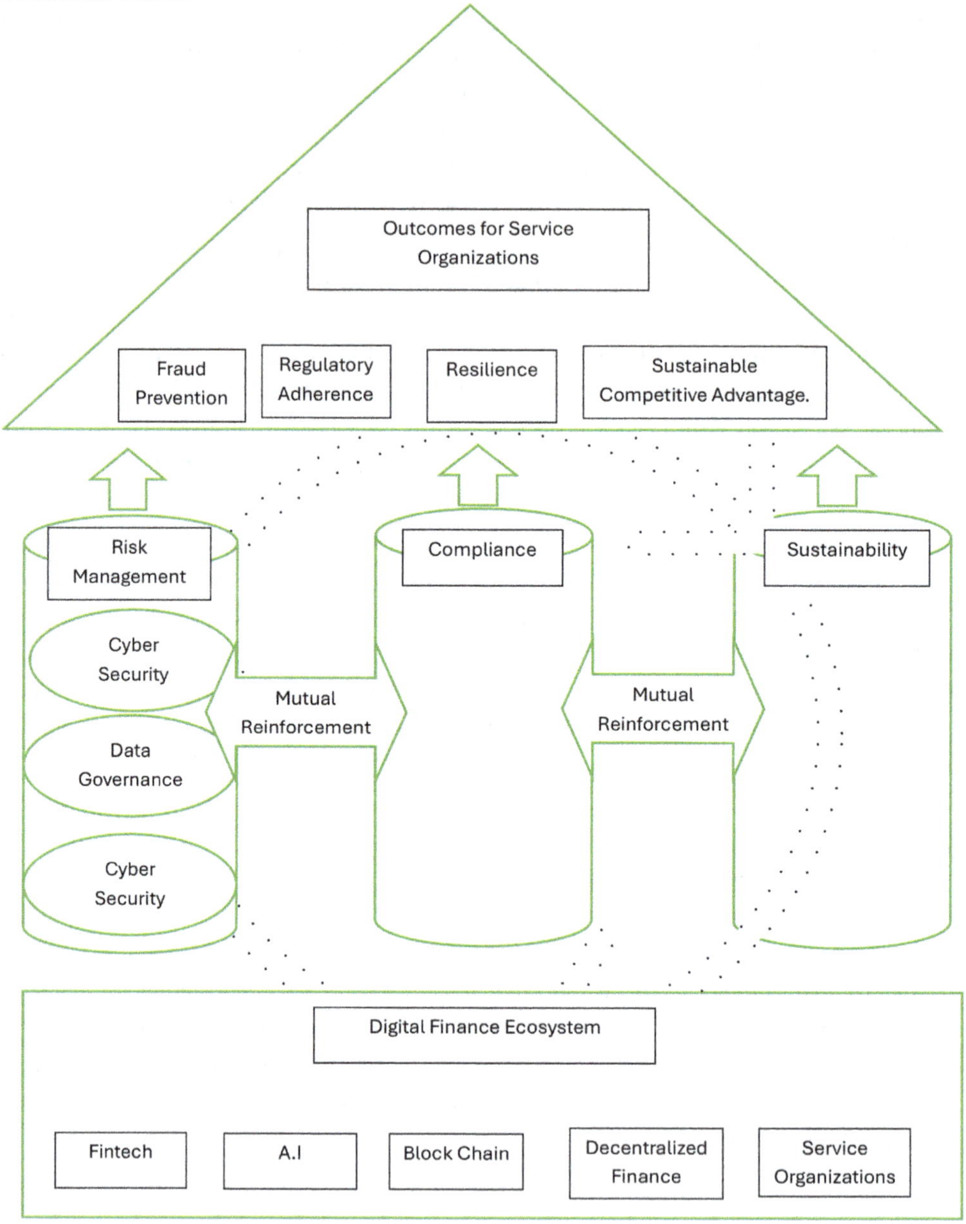

Arguably, one of the finest ways through which regulatory compliance in digital finance is managed is through the adoption of Regulatory Technology (RegTech)

solutions. RegTech is all about the use of technology for easing the process of compliance, generating reports and monitoring changes in regulations (Michailidou, 2020; Nair, Manohar, Mittal, & Chaudhry, 2024). With the likes of AI, machine learning and big data analytics, advanced technologies can be leveraged to provide the much needed efficiencies for organizations through RegTech solutions to handle their compliance obligations. For example, AI-powered RegTech platforms automatically monitor changes in regulations and flag any alterations that would affect how an enterprise operates. Machine learning algorithms can identify suspicious patterns in financial transactions, which enables organizations to meet their AML/CTF obligations. Besides that, RegTech solutions can automate the generation of reports needed by compliance and reduce some of the administrative burdens on compliance teams while ensuring that such reports are completed timely by organizations. Another important way to achieve and maintain compliance is by developing a compliance culture. This means setting compliance at the core values of the organization, decision making and daily operations. It requires senior leadership to lead a compliance first attitude and philosophy throughout the organization, ensure employees understand why compliance with regulatory requirements is important and give them the necessary tools and knowledge to do so (J. Nair et al., 2024). In addition, training programs are a very critical building block in developing a compliance culture by equipping staff with the latest information regarding applicable regulations and the best practice in managing those risks. There needs to be periodic training, which ensures that all the employees-from the front-line staff to the senior executives-know their duties regarding compliance. More importantly, organizations need to have a well-communicated process for reporting an identified compliance issue and give assurance that retaliation will not be carried out against an employee upon reporting any violation.

Second, keeping open communication with the regulatory authorities is some of the key strategies in achieving compliance. To that effect, service organizations need to interact with regulators on problematic regulations that are complex, join industry consultations and give feedback whenever there are proposed regulatory changes. Through this, working collaboratively with the regulator will assist an organization in gaining valuable insights into the expectations of regulatory mechanisms and hence make sure its compliance strategies are aligned to the current and future regulatory requirements. Third-party involvement in the early stages will also enable an organization to leverage new and emerging regulations and guidelines. For example, when new technology crops up, such as blockchain or cryptocurrencies, the regulators at that point issue some guidelines or sandbox programs that enable an organization to test such technologies in a controlled environment (Li et al., 2023; Nair et al., 2023). By being part of these initiatives, organizations can stand ahead of regulatory changes and ensure their digital finance offerings remain compliant with those changes. In the ever-increasingly dynamic regulatory environment of digital finance, one would think it impossible to interpret compliance as a one-time effort. An organization needs to be observant about regulatory changes and monitor its impact on operations in relation to whether modifications in compliance strategies are called for. In this respect, compliance monitoring systems needs to be installed that can trace the variations in regulations on a real-time basis and ensure internal policies and procedures are adjusted correspondingly (Nair, Manohar, Mittal, & Ahmed, 2024). Besides keeping the organization current with changes in laws and regulations, another necessary function of auditing the compliance program on a regular basis needs to be performed. The internal auditing needs to provide assurance that operating compliance controls are functioning properly and employees are following the required procedures. Regular auditing will also demonstrate to regulators that the organization is not only committed to maintaining compliance but also committed to continuous improvement of their practices pertaining to risk management.

4. SUSTAINABILITY AND DIGITAL FINANCE

Sustainability, in the traditional sense, is defined as the ability of a system to sustain itself over time and function within the balancing of economic, social and environmental factors. Sustainability in digital finance has a different meaning that includes not only environmental aspects but also the broader dimensions of financial stability, ethics in governance and long-term economic viability. It means incorporating digital finance technologies and services in a manner that ensures environmental stewardship, social responsibility, sound risk management, operational efficiency and profitability (Chueca Vergara & Ferruz Agudo, 2021; Nag et al., 2024). In the realm of digital finance, sustainability can be viewed through various interrelated lenses. First and foremost, it entails the environmental sustainability of the technologies and infrastructures underpinning digital finance. As financial transactions increasingly move online, the energy demands of data centres, blockchain networks and digital currencies become important considerations. For instance, cryptocurrencies like Bitcoin, which rely on energy-intensive proof-of-work algorithms, have come under scrutiny over their environmental impact. Sustainable digital finance will thus have to be realized through the adoption of more energy-efficient technologies and the pursuit of greener alternatives, such as proof-of-stake algorithms or hybrid consensus mechanisms that reduce the carbon footprint of financial systems. A second aspect of sustainability in digital finance is financial resilience at an institutional level-the capabilities thereof to mitigate systemic risks. Such a digital financial system needs to have its building blocks in the form of risk management principles that keep pace with evolving threats, whether in the form of cybersecurity risks, market volatility, or changes in regulation. This means maintaining financial stability in response to technological disruption, while making digital financial services accessible, inclusive and reliable for all users, irrespective of economic or social status (Nair & Rao A. B, 2025). Third, sustainability encompasses social and ethical considerations and hence digital finance needs to be inclusive, reducing the gap in financial facilities available to the underprivileged group. The use of digital platforms has emerged as one of the main possible ways through which monetary services can reach those negligible communities that have so far been kept out of the reach of conventional banking. This also contributes to the wider objective of sustainable development: a reduction in inequality to ensure that economic progress offers its fruits to every single member of the society. In this respect, sustainable digital finance is a strong enabler of social equity and economic empowerment. Sustainability in digital finance is finally linked to ethical governance and transparency. Digital financial institutions have to apply strict regulatory standards so as to protect consumer rights, ensure data privacy and prevent fraudulent activities. Trust and accountability give organizations the potential to create long-term, trust-based relationships with customers, investors and regulatory authorities. In this way, it will definitely reinforce their reputational capital and, finally, their possibilities of success in a continuously changing financial environment.

Generally, integration of sustainability into the risk management strategies reaps many long-term benefits to organizations operating within the realm of digital finance. Indeed, when financial objectives align with environmental and ESG factors, the ability of an organization to increase its resilience while better mitigating risks and creating value for a variety of stakeholders improves. The following section considers some of the key benefits derived from integrating sustainability into risk management.

4.1. Increased Organizational Resilience

Probably the most important reason why integrating sustainability into risk management is so valuable is that it enhances organizational resilience-in other words, helps organizations prepare and adapt to all kinds of risks that include environmental and climate-related challenges, as well as ESG issues. For example, the companies focused on environmental sustainability by optimizing energy use and adding renewable sources of energy into their portfolios are much better positioned to be resilient under changing economic and regulatory dynamics shifting toward reduced carbon emissions. Similarly, practices of social sustainability, which nurture organizational diversity, inclusion and just labor practices, are more likely to retain the best talent and improve overall employee satisfaction with a promise of maintaining good workplace culture. This would not only reduce some operational risks emanating from employee turnover and cases of labor disputes but would also culminate in increasing the innovative capability of an organization and its adaptability towards changing market conditions. Moreover, good governance practices for sustainability involve ethical leadership and transparent decision-making that protects an organization from reputational risks and regulatory penalties. Companies with a high level of commitment to ESG principles will be more capable of going through regulatory scrutiny and avoiding legal liabilities while sustaining stakeholders' trust.

4.2. Mitigation of Environmental and Climate-Related Risks

Whereas in most economies around the world, climate change still is a big concern, this implies that the financial sector faces climate-related risk on an increasing order of magnitude. Such risks could take the form of physical risks, such as the actual damage of infrastructure resulting from extreme weather conditions, or transition risks in terms of regulatory changes imposed to reduce carbon emissions. In that respect, digital finance organizations are no exception, especially those relying on large-scale data centers and blockchain infrastructures. In this regard, integrating environmental sustainability into a risk management framework could help digital finance organizations reduce potential consequences emanating from climate-related risks. This includes embracing energy-efficient technologies, lowering carbon emission rates and aligning operations with international climate change commitments such as the Paris Agreement. Those firms that proactively act on environmental risks are in a better position to meet new regulations and minimize sudden losses due to environmental catastrophes, hence protecting long-term profitability. In addition, embedding sustainability into the risk management framework provides access to new corporate growth and innovation opportunities. Consider, for example, the recent surge in green finance and sustainable investment products, allowing digital finance firms to create environmentally friendly financial solutions for their ecologically aware customers and investors. By positioning themselves as leaders in sustainable finance, organizations can differentiate themselves in the marketplace and attract a growing segment of customers who prioritize ESG values.

4.3. Better Regulatory Compliance and Mitigation of Risk

The regulatory environment with regard to digital finance has been increasingly getting strict, whereby governments and different regulating bodies across the globe introduce new laws and standards concerning the sustainability and responsible business practices of this industry. For example, the European Union's Sustainable

Finance Disclosure Regulation requires financial institutions to disclose how they integrate sustainability risks into their investment decisions, while guidelines from the Task Force on Climate-related Financial Disclosures provide guidelines on how companies are supposed to assess and disclose their climate-related risks. The integration of sustainability into digital finance organizations' risk management processes will help improve their compliance with such regulatory demands, reducing the chances of penalties or sanctions. Moreover, organizations whose operations are aligned with global sustainability frameworks-for example, the United Nations' SDGs-are well-placed for favorable treatment by regulators, investors and customers. Apart from regulatory compliance, sustainability-based risk management can enable organizations to moderate reputational risks. In today's interconnected world, consumers and investors increasingly demand more transparency and accountability from companies with which they deal directly or indirectly. Organizations that fail to protect ESG expectations are at the risk of facing public outcry, consumer boycotts and loss of investor confidence. By integrating sustainability into the risk management processes, digital finance organizations can demonstrate their commitment to ethical behavior through building stakeholder trust and maintaining brand reputation.

4.4. Long-term Financial Performance and Risk Reduction

Sustainability is not only a moral issue but also financial. Several studies proved that companies with an outstanding ESG performance tend to outperform others in terms of long-term financial performance. In addition, sustainability integrated into risk management can help digital finance organizations reduce operating expenses, increase efficiency and strengthen their financial resilience. For instance, organizations that invest in renewable sources of energy and energy-efficient technologies can realize tremendous operating expense reductions, especially where the cost of energy is prohibitively high or highly volatile. Companies that take a more proactive approach to sustainability in their supply chain are better positioned to reduce the risks associated with resource scarcity, price volatility and supply disruptions. Sustainability-oriented risk management can also prevent an organization from being involved in costly legal cases, regulatory fines and other types of damage to brand reputation. Besides, proactive ESG risk control reduces the possibility of severe financial losses caused by sudden environmental disasters, societal crises, or corporate governance failures. Accordingly, it contributes to improved financial stability and long-term profitability.

4.5. Encouraging Sustainable Investment and Capital

Sustainability has become one of the key drivers for investors and capital markets. An increasing number of investors are trying to make their funds comply with ESG principles. According to the Global Alliance, the assets under management already reached trillions of US dollars worldwide, which surely reflects the growing demand for responsible options of investment. A digital finance organization that has a risk management system that integrates sustainability will be more attractive for sustainable investment and access to capital by ESG-focused investors. In this way, demonstrating a commitment to long-term value creation, environmental stewardship and social responsibility will make companies more appealing to institutional investors, pension funds and impact investors who take the aspect of sustainability into consideration when making their investment decisions. Besides, companies embracing sustainability might enjoy cheaper borrowing costs and better access to credit. Financial institutions of late offer green bonds, sustainability-linked loans and other financial products that make businesspeople more inclined towards sustainability. Through the alignment of risk management strategies with the goals of sustainability, digital finance organizations can unlock newer sources of capital and enhance their financial flexibility.

5. CASE STUDIES

The management of risk and compliance is paramount in digital finance, given the myriad threats this domain has to face arising out of evolving technology advances, vulnerabilities in operations and altering regulatory environment. To the extent that service organizations are increasingly integrating digital finance into their operations, they are exposed to some complex risks, cybersecurity threats, fraud, data breaches and volatility associated with digital assets. Effective risk management and compliance are the major concerns for any organization in order to ensure continuity of operations, stakeholder confidence and conformance with various national and international regulations. This section explores some case studies with regard to service organizations that have implemented efficient risk management and compliance practices. Drawing from these, we bring out key lessons and best practices that can be helpful guidelines for other organizations operating in the field of digital finance.

Case Study 1: JPMorgan Chase Leading in Cybersecurity and Digital Risk Management (Mızrak, 2023)

Background: JPMorgan Chase is among the largest and most influential organizations within the financial sector across the world, with several digitally provided services like online banking, mobile applications and digital wealth management platforms. Having been an early adopter of various Digital Finance solutions, JPMorgan has indeed faced most of the cybersecurity risks associated with these digital offerings since their inception.

Risk Management Strategy: JPMorgan Chase alone has invested hugely in cybersecurity to protect all its digital platforms and financial transactions. The bank spends over $600 million every year enhancing its cybersecurity defense and takes a multilayer security approach that includes encryption, multifactor authentication and state-of-the-art advanced threat detection systems. One of the major strategies pursued is to apply artificial intelligence and machine learning in order to identify anomalous activity in real time and, hence, proactively enable organizational responses to possible cyber-attacks. Even further, JPMorgan has thus far created an enterprise-wide risk management framework known as the Risk Appetite Framework, or RAF. This framework allows finer tuning of the business strategy with the policies of risk management by clearly defining acceptable levels of risks, especially with regard to operational vulnerabilities and cyber-attacks.

Compliance Approach: The company, in this context, collaborates with the regulatory bodies towards complete compliance with the latest financial regulations. JPMorgan has, hence, an integrated compliance function throughout its operations across the world so that it is able to respond promptly to changed regulations across a wide range of jurisdictions. JPMorgan further uses RegTech, or regulatory technology, to ensure automation of compliance monitoring and reporting, a state of affair that reduces the occurrence of non-compliance by a huge margin.

Lessons Learned

Invest in Top-Class Cybersecurity Solutions: The very latest investment in cybersecurity technologies is highly important in safeguarding the digital finance platform from various types of threats. In addition, it's immensely critical for an organization not to consider cybersecurity as one time investment issue but as a continuous investment which would evolve over time with evolving threats.

Adopt AI for Risk Detection: AI and ML can significantly enhance risk detection capabilities through pattern analysis in real time and flag those that appear anomalous, that would indicate fraud or cyber-attacks.

In a world where the regulations keep on changing, organizations will need to bake compliance into their digital finance strategies. Compliance functions will be well-served in applying appropriate RegTech tools in order to speed up the compliance process and ensure timely compliance with regulatory requirements.

Case Study 2: PayPal Fraud Detection and AML Compliance (RAMAKRISHNAN & LAKSHMI, 2023)

Background: With millions of transactions taking place every day for customers around the globe, PayPal is among the largest online payment platforms. By nature, it opens up to tremendous fraud risks, including account takeovers, unauthorized transactions and money laundering activities.

Risk Management Strategy: As the incidences of fraud have increased, so has PayPal continued to develop an advanced risk management system that includes complex algorithms, behavioral analytics and monitoring of each and every real-time transaction. This company makes use of machine learning in analyzing transaction information for the detection of suspicious behavior that might indicate fraudulent activity. The risk management team at PayPal also utilizes fraud detection models, which foresee fraud risk based on user behavior, geolocation data and transaction patterns. Moreover, PayPal has established a special fraud investigators team that works closely in cooperation with law enforcement agencies all over the world. Company proactive attitude concerning fraud prevention helped it retain users' trust and reduce financial losses.

Compliance Approach: PayPal has in place an effective AML program based upon the Financial Action Task Force and other international AML requirements. Its compliance team shall monitor suspicious activities of the transactions and reports cases of money laundering to the appropriate authority. It has also had in place a KYC protocol where customers identities need to be verified to curb the use of the site for illegitimate transactions.

Lessons Learned

Use Behavioral Analytics: Including behavioral analytics in risk management enhances fraud detection capability significantly. An organization needs to make use of transaction data to generate user profiles and detect various pattern sets those points toward fraud.

Collaborate with Law Enforcement Agencies: Building relationships with law enforcement agencies enhances the ability of an organization to respond to fraud cases happening at a large scale. Close collaboration ensures that when fraudsters are investigated and prosecuted, it is done as quickly as possible.

Institute effective AML programs: Following international standards of AML and introducing strict KYC could save the money laundering hazard. The organizations need to refresh their AML programs to meet the changing regulatory requirements.

Case Study 3: Ant Financial-Alipay Ensuring Compliance with Regulators in Cross-Border Payments (Zhou et al., 2022)

Background: Ant Financial, parent company of Alipay, is one of the biggest digital payment platforms in the world. Operating in several global markets, Ant Financial has to overcome a number of compliance complexities, especially around cross-border payments, foreign exchange controls and consumer protection laws.

Risk Management Strategy: Ant Financial utilizes a centralized risk management framework that consolidates risk data from all its global operations for handling risks in cross-border transactions. Predictive analytics are used by the company to determine the risk for every transaction, considering factors like destination country regulations, transaction amount and historical data.

Ant Financial embeds real-time risk assessments within its payment products so that the platform would dynamically adjust the risk threshold for transactions given the prevailing conditions at any particular moment. That guarantees the firm identifies high-risk transactions, takes measures to mitigate the risks before the completion of the payment.

Approach to Compliance: At Ant Financial, compliance is paramount, in particular, in jurisdictions with very strict regulatory requirements concerning the offering of fintech services. In each country in which it operates, the company teams up with regulators so that it complies with the respective local laws related to consumer data protection, AML and taxation. Alipay also automates compliance reporting to accelerate the reporting process and ensure it captures all regulatory requirements in real time.

Lessons Learned

Adopt Centralized Risk Management Systems: Centralized risk management systems, aggregating information for different operations, help an organization spread across various jurisdictions ease its monitoring of risks and making informed decisions.

Leverage Predictive Analytics to Manage Cross-Border Payments: With predictive analytics, an organization will be able to make an informed judgment on the risk associated with each cross-border transaction in real time by correctly assessing the risk and proactively mitigating the risks that come along.

Focus on Automating Compliance: Compliance automation will go a long way in reducing the burden of compliance to specific regulations. Companies operating in many countries risk being confronted with a host of different regulations.

Case Study 4: ING Group Integrating Sustainability into Risk Management and Compliance (Singh et al., 2024)

Background: The ING Group was one of the first few global banking and financial services institutions that began to implement sustainability within its risk management and compliance practices. It is aware that the threats accompanying sustainability, such as through climate change or environmental degradation, are significant deterrents to long-term financial stability.

Risk Management Strategy: ING Group has included environmental and ESG concerns into risk management. The company has provided a framework for ESG risk management; this enables analysis of the environmental and social impacts of lending by the bank. For example, ING has set strict standards in providing finance to projects dealing in sectors with high environmental impacts, such as energy and agriculture. The bank actively tries to stay away from financing companies that are known for deforestation, fossil fuel business, or other environmentally destructive activities.

ING has also moved to introduce a sustainability-linked lending model, in which the interest rates would be pegged to the ESG performance of the borrower. This acts as an incentive for the borrowers to attain certain targets of sustainability, thereby aligning the financial incentives with the environmental ones.

Approach to Compliance: ING Group collaborates with the regulating body in ensuring that its initiatives in sustainability operate within the internationally set standards, which include the United Nations' SDGs and the Green Deal of the European Union. It also publishes periodic sustainability reports that indicate the progress toward meeting ESG targets and adhering to globally instituted frameworks of sustainability.

Lessons Learned

Embed ESG in Risk Management: Integrating environmental and other ESG factors into risk management strengthens the organization's potential to identify and mitigate risks regarding sustainability. This ESG-driven assessment of risk could eventually help align financial decision-making with long-term sustainability goals.

Embed Sustainability in Lending Practices: Sustainability-linked loans are a new way to incentivize borrowers to achieve predetermined environmental and social targets. Tying interest rates to ESG performance will further enable organizations to encourage their clients toward more sustainable ways of doing business.

Aligning compliance with global sustainability standards: Such collaboration with international regulatory bodies and an array of global sustainability standards, the SDGs, aids organizations in handling issues of compliance while meeting bigger objectives tied to global sustainability.

6. FUTURE DIRECTIONS

The unprecedented evolution of digital finance has turned the risk landscape in service organizations more complex and multi-dimensional. New technologies, including Artificial Intelligence, blockchain and digital currencies, power a financial services marketplace characterized by efficiency, scalability and innovation. These have also rendered new and complex risks that call for proper management strategies. For instance, service organizations will have to move with the emerging set of trends in risk management if they are to be resilient and foster safety against financial fraud. This would imply updating the operating frameworks within an externally dynamic environment.

6.1. Artificial Intelligence and Machine Learning: Rising Trends in Risk Management

Artificial intelligence and machine learning have become key tools in the management of risk within digital finance, as these technologies allow an organization to detect and mitigate its risks with unprecedented levels of precision and speed. The AI-driven systems process large volumes of data in real time and can make out anomalies, patterns and fraud risks that no human analyst could. It is, however, absolutely indispensable when it comes to the enhancement of fraud detection by means of predictive analytics and behavioral algorithms. A growing number of financial institutions are making use of artificial intelligence in tracking customer transactions, assessing credit risk and raising red flags regarding suspicious activities. Through analysis of user behavior, AI can uncover irregularities that indicates fraudulent activity, including sudden changes in spending patterns, geographical anomalies in transactions and unauthorized account access attempts. Furthermore, AI and ML are also used in enhancing risk modeling, including credit risk assessment and market risk analysis. Such technologies further ensure more effective market condition forecasting, customers' creditworthiness and operational risks, while enhancing decision-making and bolstering the overall effectiveness of risk management strategies.

6.2. Blockchain Technology: Enhancing Transparency and Reducing Fraud

It is fast becoming an increasingly critical part of digital finance risk management due to blockchain's decentralized and immutable ledger nature. The transparency of blockchain transactions allows for more accountability, decreasing the fraudulent use of cases. It will turn out to be extremely tough on the bad actors to manipulate the transaction data as blockchain records are time-stamped and could not retrospectively be altered. Moreover, blockchain has the added capability for smart contracts-self-executing contracts whose terms of agreement are directly written into lines of code. This reduces human mistakes and fraud in contractual obligations. These contracts automatically enforce compliance and reduce the need for intermediaries, hence reducing risks associated with traditional finance transactions, such as breach of contract or manipulation of contractual terms. Blockchain, in the case of service organizations, could integrate with digital finance and thereby increase the transparency in operations and reduction of operational risks considering the enhanced trust that stakeholders could have. This is a technology still in development and it will see wider usage in risk management in cross-border payments, supply chain financing and digital asset management.

6.3. Rise of Digital Currencies and DeFi

While digital currencies and DeFi platforms present, on the one hand, opportunities that have opened a number of avenues, they also create some challenges in terms of risk management within the context of the service organization. While digital currencies like Bitcoin and Ethereum offer faster and more efficient solutions to make payments, they also come with quite considerable risks: extreme volatility in prices, uncertainty regarding regulation and the growing threat of cybersecurity. DeFi platforms, by their very nature self-sovereign and independent of any traditional financial intermediary, are increasingly popular alternatives to centralized finance systems. In addition, without any regulatory oversight of DeFi markets, these organizations are more at risk from fraud, vulnerability to liquidity and holes within their smart contracts. The inability of organizations involved in digital currency transactions to practice poor risk management results in their inability to avoid market manipulation that creates financial loss. As digital currencies continue to increase with the growth of DeFi, proactive service organization risk management as a countermeasure against various risks is needed. This includes surveillance of markets, change in regulatory compliances and addition of security features within to keep fraudsters and cyberattacks at bay.

6.4. Increased Scrutiny by Regulators and Challenges from Global Compliance

Digital finance is one sector where growth is rapid. Different regulatory bodies around the world are putting more stringent control to ensure stability in the financial sectors, consumer protection and prevention of illegal activities. But the regulatory environment still remains fragmented, with different jurisdictions adopting different stances on digital finance regulation. For instance, while the European Union has introduced the MiCA regulation that has established a legislative framework to regulate digital currencies, others have not yet adopted such holistic frameworks. Service organizations operating across several states are thus facing Gordian complexity and, in some instances, conflicting regulatory demands. This is where organizations are turning to RegTech solutions for automating compliance processes, timely reporting and keeping up with regulatory changes. Integrating RegTech into operations would better position an organization to reduce the risks of non-compliance and less operational exposure to follow global regulatory requirements.

6.5. Cybersecurity: An Agenda of Great Concern in Management of Risk within Digital Finance

As increasingly more business is relying on digital platforms for offering their services, cybersecurity remains a key concern for financial service organizations. Cyberattacks on financial institutions have increased in frequency and complexity, taking on many forms, including phishing scams, ransomware attacks and DDoS attacks. According to industry reports, global cybercrime damages will cost $10.5 trillion annually by 2025, thereby setting up a strong case for cybersecurity measures in digital finance. Current trends in the management of cybersecurity risks involve the adoption of zero-trust security frameworks, assuming that threats could emanate from both inside and outside. This approach would involve continuous verification of users and devices accessing an organization's systems to reduce the possibility of unauthorized access. In addition, the organisations are investing in advanced encryption technologies and secure cloud computing solutions to ensure data protection for sensitive financial information. AI in cybersecurity also enables the organization to stay prepared for real-time threat detection and fast response in case potential breaches are detected. Automating threat detection and incident response with AI-driven systems significantly reduces damage due to cyberattacks, hence minimizing financial loss and retaining customer trust.

7. CONCLUSION

For this chapter, the complex interdependency between the field of digital finance and the operations of risk management, compliance and sustainability are explored against their very important roles in service organization protection. Digital finance continues to enhance efficiency, accessibility and innovation at an unprecedented scale in service delivery. However, with this scaling up, risks have also increased, including cyber threats, operational vulnerabilities and regulatory challenges. For this reason, it would be apt for organizations to adopt an integrated risk management framework that integrates robust compliance along with forward-looking principles of sustainability. Various case studies of high-performing organizations underline the appropriateness of the approach and prove that effective proactive risk mitigation and compliance safeguards not only against financial fraud but also guarantees long-term resilience. The underlying core-interconnection of risk management, compliance and sustainability is for organization success in the digital finance environment. Stronger frameworks of risk management are fortified by conformable compliance frameworks that help organizations maintain a valid legal standard, keeping pace with changing requirements and ensuring that operational and cyber risks are avoided. Principles of ESG factors that help solidify long-term risk mitigation comprise sustainability. But with the holistic approach, besides expecting better immediate and future challenges, service organizations can actually do well amid technological advancement and changing regulatory landscapes.

REFERENCES

Akartuna, E. A., Johnson, S. D., & Thornton, A. E. (2023). The money laundering and terrorist financing risks of new and disruptive technologies: A futures-oriented scoping review. *Security Journal*, *36*(4), 615–650. PMID: 40479271

Alabi, A. M., Oguntoyinbo, F. N., Abioye, K. M., John-Ladega, A. A., Obiki-Osafiele, A. N., & Daraojimba, C. (2023). Risk management in Africa's financial landscape: A review. *International Journal of Advanced Economics*, *5*(8), 239–257.

Bakare, S. S., Adeniyi, A. O., Akpuokwe, C. U., & Eneh, N. E. (2024). Data privacy laws and compliance: A comparative review of the EU GDPR and USA regulations. *Computer Science & IT Research Journal*, *5*(3), 528–543.

Benedek, P., & Bognár, F. (2024). Compliance Risk Assessment–Results of a Comprehensive Literature Review. *Acta Polytechnica Hungarica*, *21*(6).

Bueno, L. A., Sigahi, T. F., Rampasso, I. S., Leal Filho, W., & Anholon, R. (2024). Impacts of digitization on operational efficiency in the banking sector: Thematic analysis and research agenda proposal. *International Journal of Information Management Data Insights*, *4*(1), 100230.

Chueca Vergara, C., & Ferruz Agudo, L. (2021). Fintech and sustainability: Do they affect each other? *Sustainability*, *13*(13), 7012.

Comunale, M., & Manera, A. (2024). The economic impacts and the regulation of AI: A review of the academic literature and policy actions.

Erkan-Barlow, A., & Wells-Dietel, B. P. (2023). The Current State of Cyber Insurance and Regulation in the Context of Investment Efficiency and Moral Hazard: A Literature Review. *Journal of Insurance Regulation*. https://content. *naic. org/sites/default/files/cipr-jir-2023-4. pdf*

Gounari, M., Stergiopoulos, G., Pipyros, K., & Gritzalis, D. (2024). Harmonizing open banking in the European Union: An analysis of PSD2 compliance and interrelation with cybersecurity frameworks and standards. *International Cybersecurity Law Review*, *5*(1), 79–120.

Ibrahim, H. (2022). A Review on the Mechanism Mitigating and Eliminating Internet Crimes using Modern Technologies: Mitigating Internet crimes using modern technologies. *Wasit Journal of Computer and Mathematics Science*, *1*(3), 50–68.

Javaheri, D., Fahmideh, M., Chizari, H., Lalbakhsh, P., & Hur, J. (2023). Cybersecurity threats in FinTech: A systematic review. *Expert Systems with Applications*, ●●●, 122697.

Katsaliaki, K., Galetsi, P., & Kumar, S. (2022). Supply chain disruptions and resilience: A major review and future research agenda. *Annals of Operations Research*, ●●●, 1–38. PMID: 33437110

Li, J., Maiti, A., & Fei, J. (2023). Features and Scope of Regulatory Technologies: Challenges and Opportunities with Industrial Internet of Things. *Future Internet*, *15*(8), 256.

Lyle, P. (2024). GLOBAL TERRORISM AND NATURAL DISASTERS: Path to Environmental Sustainability, Social and Economic Justice.

Manohar, S., Nag, I., Mittal, A., & Nair, A. J. (2023, 18-19 Aug. 2023). Omni Channeling Healthcare: Chaining Details, Information and Predictions for Extemporize Service Delivery. 2023 7th International Conference On Computing, Communication, Control And Automation (ICCUBEA), Michailidou, F. (2020). RegTech and SupTech: Opportunities and Challenges in the Financial Sector.

Mızrak, F. (2023). Integrating cybersecurity risk management into strategic management: A comprehensive literature review. *Research Journal of Business and Management*, *10*(3), 98–108.

Molaro, M. (2023). Analysis of the Open API services in Europe.

Nag, I., Manohar, S., Mittal, A., & Nair, A. J. (2024). Thought clarity to execution chaos: A review on core competencies of grassroots entrepreneurs for instigation, growth and sustainability of startups. *Journal of Innovation and Entrepreneurship*, *13*(1), 89. DOI: 10.1186/s13731-024-00453-w

Nair, A. J., & Manohar, S. (2024). Green Service Consumption: Unlocking Customer Expectations on Technological Transformations Enhancing Purchase Experience in Retail Store. *International Journal of Information Management Data Insights*, *4*(2), 100277. https://doi.org/https://doi.org/10.1016/j.jjimei.2024.100277

Nair, A. J., Manohar, S., & Chaudhry, R. (2024a). Role of Knowledge Management in Enhancing the Effectiveness of the Gig Economy. In Ordóñez de Pablos, P., Almunawar, M. N., & Anshari, M. (Eds.), *Strengthening Sustainable Digitalization of Asian Economy and Society* (pp. 161–175). IGI Global., DOI: 10.4018/979-8-3693-1942-0.ch009

Nair, A. J., Manohar, S., & Chaudhry, R. (2024b). Securing the Metaverse: Exploring the Role of Artificial Intelligence in Mitigating Emerging Threats in Manufacturing and Service Industries. In B. Verma, A. Mittal, M. Raman, & B. Sindhav (Eds.), *Augmenting Retail Reality, Part B: Blockchain, AR, VR, and AI* (pp. 67-84). Emerald Publishing Limited. https://doi.org/DOI: 10.1108/978-1-83608-708-320241013

Nair, A. J., Manohar, S., & Mittal, A. (2023, 14-16 Dec. 2023). Robotic Vision with Micro Expression Analysis: Revolutionizing Customer Experiences in the Tourism and Hospitality Industry. 2023 IEEE Technology & Engineering Management Conference - Asia Pacific (TEMSCON-ASPAC),

Nair, A. J., Manohar, S., Mittal, A., & Ahmed, W. (Eds.). (2024). *Balancing Automation and Human Interaction in Modern Marketing*. IGI Global., DOI: 10.4018/979-8-3693-2276-5

Nair, A. J., Manohar, S., Mittal, A., & Chaudhry, R. (2024). Unleashing Digital Frontiers: Bridging Realities of Augmented Reality, Virtual Reality, and the Metaverse. In Krishnan, C., Behl, A., Dash, S., & Yadav, P. D. (Eds.), *The Metaverse Dilemma: Challenges and Opportunities for Business and Society* (pp. 85–112). Emerald Publishing Limited., DOI: 10.1108/978-1-83797-524-220241006

Nair, A. J., & Rao, A. B. S. (2025). Mitigating Financial Anomalies Dimensions Vulnerability and Stratagem in Service Organizations: Policy and Ethical Considerations in Public Administration. In Akkucuk, U., & Onder, M. (Eds.), *AI Driven Tools for Sustainable Public Administration* (pp. 361–388). IGI Global., DOI: 10.4018/979-8-3693-8372-8.ch013

Nair, A.J., Manohar, S., & Mittal, A. (2024). AI-enabled FinTech for innovative sustainability: promoting organizational sustainability practices in digital accounting and finance. *International Journal of Accounting & Information Management, ahead-of-print*(ahead-of-print). https://doi.org/DOI: 10.1108/IJAIM-05-2024-0172

Orelaja, A., Nasimbwa, R., & OMOYIN, D. D. (2024). Enhancing Cybersecurity Infrastructure, A Case Study on Safeguarding Financial Transactions. *Australian Journal of Wireless Technologies, Mobility and Security, 1*(1).

Pandey, A. B., Tripathi, A., & Vashist, P. C. (2022). A survey of cyber security trends, emerging technologies and threats. *Cyber Security in Intelligent Computing and Communications*, 19-33.

Rabbani, M. R. (2022). Fintech innovations, scope, challenges, and implications in Islamic Finance: A systematic analysis. *International Journal of Computing and Digital Systems*, *11*(1), 1–28.

RAMAKRISHNAN, R., & LAKSHMI, C. (2023). UNVEILING THE WORLD OF ONLINE PAYMENT GATEWAYS. SEKULIĆ, J., & LENDÁK, I. An Overview of Cyber Insurance Field Cyber Insurance as.

Sharifi, A., Allam, Z., Bibri, S. E., & Khavarian-Garmsir, A. R. (2024). Smart cities and sustainable development goals (SDGs): A systematic literature review of co-benefits and trade-offs. *Cities (London, England)*, *146*, 104659.

Singh, A. V., Varma, M., Rai, M., Pratap Singh, S., Bansod, G., Laux, P., & Luch, A. (2024). Advancing Predictive Risk Assessment of Chemicals via Integrating Machine Learning, Computational Modeling, and Chemical/Nano-Quantitative Structure-Activity Relationship Approaches. *Advanced Intelligent Systems*, *6*(4), 2300366.

Yaacoub, J.-P. A., Noura, H. N., Salman, O., & Chehab, A. (2022). Robotics cyber security: Vulnerabilities, attacks, countermeasures, and recommendations. *International Journal of Information Security*, *21*(1), 115–158. PMID: 33776611

Yeoh, P. (2020). Banks' vulnerabilities to money laundering activities. *Journal of Money Laundering Control*, *23*(1), 122–135.

Zhou, J., Chen, C., Li, L., Zhang, Z., & Zheng, X. (2022). FinBrain 2.0: When finance meets trustworthy AI. *Frontiers of Information Technology & Electronic Engineering*, *23*(12), 1747–1764.

Chapter 7

The Impact of COVID-19 on Financial Markets and the Role of Regulation in Recovery

Jyoti Rani
https://orcid.org/0000-0002-5577-7808
Parul University, India

Ramratan Guru
https://orcid.org/0000-0001-6142-2643
Mody University of Science and Technology, India

Bhaskar Mitra
Parul University, India

Sakthivel Santhanam
Presidency University, India

ABSTRACT

The COVID-19 pandemic triggered unprecedented disruptions in global financial markets, characterized by steep asset price declines, heightened volatility, and a liquidity crisis. As governments prioritized public health, financial systems faced severe strain, prompting swift regulatory and monetary interventions. This chapter explores the pandemic's impact on stock, bond, commodity, and currency markets and investigates the behavioral shifts in investor strategies during the crisis. It analyzes the temporary and long-term regulatory measures implemented by governments, central banks, and international bodies to stabilize markets and support

DOI: 10.4018/979-8-3373-1404-4.ch007

economic recovery. Key trends, such as the rise of digital finance and sustainable investments, are examined alongside the challenges of addressing emerging risks like cyber threats and climate change. The chapter highlights the evolution of financial regulation post-pandemic, emphasizing the importance of adaptive and resilient frameworks to ensure long-term market stability in an increasingly interconnected and digital economy.

INTRODUCTION

Since March 2020, the COVID-19 pandemic has already transformed the world and of financial markets, with the biggest disruptions and volatility ever seen. Things were different in the globe, and all the sectors and economies were affected by the pandemic resulting in economic depressions and changes in the market dynamics. Financial markets were impacted by the global response to the pandemic, including lockdowns and other policy interventions, further emphasizing the interdependence of global economies. To this end, the following sections review the impact of the pandemic on the financial markets, synthesized from various studies.

Volatile Markets and Economic Disruption

The COVID-19 pandemic brought unprecedented damage to economies across the globe, with the output of countries having declined dramatically across sectors. The hardest-hit sectors ranged from charter real industries such as forestry and fisheries to hotel and restaurant services (N. Sun et al., 2024).

The overall equity index returns discovery showed a significant negative impact on global equity markets. In European countries, the effect was more significant than in East Asian economies (Hui & Chan, 2022).

The COVID-19 pandemic has resulted in an increase in the volatility connectedness of global stock markets, with stronger connections being observed across continents. But China was almost apathetic to this volatility network until late 2020 (Chen, 2022).

Policy Responses and the Track Towards Recovery

The crises policies aided adaptation by showing stability in strategic corporate choices capital supply and corporate taxes and individual choices individual subsidies in response to the pandemic's economic impact (N. Sun et al., 2024).

Public health responses were key in managing the pandemic and restoring confidence among economic agents. It will require global coordination in managing pandemic challenges and stabilizing economies (McKibbin & Fernando, 2023).

But in fact, realized GDP paths for 2020 and 2021 tracked scenarios, confirming the significance of optimal policy responses (McKibbin & Fernando, 2023).

Emerging Trends and Sectoral Impacts

Food insecurity: Effects guided by income shocks rather than effects of prices in low- and lower-middle-income countries and effects were exacerbated by the pandemic. Markets were further disrupted by trade policies restricting food imports and exports (Du et al., 2024).Finding ramifications reverberated across global supply chains, interrupting every linkage from the sourcing of raw materials to the delivery of consumer goods. But after international trade was initially deaccelerated, a global dynamic gradually tended to r establish, indicating no acceleration in the trends of deglobalization. Three Industries showed resilience, seeing positive CARs cumulatively despite the uncertain climate. This means that there are opportunities for certain sectors to develop in the middle of the pandemic.

Broader Implications and Future Considerations

The COVID-19 pandemic has highlighted the susceptibility of global trading systems to health crises and the need for sound policy structures to minimize the impacts. Despite severe economic disruptions due to the pandemic, many sectors emerged resilient with the prospect of recovering thanks to coordinated global efforts. Lessons from this experience can be used to implement future actions aimed at improving market stability and economic resilience when faced with similar challenges in the future.

Initial Economic Disruptions Caused by the Pandemic.

Global disruptions occurred due to the COVID-19 pandemic, affecting sectors and demographics of different combinations. The initial impact of the pandemic resulted in massive economic closure, unemployment surge, and productivity drop in several industries. Governments around the world instituted fiscal and monetary measures to counter these effects, but the economic damage was acute and uneven across regions and age groups. The next sections describe the first economic disruptions of the pandemic.

Global Economic Impact

- Pandemic shocks to labour and sectoral productivity, consumption, and government expenditure have led to a reduction in GDP in many countries. G-Cubed simulated these effects and showed how public health measures played the most important role in controlling the pandemic and restoring confidence in the economy (McKibbin & Fernando, 2023).
- The repercussions were uneven, with developed countries seeing substantial declines in investment and the fiscal context helping to buffer the effects.

Disruptions in the United States Economy

- For the U.S. the pandemic resulted in widespread economic shutdowns where jobless claims soared. The government responded with stimulus payments as well as expanded unemployment insurance and programs like the Pay check Protection Program (PPP) to support businesses and individuals.
- Displacement was very widespread, and younger age groups faced the highest rates of job loss. The economic toll was more geographically spread in contrast to mortality impacts that were concentrated in states such as New York and New Jersey.

Real Economy & Financial Markets

- Financial markets underwent extreme dislocations, leading to massive monetary and fiscal actions. The unique nature of the pandemic spurred a wealth of research measuring its economic impact and policy response (Goldstein et al., 2021).
- On the upside, though the economic ruptures were ugly, the presence of fiscal space and policy response played an immensely significant role in attenuating economic damage. That the effects are different for different demographics and in different geographic areas indicates that we need a more tailored policy response to the different challenges posed by such global catastrophes.

Regulatory response crises Financial Market COVID-19 pandemic data Understanding the effects of the COVID-19 pandemic on financial markets and the ensuing regulatory responses is of utmost value. Financial systems reveal essential vulnerabilities that the pandemic has exposed, such as over-leveraging, poor risk management and dependence on specific sectors. By studying these failings, policymakers and market participants can formulate plans to create more resilient systems. The acute volatility we have witnessed in the financial markets during the course of the crisis also acts as an important lesson in terms of market behavior, liquidity strains, credit risks and asset price movements during periods of stress. Studying and assessing the impact of government and central bank interventions, including interest rate cuts and fiscal stimulus, is important to understand how to best respond in the future.

This is particularly relevant given that the crisis brought the urgent need to adjust regulatory frameworks to the new and old risks such as risks to digital finance and global interconnectivity. It also spurred interest in sustainable and socially responsible investing, making it critical to understand how financial markets can align with broader environmental, social and governance (ESG) objectives. Transparent analysis of the pandemic's impact bolsters investor confidence, contributing to the continued participation of investors in the markets. Last but not least, the pandemic illustrated the critical importance of global collaboration to minimize systemic risks providing crucial lessons learned for unifying worldwide regulatory regimes. Through the analysis of these factors, stakeholders can create stronger financial infrastructures that can avert similar shocks in the future.

FINANCIAL MARKET IMPACT OF COVID-19

Stock Markets

The global stock markets have been hit hard by the COVID-19 pandemic, experiencing a great deal of turmoil and volatility. This uncertainty induced by the pandemic resulted in heavy losses and high volatility across key global stock indices. This volatility was exacerbated by the rapid spread of the virus, government-mandated lock downs and economic slowdown that followed. The pandemic heightened these effects due to the "spillover" of fluctuations from global financial markets. The next sections will go into the details of these events.

Market Dips And Volatility

- The outbreak of COVID-19 caused record-breaking spikes in stock market volatility and devastating negative returns in developed economies. The analysis using the GJR-GARCH model showed that the volatility was clustered, and the leverage effect existed, indicating that the negative news had a more significant impact on volatility than positive news (Kayani et al., 2024).

- Stock prices went into free fall, with world markets down by about 30 percent from mid-February to mid-March 2020. This drop was succeeded by a partial recovery, nonetheless, volatility continued high through period (Davis et al., 2021).
- The effects of the pandemic on stock returns and volatility have not been uniform across countries. Such as the more devastating effects on the United States compared to China (in particular containment measures and economics response (Davis et al., 2021) (Fasanya et al., 2023).

Transmission of Volatility and Network Effects

- Generalized outbreak of pandemic has fed through the volatility spillover effects among international diverse stock markets. The historical correlation of these markets grew, reflected in a denser volatility spillover network and a smaller network diameter, which again confirmed a faster spread of volatility information (Lan et al., 2023).
- Using the Diebold-Yilmaz volatility network model, the level of global connectedness was high during the whole year of 2020 and international connectedness was stronger across continents. Indeed, until late 2020, China was relatively isolated from this network, indicating that it was not a major source of volatility spillover in the pandemic (Cheng et al., 2022).

Market Reactions and Asymmetric Effects

- The asymmetric influence of the pandemic on stock market volatility, where negative shocks (e.g., death rates) was found to have a greater impact than positive shocks (e.g., recovery rates).
- According to the analysis with the AR(1)-GARCH (1,1) model, fear of COVID-19 was a significant contributor to stock market volatility, with 1% rise in COVID-19 cases resulting in 0.8% drop in stock returns (Latif et al., 2021).
- Moreover, the quantile regression analysis reaffirmed the positive effect of new COVID-19 cases and deaths on market volatility at higher quantiles, which highlighted the necessity for global policies to stabilize the market.

The COVID-19 pandemic resulted in dramatic declines and greater volatility of global stock markets, but it also underscored the resilience and adaptability of these markets. Though it was devastating at first, many forgiving markets started to rebound as governments and central banks rolled out monetary and fiscal packages to cushion economies. This recovery came as a patchwork, with some countries and sectors recovering more quickly than others, an indicator of varying styles of pandemic management and economic architectures. Most importantly, the pandemic highlighted the role that pre-emptive policy responses and international coordination can play in dampening the impact of future shocks on financial markets.

Bond Markets

COVID-19 had far-reaching effects on financial markets, with a pronounced impact on yields, credit spreads, and government bonds. Origins of the pandemic-induced market disruptions were most characterized by extreme volatility and elicited historic intervention from central banks in an effort to stabilize markets. Different parts of the bond market reacted differently, with each required to deal with the distinct challenge the pandemic presented. Here, they are discussed in detail, the key aspects of these changes.

Changes in Yields

- Government Bond Yields: The pandemic has shown as varied a picture in government bond yields as in M.A.D. countries. Yields in the United States rose, a product of increased perceptions of risk and economic uncertainty. On the contrary, yields fell in Germany, signalling a flight to safety and higher demand for safe assets (Zhou et al., 2022). Yields on euro area sovereign bonds also fell because of the Eurosystem's asset purchase programs, although the impact varied across countries Depending on their credit-ratings (Wu et al., 2022).
- Sovereign Yield Curves in EM: In response to the pandemic, emerging market sovereign borrowing costs rose, reflecting increased default considerations and greater global financial interdependence. Yet, policy interventions contributed to the stabilization of the bond risk premia in time (Candelon & Moura, 2023).

Credit Spreads

- Corporate Credit Energy: The bond buying by Buckingham The Fed, in particular, on corporate bonds crushed credit spreads due to falling default risk. On the other hand, the result for the liquidity channel was mixed, suggesting that market segmentation by credit ratings had made initial reactions depend on that ranking.

- Municipal Bond Spreads: Municipal bond spreads in the United States rose following announcements of state lockdowns, indicating an increase in the risk premiums demanded by investors. These spreads helped to cap the steep rise in spreads during the pandemic, with the assistance of the Federal Reserve's Municipal Liquidity Facility.
- Tranquillity of the CDS market: Sovereign credit default swap (CDS) spreads have widened increasingly since the pandemic, especially in developing countries with weaker healthcare systems. While political responses somewhat buffer this effect, they also facilitate spread expansion.

Government Bond Responses

- Federal Reserve Interventions: The Federal Reserve played a crucial role in stabilizing bond markets through a range of liquidity measures, including the purchase of corporate bonds. The March 23 announcement moved investment-grade debt, whereas the April 9 announcement had consequences for both investment-grade and high-yield bonds (Haddad et al., 2020).
- Eurosystem Asset Buy-Downs: The ECB's asset purchase programs significantly compressed sovereign bond spreads within the euro area, with countries with lower ratings particularly enjoying the benefits. These interventions helped avoid financial fragmentation during the pandemic.

However, massive disruptions to bond markets during the pandemic may have been offset to a large extent by fast and decisive action by central banks that helped to stabilize these markets. In an increasingly interconnected global economy and capital market where the tendencies of an economy can affect other markets around the world, the disparate effects provide a complex picture of the financial system and the difficulty in navigating a global crisis. The pandemic highlighted the need for coordination among policy interventions to manage financial instability and facilitate economic recovery.

Commodity Markets

Different commodities such as oil and gold faced significant implications during the pandemic, impacting global commodity markets. U.S. treasuries, equities, commodities, and the rest of it, these markets experienced crippling volatility and price dislocations as the pandemic wreaked havoc on the underlying economy. Crude oil prices plummeted on fears of demand destruction through travel bans and economic slowdowns, while gold, historically a safe-haven investment-variable in volatility but ultimately a risk stabilizer. Other commodities, from industrial metals to food, also went through price fluctuations, though not by the same margins. The effects of these changes are outlined in the following sections.

Oil Prices

- An oil price shock happened due to the pandemic(killing oil prices based on a crash in demand, while temporary travel and lockdown takes place all over the world (Figiel et al., 2023) (Rajput et al., 2021).
- The crude oil market emerged as a significant source of contagion risk in volatility, with a considerable increase in volatility spillovers during the pandemic (Tan et al., 2022).

Gold Prices

- The safe-haven property of gold became evident during the pandemic, where one of its markets acted as a risk stabilizer even with higher volatility (Tan et al., 2022).
- In the long run, the gold market continued to transmit shocks and kept its relevance to financial networks during the pandemic (Ha, 2022).

Other Commodities

- Minerals and food commodities also fell in price, though not as sharply as oil. Because of its indirect relation to economic activities, the agriculture sector was relatively less affected (Rajput et al., 2021).
- As a result of the pandemic, the effects on the prices of food and energy were also visible, with energy prices being affected to a greater extent than food prices, and the global economic growth having differential effects on sectors (Figiel et al., 2023).

Currency Markets

COVID-19 pandemic has had significant implications in exchange rates and capital flows and has hit emerging market economies (EMEs) especially hard. The pandemic led to sharp capital outflows and exchange rate volatility, with the EMEs being more affected by these developments than advanced economies. These fluctuations were simply the result of the pandemic's direct impacts and the myriad of fiscal and monetary policy responses being enacted across the globe. The next sections discuss these dynamics in detail.

Exchange Rate Fluctuations

- Exchange rates depreciated on the back of COVID-19 intensification, particularly in severely afflicted countries. Containment measures and stabilization policies meanwhile contributed to currency value adjustments (Klose, 2023).
- Stricter movement restrictions and healthcare measures have led to local currencies depreciation and expansionary fiscal policies led to local currencies appreciation in general (Klose, 2023).

Capital Flow Dynamics

- From March onwards, EMEs experienced sudden stops in capital flows, with rapid dollar funding outflows that were larger in scale than during the Global Financial Crisis (Akinci et al., 2020).
- As the majority of the capital outflows due to the pandemic were motivated by decreased portfolio investments invested by non-bank financial intermediaries.
- The quantitative easing and fiscal stimulus measures across advanced economies had a positive spillover effect both helping to stabilize capital flows and boost stock markets in EMEs (Beirne et al., 2021).

Policy Responses and Effects

- To respond to the shock of capital outflows and the associated economic downturn, EMEs adopted expansionary fiscal and monetary policies (Martin et al., 2020).
- As sovereign bond yields fell in advanced countries and stock markets were propped up thanks to central banks' quantitative easing in those countries, this indirectly benefited EMEs (Beirne et al., 2021).

Though the resolution of the pandemic may ultimately result in market corrections, the research indicates that some of these impacts on financial markets and capital flows could prove to be permanent, especially in the case of EMEs (Beirne et al., 2021). This points towards the importance of extensive global financial architecture to deal future international financial turmoil.

Investor Behavior

The COVID-19 pandemic has had a profound impact on investor behaviour resulting in increased risk aversion and movement toward safety. Investors used this period to re-assess their portfolio allocations, frequently opting away from riskier assets towards comparatively safer investments. Importantly, this added behaviour change was uniquely amplified due to the nature of the pandemic as compared to previous crises. The next sections focus on these changes on specific levels.

Flight to Safety

- This led investors to engage in a classic "flight to safety", reallocating investments from stocks to gold, which is a traditional safe haven in times of uncertainty. On one hand, gold's importance as an asset to shield against pandemics increased, evidenced by greater volatility in gold prices, which indicates greater demand (Löwen et al., 2021).
- The causality between stock market volatility and gold-price volatility appeared most profoundly in that positive shocks of stock market volatility transmit to positive shocks of gold volatility propagating the flight to safety (Löwen et al., 2021).

Risk Aversion

- Investor risk aversion, as reflected in the actions of female investors in the U.S., increased significantly during the pandemic as they slashed unpopular risk assets. This transformation illustrates that the pandemic is a negative externality which affects the portfolio choice (Apergis, 2024).
- Moreover, it has been found that investors were regret averse and exhibited conservatism while investing during the pandemic, reinforcing the general theme of increased risk aversion.

Changes in Portfolio Allocations

- After the market crash, investor expectations about short-term economic and stock market performance slowly got more pessimistic, and investors reallocated their portfolios accordingly. In contrast, long-run expectations were stable on the whole, indicating that there was not a drastic overhaul of portfolio decisions and parameterizations (Giglio et al., 2021).

- Investor sentiment was positive in medical stocks which was known from coronavirus-related news and economic announcements, as a result medical stock portfolios in some markets had a positive effect (X. Sun et al., 2021).

The pandemic created a general trend towards risk aversion and safety, but it also illustrated the complexity of the investor psyche. For example, some investors went into safe havens, while others stayed invested or even added to sectors seen as coronavirus winners, like all things medical. That duality reflects the different ways in which people are responding to the crisis, as informed by their perception of risk and the businesses that are presenting themselves in the market.

THE ROLE OF GOVERNMENT AND CENTRAL BANKS

Governments and central banks have intervened extensively in attempts to stabilize economies and lay the groundwork for recovery. The economic policy response to the pandemic induced economic crisis was multi-dimensional involving both fiscal and monetary policies to address disruptions in the financial markets and the wider economy. Such a response has been vital in addressing the short-term effects of the pandemic and in laying the foundation for recovery. This article walks through the roles played by government and central banks, the financial market impacts, and the regulatory measures to facilitate recovery.

Government Interventions

- Various policies have been implemented by governments, globally, while combating economic recovery due to COVID-19 pandemic. This includes job retention schemes, business financial support, and sector-targeted assistance to avoid bankruptcies and widespread unemployment (Naqvi, 2022).
- Fiscal intervention policies have been crucial to stabilise financial markets, and in particular, corporate credit market bail outs have averted deeper crises by curbing bankruptcies of large corporations and maintaining stability in the financial sector (Sharma et al., 2021).
- Moreover, the impact of government policies vis-à-vis banks' lending decisions, which often involve procyclical measures that can both amplify economic shocks and deepen the recession, underscores the significance of coordinated policy responses to mitigate the severity of economic downturns.

Central Banks' Role

- To bolster economies during the pandemic, central banks have adopted expansionary monetary policies, such as by engaging in asset purchases and keeping interest rates at record lows. These measures have been essential to financing growing public debt and restoring financial market stability (Echarte Fernández et al., 2021).
- In light of the rising competition of decentralized cryptocurrencies, the design and introduction of central bank digital currencies (CBDCs) is being contemplated; for instance, in the case of projects like the digital euro (Echarte Fernández et al., 2021).
- In addition, due to the inconsistency of monetary policy interventions, it has caused the stock market to have more volatility while the bond market has given a positive effect (Liu et al., 2022).

Impact on Financial Markets

- Widespread price swings and market dislocations in equity and fixed-income markets are among the most notable disruptions in financial markets due to the pandemic (Gormsen & Koijen, 2023).
- With the pandemic, financial markets have witnessed increasing volatility, with fiscal and monetary policy countermeasures critical to stabilisation of these markets (Goldstein et al., 2021).
- Furthermore, the pandemic has underscored the role of regulatory frameworks in supporting stability in financial markets and averting financial fragility, while studies are being conducted to assess these measures in (Goldstein et al., 2021).

Governance Interventions and Recovery

- Strengthening of Regulatory Frameworks for Financial Market Recovery and Resilience Furthermore, the COVID-19 pandemic has highlighted the need for strong regulatory frameworks that support recovery and resilience in the financial market. These include the measures taken to strengthen energy security and shift to more secure forms of energy solutions that are essential for economic resilience amid dual crises of COVID-19 and the energy crisis.
- These shifts in global finance in the forms of regulatory slowdown intertwined with the development of financial technologies are likely to reshape the future of finance, the structure of financial centers and state-finance nexus as well (Wójcik & Ioannou, 2020).

Although the immediate priority has been to stabilize financial markets and support the recovery of the economy, the pandemic has also brought into sharp focus the need for long-term strategies to bolster economic resilience. This also means confronting systemic risks, including that of climate change, and making financial systems more resilient for the crisis to come. It is the government policies, the response of the central banks and regulatory measures that will be decisive in determining the nature of the post-pandemic economy.

REGULATION AND FINANCIAL MARKETS: A HISTORICAL CONTEXT

The context of finance and also most of the history of regulation has been also the case. They have become incessantly molded through the years determining the general structure of finance, and directing the changing of finance. Crisis and Reform in Financial Regulation: Past, Present, and Future Read this answer for a deep dive into the historical context of financial regulation, then read about key developments that shaped financial markets.

Technological Advancements and Early Financial Regulation

- Let me now trace a brief history of American financial regulation. Technological revolutions like the railway and the telegraph helped unify these markets and resulted in national-scale financial crises (Vetter, 2023).
- In this era, there was little regulation over financial markets, leading to stock price manipulation and poor corporate disclosure. The absence of regulation, however, often resulted in crises and an unstable market (Previts & Bricker, 1994).

Centralized Regulation and the Great Depression

- Even before the Great Depression, there were significant moves toward centralized regulation, with federal agencies like the Securities and Exchange Commission (SEC) being created to stabilize the financial system. The period of 1933–2008 enabled new New York financial headquarters, and new mass, growing middle class, by restructured regulations. (Vetter, 2023).
- This one-size-fits-all approach13 to regulation didn't come without hurdles. Challenges in balancing the interests of the financial sector participants and the regulators occasionally resulted in less than sufficient regulatory out-

comes, indicating a complexity of effective regulation (Peretz & Schroedel, 2009).

The Shift to Micro-Prudential Regulation

- Starting from the 1960s, the macro-prudential approach became gradually replaced by a micro-prudential one, heavily influenced by the private interest theory of regulation. This transformation played a major role in the 2007–2008 financial crisis, since micro-prudential regulations did not take into account the inherent global character of banking activities (Harnay & Scialom, 2016).
- The crisis highlighted the importance of developing a more integrated regulatory approach that takes into account the systemic risk associated with financial transactions (Harnay & Scialom, 2016).

The Digital Age and the Challenges of Regulation

- From 2008 to 2020 we saw the emergence of financial technologies like bitcoin and crowdfunding that exceeded existing regulatory structures. The period of digital finance revealed the struggles of traditional regulation to keep pace with the myriad complexities of digital finance (Vetter, 2023).
- This led to a dichotomy where market forces and regulations were increasingly in conflict, with agents of the market frequently working to avoid regulatory implementation. This phenomenon highlights the importance of flexible and reactive regulatory systems.

A Perspective on Financial Regulation

- Specific views of financial regulation in history argue evolving financial regulation because of changing market environments and technology. Integrating historical analysis into regulatory decision-making can improve the effectiveness of regulatory governance.
- However, the COVID-19 pandemic experience proved that robustly designed regulatory frameworks are resilient against challenges, and those frameworks need to improve and adjust constantly (Moloney, 2024).

Historical analysis provides useful insights into the evolution of financial regulation but also highlights the limits of past approaches. Yet as the tug-of-fall continues between market forces and regulatory scrutiny, it is unlikely that regulation will attain perfection. A nuanced understanding of the interaction between economic theories, technological advancement, and regulatory frameworks is critical for creating effective regulatory strategies. This view underscores the importance of flexible regulation that can adjust to the constantly changing landscape of financial markets and the challenges they pose.

REGULATORY RESPONSES TO COVID-19

The COVID-19 pandemic spurred a myriad of regulatory actions to stabilize financial markets, many of which were highly disturbed by the crisis. These ranged from fiscal and monetary policy responses to government containment measures, to regulations on financial markets. The success and impact of these measures were region and market condition dependent. In the next two sections, we outline the key regulatory responses and their implications on financial markets over the course of the pandemic.

Interventions Using Fiscal and Monetary Policy

- Interest rates were slashed to near-zero levels and massive asset purchase programs were introduced in an effort to provide liquidity and calm financial markets. Monetary policy was deemed effective in terms of its ability to support the real economy and reduce pressures on government finances particularly through asset purchases in Europe (Klose & Tillmann, 2021). Meanwhile in the UK, the Bank of England mulled radical money-printing operations to stave off the economic emergency (Paterson et al., 2024).
- Fiscal Policy: Governments announced spending packages in an effort to cushion the economic impact of the pandemic. Such economic measures, such as direct payments to businesses and households, led to the relief of the market by increasing the confidence of investors (Goldstein et al., 2021) (Klose & Tillmann, 2021).

Containment Measures by Governments

- Stringency and Economic Support The oxford covid-19 government response tracker noted the importance of containment and closure policies, economic support, and health measures in mitigating the pandemic's impact on financial markets. Although containment measures disproportionately dented economic activity and stirred up negative market reactions initially, they eventually aided in stabilizing market through new normal adjustment by investors to these measures (Beer et al., 2023).

- Differential Effects across Countries: How government interventions affected different countries. Examples include areas like China and the USA, where anti-epidemic policies exacerbated market liquidity conditions, but pre-COVID situations in Finland, Hong Kong, and Japan, where anti-epidemic policies alleviated them (Li et al., 2023). In developing economies, policy responses were more common in wealthier and more populous countries, and those countries that were in monetary unions reacted more quickly (Feyen et al., 2021).

Regulations Specific to Financial Markets

- Interventions for Market Functioning: To curb the volatility in the market, things like short selling bans and circuit-breakers were introduced. Such interventions were shown to enhance the effectiveness of containment measures on the stock market performance after the first wave of the pandemic.
- Support by Sector: In developed countries, specific support for small and medium-sized enterprises (SMEs) came first, followed by stimulus packages to prevent the pandemic from affecting financial markets. Financial support for vulnerable households in developing countries was recognised as being critical (Zhao et al., 2022).
- Investor Sentiment: Investor psychology was profoundly shaped by frequent government policy announcements, which impacted market behavior. While COVID-19 and Brexit overlapped in the UK, leading to increased investor concerns and market instability (Paterson et al., 2024).
- Market Volatility and Returns: Policies for prevention tended generally to increase market volatility and impacted negatively returns. However, health policies had a larger impact in increasing volatility than other policy indicators (Li et al., 2023).

Regulatory responses to the COVID-19 pandemic were critical for stabilizing financial markets overall, but the effectiveness of different interventions varied by the nature of the intervention and the regional dimension. The pandemic pointed out the important need for targeted and time-sensitive policy measures to address financial distress. Still, the long-term effects of these government interventions, and whether they will create market dependency, are something to be studied more closely.

POST-COVID-19 RECOVERY: REGULATORY CHALLENGES AND OPPORTUNITIES

Many of the unprecedented regulatory responses taken have been designed to help manage the significant effects of COVID-19 on financial markets. The actions taken were complex, entailing fiscal and monetary measures, regulatory revisions, and systemic stabilization actions. The pandemic acted as a stress test to identify the strengths and weaknesses of existing financial regulations. The subsequent sections describe the different regulatory responses and how they affected financial markets during the pandemic.

Interventions of Fiscal and Monetary Policy

- International governments and central banks pumped fiscal and monetary policy into the system to stabilize financial markets. They available were interest rate cuts, quantitative easing, as well as fiscal stimulus packages that were designed to support economies and financial systems during the pandemic (Gormsen & Koijen, 2023) (Liu et al., 2022).
- In the US, the resilience of the banking system was also partly credited to the strong capital and liquidity requirements put in place following the Global Financial Crisis, which kept banks able to continue lending and market-making activities during the pandemic.

Effect on FinTech and P2P Lending

- This has drawn increasing attention to the need for regulatory frameworks in the FinTech sector, including the P2P lending industry, particularly in the wake of the pandemic. Risk of increased liquidity, which requires regulatory involvement to ensure a stable market, was noted. Wiences and veterans rule with multi-different market (Nigmonov et al., 2024).
- COVID-19 policies were particularly favourable for financial services driven by technology, as government restrictions and economic support measures benefitted their development. This highlights the importance of targeted regulatory responses to enable innovative financial technologies to support the economy during periods of high uncertainty.

Structural Changes and Market Efficiency

- Structural breaks in the efficiency of credit derivative and equity markets and equity market forecastability caused by the pandemic These changes were attributed to governmental measures to stabilize markets, indicating that novel regulatory strategies will be required to manage the flow of up-to-date information, and investor behaviours in crises (Procasky & Yin, 2023).

- In China, regulatory measures were put in place to stabilize the financial markets, highlighted a small yet significant degree of stabilization in response to government policies of stay-at-home orders and social distancing measures (Liu et al., 2022)

Regulatory Repercussions and Financial Frauds

- This has accelerated digital transformation and, therefore, the risks of financial fraud. This required additional regulatory efforts to identify and prevent fraud, particularly through data- and technology-based supervision (Zhu, 2024).

Response from World and Country Level

- COVID-19's effects on financial markets were country-specific due to the severity of the outbreak as well as the strictness of government measures. This highlights the importance of drafting market-specific regulatory responses: other countries with less strict measures also experienced market reactions.
- Emerging markets experienced similar challenges, as currency depreciation and a decline in futures derivatives positions each reflect the need for regulatory frameworks capable of addressing market volatility and investor confidence during crises.

Although pandemic-related regulatory responses were generally effective in restoring calm to financial markets, they also identified some shortcomings. Adaptive and context-specific regulatory frameworks that are able to respond to dynamic market conditions and emerging risk were also highlighted as critical issues to address as the pandemic unfolded. Furthermore, the crisis further exposed the need to enhance preventive measures in the field of FinTech and to be more vigilant with respect to financial fraud. As we navigate through this landscape, the need for continuous research and policy reform will be imperative to safeguard against the eventualities of the next crisis.

LONG-TERM EFFECTS ON FINANCIAL MARKETS AND REGULATION

The impact on the long-term effect of financial markets and the regulation in the marketing of finance is a complex interrelationship between financial technology, regulation and the dynamism of the market. These factors menace the financial multidimensionality a danger to innovativeness, competition, and market balance. Extending the paradigms of legal principles, ethics, anthropology and sociology into the very center of financial markets is a complex human endeavor.

Fintech & Regulations, their Impact

- But there is a complicated relationship between financial technology and regulation of market-based financial structures. These can dampen the positive effects of financial structures on innovation, but these factors can strengthen each other to encourage an environment conducive to technological progress (Zheng et al., 2023).
- Technologies for regulation shape the boundaries of the financial markets and undergird enforcement processes, including for example, surveillance and data mining overlayers. In this way, these technologies function to flag potentially larger market problems and to direct regulatory responses and thereby shape the reach and intensity of financial governance (Williams, 2013).

Competition and Market Structure

- Financing can be a big determinant of competitive rivalry in product markets. The relief of these restrictions leads to an increased competition as shown by a declining market concentration and an rising amount of firms (Dellas & Fernandes, 2014).
- Regulatory harmonization like the Financial Instruments Markets Directive (FIMD) in the EU seeks to create single capital markets around the world and provide foster investor's protection. On the other hand, these changes can increase compliance costs and create concentration in markets, which could reduce competition.

Innovating for Regulations

- As we have noticed a lot of importance being given to regulatory frameworks after the financial crisis, a there has been a massive increase in compliance mandates. Indeed, regulatory technology has played a critical role in the ability of financial firms to meet these obligations but at the same time bring dialectic tensions between transparency and operational efficiency (Currie et al., 2018).

- Increased capital requirements and rigid compliance costs can help to diminish competition in banking markets. These regulations affect the decisions banks make about their portfolios and monitoring, thus affecting the general quality of bank's loans.

Speculation and Market Volatility

- Welfare can be improved when speculative trading is regulated in the financial market, such as limited short selling in order to decrease the excess volatility of asset returns and the equity risk premium. Borrowing limits and taxes on transactions as regulatory measures can directly be applied to reduce these effects by avoiding speculative activities in the DLT market.

Changes in Structure Drive Policy Implications

- Rapid structural changes in financial markets require policy responses that aim to balance financial stability, macroeconomic performance, and efficient financial intermediation. Policymakers face changing economic and political constraints that make it difficult to achieve the best regulatory results.
- New financial regulations and their impact on market quality and price dynamics have been studied (news/selling bans, transaction taxes, etc. The evidence to suggest that these measures are as good or as bad as they are made out to be is a lot less compelling than people argue for, creating hesitation in the regulation.

There is no doubt that financial technology and regulation have changed the face of financial markets, but they also have spawned challenges to be managed carefully. To a large extent, this balance between innovation and stability must be continuously determined, resulting in the emergence of new regulations. The combination of competition, market structure and regulatory measures will continue to define our financial landscape for market participants and policymakers alike.

CONCLUSION

The COVID-19 pandemic has highlighted the interdependence and fragility of international financial markets. The initial shock exposed major vulnerabilities within market infrastructures, investor behaviours, and institutional readiness that triggered and amplified an unprecedented economic disruption. Yet, the rapid and coordinated actions taken by governments, central banks, and regulatory agencies were instrumental in restoring confidence in financial markets and preventing a deeper financial crisis. Key among these were regulatory interventions (including monetary policy, fiscal policy and temporary relaxation of capital and liquidity regulations) which helped keep markets afloat. The crisis also exposed weaknesses in current regulatory structures, particularly in emerging sectors such as digital finance and cryptocurrency and systemic threats like pandemics and climate change. As the world recovers from the immediate crisis, there are important lessons to inform the future of financial regulation from how financial regulators and government officials responded to the pandemic. Development of enhanced and forward-looking regulatory approaches are required with the expedited adoption of the digital technologies as well as the heightened significance of sustainable finance. The prospects of global coordination, shifting market distortions, encouraging innovation while maintaining stability would all need to be addressed by policymakers. The COVID-19 crisis has been a stress test for financial markets as well as regulatory architectures. That said, significant progress on mitigating its impacts was made, but the experience has also shown the necessity of keeping regulatory practices in a state of evolution so that they can provide protection against future shocks. Our global financial systems can be better fortified, more inclusive, and more resilient through these lessons, and in an increasingly uncertain world, that ensures stability.

REFERENCES

Akinci, O., Benigno, G., & Queralto, A. (2020). Modeling the Global Effects of the COVID-19 Sudden Stop in Capital Flows. *FEDS Notes, 2020.0*(2586). https://doi.org/DOI: 10.17016/2380-7172.2586

Apergis, N. (2024). COVID-19 and US females' portfolio decisions. *International Review of Economics & Finance, 95*, 103491. DOI: 10.1016/j.iref.2024.103491

Beer, C., Maniora, J., & Pott, C. (2023). COVID-19 pandemic and capital markets: The role of government responses. *Journal of Business Economics, 93*(1–2), 11–57. DOI: 10.1007/s11573-022-01103-x PMID: 38013855

Beirne, J., Renzhi, N., Sugandi, E., & Volz, U. (2021). COVID -19, asset markets and capital flows. *Pacific Economic Review, 26*(4), 498–538. DOI: 10.1111/1468-0106.12368

Candelon, B., & Moura, R. (2023). Sovereign yield curves and the COVID-19 in emerging markets. *Economic Modelling, 127*, 106453. DOI: 10.1016/j.econmod.2023.106453

Chen, B. (2022). The Craft of Color and the Chemistry of Dyes: Textile Technology in the Ryukyu Kingdom, 1700–1900. *Technology and Culture, 63*(1), 87–117. DOI: 10.1353/tech.2022.0003 PMID: 35000960

Cheng, T., Liu, J., Yao, W., & Zhao, A. B. (2022). The impact of COVID-19 pandemic on the volatility connectedness network of global stock market. *Pacific-Basin Finance Journal, 71*, 101678. DOI: 10.1016/j.pacfin.2021.101678

Currie, W. L., Gozman, D. P., & Seddon, J. J. M. (2018). Dialectic Tensions in the Financial Markets: A Longitudinal Study of pre- and Post-Crisis Regulatory Technology. *Journal of Information Technology, 33*(4), 304–325. DOI: 10.1057/s41265-017-0047-5

Davis, S., Liu, D., & Sheng, X. S. (2021). *Stock Prices and Economic Activity in the Time of Coronavirus* (No. w28320; p. w28320). National Bureau of Economic Research. https://doi.org/DOI: 10.3386/w28320

Dellas, H., & Fernandes, A. (2014). Finance and Competition. *Economic Journal (London), 124*(575), 269–288. DOI: 10.1111/ecoj.12055

Du, C., Hu, M., Wang, T., & Kizi, M. D. D. (2024). Research on the Impact of Digital Inclusive Finance on Green Innovation of SMEs. *Sustainability, 16*(11), 4700. DOI: 10.3390/su16114700

Echarte Fernández, M. Á., Náñez Alonso, S. L., Jorge-Vázquez, J., & Reier Forradellas, R. F. (2021). Central Banks' Monetary Policy in the Face of the COVID-19 Economic Crisis: Monetary Stimulus and the Emergence of CBDCs. *Sustainability*, *13*(8), 4242. DOI: 10.3390/su13084242

Fasanya, I., Periola, O., & Adetokunbo, A. (2023). On the effects of Covid-19 pandemic on stock prices: An imminent global threat. *Quality & Quantity*, *57*(3), 2231–2248. DOI: 10.1007/s11135-022-01455-0 PMID: 35789758

Feyen, E., Alonso Gispert, T., Kliatskova, T., & Mare, D. S. (2021). Financial Sector Policy Response to COVID-19 in Emerging Markets and Developing Economies. *Journal of Banking & Finance*, *133*, 106184. DOI: 10.1016/j.jbankfin.2021.106184 PMID: 34898821

Figiel, S., Floriańczyk, Z., & Wigier, M. (2023). Impact of the COVID-19 Pandemic on the World Energy and Food Commodity Prices: Implications for Global Economic Growth. *Energies*, *16*(7), 3152. DOI: 10.3390/en16073152

Giglio, S., Maggiori, M., Stroebel, J., & Utkus, S. (2021). The joint dynamics of investor beliefs and trading during the COVID-19 crash. *Proceedings of the National Academy of Sciences of the United States of America*, *118*(4), e2010316118. DOI: 10.1073/pnas.2010316118 PMID: 33468667

Goldstein, I., Koijen, R. S. J., & Mueller, H. M. (2021). COVID-19 and Its Impact on Financial Markets and the Real Economy. *Review of Financial Studies*, *34*(11), 5135–5148. DOI: 10.1093/rfs/hhab085

Gormsen, N. J., & Koijen, R. S. J. (2023). Financial Markets and the COVID-19 Pandemic. *Annual Review of Financial Economics*, *15*(1), 69–89. DOI: 10.1146/annurev-financial-110821-020444

Ha, L. T. (2022). Effects of digitalization on financialization: Empirical evidence from European countries. *Technology in Society*, *68*, 101851. DOI: 10.1016/j.techsoc.2021.101851

Haddad, V., Moreira, A., & Muir, T. (2020). *When Selling Becomes Viral: Disruptions in Debt Markets in the COVID-19 Crisis and the Fed's Response* (No. w27168; p. w27168). National Bureau of Economic Research. https://doi.org/DOI: 10.3386/w27168

Harnay, S., & Scialom, L. (2016). The influence of the economic approaches to regulation on banking regulations: A short history of banking regulations. *Cambridge Journal of Economics*, *40*(2), 401–426. DOI: 10.1093/cje/bev023

Hui, E. C. M., & Chan, K. K. K. (2022). How does Covid-19 affect global equity markets? *Financial Innovation*, *8*(1), 25. DOI: 10.1186/s40854-021-00330-5 PMID: 35251895

Kayani, U. N., Aysan, A. F., Khan, M., Khan, M., Mumtaz, R., & Irfan, M. (2024). Unleashing the pandemic volatility: A glimpse into the stock market performance of developed economies during COVID-19. *Heliyon*, *10*(4), e25202. DOI: 10.1016/j.heliyon.2024.e25202 PMID: 38370210

Klose, J. (2023). European exchange rate adjustments in response to COVID-19, containment measures and stabilization policies. *Economic Modelling*, *128*, 106494. DOI: 10.1016/j.econmod.2023.106494

Klose, J., & Tillmann, P. (2021). COVID-19 and Financial Markets: A Panel Analysis for European Countries. *Jahrbücher für Nationalökonomie und Statistik*, *241*(3), 297–347. DOI: 10.1515/jbnst-2020-0063

Lan, T., Shao, L., Zhang, H., & Yuan, C. (2023). The impact of pandemic on dynamic volatility spillover network of international stock markets. *Empirical Economics*, *65*(5), 2115–2144. DOI: 10.1007/s00181-023-02422-w PMID: 37361958

Latif, Y., Shunqi, G., Bashir, S., Iqbal, W., Ali, S., & Ramzan, M. (2021). RETRACTED ARTICLE: COVID-19 and stock exchange return variation: empirical evidences from econometric estimation. *Environmental Science and Pollution Research International*, *28*(42), 60019–60031. DOI: 10.1007/s11356-021-14792-8 PMID: 34155586

Li, G., Wu, H., Jiang, J., & Zong, Q. (2023). Digital finance and the low-carbon energy transition (LCET) from the perspective of capital-biased technical progress. *Energy Economics*, *120*, 106623. DOI: 10.1016/j.eneco.2023.106623

Liu, F., Kong, D., Xiao, Z., Zhang, X., Zhou, A., & Qi, J. (2022). Effect of economic policies on the stock and bond market under the impact of COVID-19. *Journal of Safety Science and Resilience = An Quan Ke Xue Yu Ren Xing (Ying Wen)*, *3*(1), 24–38. DOI: 10.1016/j.jnlssr.2021.10.006 PMID: 40477849

Löwen, C., Kchouri, B., & Lehnert, T. (2021). Is this time really different? Flight-to-safety and the COVID-19 crisis. *PLoS One*, *16*(5), e0251752. DOI: 10.1371/journal.pone.0251752 PMID: 34038444

McKibbin, W., & Fernando, R. (2023). The global economic impacts of the COVID-19 pandemic. *Economic Modelling*, *129*, 106551. DOI: 10.1016/j.econmod.2023.106551

Moloney, N. (2024). EU financial market regulation a decade from the financial-crisis-era reforms: Crisis, uncertainty, and capacity. *Yearbook of European Law, 42*, 169–209. DOI: 10.1093/yel/yead008

Naqvi, H. A. (2022). Role of government policies to attain economic sustainability amid COVID-19 environment. *Frontiers in Environmental Science, 10*, 983860. DOI: 10.3389/fenvs.2022.983860

Nigmonov, A., Shams, S., & Alam, K. (2024). Liquidity risk in FinTech lending: Early impact of the COVID-19 pandemic on the P2P lending market. *Emerging Markets Review, 58*, 101084. DOI: 10.1016/j.ememar.2023.101084

Paterson, A., Sakariyahu, R., Lawal, R., & Alabi, A. (2024). The Impact of Government Policy Responses to the COVID-19 Pandemic and Brexit on the UK Financial Market: A Behavioural Perspective. *British Journal of Management, 35*(1), 174–191. DOI: 10.1111/1467-8551.12702

Peretz, P., & Schroedel, J. R. (2009). Financial Regulation in the United States: Lessons from History. *Public Administration Review, 69*(4), 603–612. DOI: 10.1111/j.1540-6210.2009.02009.x

Previts, G. J., & Bricker, R. (1994). Fact and Theory in Accounting History: Presentmindedness and Capital Market Research*. *Contemporary Accounting Research, 10*(2), 625–641. DOI: 10.1111/j.1911-3846.1994.tb00408.x

Procasky, W. J., & Yin, A. (2023). The impact of COVID-19 on the relative market efficiency and forecasting ability of credit derivative and equity markets. *International Review of Financial Analysis, 90*, 102926. DOI: 10.1016/j.irfa.2023.102926

Rajput, H., Changotra, R., Rajput, P., Gautam, S., Gollakota, A. R. K., & Arora, A. S. (2021). A shock like no other: Coronavirus rattles commodity markets. *Environment, Development and Sustainability, 23*(5), 6564–6575. DOI: 10.1007/s10668-020-00934-4 PMID: 32837284

Sharma, S., Koehl, L., Bruniaux, P., Zeng, X., & Wang, Z. (2021). Development of an Intelligent Data-Driven System to Recommend Personalized Fashion Design Solutions. *Sensors (Basel), 21*(12), 4239. DOI: 10.3390/s21124239 PMID: 34205598

Sun, N., Cao, B., & Mu, X. (2024). Research on the Future Trends of the Integration of Artificial Intelligence and Fashion Design of Clothing. *Applied Mathematics and Nonlinear Sciences, 9*(1), 20242181. DOI: 10.2478/amns-2024-2181

Sun, X., Wang, X., Sun, F., Tian, M., Qu, L., Perry, P., Owens, H., & Liu, X. (2021). Textile Waste Fiber Regeneration via a Green Chemistry Approach: A Molecular Strategy for Sustainable Fashion. *Advanced Materials, 33*(48), 2105174. DOI: 10.1002/adma.202105174 PMID: 34561908

Tan, X., Wang, X., Ma, S., Wang, Z., Zhao, Y., & Xiang, L. (2022). COVID-19 Shock and the Time-Varying Volatility Spillovers Among the Energy and Precious Metals Markets: Evidence From A DCC-GARCH-CONNECTEDNESS Approach. *Frontiers in Public Health, 10*, 906969. DOI: 10.3389/fpubh.2022.906969 PMID: 35968447

Vetter, F. (2023). A History of Financial Technology and Regulation: From American Incorporation to Cryptocurrency and Crowdfunding by Seth C. Oranburg. *Technology and Culture, 64*(2), 615–616. DOI: 10.1353/tech.2023.0084

Williams, J. W. (2013). Regulatory technologies, risky subjects, and financial boundaries: Governing 'fraud' in the financial markets. *Accounting, Organizations and Society, 38*(6–7), 544–558. DOI: 10.1016/j.aos.2012.08.001

Wójcik, D., & Ioannou, S. (2020). COVID-19 and Finance: Market Developments So Far and Potential Impacts on the Financial Sector and Centres. *Tijdschrift voor Economische en Sociale Geografie, 111*(3), 387–400. DOI: 10.1111/tesg.12434 PMID: 32836484

Wu, B., Xie, X., Ke, W., Bao, H., Duan, Z., Jin, Z., Dai, X., & Hong, Y. (2022). Merchandising for Sustainable Fashion: A Systematic Literature Review. *Sustainability, 14*(20), 13422. DOI: 10.3390/su142013422

Zhao, W., Yin, C., Hua, T., Meadows, M. E., Li, Y., Liu, Y., Cherubini, F., Pereira, P., & Fu, B. (2022). Achieving the Sustainable Development Goals in the post-pandemic era. *Humanities & Social Sciences Communications, 9*(1), 258. DOI: 10.1057/s41599-022-01283-5 PMID: 35967482

Zheng, C., Wang, Z., Pan, S., Chen, X., & Jia, S. (2023). Does financial structure still matter for technological innovation when financial technology and financial regulation develop? *Technological Forecasting and Social Change, 194*, 122747. DOI: 10.1016/j.techfore.2023.122747

Zhou, Y., Teresienė, D., Keliuotytė-Staniulėnienė, G., Kanapickiene, R., Dong, R. K., & Kaab Omeir, A. (2022). The Impact of COVID-19 Pandemic on Government Bond Yields. *Frontiers in Environmental Science, 10*, 881260. DOI: 10.3389/fenvs.2022.881260

Zhu, A. Y. F. (2024). Upgrading financial education by adding Python-based personalized financial projection: A randomized control trial. *British Journal of Educational Technology*, *55*(2), 731–750. DOI: 10.1111/bjet.13401

Chapter 8
Examining Financial Health of Companies by Applying the Altman's Z-Score Model With Special Reference to the Indian IT Sector

Mayur Ajaykumar Waghmare
https://orcid.org/0009-0004-2243-3699
Indira Institute of Management, India

Sonali Suresh Shrotri
https://orcid.org/0009-0001-5895-2675
Indira Institute of Management, India

ABSTRACT

The research presumes an in-depth assessment of the financial standing of the Information Technology sector, adopting the model of Altman Z-score for analysis of 14 renowned IT companies. This study articulates the core importance of financial stability for the Information Technology firms, especially considering volatile market conditions and galloping technological changes. By calculating the Z-scores and their financial ratios the evaluation and interpretation are drawn, to justify financial position of these companies. To strengthen the perfection of financial analysis, statistical tests like Z-test and Shapiro-Wilk test, were utilized for the assessment of data normality. By demonstrating the relevance of the Altman Z-score, the result shows important aspects of financial stability and potential weaknesses of IT com-

DOI: 10.4018/979-8-3373-1404-4.ch008

panies. The research proves that Z-score model predictive strength and accuracy, provides mighty support for evaluating financial health in various hurdles faced by IT companies.

1. INTRODUCTION

1.1. Introduction of Company

In the constantly-changing field of the Information Technology (IT) sector, financial steadiness is required to maintain competitive environment and sustainable growth. By assisting in overcoming hurdles of market demands and change in economy, evaluation of financial health becomes necessary for IT companies. The research focuses on 14 renowned IT companies, by applying the Altman Z-score as accurate and proven model for predicting bankruptcy and financial position. It precisely emphasis on financial assessment of the data, which provides a complete overview of financial health.

The Altman Z-Score model, usually applied beyond several industries, work as predictive tool in analysis. By evaluating the Z-Scores and analyzing their financial ratios such as profitability, liquidity, solvency, and leverage, for these selected companies to check their financial stability. In addition, statistical tests such as the Z-Test, and the Shapiro-Wilk test were used for assessment of data normality. The methods used during this research for distribution of data provides the detailed analysis, which strengthens the reliability and sustainability of Z-score model. The research objectifies to exhibit how predictive tools, similar to the Altman Z-score approach, can help to disclose the IT companies' financial health and future developments. By evaluating detailed patterns and outcomes derived from statistical tests, planning strategies and risk management can be done within the IT sector. The study highlights the usefulness of Altman's Z-score model in the specific industries it applies to and its importance and future prediction ability in today's empirical world. It justifies that this model is still a creditworthy tool for measurement of company's financial health and forecasting, even by assisting new overcoming hurdles.

The 14 IT companies which were selected for the research for the purpose of research to analyze the financial position and the associated risk for decision making are such as:

- Infosys Ltd.-

Infosys Ltd. is one of the leading IT companies, which is providing the IT services and consulting. It was established in 1981, headquartered in Bangalore, and specifically focuses on providing the consulting to businesses, outsourcing solutions for across the industries, which include financial services, banking, insurance and healthcare. The company holds strong global presence with clients over 50 countries.

- eClerx Ltd.-

eClerx Ltd. founded in 2000 is the most admired one which is known for the Knowledge process outsourcing (KPO) and is headquartered in India. eClerx delivers so unique expertise in customer operations, digital transformation and management process of business.

- Saksoft Ltd.-

The IT company which is specialized in providing end-to-end business transformation services is the Saksoft Ltd. Founded in 1999, focuses on the information management, digital solutions and data analytics. The company looks over the sectors such as banking, insurance, e-commerce and healthcare. There is also a wide demand for data analytics, cloud computing and IT services.

- Compucom Software Ltd.-

Compucom Software Ltd. is an IT company which focuses on the IT services, Software development and some educational services. Founded in 1991, headquartered in Jaipur, the company offers a wide range such as e-learning platform, web application and software development. The company also shows the expertise in education, private enterprises and government.

- Intrasoft Technologies Ltd.-

Infrasoft Technologies Ltd. founded in 1996, focuses on the e-commerce and IT services. The company offers services like web development, software solutions and business process outsourcing (BPO). The main aim of the company is to do innovations and Operational efficiency to stay competitive in the IT industry.

- Kellton Tech Solutions Ltd.-

Kelton Tech Solutions Ltd. is one of the prominent players in globe provider of IT service, enterprises solutions, and digital transformation. Founded in 1993, headquartered in Hyderabad, specialized in some areas such as Internet of Things

(IoT), AI, blockchain and cloud computing. Provides services for diverse industries such as retail, healthcare, financial services and manufacturing.

- Infobeans Technologies Ltd.-

Infoeans Technologies Ltd. is an Indian IT company which indulge in IT services and software development. Established in 2000 and headquartered in Indore, Madhya Pradesh, serves across industries such as BFSI, media, healthcare and retail. Specialized in providing customized digital transformation solutions.

- 63 Moons Technologies Ltd.-

63 Moons Technologies Ltd. leading IT company, specialized in development of next-generation financial market solutions. The company focuses on providing payment systems, software and infrastructure for electronic trading and commodities. It serves the offers such as banks, brokers, exchanges, regulators and financial market participants.

- Sonata Software Ltd.-

Sonata Software Ltd. is IT service and technology solutions company, specialized in platform-based solutions, digital transformation services and software product engineering. Serves multiple industries retail, manufacturing, distribution and travel, the company is growing in technologies such as cloud, analytics, AI and Internet of Things (IoT).

- Birlasoft Ltd.-

Birlasoft Ltd. is an IT company which indulges in consulting and IT services, part of CK Birla Group. The company offers technology solutions such as cloud, IT modernization, (ERP) and digital transformation. Serves diverse industries like healthcare, retail, banking and manufacturing. Birlasoft's is expert in providing innovative solutions and services to help businesses improve their operational efficiency.

- Infibeam Avenues-

Infibeam Avenues is a prominent player in IT sector, includes e-commerce and payment solutions. The company offers a wide range of services such as digital banking, e-commerce platform and payment gateway solutions. In India Fintech sector is growing characterized by digital banking, mobile wallet and innovation in payment solutions.

- CILO Infotech Ltd.-

CILO Infotech Ltd. is a company which provides a range of solutions such as IT consulting, Software development and system integration. The company serves in diverse industry like finance, retail and healthcare, offering in customized technology. In the competitive field like IT CILO Infotech Ltd. is standing in the strong position.

- Rolta India Ltd.-

Founded in 1989, Rolta India Ltd. is multinational technology and engineering company. Operates in Engineering, Geospatial sector and IT, which offers wide range of services like enterprise solutions, geographic information systems (GIS) and cloud computing. Serves to industries like government, healthcare, energy, utilities and defense. Rolta is one of the prominent players in IT and engineering.

- Bharatiya Global Info-Media Ltd.-

Bhartiya Global Info-Media Ltd. is an Indian IT company which operates in entertainment and media sector. Various areas where the company has indulged in are such as distribution, digital media and event management and film production. Established in 1999, serves into diverse industry such as tourism and leisure.

1.2. Introduction of formula:

The Altman Z-score is a financial performance indicator (FPI) created by Edward Altman, a finance professor at New York University, during 1960s. The equation is employed to assess the financial health bankruptcy and accuracy of the companies. It is particularly important to investors, stakeholders, and financial experts in the Z-score model, because it clearly shows quantitative evaluation of companies upcoming risks of bankruptcy.

The Altman's Z-Score Formula

The z-score is computed by mixture of financial ratios, which has its own specific weight according to its predictive relevance. The formula is framed as:

$\{Z=1.2A+1.4B+3.3C+0.6D+1.0E\}$

Where:
A = Working Capital / Total Assets
B = Retained Earnings / Total Assets
C = Earnings Before Interest and Taxes (EBIT) / Total Assets
D = Market Value of Equity / Total Liabilities
E = Sales / Total Assets

Table 1. Values of Altman's Model

Score	Zone	Results
Z < 1.81	Distress	Likely to be bankruptcy
1.81 < Z < 2.99	Gray Zone	Stable
2.99 < Z	Safe Zone	Safe

Gray zone (1.81< Z-score < 2.99): - The gray zone is a range in which usually the company is said to be stable.

Safe zone (Z-score >2.99): - The safe zone is the range in which the company is said to be safe, where the Z-score is greater than 2.99, which shows the financial stability and strength of the companies.

Distress zone (Z-score <1.81): - The distress zone is the category where some of the companies fell in this range which shows the poor liquidity ratios and the high liability.

2. REVIEW OF LITERATURE

(Lohana, 2014) The research was based on "Measuring Financial Sustainability in Reliance Industry limited". The one popular tool for financial analysis is ratio analysis. Financial ratios are analytical techniques that are used to financial data to determine the viability of the organization by identifying strengths and weaknesses, positive and negative trends, and investment features. With the average value of 0.92, the sales and total asset ratio for Reliance Group of Industries were observed to be consistently rising. This study uses 'Z'-score model, which captures the predicate viability of company financial health by using combination of ratios.

(Bzour, 2011) Attempted to have a sagacity to investigate financial health and ratios, in listed firms in Jordan by applying the Kida and Altman models, in for bankruptcy prediction. Non-financial services and industrial enterprises during the years 1990-2006 are included in the study sample. To accomplish the goals, the models developed by Altman and Kida were applied to the industrial and service sector, excluding the banking, insurance, and finance sector. After that, the two model's outputs were compared to determine which one is the best suited to provide an early warning regarding the likelihood of bankruptcy for each of those years. According to the study, the Altman Z-score model was able to accurately forecast the bankruptcy of Jordanian businesses five years prior to the bankruptcy incidence, with high rates of 75% for the fifth year, 94% for the fourth year, and 100% for the third, second and first year, as indicated in table. Additionally, it was discovered that the Altman Z-score's percentage rates and prediction frequencies outperform Kida's Z-score.

(Afrin, 2014) Altman Z-score is universally accepted for predicting bankruptcy risk and financial distress across industries. In the cement industry of Bangladesh analyzing, prediction of performance and shares returns is done. The purpose of the study is to find out if the Altman's z-score can provide any insights into performance and stability of a company's finances. All the cement companies enlisted in the Dhaka Stock Exchange were taken and the data for the last ten years analyzed with the application of advanced statistical tools.

(Panigrahi, 2019) To reduce the gap and contribute to the existing literature, the study seeks to conduct an empirical analysis to ascertain whether Altman's Z-score model is a reliable indicator of financial distress within the pharmaceutical sector. The highest Z-score ratio was recorded for the year 2015-2016 was 7.93, and were the successful years for the pharmaceutical industry. But one must remember that when firms adopt aggressive working capital policies, the risk of default and bankruptcy increases.

(Hoe et al., 2018) The efficacy of Altman's Z-score methodology in evaluating the financial performance and distress of businesses. The study focuses on the Malaysian technology sector, utilizing the Z-score model to evaluate companies' financial health from 2013 to 2017. It shows a consistent presence of companies in the safe zone, with a decreasing trend in distress zone companies indicating overall economic growth. Market value of equity to total liabilities emerges as the most influential ratio, alongside working capital to total assets and sales to total assets, in determining financial distress levels among technology-based companies. The findings offer valuable insights for investors and policymakers to devise strategies for mitigating financial risks and ensuring sustainable growth.

(Chouhan, et al., 2014) Edward Altman created the Altman Z-score in 1968, and it has since grown to be a key component of models used to forecast company bankruptcy and financial stability. Ratio analysis is the phrase used in various regions the world for measuring financial soundness and creditworthiness of the firms, but it's going toward elimination because analytical techniques are assessing the performance Sample Kolmogorov- Smirnov test for 10 BSE companies, but the outcomes say that Altman's model remains Encouraging and challenging.

(Anuj, C. S., et al., 2018) Investigates the use of the Altman Z-score model to predict financial health and potential bankruptcy in steel companies. This research highlights the model's effectiveness in assessing the viability and future challenges of businesses within the steel industry. By applying the Altman Z-score, the study not only demonstrates the model's relevance but also its critical role in helping stakeholders make informed decisions about financial distress. This paper proves creditworthy of the Altman Z-score model as a beneficial tool in financial analysis over several sectors.

(Suresh C, 2016) Altman's Z-score model analysis of NIFTY 50 firms discloses its value in predicting financial health within various sectors, except financial institutions. Derived by Edward Altman in 1968, the model aggregates of five ratios to analyze and predict the bankruptcy, using Z-score model which is accepted and applied over several markets, including India's NIFTY 50. As research demonstrates that, Z-scores provides worthy predictions of financial health of companies and its accuracy differ by sectors, while doing required adjustments and updates to enhance reliability Research boosts the Z-scores importance in helping investors for decision-making, by analyzing the risk and bolstering its relevance in financial analysis and investment strategy.

(Tanjung, 2020) The investigation comparing the Altman, Springate, Zmijewski, and Ohlson models for forecasting financial health shows substantial variations in their effectiveness and accuracy over samples from the pharmaceutical sector listed on the Stock Exchange from 2013 to 2017. The Altman Z-score, don't provide any immediate prediction of financial health, but it marked 8 samples at risk, indicating traditional approach for forecasting. In contrast, the Springate model marked seven samples as currently discomfort and two as likely to distress, demonstrating a higher accuracy to current discomfort conditions. The Zmijewski model didn't find discomfort and distress in any of the samples, showing a lower accuracy or different criteria. However, the Ohlson model predicted that 10 samples were in the financial discomfort, showing the greater accuracy among the models reviewed. Particularly, the most accurate model for predicting the financial health of the examined industry was discovered to be the Altman Z-score model, addressing to its predictivity and reliability in precise industrial applications, regardless of its traditional output in some cases. This variation in model effectiveness and analysis emphasizes the importance of selecting the correct predictive tool based on precise sector conditions and the characteristics of the financial health indicators used in each model.

(Abbas, 2015) The research provides the detailed view on the Altman Z-score model and the Z-score's adaptability and reliance. Abbas mentions uniqueness of financial ratios, like working capital, retained earnings, and asset turnover, while analyzing the company's financial distress. The paper talk about modifications over the years in the evolution of prediction models of bankruptcy which provides the improved accuracy. The comparison of Z-score model is done with other prediction models performances, noticing reliability and limitations. The Altman Z-score is tested across various different markets and periods. As the Z-score is widely used instrument, but is degraded because of the less applicability to non-manufacturing firms and smaller companies. Abbas has done the sector-specific modification s in the Altman Z-score formula, while Z-score serves as reliable and trustworthy for predicting bankruptcy. Adding more financial indicators, can be incorporated for improvement in accuracy of models. The paper discusses on Z-scores effectiveness during instability in economic and relevance in contemporary financial analysis.

(Anjum, 2012) The study by researcher mentions the relevance of the Altman's Z-score model in predicting the bankruptcy of businesses. The Altman Z-score model is widely used mode in analyzing the financial health and predict the companies in financial distress. The papers tell despite various new models and technologies for prediction of bankruptcy, Altman Z-score remains the important tool for measuring financial health. The research also concludes about the limitations and challenges which are faced by Z-score model in different business environment. Z-score model reliance my not fully capture the historic financial data or the chances in nature of modern business. The researcher suggests that to remain accurate across different sector, Z-score needs to adapt some combinations of financial metrics. For the corporate decision-making Z-score model continues to remain the important tool in analyzing the financial health and associated risks.

(Kannadhasan, 2007) The study is done on the analysis of financial health of public limited companies with the help of Z-score model. The paper mentions that the various changes and modification done in the Z-score provides improved accuracy and used in the Indian public companies. The discussion on the early developments in predicting financial health, and later improvements were made in his Z-score formula. The key financial indicators identification is important for knowing bankruptcy or the financial distress. The researcher tells importance of Z-score in both developed as well as emerging market and stays as a reliable tool. Several modifications are been suggested by researcher as compared to original model, considering local market conditions. As the Z-score model remains the dominant model despite the various models for predictions of bankruptcy. For the improved accuracy the modification in the Z-score could be done.

(Mulla, 2019) The study on relation between customer satisfaction and operational efficiency in banking sector is done. In context of Isamic banking operational efficiency, mentions the effective utilization of bank resources to provide some services while maximizing outputs and minimizing costs. In the UAE, bank faces many challenges of balancing operational efficiency with maintaining customer satisfaction. The researcher found that banks mostly invest in the new emerging technologies, employee traning and streamline operations while competating with the competitors.

(Farahaan Rashid, 2023) The study provides the in-depth review of Altman's Z-score model, which is mostly used model to analyze financial health of business across the diverse industries. The model invented by Edward Altman in 1968, utilizes the combination of financial ratios to predict the bankruptcy of businesses. The study discusses how Z-score is been applied for various different sectors, from manufacturing to service industries, and signifies the effectiveness in identifying the financially distressed companies. The researcher discusses on the relevance of Z-score in modern business environment, consisting both strength and limitations. While going under the various modifications the Z-score model remains highly reliable and valuable for assessing financial health. The new complementary tools could be introduced along with Z-score to improve financial risk assessment. Combined Ohlson O-score or Springate model with Z-score, could enhance the accuracy of predictions. As changing economic landscape Altman's Z-score remains the reliable and recognized model for prediction of bankruptcy.

(Joshi, 2020) The research is conducted on the in-depth analysis of Indian public sector banks, using Altman's Z-score model which is widely accepted tool for predicting the financial health. Macroeconomic challenges are faced in the applicability in economics like India evaluating the banks financial health. The study demonstrates the relevance of Z-score model while evaluating the financial health of Indian banks. The study was carried on selected public sector banks in India, to look over the financial stability. There are various factors which influence the Z-score outcomes in the banking sector such as regulatory changes, government policies and Banking sectors financial health. The Z-score model is usually recognized for its accuracy, there are some limitations when applied to the Indian banking sector compared to Western counterparts in terms of regulatory environment. In the diverse banking environments, the research work is valuable in terms of contribution to the ongoing debates.

(Singh, 2021) The study shows that various models of prediction of financial health are used to explore the Indian commercial banks, for the assessment various tools are used in the Indian banking sector. The study mentions importance of using financial ratios and different models for measuring financial health. The models which were used include Altman Z-score model and the Ohlson O-score, which are used to examine the profitability, liquidity, operational efficiency and leverage. In the market like India financial distress models can be helpful for the prediction of insolvency risk in banking operations, factors which could affect are economic changes, increased competition and policy shift. The study finds that these models are the best tools for identifying banks at risk, providing early notices and actions to prevent crises. Despite the adaptability of the financial distress models, some researcher found limitations in capturing the new emerging market conditions. The study says that the interference of the government and regulatory environment slightly affects the financial indicators in distress models. The contribution made by researcher by refining the use of financial distress models is providing the stability of Indian commercial banks and the Altman Z-score despite all other model remains the one of the most convenient tools for prediction of financial health.

(Srinivas, 2023) Early Altman's Z-score focused on the developed markets, predicting bankruptcy with accuracy rates exceeding 70% in many cases. In case of Indians prominent indices NIFTY 50, researchers utilize the model for the evaluation of the financial stability, adapting the necessary changes in new emerging market. In context of India the Z-score is applied in various sectors like banking, healthcare, manufacturing and information technology, showing the adaption of model in different industries. In the study application to NIFTY 50 companies, are 50 companies from different industry and are leading entities in Indian stock market. The researcher applies the Z-score in emerging economy, for knowing the relevance of the model on the subset of NIFTY 50 companies. The study faced sector-specific challenges while applying the Z-score model, but the accuracy gained was the accurate in prediction. By making some financial metrics changes according to the market-specific conditions, and making some modifications Altman's Z-score remains the accepted tool for decision-makers like investors, analysts, and policymakers

(Runkle, 1993) The study provides empirical analysis to test theoretical predictions on performance in implication of bank size, and understanding the economics of scales with the scope for banking sector. The research tells the importance of asset size, while evaluation of profitability and risk, as determining larger banks may often benefit from scale efficiency, but could also face challenges related to risk management and operational complexities. The study is usually based on the size, risk and performance regarding to the market conditions. By utilizing the key financial ratios, the advanced methodologies were used to analyze the firm's performance as well as the risk metrics were adjusted.

(Beltratti, 2012) In the study the major instance was noticed such as why some banks done well than others during the global financial crisis of 2008. Despite the influencing factors to the performance and cause for financial distress, how institutional and macroeconomics factors contributed to the resilience. The study quotes the importance of governance structure, risk management and capital adequacy in demonstrating the bank's ability to be financially stabilized. The research focuses on the cross-country differences, in strong governance, regulatory environments and bank performances. While facing financial challenges in banking sector the leverage level and asset quality could play a crucial role. The research extends beyond the crisis itself, which indeed is a lesson for policymakers and financial institutions. To enhance the financial stability the variations in performance could be analyzed and policies could be designed accordingly, because of which the balance between regulatory stringency and market efficiency is maintained. The research suggests that proactive risk management and sound governance plays crucial role building resilient banking system. This continues financial institutions and regulators to adapt evolving global economic uncertainties.

(Chatterjee, 2018) The study is conducted on the local market conditions using financial distress models. Altman's Z-score model being most admired need to be customized based on the diverse industries as it demonstrates the viability of the predictive accuracy across sectors. As on other hand Ohlson model provide more statistical rigor for the predictive framework, as it requires the huge data inputs and complex computations that can't always be available. The describes the nature of the models rather than finding the substitutes for them. Applying both the models can provide the better view of a company's financial health, balancing the reliability of Altman Z-score with analytical depth in Ohlson models. By utilization of these methodologies, researchers, investors and practitioners can develop an advanced framework for financial predictivity, applying theoretical models with real-world complexities in Indian emerging markets. The research continues to inspire further researchers to research into hybrid approaches for financial distress prediction.

3. STATEMENT OF PROBLEM

The accommodation of digital technologies in various industries, form's assessment of financial strength within the Information Technology sector, which is important in global economics. Although, traditional key performance indicators might not follow, the IT companies revenue model and capital structures. This study aims to utilize Altman Z-score model, for prediction of bankruptcy and analysis of financial health of the companies in the Information technology (IT) sector. By applying and improving the model, the research objectifies to unveil the qualitative terms into the financial stability and risk factors particularly to the digital economy. This research will determine the Altman Z-Score's sustainability and effectiveness in forecasting the financial health of IT companies, considering their different economic factors and market performance.

The study analyzes the relevance and accountability of the Altman Z-Score model particularly within the IT sector, to provide a better understanding of its predictive analysis power and potential limitations when applied on technologically evolving industry. For the better understanding of stakeholders this analysis is required, which provides stronger extent financial health, mitigates risk, and makes wise decisions in the developing IT sector, for the investors.

4. OBJECTIVES OF STUDY

- To analyze and calculate the data of 14 IT companies for the prediction of financial health and distress.
- To assess the likelihood of a company facing financial distress or going bankrupt soon.

5. LIMITATIONS OF STUDY

- The Altman Z-score algorithm was first created for American manufacturing firms and along time it was used broadly. But, while applying these formulas for Indian IT companies, maybe limited due to difference in economic factors.
- Majorly, the future financial health of companies is predicted considering previous financial performance using Z-score model, but in IT sector it is unreliable for predicting future as it is a fast-growing industry.
- The Z-Score majorly focuses on financial ratios, and does not consider qualitative factors like management quality, market competition, or technological advancements.

6. RESEARCH METHODOLOGY

Research Type: Quantitative research
Population: Listed IT companies in BSE and NSE
Sampling Technique: Purposive sampling
Sample Size: 14 listed IT companies in BSE and NSE

6.1. Background of Sample Selection

Researchers have selected the 14 listed IT companies in BSE and NSE, which have prominently worked from more than 3 decades, (1980-2011). For this study 5 years (2019-2023) Data is taken into consideration.

6.2. Sources of Data

Acquisition of Secondary Data: This foundation of this research study is secondary data. The information used in this study comes from a variety of sources including:

1. Annual reports of selected 14 IT Companies from the year 2019-2023.
2. Financial status of price per share in current market from (groww.com).
3. The Balance sheets and profit & loss sheets were taken from (moneycontrol.com).

Statistical tool used:

- Altman z-score formula: **Z=1.2A+1.4B+3.3C+0.6D+1.0E**
- Shapiro-Wilk test

6.3. Hypothesis of Study

Hypothesis of study is based upon the aim and literature review of the study

H_0: The data from (2019-2023) is taken in correspondence to Altman Z-score for each selected IT company where there is no difference during last 5 years.
H_1: The data from (2019-2023) is taken in correspondence to Altman Z- score for each selected IT company where there is a significant difference during last 5 years.

7. ANALYSIS AND DATA INTERPRETATION

The study is done to gauge Z-score of the companies in IT sector that are going towards bankruptcy to decide the accuracy and credibility of the companies, by which it becomes easy and convenient for stockholders for making investment decisions. Using Altman's Z-score, the financial health of IT organizations is examined. Ratio and the Z-scores are calculated by the Altman's formula. The trends in the IT sector are analysed to identify the patterns and outliers, which is mentioned in the Table 2.

Z=1.2A+1.4B+3.3C+0.6D+1.0E

Here:
A = Working Capital / Total Assets i.e. WC/TA
B = Retained Earnings / Total Assets i.e. RE/TA
C = Earnings Before Interest and Taxes (EBIT) / Total Assets i.e. EBIT/TA
D = Market Value of Equity / Total Liabilities i.e. MVE/TL
E = Sales / Total Assets i.e. Sales/TA

Table 2. The Values of Ratios and Altman's Z-score for IT Companies

NAME OF COMPANY	YEAR'S	WC/TA	RE/TA	EBIT/TA	MVE/ TL	SALES/ TA	Z-score
Infosys Ltd.	2018-2019	0.390130	0.195236	0.266577	19.88593	0.926225	14.47804
	2019-2020	0.352907	0.205315	0.273651	13.26363	0.975395	10.54657
	2020-2021	0.326382	0.206761	0.285536	26.33821	0.914550	18.33995
	2021-2022	0.276303	0.222825	0.303158	26.62028	1.045810	18.66105
	2022-2023	0.243149	0.237899	0.331626	17.63496	1.223778	13.52273
eClerx Ltd.	2018-2019	0.353919	0.151850	0.207196	14.58426	0.758136	10.82891
	2019-2020	0.474086	0.137842	0.197445	2.287881	0.738893	3.524331
	2020-2021	0.405493	0.177179	0.251148	7.526375	0.751555	6.830053
	2021-2022	0.372372	0.270284	0.376551	14.01471	1.003674	11.47937
	2022-2023	0.364690	0.306354	0.422193	14.15363	1.182479	11.93323
Saksoft Ltd.	2018-2019	0.066892	0.274832	0.411925	0.598938	0.679997	4.222417
	2019-2020	0.085174	0.251873	0.375692	0.311691	0.755229	2.636057
	2020-2021	0.153051	0.266666	0.362852	0.915226	0.737089	3.039890
	2021-2022	0.152281	0.352482	0.463364	3.402347	0.890845	5.136674
	2022-2023	0.233798	0.400058	0.525180	50.24170	1.021813	33.73954
Compucom Software Ltd.	2018-2019	0.555944	0.025267	0.045697	2.139039	0.411087	2.547403
	2019-2020	0.554954	0.000467	0.011217	1.221619	0.094217	1.863880
	2020-2021	0.621083	0.011501	0.022579	4.393059	0.111346	3.582979
	2021-2022	0.453035	0.079440	0.113789	7.867843	0.167624	5.918522
	2022-2023	0.489245	0.031391	0.049647	5.339588	0.307886	4.306206
Intrasoft Technologies Ltd	2018-2019	0.470964	0.046359	0.066344	24.54649	0.062740	15.63957
	2019-2020	0.555791	0.017890	0.065033	5.292527	0.052504	4.410564
	2020-2021	0.593149	0.069674	0.099665	16.45499	0.058730	11.07283
	2021-2022	0.599430	0.107388	0.134193	70.84848	0.067599	43.88911
	2022-2023	0.487875	0.065575	0.149395	10.05625	0.049278	7.253236
Kellton Tech Solutions Ltd.	2018-2019	0.088307	0.370063	0.559184	5.025684	0.535626	6.019855
	2019-2020	0.111927	0.327833	0.481128	0.803527	1.355424	4.017186
	2020-2021	0.190169	0.355262	0.497427	10.43886	0.595684	9.225507
	2021-2022	0.225901	0.341443	0.460475	11.04688	0.597004	10.69320
	2022-2023	0.254050	-0.569190	-0.461555	5.904431	0.766865	2.293619
Infobeans Technologies Ltd.	2018-2019	0.493206	0.143377	0.167438	41.71215	0.754762	27.12644
	2019-2020	0.233104	0.132229	0.172392	11.08858	0.689569	8.375769
	2020-2021	0.254469	0.182408	0.189539	18.09460	0.586053	12.62843
	2021-2022	-0.093563	0.172795	0.261832	15.46346	0.499465	10.77072
	2022-2023	0.178884	0.113331	0.266498	14.04276	0.765300	10.44296

continued on following page

Table 2. Continued

NAME OF COMPANY	YEAR'S	WC/TA	RE/TA	EBIT/TA	MVE/ TL	SALES/ TA	Z-score
63 Moons Technologies Ltd.	2018-2019	0.405876	-0.011837	-0.006696	4.231091	0.049984	3.036100
	2019-2020	0.428415	-0.164828	-0.013832	1.942178	0.048990	1.451941
	2020-2021	0.420706	-0.022816	-0.021945	2.432056	0.051615	1.911282
	2021-2022	0.483889	-0.027377	-0.027145	9.657718	0.053146	6.300483
	2022-2023	0.454778	-0.007701	0.007127	3.734959	0.096213	3.760312
Sonata Software Ltd.	2018-2019	0.649360	0.378840	0.537173	10.76030	1.262450	10.76907
	2019-2020	0.333977	0.424511	0.604997	2.300462	1.344125	5.714634
	2020-2021	0.478684	0.031175	0.469662	7.884238	0.998555	8.288570
	2021-2022	0.505633	0.468610	0.645358	12.61008	0.943793	11.90133
	2022-2023	0.447450	0.563192	0.767482	21.18204	1.147646	17.71382
Birlasoft Ltd.	2018-2019	0.313755	0.202249	0.180405	5.083760	0.602226	4.906869
	2019-2020	0.334712	0.134139	0.210659	3.588818	0.874230	4.311267
	2020-2021	0.445116	0.175023	0.255222	15.92261	0.894963	12.06903
	2021-2022	0.485090	0.230846	0.313518	31.08693	1.020389	21.61142
	2022-2023	0.350461	0.204706	0.284612	17.99734	1.492326	13.93558
Infibeam Avenues	2018-2019	0.100705	0.042192	0.053415	1.429933	0.181925	1.391082
	2019-2020	0.060171	0.038418	0.047397	1.520374	0.201965	1.396387
	2020-2021	0.059058	0.021463	0.026098	5.003214	0.176198	3.364989
	2021-2022	0.050073	0.023452	0.028117	6.557719	0.327319	4.447327
	2022-2023	0.076894	0.035697	0.048243	4.354186	0.468206	3.381696
CILO Infotech Ltd.	2018-2019	0.038561	0.010422	-0.009901	0.328550	0.004168	0.200303
	2019-2020	-0.012468	-0.025935	-0.001995	0.288622	0.008977	0.124288
	2020-2021	0.013290	-0.023391	0.002126	0.332010	0.003189	0.192607
	2021-2022	0.002179	-0.029972	-0.002724	0.963398	0.000000	0.529702
	2022-2023	0.201131	-0.018856	0.010685	0.713248	0.001257	0.690858
Rolta India Ltd.	2018-2019	0.532879	-0.000531	-0.580786	0.022949	0.098182	-2.441840
	2019-2020	0.621814	-0.114974	-0.039878	0.004622	0.010011	-1.025962
	2020-2021	-1.771730	-1.021682	-0.848585	0.009127	0.009017	-6.342277
	2021-2022	-2.202918	-0.251733	0.026704	0.013384	0.002660	-2.897116
	2022-2023	-2.760211	-0.344620	-0.075862	0.003575	0.000881	-4.042040
Bharatiya Global Info-Media Ltd.	2018-2019	0.326093	0.002389	0.006677	0.076289	0.270701	0.732892
	2019-2020	0.293284	-0.007672	-0.002056	0.049714	0.082654	0.446818
	2020-2021	0.253529	0.000455	0.001518	0.045071	0.084864	0.421702
	2021-2022	0.266873	0.005359	-0.003883	0.166535	0.027883	0.427690
	2022-2023	0.222408	-0.022795	-0.022759	0.146480	0.018073	0.269729

(Note: - The Data and terms mentioned in the Table 2. Is explained here.)

A = Working capital/ Total assets-

The company liquidity is removed by the assessment of ratios of working capital to its total assets. Although the company's higher liquidity indicates that company has enough short-term assets to manage better liquidity and financial health.

B = Retained earnings/ Total assets-

The ratio analyzes the share of retained earnings in relation to total assets. The high retained earning shows great strength in financial reserves, also reflects the company's power to reinvest in itself.

C = Earnings before interest and taxes (EBIT) / Total assets-

The ratio examines the operational ability by analyzing its earnings before interest and taxes (EBIT) to its total assets. Company can generate operational profits by using the assets in effective manner which indicates higher earnings before interest and taxes (EBIT) compared to total asset ratio.

D = Market value of equity / Total liabilities-

Market values of company is compared to its total liabilities the solvency ratio is obtained. The greater the ratio suggest the company has a strong equity relative to its debts.

E = Sales / Total assets-

Ability to generate revenue from its assets is called efficiency ratio. The increase in utilizing its assets to produce sales means the higher liquidity of the company which is important to maintain profits and growth.

Table 3. Hypothesis of Normality test of Shapiro-Wilk

Null Hypothesis	Test	Sig.	Decision
63 Moons Technology Ltd. distribution is normal, with a mean of 3.29 and a standard deviation of 1.91.	Normality test of Shapiro-Wilk	0.531	Retained the null hypothesis.
Bhartiya Global Info-media Ltd. distribution is normal, with a mean 0.45 and standard deviation 0.16.	Normality test of Shapiro-Wilk	0.263	Retained the null hypothesis.
Birlasoft Ltd. distribution is normal, with a mean 11.36 and standard deviation 7.13.	Normality test of Shapiro-Wilk	0.524	Retained the null hypothesis.

continued on following page

Table 3. Continued

Null Hypothesis	Test	Sig.	Decision
CLIO Infotech Ltd. distribution is normal, with a mean 0.34 and standard deviation 0.24.	Normality test of Shapiro-Wilk	0.196	Retained the null hypothesis.
Compucom Software distribution is normal, with a mean 3.64 and standard deviation 1.58.	Normality test of Shapiro-Wilk	0.902	Retained the null hypothesis.
eClerx Ltd. distribution is normal, with a mean 8.91and standard deviation 3.63.	Normality test of Shapiro-Wilk	0.207	Retained the null hypothesis.
Infibeam Avenues Ltd. distribution is normal, with a mean 2.79 and standard deviation 1.35.	Normality test of Shapiro-Wilk	0.229	Retained the null hypothesis.
Infobean Technologies Ltd. distribution is normal, with a mean 13.86 and standard deviation 7.56.	Normality test of Shapiro-Wilk	0.023	Rejected the null hypothesis.
Infosys Ltd. distribution is normal, with s mean 15.11 and standard deviation 3.42.	Normality test of Shapiro-Wilk	0.521	Retained the null hypothesis.
Infrasoft Ltd. distribution is normal, with a mean 16.45 and standard deviation 15.90.	Normality test of Shapiro-Wilk	0.066	Retained the null hypothesis.
Kellton tech solution Ltd. distribution is normal, with a mean 6.44 and standard deviation 3.50.	Normality test of Shapiro-Wilk	0.759	Retained the null hypothesis.
Rolta India Ltd. distribution is normal, with a mean 3.34 and standard deviation 1.99.	Normality test of Shapiro-Wilk	0.865	Retained the null hypothesis.
Saksoft Ltd. distribution is normal, with a mean 9.75 and standard deviation 13.44.	Normality test of Shapiro-Wilk	0.001	Rejected the null hypothesis.
Sonata software Ltd. distribution is normal, with a mean 10.87 and standard deviation 4.50.	Normality test of Shapiro-Wilk	0.839	Retained the null hypothesis.

(Note:-The above data was analysed with SPSS-19 software and is prominently correct. The Shapiro-Wilk Normality test was used to assess the Altman Z-scores of several IT organizations in order to test the aforementioned hypothesis and determine whether or not the Z-score of the companies had changed considerably over the previous five years. The result of hypothesis testing is reported in Table 3.)

Significance convergence is demonstrated. There is a 0.05 level of significance. The upward analysis shows that, statistically speaking, there is no change in the z-score model, despite all of the differences. Two companies, Saksoft Ltd. and Infobean Technologies, reject the test. Additionally, there is no statistically significant difference.

8. SCOPE FOR FURTHER RESEARCH

The Indian IT sector in India is growing in Emerging Technologies which are essential for a developing country to achieve its future advancements. There are some emerging Technologies which are AI, blockchain and quantum computing, etc. As well this industry contributes Space Sciences, Armed Technologies, Intelligence Bureau and cyber-crimes. IT industry has played a major role in market disruption, innovation in the adoption rates, and various future investment cycles. This could help in the assessment of financial risk associated with the IT companies. As compared to manufacturing sector the IT companies also work in surrounding determined by two intangible assets which human resource and intellectual property. The scope of future research may include the advancements in the Z-score formula which implies on impact on financial stability and non-traditional assets. Financial Persistency of IT sector in service expertise which may determine to include the factors like turnover ratios of employees, property valuation and potential client retention.

Although the research on Indian IT sector, can conclude the various opportunities across the world, which are Silicon Valley, Ireland and the growing Company of Iseral. By studying all the essential factors which specifically involves of financial health and risks, we can determine the geographical and cultural factors. The comparison across countries could reveal some outstanding strategies to remain stable and competitive in the IT sector over the globe, which will provide in-depth knowledge of regional factors in financial field. The future research could aim to incorporate sustainability, while looking over the Environmental, social and governance (ESG) as important stage and focusing on sustainability rules into the model. It may be beneficial to study how the (ESG) activities effect the financial health and bankruptcy risk of IT firms in India. Advanced model that accommodates financial indicators with (ESG's) regulations in long terms sustainability.

The present formulation of Altman Z-score majorly aims on well settled companies; nevertheless, the model has the power to predict and evaluate startups and potential IT firms. In the research the less financial background, shows potential for growth and the inconsistent revenue could conclude how the models react and perform when applied to companies. Early risk identification could be determined by reliable indicators of startups, and it offer the unique value to investors as well as the policy makers in the IT firms. Studying the startups and the environment could be the important aspect, and could provide the changes in the model by various factors.

For examining the financial health of companies, Altman Z-score model provides the essential tools. But there is a vast scope for the further research in the field of Indian IT sector. The customization of the Altman Z-score model in various areas, which will reflect the specific attributes of IT companies. The Altman Z-score model was created specifically with for industrial enterprises, that relies on assets and capital-intensive measures, which may not fully cover risk indicators and performance in asset-light, in technology sector like IT. The future research could focus on intangible assets, patented properties and human assets, which are essentials for IT companies. In another direction for research the different industries could be selected within the Indian economy for comparative analysis regarding the Altman Z-score.

Given that the model is often used to predict the probability of bankruptcy, the effect may be different across the sectors with all operation models such as manufacturing, automobiles and IT. The investigation could be done by researchers whether the Z-score is equally applicable for the all the sectors or the industry adjustments are necessary. The terms like macroeconomics and external factors would be the further research topic, to explore as, are the influencing financial stability of IT companies. Factors like economic distress, changes in government policies, shift in global trends, and technological disturbance could affect the financial health of IT firms. Future research could focus on revisiting the aspects, components or weightings of the Z-score model to reflect the better understanding about assets, trademarks, and human resources which is essential for IT companies.

9. FINDINGS AND CONCLUSION

By using Altman's z-score model, IT businesses' financial health may be assessed and their bankruptcy risk can be identified. The ratios which define companies' strong financial positions in this sector are high profitability, low leverage, and solid liquidity ratios, which evaluates the companies risk profiles and other financial operations according to the model. The Z-score model finds that the companies with diversified client base and creative service offering tend to be in better financial health. The IT companies have managed to the evolving technologies, ensuring revenue growth and higher market valuations. The IT companies which rely on limited number of clients or failed to create innovations may show weaker Z-score, noticing towards the potential challenges in maintaining financial stability.

While evaluating and examining the IT companies most of the companies are falling under the "safe" zone, which analyze the strength and stability of the model. The study done on Altman Z-score model while reviewing the Indian IT sector suggests the adaptivity and ability to evolving market conditions. As the IT sector is performing well, while some companies such as "Saksoft" and "Infobean" are performing closer to "gray" or "distress" zones. The factors which are affecting difference in the financial metrics are as financial ratios, liquidity and the profitability. The IT firms which rely on short-term liabilities or irregular profits consists of higher financial risks. For the stability in this type of firms depends upon some critical factors which are causing financial in stability. The IT companies who achieve higher liquidity, low-liabilities, and increasing assets could achieve consistent higher Z-scores with market fluctuations.

As of manufacturing companies, IT firms depend fully on intangible assets like human resources and intellectual properties. The adjustments which are necessary could be performed to analyze the unique financial properties of IT sector, as well as the financial health and risk can be obtained. The statistical test which includes the Shapiro-Wilk test and Z-test, says that the data set and the analysis of the test is reliable and stable. The normal distribution of the financial data is done which demonstrate strength and credibility of findings during the test. The research shows that the tests which were applied was appropriate and where reliable while it mentioned both the bankruptcy and the financial risks of the IT companies which were being selected. The study demonstrates the evaluation of the Altman Z-score model as a trustworthy asset for analyzing financial health of Indian IT companies.

Although the model is formed for the manufacturing companies, but while making some changes in financial metrics provides the financial health of IT companies as well as the risk associated with it. The findings show the importance of analyzing profitability, the current liquidity as well as past liability, and the relevance of the financial ratios. IT companies which have weak financial indicators which shows higher risk distress. Till the time Altman Z-score defines the reliability and effectiveness, such applications can be applied for the incorporating metric changes in Environmental, social and governance (ESG). The advancements and modifications could enhance the stability and reliability of IT companies. The study provides with the stages of financial planning and risk associated with it ensuring the stability of IT firm. The IT companies with the higher liquidity are firms which could handle uncertainties while minimizing the leverage.

The firms which are well positioned and are well maintained shows the stronger Z-score and promising financial health. Altman Z-score model proves to be trustworthy tool for examining the financial health of companies in the IT sectors. While the substantial IT companies show flexibility and strong financial health, the model reflects potential weaknesses, particularly in the smaller IT companies which are with limited market presence or are slower for adoption of new technologies. The overview provides valuable information for stakeholders, including investors and management, to make decision-making process easy for them on future investments, risk mitigation and strategies for growth within this rapid growing sector. The model provides a broad view on financial health, which allows businesses and investors to tackle challenges actively and freeze new opportunities. By utilizing and applying the Altman Z-score model the stake holders can make informed decisions to increase the sustainable growth and reduce financial risk present over the IT companies in India.

REFERENCES

Abbas, D. M. (2015). Companies Bankruptcy Prediction by using Altman Models And Companring Them. *Research Jounral of Fianance and Acoounting, 6*(14), 16. Retrieved from http://www.iiste.org

Afrin, R. (2014, January & July). Analysing the potential of Altman's Z-score for prediction of market performance and share returns- A case study of the cement industry in Bangladesh. *The AUST JOURNAL OF SCIENCE AND TECHNOLOGY, 6*(1 & 2), 1-16. Retrieved from https://www.aust.edu/aust_journal_v6i1_2

Anjum, S. (2012). Business Bankruptcy prediction model: A significant study of the Altman's Z-score model. *Asain Journal of management research, 3*(1), 212-219. Armutlulu, Z. C. (2021). A revision of Altman Z-Score model and a comparative analysis of Turkish

Anuj, C. S., Narayanan, A., Nandan, S., & Thangjam, R. (2018). The relevance of Altman Z-score analysis. [IJRAR]. *International Journal of Research and Analytical Reviews, 5*(4), 233–240.

Beltratti, A. B. (2012). The credit crisis around the globe: Why did some banks perform better? *Journal of Financial Economics, 105*(1), 1–17. https://econpapers .repec.org/scripts/redir.pf?u=http%3A%2F%2Fwww.sciencedirect.com%2Fscience %2Farticle%2Fpii%2FS0304405X11002790;h=repec:eee:jfinec:v:105:y:2012:i:1: p:1-17

. Bzour, K. A. (2011, March). Predicting Corporate Bankruptcy of Jordanian Listed Companies: Using Altman and Kida Models. *International Journal of Business and Management, 6*(3), 208-215. doi:. v6n3p208DOI: 10.5539/ijbm

Chatterjee, A. (2018). Predicting Corporate Financial Distress for Widely Held Large - Cap Companies in India: Altman Model vs. Ohlson Model. *Indian Journal of Finance, 12*(8), 36–49. DOI: 10.17010/ijf/2018/v12i8/130743

Chouhan, ., V (2014, April). Predicting Financial Stability of Select BSE Companies Revisiting Altman Z score. *International Letters of Social and Humanistic Sciences, 26*, 92–115. DOI: 10.18052/www.scipress.com/ILSHS.26.92

Farahaan Rashid, R. A. (2023, July). A Comprehensive Review of the Altman Z-Score Model Across Industries. *The Business Review, 27*(2).

Joshi, M. K. (2020, July-December). FINANCIAL PERFORMANCE ANALYSIS OF SELECT INDIAN PUBLIC SECTOR BANKS USING ALTMAN'S Z-SCORE MODEL. *SMART Journal of Business Management Studies*, *16*(2), 74–87. DOI: 10.5958/2321-2012.2020.00018.4

KANNADHASAN, M. (2007, June). Measuring Financial Health of A public Limited Company Using 'Z' Score Model. *The Management Accountant*, *42*(6), 469–473.

Lohana, D. (2014, May). Measuring Financial Sustainability of Reliance Industries Limited by using 'Z'-score Model. *International Journal of Scientific and Engineering Research*, *5*(5), 61–72.

Mulla, M. (2019). Sepetember). impact of Operational Efficiency and Customer Satifaction on Banking Performance: Emperical Examination on UAE Islamic Banking. *International Jorunal of Recent Technology and Engineering*, *8*, 304–309. DOI: 10.35940/ijrte.B1051.0982S1019

Panigrahi, A. (2019, January). Validity of Altman's "z" Score Model in Predicting Financial Distress of Pharmaceutical Companies. *NMIMS JOURNAL OF ECONOMICS AND PUBLIC POLICY*, *4*(1), 65-73. Retrieved from https://ssrn.com/abstract=3326312

Runkle, J. H. (1993, February). Size and performance of banking firms: Testing the predictions of theory. *Journal of Monetary Economics*, *31*(1), 47–67. DOI: 10.1016/0304-3932(93)90016-9

Singh, P. N. (2021). Decenber). An Empirical Study of Indian Commercial Banks through Financial Distress Models. *Economic Affairs*, *66*(05), 679–683. DOI: 10.46852/0424-2513.4.2021.23

. Srinivas, T. (2023, July 18). Using the Altman Z-Score Model to Forecast the Financial Distress of a Subset of NIFTY 50 Companies in the Indian Stock Market. doi: https://doi.org/DOI: 10.32388/XN0WTW

Tanjung, P. R. (2020). COMPARATIVE ANALYSIS OF ALTMAN Z-SCORE, SPRINGATE, ZMIJEWSKI AND OHLSON MODELS IN PREDECTING FINANCIAL DISTRESS. *EPRA INTERNATIONAL JOURNAL OF MULTIDISCIPLINARY RESEARCH*, *6*(3), 126–137. DOI: 10.36713/epra4162

Section 3
Sustainability, Culture, and Development

Chapter 9
Sustainable Finance and Investor Dynamics in Emerging Markets

Devesh Rajput
https://orcid.org/0009-0006-1811-9095
Christ University, India

Aashima Jindal
https://orcid.org/0009-0003-9522-5404
Christ University, India

ABSTRACT

This chapter examines the role of sustainable finance in emerging markets, focusing on the integration of Environmental, Social, and Governance (ESG) principles to promote economic growth and social impact. It discusses how ESG investments address challenges like poverty, financial inclusion, and climate change, while exploring factors influencing investor behavior and barriers such as data transparency and greenwashing. The chapter compares ESG adoption in developed and developing economies, highlights sector-specific trends, and emphasizes the importance of public-private partnerships and multilateral collaborations. It also explores sustainable finance's potential for social innovation, supporting gender equality, inclusive development, and green technologies, and advocates for improved transparency and impact measurement to build investor confidence.

DOI: 10.4018/979-8-3373-1404-4.ch009

1 INTRODUCTION

Innovation in capital allocation is being driven by sustainable finance, which combines environmental, social, and governance (ESG) considerations in financial decision making. Its goal is to maximize financial returns while supporting activities that build prosperity, environmental stewardship and social equity. Beyond the traditional financial analysis, this approach includes consideration of such issues as climate change, social inequality, and ethical governance, which results in long term value consistent with sustainability principles(Zairis et al., 2024).

Key drivers of global growth and at the same time highly vulnerable emerging markets are shaping the future development. By 2050, almost 90 per cent of the projected 2.5 billion increase in urban population will be in these region(Goel et al., 2022). But because they rely on industries with big environmental impacts like manufacturing, mining and agriculture, they are more vulnerable to climate change and ESG issues. These markets lack access to sustainable financing and urgently need innovative financial mechanisms to bridge the development and sustainability gap.

1.1 Sustainable Finance: A Global Perspective

The momentum of sustainable finance has grown on a global scale as the importance of its potential to tackle urgent environmental and social challenges has become more widely recognized. Particularly, developed markets have become leaders in ESG integration. These regions are seeing the proliferation of sustainable financial products such as green bonds and ESG focused funds as institutional investors in these regions are incorporating ESG into their decision making processes. For example, the European Union has defined benchmarks in sustainable finance policy with its Sustainable Finance Disclosure Regulation (SFDR) that requires full ESG disclosure(Eriksson, 2024).

Emerging markets, while seeing a boom in sustainable finance activity, face major obstacles. This has been a positive trend in ESG adoption in these economies(Goel et al., 2022), as green bond issuance has grown. But difficulties remain in data quality, disclosure standards and regulatory consistency. To ensure sustainable finance thrives in these regions, further policy frameworks need to evolve to provide clarity, reduce risk and attract long term investments in line with global sustainability goals.

1.2 Why Do Emerging Markets Need Sustainable Finance?

Sustainable finance is well suited to emerging markets, which have their own specific economic, social and environmental needs. In these regions, there are massive funding gaps of $2.5 trillion per year to close to meet the Sustainable Development

Goals (SDGs)(Goel et al., 2022). Sustainable finance can fill this gap by directing capital towards initiatives that support inclusive and equitable growth.

Building resilient infrastructure is a major priority in emerging economies. Funding energy, transportation and water systems that are economically viable and environmentally sustainable is a key role for sustainable finance. Green bonds, sustainability linked loans and other tools are already financing renewable energy and climate resilient projects.

Similarly, emerging markets also have serious environmental challenges, such as climate change and resource scarcity, which are threatening to key sectors such as agriculture. Investments in renewable energy, sustainable agriculture, and ecosystem restoration can mitigate environmental risks and mobilize capital to transition to a low carbon economy(Goel et al., 2022), while sustainable finance can play a role. The SDG framework is comprehensive and can help channel investments into poverty eradication, healthcare, clean energy and infrastructure through sustainable finance.

Sustainable finance aligns financial flows with the SDGs, allowing emerging markets to play a part in global sustainability and their own development. Long term sustainability is dependent on the private sector's ability to mobilize the resources and innovation required.

1.3 The Broader Implications of ESG Integration

Financial decisions incorporating ESG factors help manage a firm's risk and enhance its competitiveness(Panagopoulos & Tzionas, 2023). Companies that are in the driver's seat of ESG performance are more capable of managing market change and societal request, like investing in renewable energy to mitigate the risks posed by volatile energy prices and resource scarcity(Yucel et al., 2023).

And sustainable finance also helps social good by directing capital towards inequality. Other instruments such as social impact bonds channel investments into education, health and poverty reduction, serving underserved communities and promoting social equity.

In addition, sustainable finance plays a role in addressing systemic risks such as climate change and in transition to low carbon economy. Financial institutions are incorporating climate risks, and investments in renewable energy and climate adaptation projects reduce extreme weather and rising sea level risks, helping to build global economic resilience.

2 UNDERSTANDING INVESTOR BEHAVIOR IN DEVELOPING ECONOMIES

The behavior of investors in developing economies is a function of a complicated interaction of economic, cultural, and psychological factors. In the context of sustainable finance, these factors will impact how investors think and allocate resources. Policymakers, financial institutions and other stakeholders who want to help drive ESG integration and the growth of sustainable finance in these regions need to understand these dynamics.

2.1 Factors Affecting Investor Behaviour

2.1.1 Cultural Context

In developing economies, cultural norms and values have a tremendous impact on the investment behaviour. Investors in collectivist societies, which place high emphasis on maintaining community harmony and social responsibility, may be more open to sustainable and responsible investment (SRI) opportunities. For example, in India peer behavior and social norms have a large impact on SRI decisions, which is also reflected in a broader collectivist ethos of the society(Gupta & Goswami, 2024). Individualist cultures, that focus on individual goals and return on investment, have been associated with lower levels of ESG adoption, whereas conversely cultures with higher levels of collectivism have been associated with higher levels of ESG adoption.

Valuable insights into ESG investment trends are outlined by the distinction between collectivist and individualist cultural frameworks. Social influence mechanisms can therefore drive ESG adoption in collective cultures by aligning investment with social values(Gupta & Goswami, 2024). To be effective, ESG initiatives must be tailored to the unique cultural dynamics of developing economies.

2.1.2 Financial Literacy

Investor behavior in developing economies is strongly influenced by financial literacy, and in the domain of sustainable finance. With an understanding of ESG factors, impact investing and green bonds, investors tend to understand the long term value of sustainable investments. Such literacy enables informed decision making and enables integration of sustainability considerations into investment portfolios(Yucel et al., 2023). The studies show that people with higher sustainable finance literacy are more inclined towards sustainable investments.

Financial literacy levels across urban versus rural investors are very different, leading to barriers to market participation and reinforcing inequalities in developing economies. ESG products are also not easy for rural investors with limited access to financial education to assess the risks and opportunities associated with them. In this lack of knowledge occurs suboptimal investment choices and lack of willingness to adopt new financial instruments. It is important to address these disparities to scale up sustainable finance and increase inclusivity.

2.1.3 Economic Constraints

Financial markets in emerging economies are often underdeveloped and these markets restrict easy access to a range of investment opportunities, thereby restricting portfolio diversification. Lack of robust financial infrastructure makes it impossible for investors to enter the realm of innovative financial products, such as ESG products. In addition, micro, small and medium enterprises (MSMEs) operating in these markets face difficulties in raising capital for ESG related projects(Zairis et al., 2024). For instance, India's MSMEs are constrained by insufficient credit because of limited investor interest, preventing access to sustainable efforts.

Economic shocks and currency movements can have a big impact on the investment decisions of investors in emerging markets. There are high costs of capital — caused by perceived risks and lack of competition in the financial sector — which create additional hurdles for businesses wishing to fund sustainable projects. The implication of this research is that real capital costs have a direct negative effect on investment behavior, as unexpected changes in these costs can deter long-term commitments to ESG aligned ventures.

2.1.4 Risk Preferences

Risk aversion is a defining characteristic of investors in emerging markets, shaped by political instability, economic volatility, and regulatory uncertainty. These factors deter investors from engaging with ESG investments, which are often perceived as riskier or less profitable than traditional options(Gupta & Goswami, 2024). This perception of riskiness poses a significant challenge to the widespread adoption of sustainable finance products in developing economies.

Investors in emerging markets often exhibit a strong home bias, favoring domestic assets over international diversification opportunities. This behavior stems from a familiarity with local markets and a perceived lower risk associated with domestic investments. While home bias can provide a sense of security, it limits exposure to international ESG opportunities and restricts the flow of capital to sustainable projects in other regions, including emerging economies that might benefit from cross-border investments.

2.2 Behavioral Biases Shaping Investor Choices in Emerging Economies

Investor behavior in developing economies is often shaped by biases like herd behavior, overconfidence, and short-termism, which impact sustainable finance decisions(Gupta & Goswami, 2024). Herd behavior, driven by peer influence, can lead to large inflows into ESG funds without proper due diligence, undermining the effectiveness of ESG initiatives. Overconfidence biases investors to overestimate their abilities, potentially neglecting the complexities of ESG issues and making suboptimal investment decisions. Additionally, short-termism, the preference for immediate gains, hampers ESG adoption as investors overlook the long-term benefits of sustainable investments.Addressing these biases requires investor education, incentives for long-term investments, and regulatory measures like mandatory ESG disclosures. Educating investors on the long-term advantages of sustainable finance and aligning financial incentives with ESG goals can help promote a more informed and sustainable investment culture in developing economies.

2.3 Investor Awareness and Perceptions of ESG Factors

Investor awareness and perceptions of ESG factors are crucial for the growth of sustainable finance in emerging markets. Awareness gaps, regional disparities, and misconceptions about ESG investments hinder adoption. Motivations for sustainable and responsible investments (SRI) extend beyond financial returns, driven by altruism, ethical values, and social responsibility, with external influences like peer dynamics and societal norms shaping preferences. Extreme weather events and media coverage are prompting a shift toward sustainability-focused investments (Persad et al., 2024).However, the perception that ESG investments involve financial trade-offs remains a barrier. Many investors worry about reduced returns, though some are willing to accept this to uphold ethical values. Addressing these concerns through education, transparency, and promoting the long-term benefits of ESG investments can help align financial and sustainability goals, fostering greater adoption(Ferri & Acosta, 2019).

2.4 Socioeconomic and Political Factors

Political and economic uncertainty significantly impacts ESG adoption by undermining investor confidence and deterring long-term commitments to sustainable projects. Policy continuity risks, stemming from unstable political environments, raise concerns about the consistency of regulations, especially in sectors like sustainable transportation, where uncertainty over technologies such as electric vehicles or hydrogen can delay investments(Rahman & Hossain, 2024). Market volatility caused by political instability makes investors cautious about allocating capital to ESG projects perceived as higher risk.

Regulatory frameworks are key in shaping sustainable finance markets. Effective policies mandating ESG disclosures and offering incentives for sustainable practices can foster ESG adoption, influencing investor behavior and corporate strategies. Economic factors like GDP growth, industrialization, and urbanization influence ESG adoption in developing economies by creating new investment opportunities in infrastructure, while also presenting environmental and social challenges that demand ESG integration. Mature economies with more sophisticated financial systems can better align with ESG principles, while emerging markets face challenges related to transparency and data quality, limiting their ability to fully embrace sustainable finance.

2.5 Strategies to Influence Investor Behavior

Influencing investor behavior in emerging markets is essential for fostering the adoption of sustainable finance and Environmental, Social, and Governance (ESG) principles. This requires a multi-faceted approach, including educational initiatives, behavioral nudges, and technological advancements to improve access and transparency in ESG investing(Goel et al., 2022). Such strategies are designed to overcome cognitive and structural barriers while aligning investment decisions with long-term sustainability objectives.

Educational campaigns and capacity-building efforts form the cornerstone of these strategies, aiming to enhance sustainable finance literacy and encourage positive attitudes toward ESG investing(Persad et al., 2024). Research highlights that individuals with a deeper understanding of sustainable finance instruments, such as green bonds and ESG funds, are more likely to participate in these markets. The primary educational objectives involve equipping investors with knowledge about ESG principles, the risk-return dynamics of sustainable finance, and the broader societal impacts of such investments.

To achieve these objectives, financial institutions and governments can implement several best practices. Workshops and awareness campaigns can be organized to educate investors on the fundamentals of sustainable finance and the benefits of ESG products. These campaigns should emphasize the environmental benefits of sustainable investments, such as energy conservation, emission reductions, and efficient resource management. Misconceptions about the risk-return profiles of sustainable finance instruments must also be addressed, underscoring their potential for portfolio diversification and competitive returns(Sharma et al., 2023). Moreover, it is crucial to highlight the societal impact of ESG investments by showcasing their contributions to social responsibility, the well-being of future generations, and the achievement of Sustainable Development Goals (SDGs).

2.6 Influence of technology on Investment Behavior

Fintech innovations democratize access to financial services, overcoming geographical and infrastructural barriers while significantly enhancing sustainable finance. User-friendly platforms simplify ESG investing through intuitive interfaces, crowdfunding connects investors with sustainable projects in underfunded regions, and data analytics and AI personalize educational content and investment recommendations, fostering engagement(Yucel et al., 2023). AI enhances ESG investing by efficiently processing data on corporate sustainability, regulatory changes, and market trends, enabling precise investment decisions and personalized portfolios aligned with ethical values. Blockchain addresses transparency and trust issues by providing immutable records of ESG performance, simplifying impact reporting, and ensuring secure, fraud-resistant transactions, thus boosting confidence in ESG markets(Rahman & Hossain, 2024).

3 COMPARING DEVELOPED AND DEVELOPING ECONOMIES

The adoption and integration of ESG principles vary significantly between developed and developing economies due to differences in awareness, cultural norms, regulatory frameworks, and corporate practices. These disparities influence the pace and effectiveness of ESG adoption, highlighting the need for context-specific strategies to promote sustainable finance globally.

3.1 ESG Awareness and Cultural Norms

Developed economies exhibit higher ESG awareness and cultural alignment with sustainability, driven by widespread education and advocacy, robust regulatory frameworks mandating ESG disclosures, and growing consumer demand for ethical products. These factors create an environment where sustainability is integral to business and investment decisions. In contrast, developing economies face challenges such as educational gaps in sustainable finance, a focus on immediate societal priorities like poverty alleviation and infrastructure, and weaker regulatory frameworks, which make ESG integration less prioritized and more voluntary(Sharma et al., 2023).

3.2 Corporate ESG Practices

In developed economies, stringent regulatory requirements, such as the European Union's Non-Financial Reporting Directive (NFRD) and Corporate Sustainability Reporting Directive (CSRD), have compelled businesses to disclose their Environmental, Social, and Governance (ESG) practices(Eriksson, 2024). These mandates drive organizations to actively manage and transparently report their sustainability performance. Alongside regulatory pressures, socially conscious consumers in developed markets increasingly demand ethical practices from companies. This consumer behavior is mirrored by institutional investors, who prioritize businesses with high ESG ratings, thereby creating significant financial incentives for compliance.

While in emerging markets, many companies embrace ESG practices voluntarily, not because they have to, but because they recognize the growing expectations of investors and the global market's push for sustainability. This proactive approach also opens doors to international funding opportunities, like green bonds and ESG-focused funds, which reward businesses committed to positive change. Being listed in respected sustainability indices, such as those in Brazil and South Africa, becomes a proud milestone, inspiring companies to further improve their efforts and make a meaningful impact.

3.3 Key Drivers of ESG Integration

Developed economies benefit from strong consumer demand for sustainability, advanced regulatory frameworks mandating ESG disclosures, and institutional investor activism promoting corporate accountability. In contrast, developing economies focus on attracting international funding, aligning with global standards, leveraging emerging sustainability indices, and gradually recognizing the long-term economic and environmental benefits of sustainable practices(Vives & Wadhwa, 2012).

3.4 Stringency of Regulations

Developed markets, particularly in the EU, lead in stringent ESG regulations, ensuring transparency and accountability through initiatives like the Non-Financial Reporting Directive (NFRD), Corporate Sustainability Reporting Directive (CSRD), and the EU Green Deal, which integrates ESG principles into economic decisions. In contrast, developing economies face fragmented and less enforceable regulatory frameworks, with limited standardization creating uncertainty for investors(Eriksson, 2024). However, select markets, such as China, show progress with initiatives like green bond guidelines, though advancements remain uneven across regions.

3.5 Data Availability and Reporting Standards

Developed economies benefit from standardized ESG reporting frameworks like GRI, SASB, and TCFD, which enhance transparency, build investor confidence, and enable efficient capital allocation to ESG-focused companies(Persad et al., 2024). In contrast, developing economies face challenges such as inconsistent reporting frameworks, limited independent verification, and unreliable data, which hinder comparability, raise concerns about greenwashing, and undermine investor confidence in assessing sustainability risks and opportunities.

3.6 Market Maturity and Capital Access

Developed economies have mature ESG markets offering a wide range of sustainable financial products, such as green bonds, social bonds, and sustainability-linked loans, with established indices and funds catering to both institutional and retail investors(Aggarwal & Elembilassery, 2018). In contrast, ESG markets in developing economies are still emerging, with limited product offerings and slower growth due to regulatory gaps, data challenges, and lower awareness. However, international incentives, including access to global capital markets and investor expectations, are driving incremental progress in ESG adoption.

3.7 Examining Investor Profiles and Behavioral Trends

In developed economies, ESG investing is dominated by institutional investors with the expertise and resources to analyze complex ESG data and advocate for sustainable practices. Conversely, retail investors play a larger role in developing economies, often limited by financial literacy and access to reliable ESG information(Pilaj, 2017). Developed economies leverage ESG factors for risk mitigation and long-term goals, supported by robust regulations and fiduciary duties, while developing economies perceive ESG investments as riskier due to market volatility and short-term investment horizons. Behavioral biases like herding and overconfidence affect both markets, but in developing economies, collectivist cultures and peer influences strongly shape socially responsible investment behavior.

4 CHALLENGES AND OPPORTUNITIES FOR ESG INTEGRATION

The integration of ESG principles in developing economies faces several significant challenges. These challenges range from data deficiencies and regulatory gaps to cultural barriers and higher costs of capital. However, overcoming these obstacles also presents numerous opportunities for growth, innovation, and the development of sustainable finance frameworks tailored to emerging markets. Addressing these barriers can foster a more inclusive and resilient financial ecosystem that aligns with global sustainability goals.

4.1 Major Challenges to ESG Integration in Developing Economies

4.1.1 Data and Transparency Deficiencies

Emerging markets face significant challenges in addressing data and transparency deficiencies related to ESG practices. The scarcity of reliable data, stemming from limited disclosure practices, inconsistent reporting frameworks, and difficulties in data collection and verification, makes it challenging for investors to accurately assess a company's ESG performance. This lack of accurate data hinders informed investment decisions. Additionally, the absence of globally standardized ESG reporting frameworks further complicates the issue(Sharma et al., 2023). Varying standards across countries and industries make consistent benchmarking nearly impossible, discouraging investors from making confident comparisons and decisions. This lack of standardization ultimately undermines trust in the quality and comparability of ESG information.

4.1.2 Regulatory and Institutional Gaps

In many developing economies, the lack of comprehensive ESG regulations and effective enforcement mechanisms presents a significant challenge. Without strong oversight, there is a risk of greenwashing(Eriksson, 2024), where companies may claim to be more environmentally and socially responsible than they truly are, undermining the credibility of ESG investments and eroding investor trust in sustainable finance markets. Additionally, the limited institutional capacity in financial institutions and government agencies in emerging markets further exacerbates this issue(Panagopoulos & Tzionas, 2023). Many of these institutions lack the necessary resources and expertise to implement and monitor ESG principles effectively. To address this, capacity-building initiatives, such as training, knowledge-sharing, and technical assistance, are essential to enable proper implementation and oversight of ESG standards, helping to strengthen the sustainability framework in these regions.

4.1.3 Higher Costs of Capital

Companies in emerging markets often struggle with elevated borrowing costs for green and sustainable projects, which can be significantly higher than those for traditional investments. This disparity creates a challenge for businesses, particularly in sectors with tight profit margins, making it harder for them to pursue sustainability initiatives. The higher cost of capital is largely due to the perceived risks of operating in these markets, deterring both domestic and international investors from funding green projects(Rahman & Hossain, 2024). Additionally, the financial burden of complying with ESG standards, such as obtaining green certifications and meeting reporting requirements, can be overwhelming for smaller enterprises. For many of these businesses, the costs associated with ESG reporting and certification may be too high, ultimately delaying or preventing their ability to engage in sustainable finance and adopt ESG practices.

4.1.4 Cultural and Behavioral Barriers

In many developing markets, there is often a strong emphasis on short-term profit, driven by economic instability and a lack of patient capital(Goel et al., 2022). This focus on immediate financial returns tends to limit the willingness of both investors and corporations to embrace long-term sustainability initiatives. ESG strategies, which require long-term commitments and may not offer immediate benefits, struggle to gain buy-in in such environments. Additionally, public awareness of ESG benefits in these economies remains limited, with many people still unfamiliar with the long-term financial advantages of ESG investing. As a result, there is skepticism regarding its financial value(Aggarwal & Elembilassery, 2018), and ESG investments are often seen as less profitable than traditional ones. This lack of understanding is further exacerbated by misinformation and misconceptions about ESG risks and returns, creating significant barriers to broader adoption.

4.2 Opportunities for Overcoming Barriers to ESG Integration

4.2.1 Addressing Data and Reporting Gaps

To address data and reporting gaps, it is crucial to encourage the adoption of globally recognized reporting standards, such as the Global Reporting Initiative (GRI) or the Task Force on Climate-Related Financial Disclosures (TCFD). These frameworks help emerging economies align their ESG reporting with global best practices(Yucel et al., 2023). Additionally, investing in data infrastructure is key to overcoming data deficiencies. By improving ESG data collection systems, developing markets can ensure the availability of high-quality, comparable data, enhancing the transparency and reliability of ESG disclosures.

4.2.2 Addressing Greenwashing and Credibility Issues in ESG Integration

Greenwashing, the practice of making false or exaggerated sustainability claims, poses a major barrier to the growth of sustainable finance, especially in emerging markets. This practice not only undermines investor confidence but also detracts from the effectiveness of ESG integration, making it more difficult to distinguish genuine sustainability efforts from mere marketing tactics. Greenwashing occurs when companies inflate their ESG commitments or misrepresent their sustainability practices for reputational gain without taking meaningful action. As a result, skepticism grows, eroding trust in ESG products and impeding the progress toward global sustainability goals(Nicholls, 2021). The consequences are far-reaching, including reduced capital flows to truly sustainable projects, diminished interest in ESG products, and slower progress in achieving sustainability objectives.

Several factors contribute to the persistence of greenwashing, particularly in emerging markets. ESG ratings from various agencies can differ significantly, with some, like MSCI, placing emphasis on factors such as exposure to environmental regulations or profitability instead of a company's actual environmental impact. This can lead to misleading ratings that misrepresent a company's true sustainability performance. Similarly, impact washing, where funds or products are labeled as "sustainable" without meeting rigorous standards, further compounds the issue. Moreover, weak regulatory frameworks and limited enforcement in many developing economies allow companies to make misleading ESG claims with little consequence, perpetuating greenwashing and diminishing the reliability of ESG reporting.

To address these challenges, robust verification mechanisms and standardized frameworks are essential. Independent third-party certifications and audits play a crucial role in validating ESG claims, ensuring data accuracy, and deterring greenwashing practices. Recognized reporting frameworks like GRI, SASB, and TCFD provide a credible and consistent basis for ESG reporting, reducing the likelihood of misleading claims and boosting investor confidence. Moreover, globally recognized ESG taxonomies, such as the EU Taxonomy and China's Green Bond Guidelines, offer clear definitions and standardized classifications for sustainable activities. These taxonomies help reduce greenwashing by providing a uniform standard that companies can adhere to, making it easier for investors to compare ESG performance across companies and industries(Panagopoulos & Tzionas, 2023).

Improving disclosure practices is equally vital to ensure transparency and build trust in ESG investments. Mandatory disclosure requirements can help standardize ESG reporting, making data more comparable across markets. By incentivizing companies to report ESG data systematically, regulators can create a level playing field and empower investors with consistent, reliable information to make informed decisions. Furthermore, enhancing the quality, accessibility, and comparability of ESG data is critical(Aggarwal & Elembilassery, 2018). Standardized methodologies and technologies, like data analytics and AI, can improve data management and risk assessment, while capacity-building programs within companies can support accurate and transparent reporting. The development of standards like SASB and the ongoing use of technology are crucial steps toward improving ESG data quality and accessibility.

4.2.3 Innovation in Financial Instruments

Instruments like green bonds, sustainability-linked loans, and social impact bonds are not only gaining popularity but are also paving the way for more impactful financial markets that prioritize environmental, social, and governance (ESG) goals. Green bonds, for instance, have become a prominent tool to fund projects aimed at mitigating climate change, from renewable energy to sustainable infrastructure. As more investors focus on aligning their portfolios with climate action, green bonds have seen an impressive rise in demand.

Sustainability-linked loans, another innovative instrument, are pushing companies to improve their ESG performance by linking the cost of borrowing to sustainability targets(Nicholls, 2021). This creates a financial incentive for companies to enhance their environmental practices or social impacts, fostering a culture of accountability and long-term thinking. As businesses strive to lower their borrowing costs by meeting specific ESG goals, these loans help align corporate behavior with broader sustainability objectives.

Social impact bonds, meanwhile, offer a unique approach by focusing on funding social projects that deliver tangible outcomes, such as poverty reduction or healthcare improvements. The innovative aspect of these bonds lies in their structure: financial returns are tied to the achievement of measurable social impacts, aligning investor interests with the welfare of communities(Nicholls, 2021). Additionally, new financial instruments like transition bonds and blue bonds are expanding the scope of sustainable finance, addressing specific areas like ocean conservation and the transition to a low-carbon economy.

4.2.4 Development of New Instruments

There is significant potential for developing new financial instruments that can address specific local challenges and expand the scope of sustainable finance beyond traditional green initiatives. For example, biodiversity-linked bonds could be introduced to fund projects dedicated to preserving natural ecosystems, with returns tied to the successful protection of biodiversity(Nicholls, 2021). Similarly, water-resource bonds could be developed in emerging markets facing water scarcity, providing a financial mechanism to support the development of water infrastructure and promote sustainable water usage and management. Innovations like these broaden the impact of sustainable finance, allowing it to address a wider range of environmental and social challenges, from biodiversity conservation to water resource management, and create tailored solutions that resonate with local needs.

4.2.5 Public-Private Partnerships (PPPs)

Public-private partnerships (PPPs) play a crucial role in scaling ESG initiatives and advancing sustainable finance projects, particularly in emerging markets. These collaborations combine the strengths of both sectors to address barriers to ESG adoption. Governments can serve as anchor investors, offer credit enhancements, and establish regulatory frameworks that foster sustainable finance, as seen with the green bond markets in India and China, which have flourished due to government support(Panagopoulos & Tzionas, 2023). On the other hand, the private sector brings essential capital, innovation, and market expertise, while governments create the enabling environments that allow sustainable projects to thrive. Through PPPs, the public and private sectors can share knowledge, technology, and best practices, empowering emerging markets to tailor sustainable finance solutions to their unique local contexts.

4.2.6 Leveraging Technology

Fintech innovations are playing a pivotal role in enhancing ESG data management, leveraging technologies like artificial intelligence (AI), big data analytics, and cloud computing to improve data collection, transparency, and accessibility. AI can automate the process of gathering and analyzing vast ESG datasets, while big data analytics offers deep insights into ESG performance, helping investors make more informed and accurate decisions. In parallel, blockchain technology is revolutionizing traceability and accountability in sustainable finance by providing a secure, transparent platform to track ESG data throughout the supply chain. This not only boosts the credibility of ESG reporting but also reduces the risk of data manipulation and enhances audit efficiency(Aggarwal & Elembilassery, 2018). Additionally, blockchain facilitates secure transactions within sustainable finance markets, fostering greater trust and confidence in the ecosystem. Together, these fintech innovations are driving the transformation of ESG data management and ensuring greater integrity and transparency in the finance sector.

5 CASE STUDIES: EMERGING MARKETS AND SUSTAINABLE INVESTMENT TRENDS

This section explores both successful and challenging examples of ESG investment initiatives in emerging markets. The case studies illustrate the growing adoption of sustainable finance practices and highlight lessons learned from projects that faced setbacks. Through these examples, we gain valuable insights into how ESG integration is evolving in developing economies and how it can be further scaled.

5.1 Success Stories of ESG Investment in Emerging Markets

5.1.1 Green Bond Pioneers

Chile: Chile has emerged as a leader in sustainable finance among emerging markets, particularly through its innovative use of green bonds. These bonds currently comprise nearly 12% of Chile's GDP, highlighting the country's strong commitment to financing environmentally sustainable projects(Goel et al., 2022). Chile's pioneering efforts began in 2019 when it became the first sovereign issuer of green bonds in the Americas, raising €861 million ($950 million) through a 12-year green bond at an impressively low yield. This success paved the way for further expansion in sustainable finance, with Chile issuing its first social bond in 2020 and its inaugural sustainable bond in 2021. By the end of January 2022, the country's ESG instruments totaled approximately $31 billion, representing 28.3% of its total debt.

Chile has strategically used green bonds to fund large-scale projects in renewable energy, water management, and sustainable infrastructure. The country's efforts have been crucial in attracting responsible investments and positioning itself as a model for other developing economies seeking to leverage financial instruments for environmental impact. In 2022, Chile issued its first sustainability-linked bond (SLB), a $2 billion, 20-year bond, underscoring its ongoing commitment to sustainable finance. These efforts have firmly established Chile as a global leader in green finance, setting an example for how emerging markets can harness the power of financial instruments to drive environmental sustainability(Environmental Finance, 2020).

Peru: Peru has increasingly embraced sustainability-linked financial instruments, such as sustainability-linked bonds (SLBs), to promote sustainable development across various sectors. Unlike traditional green bonds, which fund specific environmentally sustainable projects, SLBs tie interest payments to a company's performance on predefined environmental, social, and governance (ESG) key performance indicators (KPIs). This innovative approach incentivizes companies to improve their sustainability practices by linking financial rewards to their ESG performance(Goel et al., 2022). Peru's commitment to these instruments is further reflected in its active engagement with the global sustainable finance market. In 2021, the country's green, social, and sustainability-linked (GSS+) deals reached USD 4.8 billion, signaling a significant shift towards sustainable finance. Additionally, in June 2023, Peru issued its first sovereign green bond, raising S/ 16.358 million, with the aim of strengthening public debt management and advancing its transition to an environmentally responsible economy. The country's use of sustainability-linked bonds, along with other sovereign bonds such as a social bond for €1 billion in late 2021, demonstrates Peru's dedication to aligning financial incentives with long-term ESG goals and driving positive environmental and social outcomes.(Global Green Growth Institute, 2024)

5.1.2 Renewable Energy Projects

India and Brazil: India and Brazil have emerged as significant players in the renewable energy sector, particularly in solar and wind power, with green finance playing a crucial role in funding these projects. Both countries have heavily invested in green energy to reduce carbon emissions and enhance energy independence(-Goel et al., 2022). Green bonds have become a key financial instrument, helping to fund the infrastructure needed for large-scale solar and wind projects. In Brazil, the government has been proactive in promoting sustainable finance, launching the Sovereign Sustainable Bond Framework in 2023 to enable the issuance of green, social, and sustainability bonds for financing budgetary programs with positive environmental and social impacts. Additionally, the Brazilian Development Bank (BNDES) has been instrumental in financing renewable energy projects, and the establishment of Fundo Clima, a $10 billion climate fund, has further supported sustainable initiatives.

Similarly, India has made significant strides in green finance and is now the world's second-largest market for green bonds, with $28.2 billion worth of bonds issued to date. In early 2023, India launched its first sovereign green bond, raising about $2 billion for projects focused on climate change mitigation and adaptation. Moreover, municipal corporations in India, such as the Indore Municipal Corporation, have started issuing green bonds to finance renewable energy projects, including a

60-megawatt solar power plant. These efforts reflect the importance of green finance in helping both nations scale up their renewable energy capacities and contribute to the global transition to a low-carbon economy. By harnessing the potential of green bonds and other financial instruments, India and Brazil are playing a pivotal role in financing the renewable energy infrastructure necessary for a sustainable future. (U.S. Agency for International Development, 2020; World Bank Group, 2024)

5.1.3 Sustainability in Agriculture

Southeast Asia: Southeast Asia's agriculture sector is playing a crucial role in the region's ESG landscape, with many small and medium enterprises (SMEs) adopting sustainable farming practices to address climate change challenges(Goel et al., 2022). These initiatives focus on improving resource efficiency, boosting productivity, and enhancing social equity. Microfinance institutions, often supported by impact investment, are helping SMEs integrate sustainable agriculture practices, thereby contributing to broader ESG goals. Programs like USAID's Green Invest Asia connect investors with sustainable agriculture and forestry businesses in the region, helping companies improve their commodity production and manage environmental risks. These efforts are vital for achieving the region's sustainable development objectives.

However, the region faces significant challenges, such as the dominance of family-owned conglomerates in industries like sugar, palm oil, timber, and mining. These conglomerates often exert considerable influence over local banks, reducing their dependence on capital markets and hindering the widespread adoption of sustainable practices. Despite these obstacles, the growing interest in sustainable investing has led to the development of new financial instruments tailored to local challenges. For instance, biodiversity-linked bonds can fund projects aimed at preserving natural ecosystems, with returns tied to the successful protection of biodiversity. Similarly, water-resource bonds can finance infrastructure projects in areas facing water scarcity, promoting sustainable water usage and management(Goel et al., 2022). These innovations broaden the scope of sustainable finance beyond traditional green initiatives, addressing a wider range of environmental and social challenges.

In summary, while Southeast Asia's agriculture sector is making significant strides toward sustainability, it faces challenges related to the influence of family-owned conglomerates and the need for tailored financial instruments. To overcome these barriers, a coordinated effort from governments, financial institutions, and businesses is needed to promote sustainable practices and develop innovative financial solutions that meet the region's unique needs. By fostering a supportive environment for ESG investments, Southeast Asia can pave the way for a more sustainable and equitable future.(Bain, 2024; UNDP, 2024)

6 CHALLENGES AS LESSONS FROM FAILED ESG INITIATIVES

While there are numerous success stories, some ESG initiatives in emerging markets have faced set-backs. These challenges underscore the importance of addressing regulatory, operational, and cultural barriers to ensure the success of future ESG projects.

6.1 Regulatory and Operational Barriers

Inconsistent definitions and unclear regulatory frameworks remain significant barriers in the ESG landscape. One major challenge is the lack of universally accepted definitions, particularly in the context of green bonds, which can lead to greenwashing—where projects are labeled as "green" without meeting rigorous sustainability criteria. This ambiguity creates confusion among investors and undermines trust in ESG investments(Persad et al., 2024). Additionally, many emerging markets face unclear regulatory frameworks that hinder the growth of sustainable finance. Without clear guidelines and effective enforcement mechanisms, companies struggle to align their operations with ESG goals, and investors hesitate to commit capital to projects without assurance that they meet required sustainability standards. Weak governance structures, characterized by a lack of transparency and accountability, further exacerbate these issues. The absence of strong governance frameworks can lead to significant setbacks, with ESG projects failing to meet their objectives(Panagopoulos & Tzionas, 2023). To overcome these challenges, clear definitions, robust regulatory frameworks, and strong governance structures are essential to ensuring the credibility and effectiveness of ESG initiatives.

6.2 Impact of Greenwashing

Greenwashing has a significant negative impact on the sustainable finance market, primarily by eroding investor trust. When companies make exaggerated or false sustainability claims, it undermines the integrity of the ESG market, causing investors to become skeptical of future ESG opportunities. This lack of trust discourages capital flow into genuinely sustainable projects. Additionally, greenwashing contributes to market confusion by applying the terms "green" or "sustainable" without clear and consistent definitions, making it difficult for investors to distinguish between authentic ESG projects and those simply seeking to capitalize on the growing trend without making meaningful changes(Aggarwal & Elembilassery, 2018). This confusion further hinders the growth of the sustainable finance market. To combat this, there is a clear need for robust standards and definitions, as well as the enforcement of transparent ESG criteria through regulatory frameworks, to promote investor confidence and ensure that ESG investments lead to real, measurable impacts(Peltonen et al., 2011).

6.3 Inadequate Stakeholder Engagement

Inadequate stakeholder engagement is a significant barrier to the success of ESG initiatives. Limited community involvement can lead to resistance and delays, preventing projects from achieving their intended outcomes. When local communities are not consulted, projects often fail to align with their needs and concerns, resulting in a lack of support or, in some cases, project abandonment. Additionally, ESG initiatives that do not take local priorities into account tend to be less effective. Top-down approaches, particularly in sectors like agriculture or infrastructure, may exacerbate existing social inequalities or environmental challenges instead of addressing them(Persad et al., 2024). To mitigate these risks, it is crucial to establish multi-stakeholder platforms that foster collaboration between businesses, investors, regulators, and local communities(Rahman & Hossain, 2024). These platforms encourage dialogue, build consensus, and ensure that ESG projects are designed with local needs and priorities in mind, promoting more inclusive and impactful outcomes(Panagopoulos & Tzionas, 2023). Engaging stakeholders from the outset helps ensure that benefits are equitably distributed and that potential challenges are addressed proactively.

7 SUSTAINABLE FINANCE AS A TOOL FOR SOCIAL INNOVATION

Sustainable finance has the potential to drive significant social change by fostering financial inclusion, alleviating poverty, and supporting social innovation. By aligning financial investments with social and environmental goals, sustainable finance offers new avenues for addressing income disparities and empowering marginalized communities. This section explores how sustainable finance tools, such as microfinance, social impact bonds, and alternative financial institutions, contribute to building more inclusive and equitable economic systems.

7.1 Financial Inclusion and Poverty Alleviation Through Sustainable Finance

Sustainable finance plays a critical role in promoting financial inclusion and addressing poverty in emerging markets. By providing access to capital and financial services for underserved populations, sustainable finance initiatives empower individuals and small businesses, facilitating greater economic participation and reducing income disparities(Aggarwal & Elembilassery, 2018).

7.1.1 Microfinance and Community Empowerment

Microfinance plays a crucial role in fostering financial inclusion by providing small loans, savings, insurance, and fund transfers to individuals and small businesses that lack access to traditional banking services. These financial services empower marginalized communities, offering the capital needed to start or expand businesses, manage financial crises, and improve overall quality of life. In many developing economies, microfinance has become a powerful tool for economic empowerment, particularly for women and marginalized groups, by helping entrepreneurs overcome barriers to credit and creating jobs that enhance community prosperity(Ferri & Acosta, 2019). With the increasing focus on Environmental, Social, and Governance (ESG) factors, microfinance institutions (MFIs) are aligning their portfolios with sustainability criteria, attracting greater funding and support for initiatives that have positive social and environmental impacts(Peltonen et al., 2011). This growing emphasis on social outcomes is expected to strengthen microfinance ecosystems, particularly in underserved regions, creating a more inclusive and sustainable financial landscape.

7.1.2 Social Impact Bonds (SIBs)

Social Impact Bonds (SIBs) represent an innovative public-private partnership model designed to address social challenges by aligning the interests of investors, service providers, and governments. In an SIB, private investors provide upfront capital for public projects aimed at achieving social and environmental outcomes(Ferri & Acosta, 2019). If the project meets predefined success metrics, such as reducing homelessness, improving education outcomes, or enhancing healthcare access, the government or an aid agency repays the investors with capital plus interest. This results-oriented approach incentivizes measurable results by linking financial returns to the successful achievement of social outcomes, ensuring that investors are directly tied to the success of the initiative, driving better accountability and performance. The potential of SIBs to create measurable social outcomes is evident in examples such as projects aimed at reducing recidivism rates in prison systems or increasing employment for at-risk populations(Nicholls, 2021). These initiatives have demonstrated that the SIB model can generate both social and financial returns, making them a valuable tool for addressing complex societal issues.

7.2 Green Technologies and Sustainable Production Models: The Intersection of Sustainable Finance and Technological Innovation

The primary role of sustainable finance is to provide the capital necessary for research, development, and deployment of green technologies. This funding supports innovations such as renewable energy sources, energy-efficient technologies, and carbon capture solutions(Zairis et al., 2024). By facilitating access to capital, sustainable finance makes green technologies more accessible to businesses and consumers alike, fostering widespread adoption and scaling up of sustainable solutions across industries.

Several financial instruments are essential in supporting the development of green technologies:

Green Bonds: Green bonds are a critical financial instrument used to fund large-scale environmental projects. They are specifically designed for investments that contribute to positive environmental outcomes, such as renewable energy infrastructure, energy efficiency improvements, and sustainable agriculture projects. By issuing green bonds, companies and governments can attract investors who are looking for both financial returns and positive environmental impacts(Ferri & Acosta, 2019). The increasing issuance of green bonds in emerging markets demonstrates their growing importance in funding green technologies and projects(Zairis et al., 2024).

ESG Investments: ESG (Environmental, Social, and Governance) investing encourages investors to consider a company's environmental and social performance alongside its financial metrics. This investment approach has led many companies to adopt greener technologies and sustainable practices, thus making their businesses more attractive to ESG-focused investors. ESG investment funds are also growing in popularity, supporting companies that are at the forefront of technological innovations for sustainability.

Green Loans: Green loans are loans designed specifically for environmentally beneficial projects. These loans often come with incentives, such as lower interest rates, if the borrower meets certain sustainability criteria. Green loans are an attractive option for companies looking to finance projects related to renewable energy or resource efficiency, and they are particularly beneficial for businesses that are transitioning to more sustainable operations.

7.3 Circular Economy Initiatives

The circular economy is a model that promotes sustainability through the reduction, reuse, and recycling of resources. This model is central to addressing global environmental challenges, such as waste generation, resource depletion, and pollution(Vives & Wadhwa, 2012).

Key components that contribute to the transition towards circularity:

Waste Reduction and Resource Recycling: One of the fundamental principles of the circular economy is minimizing waste generation and maximizing resource efficiency. Sustainable finance supports companies and initiatives focused on waste reduction, recycling, and the efficient use of materials. This approach not only reduces environmental footprints but also improves the economic viability of businesses by turning waste into valuable resources.

Green Technologies Enabling the Circular Economy: Green technologies are crucial enablers of the circular economy. For example, advanced recycling technologies can help recover and reuse valuable materials from waste streams. Energy-efficient manufacturing processes, which reduce resource consumption and minimize waste generation, are another key aspect of the circular economy. Green finance is essential in supporting the development of such technologies and ensuring they are accessible to companies across various industries.

Sustainable Finance's Role in Circular Economy: The increasing emphasis on ESG investing is creating a favorable environment for companies that are actively pursuing circular economy practices. Investors who prioritize ESG factors are more likely to direct capital toward businesses that adopt sustainable models, including those that focus on waste reduction, resource recycling, and closed-loop production systems(Zairis et al., 2024). As sustainable finance instruments such as green bonds and ESG-aligned funds gain popularity, they create new opportunities for businesses to integrate circular economy principles into their operations.

7.4 Promoting Gender Equality and Social Equity through Sustainable Finance

Sustainable finance plays an essential role in fostering inclusive development and addressing societal inequalities. By prioritizing investments that promote social equity, sustainable finance can directly contribute to advancing gender equality and tackling other critical social challenges. This section explores the role of sustainable finance in driving gender equity and social inclusion, with a focus on gender-lens investing, addressing social inequalities, and providing solutions for essential services like clean water, sanitation, and affordable housing(Pilaj, 2017).

Gender-lens investing is a growing approach that directs capital toward businesses and projects that promote gender equality and empower women(Ferri & Acosta, 2019). Sustainable finance provides a platform for investors to consider gender-specific outcomes in their investment decisions, encouraging greater social equity in the marketplace.

Women are increasingly interested in Socially Responsible Investing (SRI) and are more likely to prioritize ESG factors compared to men. For instance, women are often more inclined to support companies with fair employee compensation practices, environmentally responsible operations, and ethical business practices(Nicholls, 2021). This trend presents a unique opportunity to leverage gender-lens investing by creating financial products specifically targeted at women investors who prioritize gender equity.

Investing in Women-Owned Businesses: Gender-lens investing could involve actively channeling capital to women-owned enterprises, or supporting companies that have robust gender diversity and equity practices in place. Investors could seek businesses that offer leadership opportunities for women or have policies in place to support equal pay and opportunities for advancement.

Promoting Gender Diversity: Additionally, sustainable finance could focus on investing in companies that are committed to fostering gender diversity in the workplace. This would include companies with clear policies and practices aimed at ensuring gender equity in recruitment, pay, and career advancement, creating more inclusive work environments.

7.5 Addressing Social Inequalities

Sustainable finance plays a crucial role in addressing social disparities in education, healthcare, and access to essential services like clean water and housing. ESG investments that prioritize social outcomes help create more equitable societies by providing critical services to underserved populations (Yucel et al., 2023). In education, ESG investing encourages support for companies that offer affordable, accessible, and quality education, fostering social mobility and gender equity, particularly in low-income regions. Similarly, in healthcare, ESG investments can fund companies developing affordable healthcare technologies or providing services in underserved areas, thereby improving health outcomes and reducing disparities.

Sustainable finance mechanisms are also instrumental in addressing critical infrastructure needs. Social Impact Bonds (SIBs) can fund social projects targeting clean water access, sanitation, and poverty alleviation, with investor returns tied to measurable outcomes like improved water quality or health metrics(Ferri & Acosta, 2019). Green bonds, traditionally used for environmental projects, can finance sustainable water infrastructure in water-scarce regions, enhancing access to clean water and resilience to climate change. Additionally, ESG investments in affordable housing initiatives can direct capital toward low-cost, sustainable housing developments, addressing urban housing shortages and supporting population growth. Together, these sustainable finance strategies demonstrate their potential to drive meaningful social progress and foster inclusive development.

7.6 Encouraging Public-Private Partnerships (PPPs) for Social Innovation

Public Private Partnerships (PPPs) have emerged as a powerful model for driving social innovation by leveraging the strengths and resources of governments, private investors, and non-profit organizations. By pooling their respective assets—public funding and policy frameworks from governments, financial capital and innovation from the private sector, and community expertise from non-profits—PPPs can effectively tackle complex social challenges. This section delves into the potential of PPPs to foster scalable social innovation and highlights examples and mechanisms that contribute to their success(Pilaj, 2017).The collaboration between governments, private investors, and non-profits creates synergies that enhance the impact of social innovation projects. Each sector brings valuable resources to the table:

Governments: Provide public funding, policy frameworks, and regulatory oversight that ensure projects are aligned with public welfare goals and comply with legal standards.

Private Sector: Contributes financial capital, business expertise, and innovation, helping to design and implement efficient, market-driven solutions that scale more effectively.

Non-Profits: Offer deep knowledge of local communities, social impact expertise, and a mission-driven approach to ensure that projects are designed with the needs of vulnerable populations in mind.

This synergy allows PPPs to access a wider pool of resources and expertise, enabling them to tackle projects that might otherwise be beyond the capacity of any single sector(Ferri & Acosta, 2019). By working together, these sectors can create more sustainable and impactful solutions to social challenges, especially in areas like healthcare, education, housing, and infrastructure.

The Social Impact Accelerator (SIA), the first pan-European Public-Private Partnership (PPP) focused on social impact investing, was established to address the equity financing needs of social enterprises across Europe. Managed by the European Investment Fund (EIF), SIA strategically invested in social impact funds targeting enterprises with the potential to deliver positive social outcomes, such as alleviating poverty and reducing unemployment. Complementing this, the Public Employment Service (PES) model demonstrates the power of PPPs in integrating resources from the Recovery and Resilience Facility (RRF), the Public Investment Program, and InvestEU to collaborate with the private sector on housing policies. This approach maximizes the impact of public funds by leveraging private sector contributions to drive greater social change. Similarly, the Portuguese Social Investment Taskforce, launched in 2014, showcases the potential of multi-sector collaboration among private, public, and social sectors to support social innovation and develop a robust impact investment market in Portugal(Ferri & Acosta, 2019). Together, these initiatives underscore the transformative role of PPPs in fostering sustainable development and addressing critical societal challenges.

7.7 Incentivizing Private Investment

Government policies are pivotal in fostering an enabling environment for social impact investing by offering clear guidelines and financial incentives to attract private investment in initiatives addressing critical social challenges. Programs like InvestEU exemplify this approach, serving as a key European Union funding mechanism to mobilize private capital for social investments. By providing EU guarantees and equity schemes, InvestEU supports sustainable infrastructure, research, innovation, small and medium businesses, and social investment(Zairis et al., 2024). These initiatives demonstrate how governments can effectively incentivize private investors to fund projects that align with long-term social and environmental goals, driving impactful and sustainable development.

8 CONCLUSION

The future of sustainable finance hinges on aligning investor behavior with the United Nations' Sustainable Development Goals (SDGs) to foster long-term sustainability. As the financial landscape shifts, investors increasingly recognize that sustainability is not just an ethical consideration but a critical factor for long-term business success. This transition moves away from short-term profit maximization toward a holistic approach that integrates environmental, social, and governance (ESG) factors. Companies with strong ESG practices tend to outperform their peers, showing that sustainable investments can offer both financial rewards and positive societal outcomes.

A key challenge is encouraging both institutional and retail investors to integrate ESG factors into their portfolios. As awareness grows, investors recognize that aligning with sustainable values can promote long-term well-being. Sustainable portfolios often deliver comparable or superior risk-adjusted returns, demonstrating that sustainability and profitability can coexist. Governments also play a vital role by implementing policies, tax incentives, and regulatory frameworks to encourage long-term investments in sustainability, as seen in initiatives like the EU's InvestEU program and China's Green Bond Taxonomy.

For successful integration, investors must be equipped with knowledge of ESG factors and sustainable finance instruments. Education on ESG risks, returns, and impact measurement helps investors make informed decisions aligned with global sustainability challenges. Key institutions, including universities and financial organizations, must drive ESG education to prepare future professionals and ensure that investors and financial institutions are well-versed in integrating ESG principles into investment strategies.

Raising awareness about ESG investing requires collaboration among governments, businesses, and consumers. A shared understanding of the SDGs and the role of sustainable finance is essential for achieving global sustainability goals. Public campaigns, industry forums, and community engagement initiatives can educate consumers on the impacts of their purchasing decisions, while corporate leaders can align business strategies with sustainability objectives. Engaging local communities ensures ESG initiatives meet local needs, driving better outcomes and building trust.

Cross-border ESG investments, particularly in emerging markets, are critical for advancing the SDGs. Multilateral Development Banks (MDBs), like the World Bank, mobilize capital for ESG projects and provide technical expertise. Initiatives like InvestEU and the African Development Bank's Green Bank Initiative demonstrate the power of multilateral collaboration (Gebreysus Abegaz Yimer, 2024). Harmonizing global standards for ESG transparency, such as the Paris Agreement and frameworks like PRI, GRI, and SASB, is essential to avoid inconsistencies and risks like greenwashing.

Measuring and communicating the impact of ESG investments is vital for demonstrating their effectiveness. Frameworks like IRIS+ and GIIRS quantify outcomes such as carbon emissions reductions, job creation, and biodiversity preservation, helping investors assess social and environmental impacts. Highlighting success stories that showcase the dual value of financial returns and societal benefits will build trust and encourage broader adoption of ESG practices across the investment landscape

REFERENCES

Aggarwal, D., & Elembilassery, V. (2018). Sustainable Finance in Emerging Markets: A Venture Capital Investment Decision Dilemma. *South Asian Journal of Business and Management Cases*, *7*(2), 131–143.

Eriksson, S. (2024). The centrality of law for EU sustainable finance markets: Outlining a research agenda. *Review of European, Comparative & International Environmental Law*, *33*(1), 57–69.

Ferri, G., & Acosta, B. A. (2019). Sustainable finance for sustainable development. Center for Relationship Banking and Economics Working Paper Series, 30.

Goel, R., Gautam, D., Natalucci, F., & Natalucci, M. F. M. (2022). *Sustainable finance in emerging markets: evolution, challenges, and policy priorities (No. 2022-2182)*. International Monetary Fund.

Gupta, A., & Goswami, S. (2024). Behavioral perspective on sustainable finance: nudging investors toward SRI. Asian Journal of Economics and Banking.

Nicholls, A. (2021). Sustainable finance: a primer and recent developments. *Asian Development Outlook*, 1-51.

Peltonen, T. A., Sousa, R. M., & Vansteenkiste, I. S. (2011). Fundamentals, financial factors, and the dynamics of investment in emerging markets. Emerging Markets Finance and Trade, 47(sup2), 88-105.

Persad, K., Xu, B., & Greening, P. (2024). Institutional investor behaviour and the energy transition: A complexity framework for accelerating sustainable finance from UK investors. *Energy Economics*, •••, 107444.

Pilaj, H. (2017). The choice architecture of sustainable and responsible investment: Nudging investors toward ethical decision-making. *Journal of Business Ethics*, *140*, 743–753.

Rahman, M. M., & Hossain, M. E. (2024). Green technology, policy and sustainable finance nexus with SDG-12: Moderating effects of stakeholder awareness. *Sustainable Futures : An Applied Journal of Technology, Environment and Society*, •••, 100405.

Sharma, G. D., Talan, G., Bansal, S., & Jain, M. (2023). Is there a cost for sustainable investments: Evidence from dynamic conditional correlation. *Journal of Sustainable Finance & Investment*, *13*(2), 1009–1029.

Vives, A., & Wadhwa, B. (2012). Sustainability indices in emerging markets: Impact on responsible practices and financial market development. *Journal of Sustainable Finance & Investment*, *2*(3-4), 318–337.

World Bank Group. (2024, February 8). *Brazil Sovereign Sustainable Bond: Financing a greener, more inclusive, and equitable economy*. World Bank. https://www.worldbank.org/en/news/feature/2024/02/08/brazil-sovereign-sustainable-bond-financing-a-greener-more-inclusive-and-equitable-economy

Yimer, G. A. (2024). Sustainable Finance in Africa: A Comparative Overview. *Mizan Law Review*, *18*(1), 123–160.

Yucel, O., Celik, G., & Yilmaz, Z. (2023). Sustainable Investment Attitudes Based on Sustainable Finance Literacy and Perceived Environmental Impact. *Sustainability*, *15*(22), 16026.

Zairis, G., Liargovas, P., & Apostolopoulos, N. (2024). Sustainable finance and ESG importance: A systematic literature review and research agenda. *Sustainability*, *16*(7), 2878.

Chapter 10
The Impact of Dividend Declaration Timing on Stock Returns: Evidence From Announcement Date and Ex-Dividend Date Events

Rohit Sood
https://orcid.org/0000-0002-4127-7781
Lovely Professional University, India

Rahul Madhavan
https://orcid.org/0009-0005-7256-5160
Lovely Professional University, India

ABSTRACT

This study will examine the influence of dividend declaration timing on stock returns, focusing on two critical events: the announcement date and the ex-dividend date. Numerous studies will analyze the effect of dividend announcements on the share prices of various companies to determine their impact on share prices. This study will analyze 25 companies selected from 15 sectors of the Nifty 50 index over five years (2020-2024). The event study methodology will be used in this study. Abnormal Return, Average Abnormal Return, Cumulative Average Abnormal Return, and t-statistics of CAAR will be calculated. A paired t-test will be conducted to measure the impact of a dividend announcement on the share price before and after the announcement period. For that 21-day period, i.e., 10 days before the dividend announcement date/ex-dividend date to 10 days after the announcement date and event date (announcement/ex-dividend date), the event window will be taken from the year 2020 to 2024.

DOI: 10.4018/979-8-3373-1404-4.ch010

INTRODUCTION

A stock is the ownership stake in the business. Depending on your country and how you arrived, it is traded on the exchange. Potential Indian investors can trade derivatives, equities, mutual funds, and commodities on the Bombay Stock Exchange (BSE). The primary objective of this organization is to make it easier for regular investors to trade financial products like stocks, bonds, and other comparable goods. Companies can raise money by selling shares to interested parties through public offerings, which are facilitated by the BSE. The National Stock Exchange has come a long way since launching its initial manual trading platform in 1992. The NSE is currently regarded by the majority as a state-of-the-art technological innovation.

Smooth trade, investments, and capital raising abilities from investors, institutions, and governments are necessary to maintain economic growth and development. Exchange markets are therefore essential to economic development and progress. Levine and Zervos (1996) assert that the size of the stock market has a significant role in stabilizing the methods of obtaining capital to better support investments and economic development. According to empirical research, the relationship between economic growth and stock market development has garnered a lot of attention, as seen by the quantity of scholarly studies in this area. They concluded that in developed economies, the relationship is typically positive. The proper operation of the economy depends on the financial securities that are traded on the stock exchange. The stock exchange is crucial because finance instruments need to be broadly available for an economy to thrive. The relationship between organized exchange markets and economic growth has been disputed over time. Many people, including investors, have experienced layoffs or financial difficulties as a result of the economic slowdown and the implementation of various measures, such as the Large-Scale Social Restriction. This could have an impact on the financial market's volatility during the relevant time frame. (Levine & Sara, 1996)

Dividend stocks are the shares of companies that pay out cash dividends to their shareholders on a regular basis. By reinvesting dividends, investors can grow their wealth over time and get income from these payments. Although they might be paid annually or semi-annually, dividends are often given out on a quarterly basis. The dividend payment amount is usually determined by the board of directors of the company based on cash inflows and earnings. Dividend stocks may be a wise choice for investors looking for a consistent income stream or who wish to generate income from their assets in addition to potential capital development. This article will cover a wide range of topics, including what dividend stocks are, the many kinds of dividends, which Indian stocks pay the greatest dividends, how to purchase dividend stocks, and how to calculate them. In an ideal environment, there would be no correlation between stock valuation and dividend policy, according to Miller and

(Modigliani & Miller, 1961)'s dividend irrelevance theory (1961). But according to the bird-in-the-hand argument put out by stockholders would rather get dividend payments than risky capital gains down the road. (Lintner, 1956)

Since, dividend decisions involves a major policy shift, it is assumed that the change in risk, if any, will be substantial. As a result, dividend announcements may raise doubts about the durability of earnings as well as the prospects for future cash dividends. The lesser dividend payments were associated with higher company risk. The findings of Dyl and Weigand (1998) provided credence to the theory that managers' awareness of the firm's risk was demonstrated by their choice to pay dividends. Investors saw businesses that paid cash dividends as less hazardous than those that didn't. However, stock price volatility suffers from a lack of theory underpinning the hypotheses on which tests and conclusions are based in the literature, in contrast to abnormal returns computed using event studies . It has been acknowledged that information uncertainty has a significant role in influencing fluctuations in securities prices, which represent investors' expectations of risk and return. (Acker, 1999)

There are three main categories for a going concern's dividend payments: interim, final, and special. Only if the firm declares a final dividend at its annual general meeting, after the Board of Directors' proposal, is it payable. On the other hand, where permitted by the company's articles of association, the Board of Directors may issue an interim dividend in between two annual general meetings of shareholders. Nonetheless, a special dividend is typically paid out in line with the company's unique goals. In contrast to regular payouts (interim or final), it is typically non-recurrent and somewhat uncommon. It makes sense to return excess funds to shareholders through a special dividend payment rather than a share repurchase anytime the market value of the shares above their basic inherent value. Managers can generate wealth for the company in this way. Additionally, special dividends might be utilized to change an organization. (Buckley, 2003)

The over-investment problem serves as the firm's continuous justification for allocating capital. In addition to the usual announcement effects of special dividends by Sealed Air Corporation, the manager's deliberate and effective use of financial leverage as a tool to upend the status quo and encourage internal change—including setting a new goal, altering compensation structures, and reorganizing the manufacturing and capital budgeting processes—was responsible for improved post-dividend performance. A model was to explain how special dividends, when funded by debt, help protect the current management from a takeover. Without increasing its shareholding, the management can successfully defend against a takeover attempt by using such a debt-financed special dividend. (Wruck, 1994)

According to the study, stock prices rose as cash and stock dividend announcements increased. According to the findings, there is information asymmetry, and the dividend payout policies and dividend signaling theories aim to close this gap.

The stock price of 28 businesses listed on the BSE 30 Sensex responded to 65 announcements of dividend increases between 2006 and 2009. The study revealed that dividend announcements do have signaling properties and that stock prices do respond to increases in them. The inefficiency of the Indian stock market was another finding of the study.

In underdeveloped nations, investor sentiment was not always so giving. The dividend yield on stock in emerging nations averaged 4.5 percent in 1984, which was higher than the 3.8 percent average for developed country markets at the same time. However, sentiments appear to have changed since then; in 1994, dividend yields in developing countries were just 1.9 percent, which was less than the 2.3 percent average for industrialized countries. This change demonstrates investors' conviction that stock has strong growth possibilities. However, it also needs to reflect management's deliberate conviction that reinvesting earnings is optimal for shareholders. Dividend behavior in emerging markets is examined in this article from the viewpoints of the firm and investors. It looks at how dividend payouts have changed recently and considers a range of environmental factors that could affect such payments.

In order to optimize their after-tax return, investors should choose to reinvest their earnings when their dividend tax rate is higher than their capital gains tax rate. Naturally, according to this logic, the opposite will occur when the capital gains tax rate is higher than the dividend rate. With the exception of dividend payments, earnings are essentially invisible to investors. A higher stock price today results from management's choice to raise dividends because it sends a reliable signal of high future profitability. On the other hand, cutting dividends lowers the stock price and indicates a decline in future possibilities. The notion that businesses should maintain a long-run target payout ratio has created a lot of discussion. A dividend payout ratio is defined as the percentage of earnings that dividends represent. A seasoned company with limited investment options might easily afford to pay out more dividends than a startup.

A benchmark that aids in assessing the performance of a specific industry or the market overall is a stock market index. It tracks the performance and price changes of stocks on a given exchange and chooses them according to certain standards, such as industry sector, market capitalization, etc. The BSE Sensex, which is made up of the top 30 companies listed on the Bombay Stock Exchange, is a great illustration of this. The top 50 equities listed on the National Stock Exchange are also tracked by the NIFTY 50. Before it is credited to shareholders, companies typically announce the quarterly dividend amount and the date of payment. Additionally, it declares an ex-dividend date before which people might buy its stock to become shareholders and receive dividends.

Companies with lower dividend premiums (and hence weaker catering-related incentives) have a stronger correlation between the stickiness of dividends and future earnings. Knowledge asymmetry has a greater effect on cash dividends in companies with lower dividend premiums than dividend premium. As a result, we carry out more research to investigate how catering incentives affect the connection between dividend adjustments and future profitability. More precisely, we investigate whether companies with lower catering incentives have more informational substance in their announcements of dividend revisions than do those with larger incentives. This is because, in the event of increased catering incentives, companies are more likely to alter their dividend policies in order to satisfy the shifting demands of their shareholders for cash payouts (as a dominant effect), rather than to give indications of their anticipated future profitability. In order to create two groups—those with higher and lesser catering incentives—we use the dividend premium and the market-to-book ratio as indicators of market sentiment. We next investigate the relationship between all dividend change kinds in those groups and future profitability. Our findings seem to indicate that companies with lower market attitudes do not support the catering incentives. (James & Lee, 2021)

The relationship between dividends and earnings in the US, there is a strong (insignificant) correlation between dividends and present (future) earnings. Fukuda (2000) finds that dividends' information content is not very strong. Use a nonlinear method and find no evidence of a correlation between dividend changes and future profitability. Dividend announcements don't predict future earnings; instead, they reveal information about cash flow volatility. (Benartzi et, 1997)

The ex-dividend date, which is the first trading day on which new stock purchasers are not eligible for the impending dividend payment, is a significant point in the dividend lifecycle. As previously stated, because new buyers will not be receiving the impending distribution, the stock price usually declines by a sum that is comparable to the dividend value on this date. A well-known feature of dividend announcements, this adjustment takes place independent of company news or the overall state of the market. The decline in stock prices may cause confusion for investors unfamiliar with the ex-dividend date, but this price adjustment is entirely mechanical and does not indicate a shift in the company's intrinsic value. However, investment behavior and market mood may have an impact on this decline. For instance, the stock price might not decrease by the entire dividend amount on the ex-dividend date if the market believes the dividend will indicate great future performance or if the company's dividend payout is thought to be abnormally high.

Investor loyalty and trust can be strongly impacted by a company's dividend policy's dependability and regularity. A corporation that values shareholder returns and is dedicated to giving investors a portion of its earnings is frequently linked to a consistent dividend policy. For individual investors who depend on dividends as their main source of income, this might be very crucial. These income-focused investors, who might not place a high value on capital gains, frequently support businesses that pay out a steady and increasing dividend, and they might grow rather devoted to these companies. Therefore, even in the face of larger general market swings, businesses with a solid dividend history have a higher chance of retaining long-term investors and lowering stock price volatility. The confidence of investors may be damaged by businesses that regularly change their dividend policy, particularly those that abruptly reduce or stop paying dividends. Perceptions of inconsistency or a lack of financial stability may result from such adjustments. The market can view an abrupt dividend cut as an indication of deeper problems, such diminishing cash flows or subpar management. Investors may decide to sell their shares as a result, which would lower the value of the company's stock. Investor loyalty might occasionally be lost for a long time because shareholders may become apprehensive about the company's prospects, especially if the dividend cut indicates financial instability.

The expenses related to conflicts of interest between shareholders and management are referred to as agency costs in corporate finance. Dividends can help offset these expenses in part by lowering management's cash flow, which restricts their capacity to fund initiatives that don't add value for shareholders. Management may be tempted to spend earnings for empire-building endeavors or inefficient investments that would not benefit shareholders when businesses choose to keep their profits rather than distribute dividends. Businesses guarantee that profits are distributed to shareholders rather than perhaps being abused by management by paying dividends. The "free cash flow hypothesis" is the term for this (Jensen, 1986). By bringing management and shareholders' interests into alignment, the dividend payout lowers the likelihood of reckless risk-taking or ineffective capital allocation.

Dividends can be viewed in this way as a means of enhancing company governance. Because they are answerable to shareholders who anticipate constant returns, companies that implement a consistent and clear dividend policy are less likely to engage in value-destroying actions. Because markets tend to reward companies with solid governance and congruence between shareholder interests and management actions, this can boost investor confidence and result in higher stock prices. Conversely, businesses with a history of low dividend payments can be seen as having less effective governance, which could lead to lower stock prices and a greater perception of risk.

Dividend policies, in particular, assist businesses in upholding financial discipline, coordinating management and shareholder interests, and giving investors a steady revenue stream. However, because they indicate possible financial difficulties or changes in the company's growth strategy, dividend policy changes—particularly cutbacks or omissions—can have a substantial negative effect on stock values. To preserve investor confidence and optimize stock price performance, businesses must so carefully balance their dividend payments with their growth goals, capital structure requirements, and market conditions.

Earlier studies indicate that news of dividend increases typically leads to a rise in stock prices, while announcements of dividend payout reductions tend to result in price declines. However, considerable research suggests that a company's dividend announcement may not necessarily lead to abnormal returns. The primary aim of this research paper is to delve into this issue and provide a deeper understanding of an ongoing debate. Dividends play a significant role for investors who seek a steady income. Despite ongoing discussions among investors, the impact of dividend announcements on share prices remains a contentious issue. This study aims to provide clarity on the matter.

LITERATURE REVIEW

Bao Ngoc and Chi Cuong (2016) studied the impact of dividend policy on stock returns. They investigated the reaction of stock prices on the dividend announcement date and the ex-dividend date. The study analyzed dividend-related events from 432 listed companies in Vietnam from 2008 to 2015. They used event study methodology to estimate abnormal returns to the shares around the announcement date and the ex-dividend date. The results showed that the effect of dividend announcement on stock return is positive around the announcement date. Additionally, the stock price increased as the ex-dividend date approached, but then decreased from this date onwards.

Rawat and Jessica (2016) conducted a study on the impact of the ex-dividend day on stock returns for Indian companies listed under Nifty 50 companies from 2011 to 2015. They analyzed the daily abnormal returns for event windows of 61 days, 31 days, and 11 days, using the event study methodology with an estimation period of 250 days before the ex-dividend date. They calculated the Average Abnormal Returns using parametric and non-parametric tests (paired t-test and Wilcoxon Signed Rank Test). The results indicated significantly high actual returns during the pre-announcement period, suggesting a positive market reaction.

Legenzova et al.(2017) analyzed and evaluated the dividend announcement impact on stock prices of companies listed on the NASDAQ OMX Baltic market during 2010–2015. They used the market model event study analysis and calculated AARs based on 3 strategies, where they assumed that investors bought shares 30 days before the dividend announcement and sold them either 1, 3, or 7 days after the dividend announcement. The analysis in the end revealed that positive AARs can be obtained while buying stocks on the NASDAQ OMX Baltic 30 days before the dividend announcement and selling 1, 3, or 7 days after the dividend announcement.

Jella and Shekhar (2018) conducted a study on the impact of dividend announcements on stock prices. They focused on Nifty 100 companies that declared special dividends between 2015 and 2018. The study utilized a market model and regression model to estimate beta, which was then used to calculate the expected return, Abnormal Return (AR), and Cumulative Average Abnormal Return (CAAR). Additionally, they employed event study methodology and analyzed a timeframe of 41 trading days surrounding the event (-20 days, 0 days, and +20 days). The study concluded that investors could earn abnormal returns only in the two days following a special dividend announcement.

Kreidl (2020) examined stock prices and the number of stocks traded around ex-dividend dates of German stocks with tax-free dividends. They took German stocks with tax-free dividend payments between the years 2002 and 2019 as empirical data samples and analyzed them using price drop ratios, average abnormal return, and other descriptive techniques. The results showed that an increased number of stocks were traded around ex-dates at all trading venues.

Dahal and Das (2021) conducted a study on the Indian stock market's response to corporate dividend announcements, with a specific focus on the reaction to dividend announcements by banks. They selected the top ten banking sector companies based on market capitalization as per moneycontrol.com, listed on both NSE and BSE, and collected dividend announcement dates from January 1, 2011, to December 31, 2019. The study utilized an event study methodology, including event study, event day, event window, and estimation window. The event window considered in the study is 21 days (-10 to +10), and the estimation period is 120 days prior to the event window. The OLS market model was used to calculate abnormal returns, average abnormal returns, and cumulative average abnormal returns. The study's findings indicated that public sector banks are not significantly impacted by dividend announcements.

Qadar et al. (2023) aimed to examine the movement of stock price and trading volumes around ex-dividend dates in Pakistan Stock Exchange-listed companies for the period 2018 - 2020. They used standard event study research techniques to investigate the presence of abnormal returns and trading volume by calculating price drop ratios and abnormal returns. The results indicate buying pressure before the event and selling pressure after it.

Halife and Karroum (2023) conducted a study on how share prices on the Istanbul Stock Exchange react after dividends are distributed. They utilized data from the Daily Returns Series from the Turkish Financial Market spanning the years 2011 to 2017. An event study methodology was employed to predict the security's response to an event announcement, and abnormal return, average abnormal return, and cumulative average abnormal return were calculated for analysis. The empirical findings of the study revealed that stock prices do change after dividend announcements, indicating a significant impact of dividend announcements on stock prices.

Mahirun et al. (2023) conducted a research analysis using dividend policy as an intervening variable to assess the impact of firm value and capital structure on firm value. The analysis focused on companies included in the LQ45 index on the Indonesia Stock Exchange during the 2012 - 2021 period. They utilized the Dividend Payout Ratio (DPR) as a primary indicator to examine how this ratio influences stock prices and also explored how DPR is influenced by other ratios using descriptive statistics. The study's findings indicated that dividend policy, as measured by the DPR indicator, did not mediate funding policy and firm value to increase stock prices. Additionally, the study revealed that the dividend policy did not attract investors to buy shares and increase transactions.

Dahal and Das (2023) determined the behavior of stock of the Indian banking sector around the announcements of dividends before and during the global health crisis of 2019. The study considered all the banks in the Indian banking sector that announced the dividend from January 2015 to December 2021 and conducted the analysis using event study methodology with the Multi-Index Model (MIM). In the analysis, they calculated using abnormal returns (AR), average abnormal returns (ARR), and cumulative average abnormal returns (CAAR) and both parametric and non-parametric tests were employed in the analysis.

Sharma et al. (2023) conducted a study to examine how the announcement of dividends can impact the stock market. They analyzed data from Nifty 50 companies over 10 years from 2009-10 to 2018-19. The study used event study and regression analysis for 31 companies that had continuous profit corresponding to the declared final cash dividend. The event window spanned 31 days, including 15 days before the announcement, 15 days after the announcement, and the dividend date. The study also calculated abnormal returns (AR), average abnormal returns (ARR), and cumulative average abnormal returns (CAAR). The findings suggested that dividend announcements provide new information to the market, leading to movements in share prices. The study also supported the semi-strong form of the efficient market hypothesis.

Kumar et al. (2023) conducted a study to analyze the volatility of share prices around dividend announcements for a sample of 50 firms from 2018 to 2022. They used the Ordinary Least Squares (OLS) regression model to determine alpha and beta values, which were then used to calculate the expected return, Abnormal Return (AR), and Cumulative Average Abnormal Return (CAAR). Additionally, they utilized the event study methodology of the S&P BSE 500 as a proxy to assess the excess return for the sample firms. The study also involved a 200-day estimation window (-230 to -30 days) and a 61-day event window (-30 trading days, 0 days, and +30 trading days) using the market model for analysis. Ultimately, the study found that there was a gradual increase in share price leading up to the dividend declaration and greater fluctuations in the stock price afterward.

Manurung et al. (2024) investigated how dividend announcements affect the stock price of the company on the cum and ex-dividend dates. They analyzed manufacturing companies listed on the Indonesia Stock Exchange (IDX) from 2013 to 2018 by only focusing on the closing price. The Data analysis in this study included descriptive statistical tests, classical assumption tests, and hypothesis testing. The findings of the study revealed that dividend announcements at cum-dividend date and ex-dividend date have a positive effect on stock prices.

Chatterjee et al.(2024) conducted a study on the behavior of stock prices following cash dividend announcements in the Indian equity market. They analyzed 3,671 cash dividend announcements from 2012 to 2019 and identified 817 companies that were part of the Standard and Poor BSE 500 index from April 1, 2011, to March 31, 2019. The researchers used an event study methodology, considering a 29-day event window, 14 days before and after the dividend announcement, and the announcement day itself. They also employed the market model approach to estimate expected returns and computed abnormal returns, average abnormal returns, and cumulative average abnormal returns. The findings revealed that cash dividend announcements do result in abnormal stock returns in the Indian equity market immediately after the announcement. Additionally, the study showed that firms with higher promoter shareholding experienced lower gains on dividend announcements.

Rani Singh and Nautiyal (2024) conducted a study on dividend decisions and their impact on firm performance and shareholder value. They analyzed dividend patterns across different industries and investigated how investor sentiment and market volatility influence dividend policies. The study included 30 companies selected based on their dividend policies and financial performance between 2022 and 2023. They used inferential statistical tools such as null hypothesis and alternative hypothesis to determine the impact of dividend declarations on share prices for specific companies. The study concluded that investors did not show significant sentiment when dividends were declared, and the dividends offered did not strongly attract investors to purchase their stocks. Measures like t-statistics and p-values indicated that there was no significant connection between these dividends and the decisions made by potential investors.

Kumar and Kadam (2024) conducted a study on the relationship between the market price of selected equity shares and dividend announcements. They also examined the impact of dividend decisions on shareholder value. The researchers gathered data from online financial platforms to identify companies that declared interim dividends between 2022 and 2023. They selected 30 companies that provided interim dividends during this period. The data was evaluated using null and alternative hypotheses to determine if there was a significant difference in market share price when dividend announcements were made. The study's findings suggested that companies distributing profits to investors through dividends did not significantly attract investors.

Prakash and Karthick (2024) conducted a study to examine the efficiency of the capital market and the behavior of share prices in relation to the distribution of dividends to shareholders. They focused on a 10-year period from 2013 to 2024 and selected a sample of 12 Public Sector Banks (PSBs) listed on the National Stock Exchange (NSE), analyzing 58 final dividend announcements. The researchers used an event study approach, considering the event, event window, estimate window, and investigation window, and applied a market model to calculate the predicted returns of the sample firms, along with average abnormal returns and cumulative average abnormal returns. The findings indicated that the market anticipated the dividend announcements and reacted significantly early, then corrected its overreaction after the announcement day.

Jagrutiben and Shraddhaben (2024) investigated on the impact of dividend announcements on the share prices of selected IT companies listed in the NSE in India. They used an event study methodology with an event window of 21 trading days, examining 10 days before the dividend announcement date and 10 days after the announcement date. They analyzed share price reactions including normal return, market return, Abnormal Return (AR), t-statistic of AR, Average Abnormal Return (AAR), t-statistic of AAR, Cumulative Abnormal Return (CAR), t-statistic of CAR, Cumulative Average Abnormal Return (CAAR), and t-statistic of CAAR around the dividend announcement period for the years 2016-17 to 2018-19. The study concluded that there was no significant difference between pre and post-announcement periods in the years 2016-17 and 2018-19. However, it found a significant difference between these variables in the year 2017-18.

PROBLEM STATEMENT

The declaration of dividends is a vital aspect of corporate financial management, as it impacts both investor sentiment and stock market dynamics. The timing of dividend-related announcements, particularly the announcement date and the ex-dividend date, significantly influences investor behavior and stock price movements. This research aims to fill the gap by examining the relationship between the timing of dividend announcements and stock return volatility for selected Nifty 50 companies. It seeks to analyze whether any significant patterns emerge around these critical dates, providing insights for investors and corporate decision-makers to understand better how dividend declarations affect market performance.

OBJECTIVES

To examine how the timing of dividend declarations affects stock price behaviour around the announcement and ex-dividend dates.

- To evaluate the abnormal stock returns around the announcement date and ex-dividend date for selected Nifty 50 companies.
- To assess the stock price movements and volatility around the announcement and ex-dividend dates.

RESEARCH DESIGN

This study employs a quantitative research design using secondary data to evaluate the impact of dividend declaration timing on stock returns. The research focuses on companies listed in the Nifty 50 index, selected based on their consistency in declaring dividends during the study period. There are a total of 15 sectors or industries in the Nifty 50 index from which companies have been selected for the study.

Table 1. Nifty 50 Industries/Sectors

NIFTY 50 INDUSTRIES/SECTORS
Metals & Mining
Services
Healthcare
Consumer Durables
Financial Services
Automobile and Auto Components
Capital Goods
Oil Gas & Consumable Fuels
Telecommunication
Fast Moving Consumer Goods
Construction Materials
Information Technology
Construction
Power
Consumer Services

In this study, two companies were selected from each sector of the Nifty 50 index, resulting in a total of 25 companies for analysis. Here are the companies that have been chosen for the study:

Table 2. Selected Companies for Study

COMPANY NAME	INDUSTRY/SECTOR
Adani Enterprises Ltd.	Metals & Mining
Adani Ports and Special Economic Zone Ltd.	Services
Apollo Hospitals Enterprise Ltd.	Healthcare
Asian Paints Ltd.	Consumer Durables
Bajaj Auto Ltd.	Automobile and Auto Components
Bharat Electronics Ltd.	Capital Goods
Bharat Petroleum Corporation Ltd.	Oil Gas & Consumable Fuels
Bharti Airtel Ltd.	Telecommunication
Britannia Industries Ltd.	Fast Moving Consumer Goods
Cipla Ltd.	Healthcare
Coal India Ltd.	Oil Gas & Consumable Fuels
Grasim Industries Ltd.	Construction Materials
HDFC Bank Ltd.	Financial Services
Hindalco Industries Ltd.	Metals & Mining
Hindustan Unilever Ltd.	Fast Moving Consumer Goods
ICICI Bank Ltd.	Financial Services
Infosys Ltd.	Information Technology
Larsen & Toubro Ltd.	Construction
Mahindra & Mahindra Ltd.	Automobile and Auto Components
NTPC Ltd.	Power
Power Grid Corporation of India Ltd.	Power
Tata Consultancy Services Ltd.	Information Technology
Titan Company Ltd.	Consumer Durables
Trent Ltd.	Consumer Services
UltraTech Cement Ltd.	Construction Materials

The announcement and ex-dividend dates for the 25 companies were sourced from 2020 to 2024, with data obtained from 'Prowess IQ', a database maintained by the Centre for Monitoring Indian Economy (CMIE).

The event study method has been utilized in the study to analyze the impact of dividend announcements and ex-dividend dates on stock prices and evaluate market efficiency. This methodology is well-regarded for measuring the economic effects of events by examining security prices in the time surrounding the event day. In this study, we employ the event study methodology to explore how dividend announcements and ex-dividend dates affect stock returns.

In this study, the day of dividend announcement and ex-dividend is the event day. Event day is the dividend announcement day or ex-dividend day also called day 0. Event window consists of 21 days that include 10 days pre-announcement and 10 days as post announcement day plus the dividend date or ex-dividend date.

Figure 1. Event Window

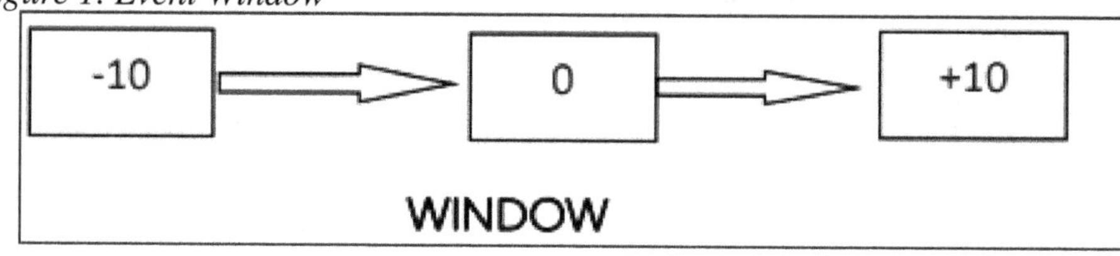

This event window study is employed for all 25 companies.

Estimation Model – The Market Model Approach

The study employs the market model to estimate expected and abnormal returns. The market model establishes a linear relationship between individual stock return and the market return that follows from joint normality:

$E(R) = \alpha + \beta \times Rm$

$E(R)$ = Expected Return on the day t by applying the market model.
α = Alpha (Intercept)
β = beta (slope)
Rm = market return on the day t using the market model

Computation of Abnormal Return

To assess the stock price volatility surrounding dividend declarations and ex-dividend date, this paper calculates the abnormal gains and losses for the event window. Abnormal Returns are determined using the following equation:

Abnormal Returns = Actual return (AR) – Expected Return(ER)

Computation of Average Abnormal Return (AAR)

The AR of all companies on each day of the event is aggregated and averaged.
AAR = 1/N ARit

Computation of Cumulative Average Abnormal Return (CAAR)

It is the sum of the AAR of the specified period.

CAAR = AAR

Computation of T-statistic of CAAR

T-statistic of CAAR = CAAR of the same day / (σ × event day) ^ (1/2)

In addition to this estimation, the present study employs a paired t-test in Excel to determine whether there is a significant difference between the pre-announcement and post-announcement periods. This analysis is conducted at a 5% level of significance. The hypotheses in the study are as follows:

> **H01**: There is no significant difference/impact in share prices during the pre and post-dividend announcement period and Ex-dividend period.
> **H02**: There is significant impact/difference during dividend announcements and ex-dividend dates on the share prices.

DATA ANALYSIS

Figure 2. Estimation of CAAR and ARR of the announcement date for the year 2020

Figure 3. Estimation of CAAR and ARR of the announcement date for the year 2021

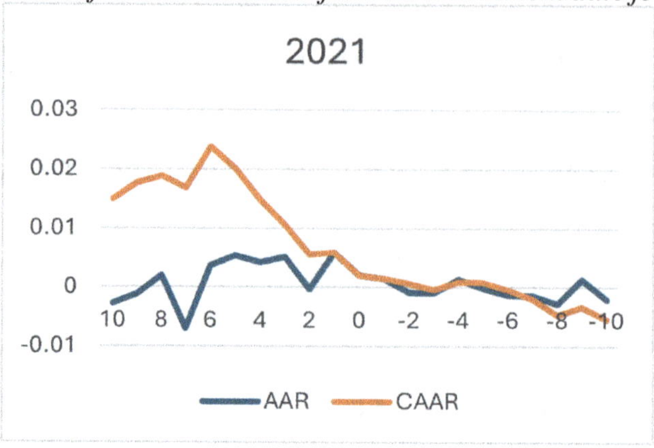

Figure 4. Estimation of CAAR and ARR of the announcement date for the year 2022

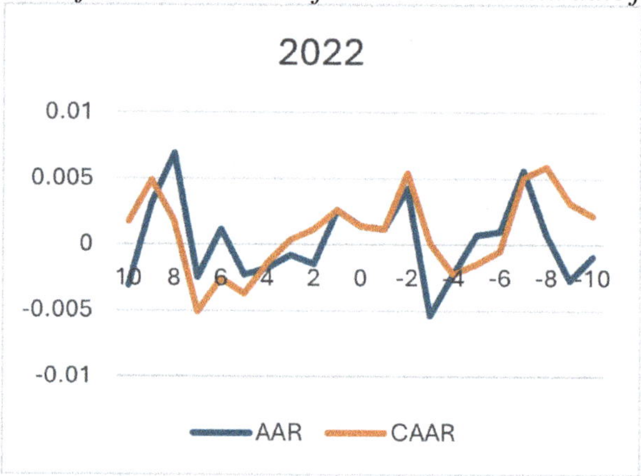

Figure 5. Estimation of CAAR and ARR of the announcement date for the year 2023

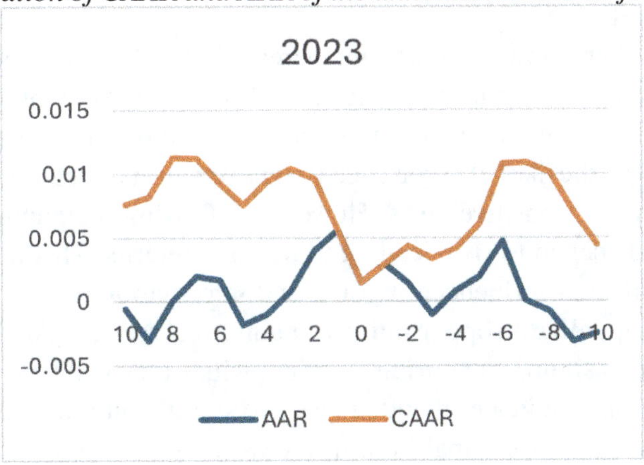

Figure 6. Estimation of CAAR and ARR of the announcement date for the year 2024

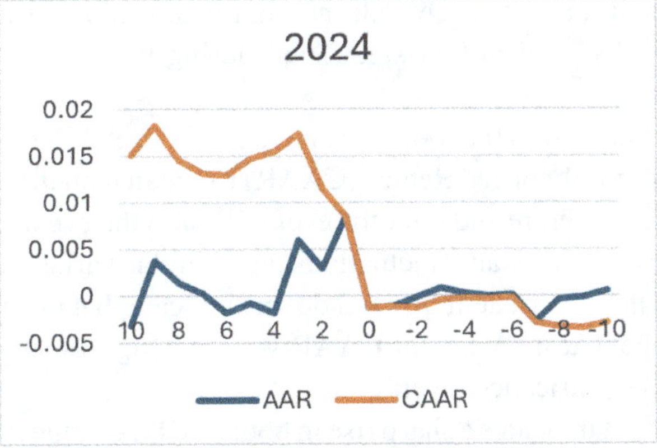

Figure 2 from 2020 illustrates that on the day of the dividend announcement, the Average Abnormal Return (AAR) and Cumulative Average Abnormal Return (CAAR) began to decline, resulting in negative returns following the announcement (event day). Before the event, the market was performing positively; however, after the dividend announcement, it started to yield negative returns. This suggests that market movements are not influenced by dividend information. Consequently, this observation cannot be used by investors to achieve abnormal returns. The T-test values for CAAR were not found significant during the event window at a 1.96 significance level.

In 2021, the chart shows a significant increase in the Average Abnormal Returns (AAR) and Cumulative Abnormal Returns (CAAR) on the day of the dividend announcement, indicating that the event has a notable impact on the market. Prior to the announcement, the market experienced negative returns, suggesting that investors were not anticipating positive news. However, following the announcement, both CAAR and AAR began to rise, leading to positive returns. This indicates that the market's movement is influenced by dividend information. Investors can use this observation to capitalize on opportunities for abnormal returns. The T-test values for CAAR were found significant during the event window at a 1.96 significance level.

In 2022, the chart indicates that there was no significant movement on the event day. Both the Average Abnormal Returns (AAR) and the Cumulative Average Abnormal Returns (CAAR) fluctuated during the pre-announcement phase. Following the dividend announcement, both CAAR and AAR experienced a negative decline for some time. Additionally, AAR and CAAR changed frequently, exhibiting ups and downs in short intervals. This indicates investor attitudes shifted abruptly due to the floating of information. Overall, no significant impact was observed. The T-test values for CAAR were not significant during the event window at a 1.96 significance level.

In 2023, the chart shows that both the Average Abnormal Return (AAR) and the Cumulative Average Abnormal Return (CAAR) fluctuated on the event day, as well as during the periods before and after the event. Prior to the event day, the AAR and CAAR experienced significant fluctuations, and similar variations were observed after the event. These consistent ups and downs indicate that no significant impact was observed. The T-test values for CAAR were not significant during the event window at a 1.96 significance level.

In 2024, the chart indicates a sharp rise in both AAR (Average Abnormal Return) and CAAR (Cumulative Average Abnormal Return) on the event day. Before the announcement, the CAAR is negative. However, on the day of the announcement, the CAAR increases significantly. Following this, the CAAR gradually declined where the AAR remained mostly negative on certain days after the announcement. This suggests that there is little lag in absorbing the dividend information, indicating that the market may not be fully efficient in processing such information. The positive Cumulative Average Abnormal Return (CAAR) suggests that investors have made profits. This indicates that the information regarding dividend announcements for Nifty companies has provided minimal new insights to the market and has had a limited effect on stock prices, as shown in the chart. Additionally, the T-test values for CAAR were found to be significant during the event window at a significance level of 1.96.

Figure 7. Estimation of CAAR and ARR of the ex-dividend for the year 2020

Figure 8. Estimation of CAAR and ARR of the ex-dividend for the year 2021

Figure 9. Estimation of CAAR and ARR of the ex-dividend for the year 2022

Figure 10. Estimation of CAAR and ARR of the ex-dividend for the year 2023

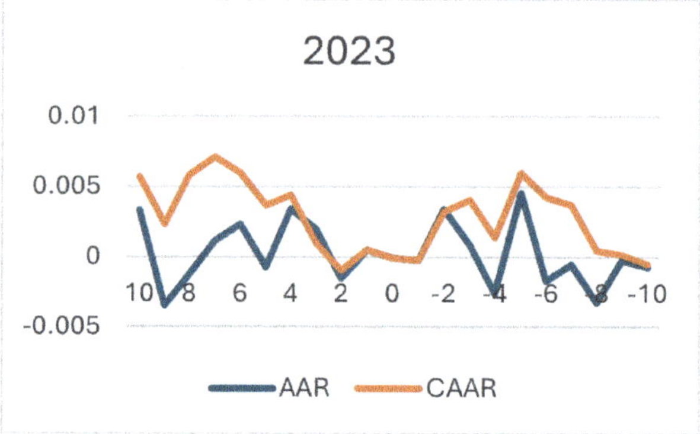

Figure 11. Estimation of CAAR and ARR of the ex-dividend for the year 2024

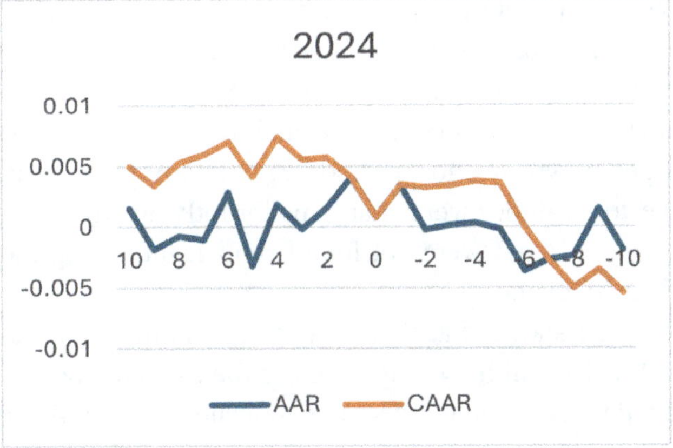

In the above, 2020 chart illustrates that on the day of the Ex-dividend date, the Average Abnormal Return (AAR) and Cumulative Average Abnormal Return (CAAR) began to decline, resulting in negative returns following the ex-dividend (event day). Before the event, the market was performing positively; however, after the ex-dividend date, it started to yield negative returns. The negative CAAR showed that investors incurred losses post the announcement. This indicates that market movements are not influenced around the ex-dividend date. The T-test values for CAAR were not found significant during the event window at a 1.96 significance level.

In 2021, the chart shows that on the Ex-dividend date, both the Average Abnormal Return (AAR) and the Cumulative Average Abnormal Return (CAAR) began to decline, resulting in negative returns following the event. Prior to the ex-dividend date, the market was performing positively. However, after this date, the market started to decline, leading to negative returns, which indicates that investors experienced losses. This suggests that market movements are not influenced by dividend information. Therefore, this observation cannot be utilized by investors to achieve abnormal returns. The T-test values for CAAR were not found significant during the event window at a 1.96 significance level.

In 2022, the chart indicates that there was no significant movement on the ex-dividend date. Before the announcement, both the Average Abnormal Return (AAR) and the Cumulative Average Abnormal Return (CAAR) were fluctuating. Following the ex-dividend, the CAAR declined negatively for a period. Overall, both the AAR and CAAR are changing up and down frequently in every short period. Investor attitudes shifted abruptly due to the floating of information, resulting in no significant impact being observed. The T-test values for CAAR were not found significant during the event window at a 1.96 significance level.

In 2023, the chart indicates that there was no significant movement on the ex-dividend date. However, prior to the event, there were considerable fluctuations in returns, and similar fluctuations were observed after the event as well. Following the ex-dividend date, the Cumulative Average Abnormal Return (CAAR) showed a temporary decline. Both the Average Abnormal Return (AAR) and CAAR exhibited frequent ups and downs in short periods. As a result, no significant impact was observed, as investor attitudes were changing abruptly due to floating information. The T-test values for CAAR were not found significant during the event window at a 1.96 significance level.

In 2024, the Chart shows that there was a fluctuating movement of the AAR and CAAR. CAAR rises initially 6 days before the ex-dividend and suddenly falls on the event day. Post-ex-dividend declines indicate a cumulative negative return, suggesting that investors may be overreacting to the information. The Average Abnormal Returns (AAR) also drop to negative values on most days. The negative Cumulative Abnormal Returns (CAAR) demonstrate that investors incurred losses post ex-dividend date. However, around the ex-dividend date, the selected Nifty 50 companies do not show a significant impact on their share prices. The T-test values for CAAR were not found significant during the event window at a 1.96 significance level.

PAIRED T-TEST

This test is used to examine the significant difference between two variables. In the current study, a paired t-test is applied to determine whether there is a significant difference between the pre-announcement and post-announcement periods at a 5% level of significance.

Table 3. Paired T-test of announcement dates

Paired Samples Test	Sig. (2-tailed)
2020	0.021399659
2021	0.133949603
2022	0.977370183
2023	0.68374261
2024	0.189281032

If the p-value is greater than α (significance level), the null hypothesis(H01) is accepted. However, if the p-value is less than α, the null hypothesis is rejected (H01 is rejected and H02 is accepted).

In the year 2020, the p-value is less than α (significance level) i.e, 0.021< 0.05, which concludes that there was a significant difference between the pre and post-announcement period, the H02 is accepted. For the years 2021, 2022, 2023, and 2024, the p-value is greater than the significance level (α). Therefore, the null hypothesis (H01) is accepted, concluding that there was no significant difference between the pre and post-announcement periods, the H01 is accepted.

Table 4. Paired T-test of Ex-Dividend dates

Paired Samples Test	Sig. (2-tailed)
2020	0.052748
2021	0.736205
2022	0.742272
2023	0.626087
2024	0.284733

For the years 2020,2021,2022,2023,and 2024 the p-value is greater than the significance level (α). Therefore, the null hypothesis (H01) is accepted, concluding that there was no significant difference between the pre- and post- ex-dividend periods. Therefore, the H01 is accepted.

CONCLUSION

In reference to the computation, graphs, and analysis from the event study, the inferences drawn are detailed below:

In 2020 for the announcement date, the data and graph for Average Abnormal Returns (AAR) and Cumulative Average Abnormal Returns (CAAR), along with the t-statistics for CAAR, indicated that no significant findings were observed on the announcement dates. Although the paired t-test showed a significant difference between the pre-and post-announcement periods, there were negative returns following the event day. This suggests that market movements are not influenced by dividend information. For the Ex-dividend date also, the data and graph for Average Abnormal Returns (AAR) and Cumulative Average Abnormal Returns (CAAR), along with the t-statistics for CAAR, indicated that no significant findings were observed on the ex-dividend dates. Even the paired t-test showed no significant difference between the pre-and post- and post-ex-dividend periods. In 2020, we can conclude that the dividend announcement and ex-dividend date did not impact share prices.

In 2021 for the announcement date, the data and graph for Average Abnormal Returns (AAR) and Cumulative Average Abnormal Returns (CAAR), along with the t-statistics for CAAR, indicated that significant findings were observed on the announcement dates. Although the paired t-test indicated no significant difference between the pre-and post-announcement periods, the Average Abnormal Return (AAR) and Cumulative Average Abnormal Return (CAAR) were increasing and yielding positive returns during the post-announcement phase. For the Ex-dividend date, the data and graph for Average Abnormal Returns (AAR) and Cumulative Average Abnormal Returns (CAAR), along with the t-statistics for CAAR, indicated that no significant findings were observed on the ex-dividend dates. Even the paired t-test showed no significant difference between the pre-and post-ex-dividend periods. In 2021, we can say that only the announcement date impacted share prices, while the ex-dividend date did not affect share prices.

In 2022 and 2023 for the announcement date, the data and graph for Average Abnormal Returns (AAR) and Cumulative Average Abnormal Returns (CAAR), along with the t-statistics for CAAR, indicated that no significant findings were observed on the announcement dates. Even the paired t-test showed no significant difference between the pre-and post-announcement periods. For the Ex-dividend date, the data and graph for Average Abnormal Returns (AAR) and Cumulative Average Abnormal Returns (CAAR), along with the t-statistics for CAAR, indicated that no significant findings were observed on the Ex-dividend dates. Even the paired t-test showed no significant difference between the pre-and post-ex-dividend periods. In 2022 and 2023, it can be concluded that neither the dividend announcement nor the ex-dividend date impacted share prices.

In 2024, for the announcement date, the data and graph for Average Abnormal Returns (AAR) and Cumulative Average Abnormal Returns (CAAR), along with the t-statistics for CAAR, indicated that minimal significant findings were observed on the announcement dates, which made a limited effect on stock prices. Even the paired t-test showed no significant difference between the pre-and post-announcement periods. For the Ex-dividend date, the data and graph for Average Abnormal Returns (AAR) and Cumulative Average Abnormal Returns (CAAR), along with the t-statistics for CAAR, indicated that no significant findings were observed on the Ex-dividend dates. Even the paired t-test showed no significant difference between the pre- and post-ex-dividend periods. In 2024, it can be concluded that neither the dividend announcement nor the ex-dividend date impacted share prices.

REFERENCES

Acker. (1999). Cash Dividend Announcements and Stock Return Volatility: Evi dence from India.

Benartzi, S., Michaely, R., & Thaler, R. (1997). Do changes in dividends signal the future or the past? *The Journal of Finance*, *52*(3), 1007–1034.

Buckley, J. (2003). Uncertain Probabilities I: The Discrete Case.

Chatterjee, C., Dutta, P., & Basu, S. (2024). Evidence-based Stock Price Behaviour Around Cash Dividend Announcements in an Emerging Market Set-up. *Global Business Review*.

Dahal, M., & Das, J. (2021). Impact of Dividend Announcements on Share Price of Indian Banking Sector Companies. *Research Gate*, Issue 1, Volume VI.

Dahal, M., & Das, J. (2023). Market Reaction to Dividend Announcements Before and During COVID-19-Evidence from Banking Sector. *SDMIMD Journal of Management*, *14*(1), 383–417.

Halıfe, H., & Karroum, S. (2023). THE IMPACT OF DIVIDEND DISTRIBUTION ANNOUNCEMENTS ON STOCK PRICES: AN EVENT STUDY AT THE ISTANBUL STOCK EXCHANGE. *Journal of Economics Finance and Accounting*, *10*(2), 76–84.

James, & Lee, C.-F. (2021). Does managerial reluctance of dividend cuts signal future earnings?

Jella, S., & Shekhar, V. (2018). A STUDY ON THE IMPACT OF SPECIAL DIVIDENDS ON SHARE PRICE IN INDIAN MARKETS.

Kreidl, F. (2020). Stock-market behavior on ex-dates: New insights from German stocks with tax-free dividend. *International journal of financial studies, 8*(3), 58.

Kumar, G., & Kadam, M. (2024). *Dividend Announcements and Share Price Dynamics: Unraveling the Connection.* Lloyd Business Review.

Kumar, R., Mittal, A. K., & Gupta, S. (2023). Share Price Volatility around Dividend Announcements in India-an Empirical investigation of S&P BSE 500 Index Companies. *Res Militaris*, *13*(1), 3525–3535.

Legenzova, R., Jurakovaitė, O., & Galinskaitė, A. (2017). THE ANALYSIS OF DIVIDEND ANNOUNCEMENT IMPACT ON STOCK PRICES OF BALTIC COMPANIES. *Central European Business Review, 6*(1).

Levine, R., & Sara, Z. (1996). Stock Market Development and Long-Run Growth .

Lintner, J. (1956). *Distribution of Incomes of Corporations among Dividends.* Retained Earnings, and Taxes.

Mahirun, M., Jannati, A., Kusher Manto, A., & Prasetiani, R. (2023). Impact of dividend policy on stock prices. -International Scientific Journal about. *Logistics (Basel).*

Manurung, A., & Machdar, N. (2024). Jacob FoEh, J., & Sinaga, J. (2024). Dividend Policy as a Moderating of the Effect of Dividend Announcement on Stock Price in Indonesian Firms. *International Journal of Economics and Financial Issues, 14*(4), 96–105.

Modigliani, & Miller, M. .. (1961). The Miller–Modigliani dividend irrelevance theory as a warning for investors looking for quick profits from investments in companies paying dividends.

Ngoc, D. B., & Cuong, N. C. (2016). Dividend announcement and ex-dividend effects on stock return. *International Journal of Economics and Finance*, *8*(7), 207–215.

Prakash, A., & Karthick, M. (2024). Dividend Announcement Effect and Informational Efficiency of Indian Capital Market – With Reference to Public Sector Banks. *African Journal of Biological Sciences.*

Qadar, A., Rehan, A., & Hussain, M. A. (2023). An Examination of Stock Price Behavior And Trading Volume Around Ex-Dividend Day: Empirical Evidence From Pakistan. *International Journal of Social Science & Entrepreneurship*, *3*(1), 129–143.

Raj, J. G., & Raj, S. G. (2024). Dividend Announcement and Stock Prices: An Analysis of Selected IT Companies in India. *RESEARCH REVIEW International Journal of Multidisciplinary*, *9*(1), 214–224.

Rawat, L., & Jessica, M. (2016). Effect of ex-dividend date on stock returns of Nifty stocks in India. *People*, *2*(1), 236–248.

Saravanakumar, S. (2011). Impact of dividend announcement on Indian bourses. *Global Business Review*, *12*(3), 401–413.

. Sharma, S., Mittal, A., & Mittal, A. (2023). Distribution of Earning Announcements in Indian Stock Markets: A Statistical Event Study. *International Journal of Applied Engineering and Technology.*

. Singh, A., & Nautiyal, A. (2024). Do dividend announcements impact share price? Lloyd Business Review, Volume III, Issue 2.

Suwanna, T. (2012). Impacts of dividend announcement on stock return. *Procedia: Social and Behavioral Sciences*, *40*, 721–725.

Woolridge, J. R. (1983). Dividend Changes and Security Prices.

Wruck. (1994). Financial policy, internal control, and performance Sealed Air Corporation's leveraged special dividend.

Compilation of References

Aave. (2021). *Aave Protocol Documentation.* https://docs.aave.com/

Abbas, D. M. (2015). Companies Bankruptcy Prediction by using Altman Models And Companring Them. *Research Jounral of Fianance and Acoounting, 6*(14), 16. Retrieved from http://www.iiste.org

Abraham, F., Schmukler, S. L., & Tessada, J. (2019). Robo-advisors: Investing through machines. *World Bank Policy Research Working Paper (134881).*

Abraham, F., Schmukler, S. L., & Tessada, J. (2019). Robo-advisors: Investing through machines. *World Bank Research and Policy Briefs*, (134881).

Acharya, V. V., & Rajan, R. (2020). Lending in the age of fintech: A decentralized alternative. *Journal of Financial Intermediation*, *44*, 100827.

Acharya, V. V., & Rajan, R. G. (2020). *Banks and Shadow Banks*. Princeton University Press.

Acker. (1999). Cash Dividend Announcements and Stock Return Volatility: Evidence from India.

Adams, H., Zins, J., & Weill, L. (2020). Automated Market Makers and the Rise of Decentralized Finance: A Comparative Study. *Journal of Financial Economics*, *56*(3), 120–145.

Adams, H., Zinsmeister, N., & Robinson, D. (2021). *Uniswap v3 Core*. Uniswap Documentation.

Aderemi, S., Olutimehin, D. O., Nnaomah, U. I., Orieno, O. H., Edunjobi, T. E., & Babatunde, S. O. (2024). Big data analytics in the financial services industry: Trends, challenges, and future prospects: A review. International Journal of Science and Technology Researh Archive, 20.

Afrin, R. (2014, January & July). Analysing the potential of Altman's Z-score for prediction of market performance and share returns- A case study of the cement industry in Bangladesh. *The AUST JOURNAL OF SCIENCE AND TECHNOLOGY, 6*(1 & 2), 1-16. Retrieved from https://www.aust.edu/aust_journal_v6i1_2

Aggarwal, D., & Elembilassery, V. (2018). Sustainable Finance in Emerging Markets: A Venture Capital Investment Decision Dilemma. *South Asian Journal of Business and Management Cases*, *7*(2), 131–143.

Akartuna, E. A., Johnson, S. D., & Thornton, A. E. (2023). The money laundering and terrorist financing risks of new and disruptive technologies: A futures-oriented scoping review. *Security Journal, 36*(4), 615–650. PMID: 40479271

Akinci, O., Benigno, G., & Queralto, A. (2020). Modeling the Global Effects of the COVID-19 Sudden Stop in Capital Flows. *FEDS Notes, 2020.0*(2586). https://doi.org/DOI: 10.17016/2380-7172.2586

Alaassar, A., Mention, A.-L., & Aas, T. H. (2023). Facilitating innovation in FinTech: A review and research agenda. *Review of Managerial Science*, *17*(1), 33–66.

Alabi, A. M., Oguntoyinbo, F. N., Abioye, K. M., John-Ladega, A. A., Obiki-Osafiele, A. N., & Daraojimba, C. (2023). Risk management in Africa's financial landscape: A review. *International Journal of Advanced Economics*, *5*(8), 239–257.

Almashhadani, I. S., Abuhashesh, M., Bany Mohammad, A., Masa'deh, R., & Al-Khasawneh, M. (2023). Exploring the determinants of FinTech adoption and intention to use in Jordan: The impact of COVID-19. *Cogent Social Sciences*, *9*(2), 2256536.

Alshari, H. A., & Lokhande, M. (2022). The impact of demographic factors of clients' attitudes and their intentions to use FinTech services on the banking sector in the least developed countries. *Cogent Business & Management*, *9*(1), 2114305.

Alt, R., Beck, R., & Smits, M. T. (2018). FinTech and the transformation of the financial industry. [Springer.]. *Electronic Markets*, *28*, 235–243.

Anderson, J. G. (1987). Structural equation models in the social and behavioral sciences: Model building. *Child Development*, •••, 49–64.

Andria, F., Ananda, D., Rahmi, A., & Bon, A. (2021). Fintech payment application in improving customer services. *Proceedings of the International Conference on Industrial Engineering and Operations Management,* Singapore.

Angeris, G., Evans, A., Chitra, T., & Minca, A. (2021). Impermanent Loss and Stability in Automated Market Makers. *Quantitative Finance*, *22*(1), 90–110.

Anjum, S. (2012). Business Bankruptcy prediction model: A significant study of the Altman's Z-score model. *Asain Journal of management research, 3*(1), 212-219.
Armutlulu, Z. C. (2021). A revision of Altman Z-Score model and a comparative analysis of Turkish

Anuj, C. S., Narayanan, A., Nandan, S., & Thangjam, R. (2018). The relevance of Altman Z-score analysis. [IJRAR]. *International Journal of Research and Analytical Reviews*, *5*(4), 233–240.

Apergis, N. (2024). COVID-19 and US females' portfolio decisions. *International Review of Economics & Finance*, *95*, 103491. DOI: 10.1016/j.iref.2024.103491

Arner, D. W., Auer, R., & Frost, J. (2020). *Stablecoins, central bank digital currencies, and cross-border payments: A new look at the international monetary system.* BIS Papers, 114.

Arner, D. W., Barberis, J., & Buckley, R. P. (2015). The evolution of Fintech: A new post-crisis paradigm. *Geo. J. Int'l L.*, *47*, 1271.

Arner, D. W., Barberis, J., & Buckley, R. P. (2020). The Evolution of FinTech: A New Post-Crisis Paradigm? *Georgetown Journal of International Law*, *47*(4), 1271–1319.

Bakare, S. S., Adeniyi, A. O., Akpuokwe, C. U., & Eneh, N. E. (2024). Data privacy laws and compliance: A comparative review of the EU GDPR and USA regulations. *Computer Science & IT Research Journal*, *5*(3), 528–543.

Balakrishnan, J., & Dwivedi, Y. K. (2021). Role of cognitive absorption in building user trust and experience. *Psychology and Marketing*, *38*(4), 643–668.

Balwani, D. N., Dash, A., Das, A., Das, L., Misra, D. S., & Ghose, D. S. (2019). Robo-Advisory: An Investor's Perception. *International Journal of Psychosocial Rehabilitation*, *23*(3).

Barile, D., Secundo, G., & Bussoli, C. (2024). Exploring artificial intelligence robo-advisor in banking industry: A platform model. *Management Decision*.

Bartoletti, M., Carta, S., Cimoli, T., & Saia, R. (2022). *Security and Stability in Decentralized Finance: A Comparative Analysis of DEX Protocols*. IEEE Transactions on Blockchain.

Batchu, R. K., & Settibathini, V. S. (2024). Sustainable Finance Beyond Banking Shaping the Future of Financial Technology. *International Conference on Sustainable Development through Machine Learning, AI and IoT* (pp. 119--129). Springer.

Beer, C., Maniora, J., & Pott, C. (2023). COVID-19 pandemic and capital markets: The role of government responses. *Journal of Business Economics, 93*(1–2), 11–57. DOI: 10.1007/s11573-022-01103-x PMID: 38013855

Beirne, J., Renzhi, N., Sugandi, E., & Volz, U. (2021). COVID -19, asset markets and capital flows. *Pacific Economic Review, 26*(4), 498–538. DOI: 10.1111/1468-0106.12368

Beltratti, A. B. (2012). The credit crisis around the globe: Why did some banks perform better? *Journal of Financial Economics, 105*(1), 1–17. https://econpapers.repec.org/scripts/redir.pf?u=http%3A%2F%2Fwww.sciencedirect.com%2Fscience%2Farticle%2Fpii%2FS0304405X11002790;h=repec:eee:jfinec:v:105:y:2012:i:1:p:1-17

Benartzi, S., Michaely, R., & Thaler, R. (1997). Do changes in dividends signal the future or the past? *The Journal of Finance, 52*(3), 1007–1034.

Benedek, P., & Bognár, F. (2024). Compliance Risk Assessment–Results of a Comprehensive Literature Review. *Acta Polytechnica Hungarica, 21*(6).

Bhatia, A., Chandani, A., & Chhateja, J. (2020). Robo advisory and its potential in addressing the behavioral biases of investors—A qualitative study in Indian context. *Journal of Behavioral and Experimental Finance, 25*, 100281.

Bishop, C. M. (2013). *Pattern recognition and machine learning*. Springer.

Boinpalli, N. R. (2023). AI-Driven Predictive Analytics for Risk Management in Financial Markets. Silicon Valley Tech Review, 41-53.

Buckley, J. (2003). Uncertain Probabilities I: The Discrete Case.

Bueno, L. A., Sigahi, T. F., Rampasso, I. S., Leal Filho, W., & Anholon, R. (2024). Impacts of digitization on operational efficiency in the banking sector: Thematic analysis and research agenda proposal. *International Journal of Information Management Data Insights, 4*(1), 100230.

Bureshaid, N., Lu, K., & Sarea, A. (2021). Adoption of fintech services in the banking industry. *Applications of Artificial Intelligence in Business, Education and Healthcare*, 125-138.

Buterin, V. (2014). *A next-generation smart contract and decentralized application platform.* Ethereum White Paper.

Buterin, V. (2021). *A rollup-centric Ethereum roadmap*. Ethereum Foundation Blog.

Candelon, B., & Moura, R. (2023). Sovereign yield curves and the COVID-19 in emerging markets. *Economic Modelling, 127*, 106453. DOI: 10.1016/j.econmod.2023.106453

Chainalysis. (2022). *The 2022 Global Crypto Adoption Index.*

Chandani, A., Sriharshitha, S., Bhatia, A., Atiq, R., & Mehta, M. (2021). Robo-advisory services in India: A study to analyse awareness and perception of millennials. [IJCAC]. *International Journal of Cloud Applications and Computing, 11*(4), 152–173.

Chandra, Y. U., Kristin, D. M., Suhartono, J., Sutarto, F. S., & Sung, M. (2018). Analysis of determinant factors of user acceptance of mobile payment system in indonesia (a case study of go-pay mobile payment. *2018 International Conference on Information Management and Technology (ICIMTech)* (pp. 454--459). IEEE.

Chatterjee, A. (2018). Predicting Corporate Financial Distress for Widely Held Large - Cap Companies in India: Altman Model vs. Ohlson Model. *Indian Journal of Finance, 12*(8), 36–49. DOI: 10.17010/ijf/2018/v12i8/130743

Chatterjee, C., Dutta, P., & Basu, S. (2024). Evidence-based Stock Price Behaviour Around Cash Dividend Announcements in an Emerging Market Set-up. *Global Business Review.*

Chellappan, K., Elanchselvan, T., & Abu-Samah, A. (2025). E-wallet Delivery Technology Architecture Adoption: A Review. *Jurnal Kejuruteraan, 37*(1), 219–232.

Chen, B. (2022). The Craft of Color and the Chemistry of Dyes: Textile Technology in the Ryukyu Kingdom, 1700–1900. *Technology and Culture, 63*(1), 87–117. DOI: 10.1353/tech.2022.0003 PMID: 35000960

Cheng, T., Liu, J., Yao, W., & Zhao, A. B. (2022). The impact of COVID-19 pandemic on the volatility connectedness network of global stock market. *Pacific-Basin Finance Journal, 71*, 101678. DOI: 10.1016/j.pacfin.2021.101678

Cheng, X., Guo, F., Chen, J., Li, K., Zhang, Y., & Gao, P. (2019). Exploring the trust influencing mechanism of robo-advisor service: A mixed method approach. *Sustainability, 11*(18), 4917.

Chen, H., Chiang, R. H. L., & Storey, V. C. (2012). Business Intelligence and Analytics: From Big Data to Big Impact. *Management Information Systems Quarterly, 36*(4), 1165–1188.

Chen, X., You, X., & Chang, V. (2021). FinTech and commercial banks' performance in China: A leap forward or survival of the fittest? *Technological Forecasting and Social Change*, *166*, 120645.

Chen, Y., & Bellavitis, C. (2020). Decentralized Finance: Blockchain Technology and the Future of Financial Markets. *Journal of Financial Innovation*, *6*(1), 45–67. PMID: 35024267

Chhabra, A. B. (2005). Beyond Markowitz: A comprehensive wealth allocation framework for individual investors. *The Journal of Wealth Management*, *7*(4), 8–34.

Chong, A. Y. L., Ooi, K. B., Lin, B., & Tang, S. Y. (2017). Predictive analytics in financial services: A review. *Decision Support Systems*, *102*, 102–114.

Cho, S., Lee, Z., Hwang, S., & Kim, J. (2023). Determinants of bank closures: What ensures sustainable profitability in mobile banking? *Electronics (Basel)*, *12*(5), 1196.

Choudhury, A. (2022). India's crypto lending sector: Growth and regulatory hurdles. *Journal of Fintech Research*, *14*(2), 67–81.

Chouhan, ., V (2014, April). Predicting Financial Stability of Select BSE Companies Revisiting Altman Z score. *International Letters of Social and Humanistic Sciences*, *26*, 92–115. DOI: 10.18052/www.scipress.com/ILSHS.26.92

Chueca Vergara, C., & Ferruz Agudo, L. (2021). Fintech and sustainability: Do they affect each other? *Sustainability*, *13*(13), 7012.

Comunale, M., & Manera, A. (2024). The economic impacts and the regulation of AI: A review of the academic literature and policy actions.

Currie, W. L., Gozman, D. P., & Seddon, J. J. M. (2018). Dialectic Tensions in the Financial Markets: A Longitudinal Study of pre- and Post-Crisis Regulatory Technology. *Journal of Information Technology*, *33*(4), 304–325. DOI: 10.1057/s41265-017-0047-5

Dahal, M., & Das, J. (2021). Impact of Dividend Announcements on Share Price of Indian Banking Sector Companies. *Research Gate*, Issue 1, Volume VI.

Dahal, M., & Das, J. (2023). Market Reaction to Dividend Announcements Before and During COVID-19-Evidence from Banking Sector. *SDMIMD Journal of Management*, *14*(1), 383–417.

Daian, P., Goldfeder, S., Kell, T., & Juels, A. (2020). On the Feasibility of Secure DeFi Arbitrage and Front-Running Prevention. *IEEE Security and Privacy*.

Daian, P., Goldfeder, S., Kell, T., & Narayanan, A. (2020). Flash loans and DeFi attacks: Systemic risks in decentralized finance. *Proceedings of the IEEE Symposium on Security and Privacy.*

Darskuviene, V., & Lisauskiene, N. (2021). Linking the robo-advisors' phenomenon and behavioural biases in investment management: An interdisciplinary literature review and research agenda. *Organizations and Markets in Emerging Economies, 12*(2), 459–477.

Davis, S., Liu, D., & Sheng, X. S. (2021). *Stock Prices and Economic Activity in the Time of Coronavirus* (No. w28320; p. w28320). National Bureau of Economic Research. https://doi.org/DOI: 10.3386/w28320

Dellas, H., & Fernandes, A. (2014). Finance and Competition. *Economic Journal (London), 124*(575), 269–288. DOI: 10.1111/ecoj.12055

Deloitte. (2016). The expansion of robo-advisory in wealth management.

Demirgüç-Kunt, A., Klapper, L., Singer, D., Ansar, S., & Hess, J. (2018). *The Global Findex Database 2017: Measuring financial inclusion and the fintech revolution.* World Bank.

Dietvorst, B. J., Simmons, J., & Massey, C. (2015). Algorithm aversion: People erroneously avoid algorithms after seeing them err. *Journal of Experimental Psychology. General, 144*(1), 114–126. DOI: 10.1037/xge0000033 PMID: 25401381

Du, C., Hu, M., Wang, T., & Kizi, M. D. D. (2024). Research on the Impact of Digital Inclusive Finance on Green Innovation of SMEs. *Sustainability, 16*(11), 4700. DOI: 10.3390/su16114700

Ebrahim, R., Kumaraswamy, S., & Abdulla, Y. (2021). FinTech in banks: opportunities and challenges. *Innovative strategies for implementing fintech in banking*, 100-109.

Echarte Fernández, M. Á., Náñez Alonso, S. L., Jorge-Vázquez, J., & Reier Forradellas, R. F. (2021). Central Banks' Monetary Policy in the Face of the COVID-19 Economic Crisis: Monetary Stimulus and the Emergence of CBDCs. *Sustainability, 13*(8), 4242. DOI: 10.3390/su13084242

Ediagbonya, V., & Tioluwani, C. (2023). The role of fintech in driving financial inclusion in developing and emerging markets: Issues, challenges and prospects. *Technological Sustainability, 2*(1), 100–119.

Elbahnasawy, N. G. (2021). Big data analytics and financial decision-making. *The Journal of Financial Data Science, 3*(1), 45–62.

Elia, G., Stefanelli, V., & Ferilli, G. B. (2022). Investigating the role of Fintech in the banking industry: What do we know? *European Journal of Innovation Management, 26*(5), 1365–1393.

Eren, B. A. (2023). Antecedents of robo-advisor use intention in private pension investments: An emerging market country example. *Journal of Financial Services Marketing*, •••, 1–16.

Eriksson, S. (2024). The centrality of law for EU sustainable finance markets: Outlining a research agenda. *Review of European, Comparative & International Environmental Law, 33*(1), 57–69.

Erkan-Barlow, A., & Wells-Dietel, B. P. (2023). The Current State of Cyber Insurance and Regulation in the Context of Investment Efficiency and Moral Hazard: A Literature Review. *Journal of Insurance Regulation. https://content. naic. org/sites/default/files/cipr-jir-2023-4. pdf*

Fadhul, S., & Hamdan, A. (2020). The role of" fintech" on banking performance. *European Conference on Innovation and Entrepreneurship* (pp. 911--XVII). Academic Conferences International Limited.

Faheem, M. A., Aslam, M., & Kakolu, S. (2022). Artificial Intelligence in Investment Portfolio Optimization: A Comparative Study of Machine Learning Algorithms . International Journal of Science and Research Archive, 8.

Farahaan Rashid, R. A. (2023, July). A Comprehensive Review of the Altman Z-Score Model Across Industries. *The Business Review, 27*(2).

Fasanya, I., Periola, O., & Adetokunbo, A. (2023). On the effects of Covid-19 pandemic on stock prices: An imminent global threat. *Quality & Quantity, 57*(3), 2231–2248. DOI: 10.1007/s11135-022-01455-0 PMID: 35789758

Fernando, E. (2019). Analysis of the influence of consumer behavior using FinTech services with SEM and TOPSIS. *2019 International conference on information management and technology (ICIMTech). 1*, pp. 93-97. IEEE.

Ferri, G., & Acosta, B. A. (2019). Sustainable finance for sustainable development. Center for Relationship Banking and Economics Working Paper Series, 30.

Feyen, E., Alonso Gispert, T., Kliatskova, T., & Mare, D. S. (2021). Financial Sector Policy Response to COVID-19 in Emerging Markets and Developing Economies. *Journal of Banking & Finance, 133*, 106184. DOI: 10.1016/j.jbankfin.2021.106184 PMID: 34898821

Figiel, S., Floriańczyk, Z., & Wigier, M. (2023). Impact of the COVID-19 Pandemic on the World Energy and Food Commodity Prices: Implications for Global Economic Growth. *Energies*, *16*(7), 3152. DOI: 10.3390/en16073152

Fulk, M., Grable, J., Watkins, K., & Kruger, M. (2018). Who uses robo-advisory services, and who does not? *Financial Services Review*, *27*(2), 173–188.

Gaunt, D., Xu, Q., & Chen, W. (2022). *Decentralized Credit Risk Management in DeFi Lending*. Blockchain: Research and Applications.

Giglio, S., Maggiori, M., Stroebel, J., & Utkus, S. (2021). The joint dynamics of investor beliefs and trading during the COVID-19 crash. *Proceedings of the National Academy of Sciences of the United States of America*, *118*(4), e2010316118. DOI: 10.1073/pnas.2010316118 PMID: 33468667

Goel, R., Gautam, D., Natalucci, F., & Natalucci, M. F. M. (2022). *Sustainable finance in emerging markets: evolution, challenges, and policy priorities (No. 2022-2182)*. International Monetary Fund.

Goldstein, I., Koijen, R. S. J., & Mueller, H. M. (2021). COVID-19 and Its Impact on Financial Markets and the Real Economy. *Review of Financial Studies*, *34*(11), 5135–5148. DOI: 10.1093/rfs/hhab085

Gopinath, S. (2021). DeFi security challenges and the need for regulation. *Economic Policy Review*, *29*(4), 45–63.

Gormsen, N. J., & Koijen, R. S. J. (2023). Financial Markets and the COVID-19 Pandemic. *Annual Review of Financial Economics*, *15*(1), 69–89. DOI: 10.1146/annurev-financial-110821-020444

Gounari, M., Stergiopoulos, G., Pipyros, K., & Gritzalis, D. (2024). Harmonizing open banking in the European Union: An analysis of PSD2 compliance and interrelation with cybersecurity frameworks and standards. *International Cybersecurity Law Review*, *5*(1), 79–120.

Gozman, D., Liebenau, J., & Mangan, J. (2018). The innovation mechanisms of fintech start-ups: Insights from SWIFT's innotribe competition. *Journal of Management Information Systems*, *35*(1), 145–179.

Gudgeon, L., Moreno-Sanchez, P., Roos, S., McCorry, P., & Gervais, A. (2020). SoK: Layer-Two Blockchain Protocols. *Proceedings of the IEEE Symposium on Security and Privacy*.

Gudgeon, L., Werner, S., Pérez, D., & Gervais, A. (2020). DeFi: The Decentralized Financial Ecosystem. *Proceedings of the Crypto Valley Conference on Blockchain Technology.*

Guo, F., Cheng, X., & Zhang, Y. (2019). A conceptual model of trust influencing factors in robo-advisor products: A qualitative study. *WHICEB 2019 Proceedings.* Available at: https://aisel.aisnet.org/whiceb2019/48

Guo, F. (2020). Regulating investment robo-advisors in China: Problems and prospects. *European Business Organization Law Review, 21*(1), 69–99. DOI: 10.1007/s40804-020-00178-3

Gupta, A., & Goswami, S. (2024). Behavioral perspective on sustainable finance: nudging investors toward SRI. Asian Journal of Economics and Banking.

Gupta, P., & Jain, R. (2021). Cryptocurrency remittances: Implications for India's financial system. *Journal of Financial Innovation, 7*(1), 23–41.

Haddad, V., Moreira, A., & Muir, T. (2020). *When Selling Becomes Viral: Disruptions in Debt Markets in the COVID-19 Crisis and the Fed's Response* (No. w27168; p. w27168). National Bureau of Economic Research. https://doi.org/DOI: 10.3386/w27168

Hakala, J. (2019). Robo-advisors: Revolutionizing financial services through algorithmic investment management. *Financial Innovation, 5*(3), 23–34.

Ha, L. T. (2022). Effects of digitalization on financialization: Empirical evidence from European countries. *Technology in Society, 68*, 101851. DOI: 10.1016/j.techsoc.2021.101851

Halıfe, H., & Karroum, S. (2023). THE IMPACT OF DIVIDEND DISTRIBUTION ANNOUNCEMENTS ON STOCK PRICES: AN EVENT STUDY AT THE ISTANBUL STOCK EXCHANGE. *Journal of Economics Finance and Accounting, 10*(2), 76–84.

Harnay, S., & Scialom, L. (2016). The influence of the economic approaches to regulation on banking regulations: A short history of banking regulations. *Cambridge Journal of Economics, 40*(2), 401–426. DOI: 10.1093/cje/bev023

Harvey, C. R., Ramachandran, A., & Santoro, J. (2021). *DeFi and the Future of Finance*. John Wiley & Sons.

High-Level Expert Group on AI. (2019). Ethics guidelines for trustworthy AI—Shaping Europe's digital future. *European Commission Report.* Brussels. Available at: https://digital-strategy.ec.europa.eu/en/library/ethics-guidelines-trustworthy-ai

Hildebrand, C., & Bergner, A. (2021). Conversational robo-advisors as surrogates of trust: Onboarding experience, firm perception, and consumer financial decision-making. *Journal of the Academy of Marketing Science*, *49*(4), 659–676. DOI: 10.1007/s11747-020-00753-z

Hohenberger, C., Lee, C., & Coughlin, J. (2019). Acceptance of robo-advisors: Effects of financial experience, affective reactions, and self-enhancement motives. *Financial Planning Review*, *2*(2), e1047.

Huang, M. H., & Rust, R. T. (2018). Artificial intelligence in service. *Journal of Service Research*, *21*(2), 155–172.

Huang, Z. (2022). Robo-advisors and the digitization of wealth management in China. In *The Digital Financial Revolution in China*. The Brookings Institution.

Hui, E. C. M., & Chan, K. K. K. (2022). How does Covid-19 affect global equity markets? *Financial Innovation*, *8*(1), 25. DOI: 10.1186/s40854-021-00330-5 PMID: 35251895

Ibrahim, H. (2022). A Review on the Mechanism Mitigating and Eliminating Internet Crimes using Modern Technologies: Mitigating Internet crimes using modern technologies. *Wasit Journal of Computer and Mathematics Science*, *1*(3), 50–68.

Investment Company Institute. (2023). ICI Research Perspective: Trends in the expenses and fees of funds, 2022. *Research.* Washington, D.C.: Investment Company Institute. Available at: https://www.ici.org/system/files/2023-03/per29-03.pdf

Jain, M., & Kumar, R. (2022). *Blockchain adoption in India: A case study*

Jalal, A., Al Mubarak, M., & Durani, F. (2023). *Financial technology (fintech). Artificial Intelligence and Transforming Digital Marketing*. Springer.

James, & Lee, C.-F. (2021). Does managerial reluctance of dividend cuts signal future earnings?

Javaheri, D., Fahmideh, M., Chizari, H., Lalbakhsh, P., & Hur, J. (2023). Cybersecurity threats in FinTech: A systematic review. *Expert Systems with Applications*, •••, 122697.

Jayanthi, M., Amudha, R., Alamelu, R., Dinesh, S., Nalini, R., & Shobhana, N. (2024). AIP Conference Proceedings: Vol. 3180. *Adoption of FinTech payment services-An extended expectation towards core constructs of technology acceptance model.* AIP Publishing.

Jella, S., & Shekhar, V. (2018). A STUDY ON THE IMPACT OF SPECIAL DIVIDENDS ON SHARE PRICE IN INDIAN MARKETS.

Joshi, M. K. (2020, July-December). FINANCIAL PERFORMANCE ANALYSIS OF SELECT INDIAN PUBLIC SECTOR BANKS USING ALTMAN'S Z-SCORE MODEL. *SMART Journal of Business Management Studies, 16*(2), 74–87. DOI: 10.5958/2321-2012.2020.00018.4

KANNADHASAN, M. (2007, June). Measuring Financial Health of A public Limited Company Using 'Z' Score Model. *The Management Accountant, 42*(6), 469–473.

Kaplan, A. D., Kessler, T., Brill, J. C., & Hancock, P. A. (2023). Trust in artificial intelligence: Meta-analytic findings. *Human Factors, 65*(2), 337–359. DOI: 10.1177/00187208211013988 PMID: 34048287

Katsaliaki, K., Galetsi, P., & Kumar, S. (2022). Supply chain disruptions and resilience: A major review and future research agenda. *Annals of Operations Research*, •••, 1–38. PMID: 33437110

Kayani, U. N., Aysan, A. F., Khan, M., Khan, M., Mumtaz, R., & Irfan, M. (2024). Unleashing the pandemic volatility: A glimpse into the stock market performance of developed economies during COVID-19. *Heliyon, 10*(4), e25202. DOI: 10.1016/j.heliyon.2024.e25202 PMID: 38370210

Khudoyorova, F., & Khusainov, F. (2024). Big Data Analytics in Financial Services: Opportunities and Challenges. Excellencia International Multi-disciplinary. *Journal of Education*, •••, 5.

Klose, J. (2023). European exchange rate adjustments in response to COVID-19, containment measures and stabilization policies. *Economic Modelling, 128*, 106494. DOI: 10.1016/j.econmod.2023.106494

Klose, J., & Tillmann, P. (2021). COVID-19 and Financial Markets: A Panel Analysis for European Countries. *Jahrbücher für Nationalökonomie und Statistik, 241*(3), 297–347. DOI: 10.1515/jbnst-2020-0063

Kreidl, F. (2020). Stock-market behavior on ex-dates: New insights from German stocks with tax-free dividend. *International journal of financial studies, 8*(3), 58.

Kumar, G., & Kadam, M. (2024). *Dividend Announcements and Share Price Dynamics: Unraveling the Connection.* Lloyd Business Review.

Kumar, A., & Ravi, V. (2016). A survey of the applications of text mining in financial services. *Computational Intelligence, 32*(1), 1–27.

Kumar, R., Mittal, A. K., & Gupta, S. (2023). Share Price Volatility around Dividend Announcements in India-an Empirical investigation of S&P BSE 500 Index Companies. *Res Militaris, 13*(1), 3525–3535.

Lan, T., Shao, L., Zhang, H., & Yuan, C. (2023). The impact of pandemic on dynamic volatility spillover network of international stock markets. *Empirical Economics, 65*(5), 2115–2144. DOI: 10.1007/s00181-023-02422-w PMID: 37361958

Latif, Y., Shunqi, G., Bashir, S., Iqbal, W., Ali, S., & Ramzan, M. (2021). RETRACTED ARTICLE: COVID-19 and stock exchange return variation: empirical evidences from econometric estimation. *Environmental Science and Pollution Research International, 28*(42), 60019–60031. DOI: 10.1007/s11356-021-14792-8 PMID: 34155586

Lee, H. J., & Han, K. S. (2018). A study on mobile easy payment service based on fintech to reduce smart divide and income gap. *Int. J. Adv. Sci. Technol, 116*, 35–48.

Legenzova, R., Jurakovaitė, O., & Galinskaitė, A. (2017). THE ANALYSIS OF DIVIDEND ANNOUNCEMENT IMPACT ON STOCK PRICES OF BALTIC COMPANIES. *Central European Business Review, 6*(1).

Leshner, R., & Hayes, J. (2020). *Liquidity Mining and the Democratization of Financial Services*. Compound Finance Whitepaper.

Levine, R., & Sara, Z. (1996). Stock Market Development and Long-Run Growth .

Liang, H., & Xue, Y. (2009). Avoidance of information technology threats: A theoretical perspective. *Management Information Systems Quarterly*, •••, 71–90.

Liaudinskas, K. (2022). *Human vs. machine: Disposition effect among algorithmic and human day traders* (No. 6/2022). Working Paper.

Li, G., Wu, H., Jiang, J., & Zong, Q. (2023). Digital finance and the low-carbon energy transition (LCET) from the perspective of capital-biased technical progress. *Energy Economics, 120*, 106623. DOI: 10.1016/j.eneco.2023.106623

Li, J., Maiti, A., & Fei, J. (2023). Features and Scope of Regulatory Technologies: Challenges and Opportunities with Industrial Internet of Things. *Future Internet, 15*(8), 256.

Lintner, J. (1956). *Distribution of Incomes of Corporations among Dividends*. Retained Earnings, and Taxes.

Liu, B. (2012). *Sentiment analysis and opinion mining*. Morgan & Claypool Publishers.

Liu, F., Kong, D., Xiao, Z., Zhang, X., Zhou, A., & Qi, J. (2022). Effect of economic policies on the stock and bond market under the impact of COVID-19. *Journal of Safety Science and Resilience = An Quan Ke Xue Yu Ren Xing (Ying Wen), 3*(1), 24–38. DOI: 10.1016/j.jnlssr.2021.10.006 PMID: 40477849

Lohana, D. (2014, May). Measuring Financial Sustainability of Reliance Industries Limited by using 'Z'-score Model. *International Journal of Scientific and Engineering Research*, *5*(5), 61–72.

Loos, B., Previtero, A., Scheurle, S., & Hackethal, A. (2020). Robo-advisers and investor behavior. *Unpublished Working Paper.*

Lou, A. T. (2017). *Integrating innovation diffusion theory and the technology acceptance model: The adoption of blockchain technology from business managers' perspective.* International Consortium for Electronic Business.

Löwen, C., Kchouri, B., & Lehnert, T. (2021). Is this time really different? Flight-to-safety and the COVID-19 crisis. *PLoS One*, *16*(5), e0251752. DOI: 10.1371/journal.pone.0251752 PMID: 34038444

Lyle, P. (2024). GLOBAL TERRORISM AND NATURAL DISASTERS: Path to Environmental Sustainability, Social and Economic Justice.

Mahirun, M., Jannati, A., Kusher Manto, A., & Prasetiani, R. (2023). Impact of dividend policy on stock prices. -International Scientific Journal about. *Logistics (Basel).*

Malhi, A. S., Kovid, R. K., & Singh, T. P. (2024). Artificial Intelligence of Things (AIoT)-Enabled Personalized Banking: Investigating Intention to Adopt. *Reshaping Intelligent Business and Industry: Convergence of AI and IoT at the Cutting Edge*, 315--324.

Manohar, S., Nag, I., Mittal, A., & Nair, A. J. (2023, 18-19 Aug. 2023). Omni Channeling Healthcare: Chaining Details, Information and Predictions for Extemporize Service Delivery. 2023 7th International Conference On Computing, Communication, Control And Automation (ICCUBEA), Michailidou, F. (2020). RegTech and SupTech: Opportunities and Challenges in the Financial Sector.

Manurung, A., & Machdar, N. (2024). Jacob FoEh, J., & Sinaga, J. (2024). Dividend Policy as a Moderating of the Effect of Dividend Announcement on Stock Price in Indonesian Firms. *International Journal of Economics and Financial Issues*, *14*(4), 96–105.

Maume, P. (2019). Robo-advisor is algorithm-based software that provides specifically tailored investment recommendations to the client based on the client's input. *Bachelor Thesis.*

Maume, P. (2019). Regulating robo-advisory. *Tex. Int'l LJ*, *55*, 49.

McKibbin, W., & Fernando, R. (2023). The global economic impacts of the COVID-19 pandemic. *Economic Modelling, 129*, 106551. DOI: 10.1016/j.econmod.2023.106551

Mehortra, A. (n.d.). Artificial Intelligence in Financial Services – Need to Blend Automation with Human Touch . 6.

Mention, A.-L. (2019). The future of fintech. [Taylor & Francis.]. *Research Technology Management, 62*(4), 59–63.

Mezzanotte, F. E. (2020). An examination into the investor protection properties of robo-advisory services in Switzerland. *Capital Markets Law Journal, 15*(4), 489–508.

Mishkin, F. S. (2007). *The Economics of Money, Banking, and Financial Markets.* Pearson.

Mızrak, F. (2023). Integrating cybersecurity risk management into strategic management: A comprehensive literature review. *Research Journal of Business and Management, 10*(3), 98–108.

Modigliani, & Miller, M. .. (1961). The Miller–Modigliani dividend irrelevance theory as a warning for investors looking for quick profits from investments in companies paying dividends.

Molaro, M. (2023). Analysis of the Open API services in Europe.

Moloney, N. (2024). EU financial market regulation a decade from the financial-crisis-era reforms: Crisis, uncertainty, and capacity. *Yearbook of European Law, 42*, 169–209. DOI: 10.1093/yel/yead008

Muhammad, F. A. (2021). AI-Driven Risk Assessment Models: Revolutionizing Credit Scoring and Default Prediction. *Iconic Research and Engineering Journals,* •••, 10.

Mulla, M. (2019). Sepetember). impact of Operational Efficiency and Customer Satifaction on Banking Performance: Emperical Examination on UAE Islamic Banking. *International Jorunal of Recent Technology and Engineering, 8*, 304–309. DOI: 10.35940/ijrte.B1051.0982S1019

Nag, I., Manohar, S., Mittal, A., & Nair, A. J. (2024). Thought clarity to execution chaos: A review on core competencies of grassroots entrepreneurs for instigation, growth and sustainability of startups. *Journal of Innovation and Entrepreneurship, 13*(1), 89. DOI: 10.1186/s13731-024-00453-w

Nair, A. J., Manohar, S., & Chaudhry, R. (2024b). Securing the Metaverse: Exploring the Role of Artificial Intelligence in Mitigating Emerging Threats in Manufacturing and Service Industries. In B. Verma, A. Mittal, M. Raman, & B. Sindhav (Eds.), *Augmenting Retail Reality, Part B: Blockchain, AR, VR, and AI* (pp. 67-84). Emerald Publishing Limited. https://doi.org/DOI: 10.1108/978-1-83608-708-320241013

Nair, A. J., Manohar, S., & Mittal, A. (2023, 14-16 Dec. 2023). Robotic Vision with Micro Expression Analysis: Revolutionizing Customer Experiences in the Tourism and Hospitality Industry. 2023 IEEE Technology & Engineering Management Conference - Asia Pacific (TEMSCON-ASPAC),

Nair, A.J., Manohar, S., & Mittal, A. (2024). AI-enabled FinTech for innovative sustainability: promoting organizational sustainability practices in digital accounting and finance. *International Journal of Accounting & Information Management, ahead-of-print*(ahead-of-print). https://doi.org/DOI: 10.1108/IJAIM-05-2024-0172

Nair, A. J., & Manohar, S. (2024). Green Service Consumption: Unlocking Customer Expectations on Technological Transformations Enhancing Purchase Experience in Retail Store. *International Journal of Information Management Data Insights*, *4*(2), 100277. https://doi.org/https://doi.org/10.1016/j.jjimei.2024.100277

Nair, A. J., Manohar, S., & Chaudhry, R. (2024a). Role of Knowledge Management in Enhancing the Effectiveness of the Gig Economy. In Ordóñez de Pablos, P., Almunawar, M. N., & Anshari, M. (Eds.), *Strengthening Sustainable Digitalization of Asian Economy and Society* (pp. 161–175). IGI Global., DOI: 10.4018/979-8-3693-1942-0.ch009

Nair, A. J., Manohar, S., Mittal, A., & Ahmed, W. (Eds.). (2024). *Balancing Automation and Human Interaction in Modern Marketing*. IGI Global., DOI: 10.4018/979-8-3693-2276-5

Nair, A. J., Manohar, S., Mittal, A., & Chaudhry, R. (2024). Unleashing Digital Frontiers: Bridging Realities of Augmented Reality, Virtual Reality, and the Metaverse. In Krishnan, C., Behl, A., Dash, S., & Yadav, P. D. (Eds.), *The Metaverse Dilemma: Challenges and Opportunities for Business and Society* (pp. 85–112). Emerald Publishing Limited., DOI: 10.1108/978-1-83797-524-220241006

Nair, A. J., & Rao, A. B. S. (2025). Mitigating Financial Anomalies Dimensions Vulnerability and Stratagem in Service Organizations: Policy and Ethical Considerations in Public Administration. In Akkucuk, U., & Onder, M. (Eds.), *AI Driven Tools for Sustainable Public Administration* (pp. 361–388). IGI Global., DOI: 10.4018/979-8-3693-8372-8.ch013

Nakamoto, S. (2008). *Bitcoin: A peer-to-peer electronic cash system.* Bitcoin White Paper.

Naqvi, H. A. (2022). Role of government policies to attain economic sustainability amid COVID-19 environment. *Frontiers in Environmental Science, 10,* 983860. DOI: 10.3389/fenvs.2022.983860

Nazareth, N., & Reddy, Y. V. (2019). Financial applications of machine learning: A literature review. *Elsevier*, 33.

Ngai, E. W., Hu, Y., Wong, Y. H., Chen, Y., & Sun, X. (2009). The application of data mining techniques in financial fraud detection: A classification framework and an academic review of literature. *Decision Support Systems*, *50*(3), 559–569.

Ngoc, D. B., & Cuong, N. C. (2016). Dividend announcement and ex-dividend effects on stock return. *International Journal of Economics and Finance*, *8*(7), 207–215.

Nguyen, L., Tran, S., & Ho, T. (2022). Fintech credit, bank regulations and bank performance: A cross-country analysis. *Asia-Pacific Journal of Business Administration, 14*(4), 445–466.

Nicholls, A. (2021). Sustainable finance: a primer and recent developments. *Asian Development Outlook*, 1-51.

Nigmonov, A., Shams, S., & Alam, K. (2024). Liquidity risk in FinTech lending: Early impact of the COVID-19 pandemic on the P2P lending market. *Emerging Markets Review*, *58*, 101084. DOI: 10.1016/j.ememar.2023.101084

Odeyemi, O., Okoye, C. C., Ofodile, O. C., Adeoye, O. B., Addy, W. A., & Ajayi-Nifise, A. O. (2024). Integrating AI with Blockchain for Enchanced Financial Services Security. Finance & Accounting Research Journal, 17.

Orelaja, A., Nasimbwa, R., & OMOYIN, D. D. (2024). Enhancing Cybersecurity Infrastructure, A Case Study on Safeguarding Financial Transactions. *Australian Journal of Wireless Technologies, Mobility and Security, 1*(1).

Pala, S. K. (2023). Role and Importance of Predictive Analytics in Financial Market Risk Assessment. International Journal of Enhanced Research in Management & Computer Applications, 6.

Pal, A., Sharma, S. S., & Gupta, K. P. (2021). The Role of Analytics and Robo-Advisory in Investors' Financial Decisions and Risk Management: Review of Literature Post-Global Financial Crisis. [IJBAN]. *International Journal of Business Analytics*, *8*(2), 46–62.

Pandey, A. B., Tripathi, A., & Vashist, P. C. (2022). A survey of cyber security trends, emerging technologies and threats. *Cyber Security in Intelligent Computing and Communications*, 19-33.

Panigrahi, A. (2019, January). Validity of Altman's "z" Score Model in Predicting Financial Distress of Pharmaceutical Companies. *NMIMS JOURNAL OF ECONOMICS AND PUBLIC POLICY, 4*(1), 65-73. Retrieved from https://ssrn.com/abstract=3326312

Paterson, A., Sakariyahu, R., Lawal, R., & Alabi, A. (2024). The Impact of Government Policy Responses to the COVID-19 Pandemic and Brexit on the UK Financial Market: A Behavioural Perspective. *British Journal of Management, 35*(1), 174–191. DOI: 10.1111/1467-8551.12702

Patnaik, A., Kudal, P., Dawar, S., Inamdar, V., & Dawar, P. (2023). Exploring User Acceptance of Digital Payments in India: An Empirical Study Using an Extended Technology Acceptance Model in the Fintech Landscape. *International Journal of Sustainable Development and Planning*, *18*(8).

Peltonen, T. A., Sousa, R. M., & Vansteenkiste, I. S. (2011). Fundamentals, financial factors, and the dynamics of investment in emerging markets. Emerging Markets Finance and Trade, 47(sup2), 88-105.

Peretz, P., & Schroedel, J. R. (2009). Financial Regulation in the United States: Lessons from History. *Public Administration Review*, *69*(4), 603–612. DOI: 10.1111/j.1540-6210.2009.02009.x

Persad, K., Xu, B., & Greening, P. (2024). Institutional investor behaviour and the energy transition: A complexity framework for accelerating sustainable finance from UK investors. *Energy Economics*, **•••**, 107444.

Phan, D. H., Narayan, P. K., Rahman, R. E., & Hutabarat, A. R. (2020). Do financial technology firms influence bank performance? *Pacific-Basin Finance Journal, 62*, 101210.

Philippon, T. (2019). *The Great Reversal: How America Gave Up on Free Markets*. Harvard University Press.

Pilaj, H. (2017). The choice architecture of sustainable and responsible investment: Nudging investors toward ethical decision-making. *Journal of Business Ethics, 140*, 743–753.

Prakash, A., & Karthick, M. (2024). Dividend Announcement Effect and Informational Efficiency of Indian Capital Market – With Reference to Public Sector Banks. *African Journal of Biological Sciences*.

Previts, G. J., & Bricker, R. (1994). Fact and Theory in Accounting History: Presentmindedness and Capital Market Research*. *Contemporary Accounting Research*, *10*(2), 625–641. DOI: 10.1111/j.1911-3846.1994.tb00408.x

Procasky, W. J., & Yin, A. (2023). The impact of COVID-19 on the relative market efficiency and forecasting ability of credit derivative and equity markets. *International Review of Financial Analysis*, *90*, 102926. DOI: 10.1016/j.irfa.2023.102926

Puntoni, S., Reczek, R. W., Giesler, M., & Botti, S. (2021). Consumers and artificial intelligence: An experiential perspective. *Journal of Marketing*, *85*(1), 131–151.

Puschmann, T. (2017). Fintech. *Business & Information Systems Engineering*, *59*, 69–76.

Qadar, A., Rehan, A., & Hussain, M. A. (2023). An Examination of Stock Price Behavior And Trading Volume Around Ex-Dividend Day: Empirical Evidence From Pakistan. *International Journal of Social Science & Entrepreneurship*, *3*(1), 129–143.

Rabbani, M. R. (2022). Fintech innovations, scope, challenges, and implications in Islamic Finance: A systematic analysis. *International Journal of Computing and Digital Systems*, *11*(1), 1–28.

Rahman, M. M., & Hossain, M. E. (2024). Green technology, policy and sustainable finance nexus with SDG-12: Moderating effects of stakeholder awareness. *Sustainable Futures : An Applied Journal of Technology, Environment and Society*, •••, 100405.

Raj, J. G., & Raj, S. G. (2024). Dividend Announcement and Stock Prices: An Analysis of Selected IT Companies in India. *RESEARCH REVIEW International Journal of Multidisciplinary*, *9*(1), 214–224.

Rajput, H., Changotra, R., Rajput, P., Gautam, S., Gollakota, A. R. K., & Arora, A. S. (2021). A shock like no other: Coronavirus rattles commodity markets. *Environment, Development and Sustainability*, *23*(5), 6564–6575. DOI: 10.1007/s10668-020-00934-4 PMID: 32837284

RAMAKRISHNAN, R., & LAKSHMI, C. (2023). UNVEILING THE WORLD OF ONLINE PAYMENT GATEWAYS. SEKULIĆ, J., & LENDÁK, I. An Overview of Cyber Insurance Field Cyber Insurance as.

Rawat, L., & Jessica, M. (2016). Effect of ex-dividend date on stock returns of Nifty stocks in India. *People*, *2*(1), 236–248.

Raykov, T., & Widaman, K. F. (1995). Issues in applied structural equation modeling research. *Structural Equation Modeling*, *2*(4), 289–318.

Romānova, I., & Kudinska, M. (2016). Banking and fintech: A challenge or opportunity? In *Contemporary issues in finance: Current challenges from across* [). Emerald Group Publishing Limited.]. *Europe, 98*, 21–35.

Runkle, J. H. (1993, February). Size and performance of banking firms: Testing the predictions of theory. *Journal of Monetary Economics, 31*(1), 47–67. DOI: 10.1016/0304-3932(93)90016-9

Ryll, L., & Sebastin, S. (2019). Evaluating the Performance of Machine Learning Algorithms in Financial Market Forecasting: A Comprehensive Survey. 22.

Sander, M. (2021). Success factors for robo-advisory: Now and then. *Robo-Advisory: Investing in the Digital Age*, 257-269. Beck, A. D. (2021). The role of artificial intelligence in robo-advisory. *Robo-Advisory: Investing in the Digital Age*, 227-243.

Saravanakumar, S. (2011). Impact of dividend announcement on Indian bourses. *Global Business Review, 12*(3), 401–413.

Schär, F. (2021). Decentralized finance: On blockchain- and smart contract-based financial markets. *Review - Federal Reserve Bank of St. Louis, 103*(2), 153–174.

Sharifi, A., Allam, Z., Bibri, S. E., & Khavarian-Garmsir, A. R. (2024). Smart cities and sustainable development goals (SDGs): A systematic literature review of co-benefits and trade-offs. *Cities (London, England), 146*, 104659.

Sharma, G. D., Talan, G., Bansal, S., & Jain, M. (2023). Is there a cost for sustainable investments: Evidence from dynamic conditional correlation. *Journal of Sustainable Finance & Investment, 13*(2), 1009–1029.

Sharma, S., Koehl, L., Bruniaux, P., Zeng, X., & Wang, Z. (2021). Development of an Intelligent Data-Driven System to Recommend Personalized Fashion Design Solutions. *Sensors (Basel), 21*(12), 4239. DOI: 10.3390/s21124239 PMID: 34205598

Sharma, V., Jangir, K., Gupta, M., & Rupeika-Apoga, R. (2024). Does service quality matter in FinTech payment services? An integrated SERVQUAL and TAM approach. *International Journal of Information Management Data Insights, 4*(2), 100252.

Shiller, R. J. (2012). *Finance and the Good Society*. Princeton University Press.

Singh, S., Sahni, M. M., & Kovid, R. K. (2021). Exploring antecendents of FinTech adoption using adapted technology acceptance model. *Advances in Systems Engineering: Select Proceedings of NSC 2019* (pp. 337--352). Springer.

Singh, A. V., Varma, M., Rai, M., Pratap Singh, S., Bansod, G., Laux, P., & Luch, A. (2024). Advancing Predictive Risk Assessment of Chemicals via Integrating Machine Learning, Computational Modeling, and Chemical/Nano-Quantitative Structure-Activity Relationship Approaches. *Advanced Intelligent Systems*, *6*(4), 2300366.

Singh, P. N. (2021). Decenber). An Empirical Study of Indian Commercial Banks through Financial Distress Models. *Economic Affairs*, *66*(05), 679–683. DOI: 10.46852/0424-2513.4.2021.23

Sironi, P. (2016). My Robo Advisor was an iPod–Applying the Lessons from Other Sectors to FinTech Disruption. *The FinTech Book: The Financial Technology Handbook for Investors, Entrepreneurs and Visionaries*, 152-154.

Sironi, P. (2016). *FinTech innovation: From robo-advisors to goal-based investing and gamification*. John Wiley & Sons.

Srivastava, S., Mohta, A., & Shunmugasundaram, V. (2024). Adoption of digital payment FinTech service by Gen Y and Gen Z users: Evidence from India. *Digital Policy. Regulation & Governance*, *26*(1), 95–117.

Streiner, D. L. (2006). Building a better model: An introduction to structural equation modelling. *Canadian Journal of Psychiatry*, *51*(5), 317–324. PMID: 16986821

Sun, N., Cao, B., & Mu, X. (2024). Research on the Future Trends of the Integration of Artificial Intelligence and Fashion Design of Clothing. *Applied Mathematics and Nonlinear Sciences*, *9*(1), 20242181. DOI: 10.2478/amns-2024-2181

Sun, X., Wang, X., Sun, F., Tian, M., Qu, L., Perry, P., Owens, H., & Liu, X. (2021). Textile Waste Fiber Regeneration via a Green Chemistry Approach: A Molecular Strategy for Sustainable Fashion. *Advanced Materials*, *33*(48), 2105174. DOI: 10.1002/adma.202105174 PMID: 34561908

Suwanna, T. (2012). Impacts of dividend announcement on stock return. *Procedia: Social and Behavioral Sciences*, *40*, 721–725.

Tanjung, P. R. (2020). COMPARATIVE ANALYSIS OF ALTMAN Z-SCORE, SPRINGATE, ZMIJEWSKI AND OHLSON MODELS IN PREDECTING FINANCIAL DISTRESS. *EPRA INTERNATIONAL JOURNAL OF MULTIDISCIPLINARY RESEARCH*, *6*(3), 126–137. DOI: 10.36713/epra4162

Tan, X., Wang, X., Ma, S., Wang, Z., Zhao, Y., & Xiang, L. (2022). COVID-19 Shock and the Time-Varying Volatility Spillovers Among the Energy and Precious Metals Markets: Evidence From A DCC-GARCH-CONNECTEDNESS Approach. *Frontiers in Public Health, 10*, 906969. DOI: 10.3389/fpubh.2022.906969 PMID: 35968447

Tao, R., Su, C. W., Xiao, Y., Dai, K., & Khalid, F. (2021). Robo advisors, algorithmic trading and investment management: Wonders of fourth industrial revolution in financial markets. *Technological Forecasting and Social Change, 163*, 120421.

Thier, P., & dos Santos Monteiro, L. (2022). Robo-advisors typically use algorithms, but those algorithms may or may not use artificial intelligence.

Thier, J., & dos Santos Monteiro, L. (2022). The role of algorithms in robo-advisors: A critical analysis. *Journal of Financial Services Research, 62*(1), 1–15. DOI: 10.1007/s10693-021-00365-0

Tran, T., Han, K., & Yun, S. (2018). Factors influencing the intention to use mobile payment service using fintech systems: Focused on Vietnam. *Asia Life Sciences*, (3), 1731–1747.

Treleaven, P., Galas, M., & Lalchand, V. (2013). Algorithmic trading review. *Communications of the ACM, 56*(11), 76–85.

Vetter, F. (2023). A History of Financial Technology and Regulation: From American Incorporation to Cryptocurrency and Crowdfunding by Seth C. Oranburg. *Technology and Culture, 64*(2), 615–616. DOI: 10.1353/tech.2023.0084

Vives, A., & Wadhwa, B. (2012). Sustainability indices in emerging markets: Impact on responsible practices and financial market development. *Journal of Sustainable Finance & Investment, 2*(3-4), 318–337.

Waller, M. A., & Fawcett, S. E. (2013). Data science, predictive analytics, and big data: A revolution that will transform supply chain design and management. *Journal of Business Logistics, 34*(2), 77–84.

Wang, S., Xie, T., & Liu, L. (2022). *Scalability and Efficiency in Decentralized Finance: A Blockchain Perspective*. IEEE Computer Society.

Wang, Y., Kang, Q., Zhou, S., Dong, Y., & Liu, J. (2022). The impact of service robots in retail: Exploring the effect of novelty priming on consumer behavior. *Journal of Retailing and Consumer Services, 68*, 103002.

Werner, S., Perez, D., & Gudgeon, L. (2021). *Decentralized finance: An emerging alternative financial ecosystem*. Journal of Financial Regulation.

Werner, S., Ko, R. K., & Gervais, A. (2021). Security Considerations in Decentralized Finance (DeFi). *IEEE Security and Privacy.*

Widiasmara, A., Retnowati, W., Alvarez, J. I., & De Guzman, E. K. (2024). The Financial Technology Investment: A Comparative Analysis of Profitability and Performance in Indonesian State-Owned and Sharia Banks. *AKRUAL: Jurnal Akuntansi, 16*(1).

Williams, J. W. (2013). Regulatory technologies, risky subjects, and financial boundaries: Governing 'fraud' in the financial markets. *Accounting, Organizations and Society, 38*(6–7), 544–558. DOI: 10.1016/j.aos.2012.08.001

Wójcik, D., & Ioannou, S. (2020). COVID-19 and Finance: Market Developments So Far and Potential Impacts on the Financial Sector and Centres. *Tijdschrift voor Economische en Sociale Geografie, 111*(3), 387–400. DOI: 10.1111/tesg.12434 PMID: 32836484

Woolridge, J. R. (1983). Dividend Changes and Security Prices.

World Bank Group. (2024, February 8). *Brazil Sovereign Sustainable Bond: Financing a greener, more inclusive, and equitable economy.* World Bank. https://www.worldbank.org/en/news/feature/2024/02/08/brazil-sovereign-sustainable-bond-financing-a-greener-more-inclusive-and-equitable-economy

Wruck. (1994). Financial policy, internal control, and performance Sealed Air Corporation's leveraged special dividend.

Wu, B., & Duan, T. (2019). The Application of Blockchain Technology in Financial markets. *Journal of Physics: Conference Series*, 6. Lewis, R., McPartland, J., & Ranjan, R. (2019). Blockchain and Financial Market Innovation. 18.

Wu, B., Xie, X., Ke, W., Bao, H., Duan, Z., Jin, Z., Dai, X., & Hong, Y. (2022). Merchandising for Sustainable Fashion: A Systematic Literature Review. *Sustainability, 14*(20), 13422. DOI: 10.3390/su142013422

Yaacoub, J.-P. A., Noura, H. N., Salman, O., & Chehab, A. (2022). Robotics cyber security: Vulnerabilities, attacks, countermeasures, and recommendations. *International Journal of Information Security, 21*(1), 115–158. PMID: 33776611

Yeoh, P. (2020). Banks' vulnerabilities to money laundering activities. *Journal of Money Laundering Control, 23*(1), 122–135.

Yimer, G. A. (2024). Sustainable Finance in Africa: A Comparative Overview. *Mizan Law Review, 18*(1), 123–160.

Yoon, C., & Lim, D. (2021). Customers' intentions to switch to internet-only banks: Perspective of the push-pull-mooring model. *Sustainability*, *13*(14), 8062.

Yucel, O., Celik, G., & Yilmaz, Z. (2023). Sustainable Investment Attitudes Based on Sustainable Finance Literacy and Perceived Environmental Impact. *Sustainability*, *15*(22), 16026.

Zairis, G., Liargovas, P., & Apostolopoulos, N. (2024). Sustainable finance and ESG importance: A systematic literature review and research agenda. *Sustainability*, *16*(7), 2878.

Zetzsche, D. A., Buckley, R. P., & Arner, D. W. (2021). Regulating decentralised finance (DeFi): Challenges and opportunities. *Capital Markets Law Journal*, *16*(1), 1–26.

Zhang, R., Xie, B., & Wang, J. (2022). Blockchain, decentralization, and the future of finance. *Financial Innovation*, *8*(1), 23–45.

Zhang, R., Xie, S., & Wang, W. (2021). *Blockchain and trust in the digital economy*. Springer.

Zhao, J., Li, X., Yu, C.-H., Chen, S., & Lee, C.-C. (2022). Riding the FinTech innovation wave: FinTech, patents and bank performance. *Journal of International Money and Finance*, *122*, 102552.

Zhao, Q., Tsai, P.-H., & Wang, J.-L. (2019). Improving financial service innovation strategies for enhancing china's banking industry competitive advantage during the fintech revolution: A Hybrid MCDM model. *Sustainability*, *11*(5), 1419.

Zhao, W., Yin, C., Hua, T., Meadows, M. E., Li, Y., Liu, Y., Cherubini, F., Pereira, P., & Fu, B. (2022). Achieving the Sustainable Development Goals in the post-pandemic era. *Humanities & Social Sciences Communications*, *9*(1), 258. DOI: 10.1057/s41599-022-01283-5 PMID: 35967482

Zheng, C., Wang, Z., Pan, S., Chen, X., & Jia, S. (2023). Does financial structure still matter for technological innovation when financial technology and financial regulation develop? *Technological Forecasting and Social Change*, *194*, 122747. DOI: 10.1016/j.techfore.2023.122747

Zhou, J., Chen, C., Li, L., Zhang, Z., & Zheng, X. (2022). FinBrain 2.0: When finance meets trustworthy AI. *Frontiers of Information Technology & Electronic Engineering*, *23*(12), 1747–1764.

Zhou, Y., Teresienė, D., Keliuotytė-Staniulėnienė, G., Kanapickiene, R., Dong, R. K., & Kaab Omeir, A. (2022). The Impact of COVID-19 Pandemic on Government Bond Yields. *Frontiers in Environmental Science*, *10*, 881260. DOI: 10.3389/fenvs.2022.881260

Zhu, A. Y. F. (2024). Upgrading financial education by adding Python-based personalized financial projection: A randomized control trial. *British Journal of Educational Technology*, *55*(2), 731–750. DOI: 10.1111/bjet.13401

Ziegler, A., & Weller, J. (2021). Robo-advisors and their role in sustainable investing: Evidence from the German market. *Journal of Sustainable Finance & Investment*, *11*(1), 1–15. DOI: 10.1080/20430795.2020.1848140

About the Contributors

Safae Ismaili is a seasoned academic and researcher in economics and finance. She currently serves as Director of Research at Fès Business School, part of the Université Privée de Fès in Morocco. Holding a doctorate in economics and management from the Faculty of Legal, Economic, and Social Sciences in Fès, she focuses her work on financial markets, fintech innovations, circular economy models, and broader topics tied to economic management. With over a decade of experience in higher education, she's taken on key academic and leadership roles. She's been a full-time professor, educational director, and managed institutional partnerships across several Moroccan institutions. Her teaching spans a wide range—market finance, portfolio management, national accounting, monetary economics, and project management. She's also supervised more than 100 master's and doctoral theses. Her research output is both prolific and internationally recognized. She has published in several indexed journals, including Finance & Finance Internationale, Revue Internationale des Sciences de Gestion, Alternatives Managériales et Économiques, and Sustainability (ISSN: 2071-1050). Dr. Ismaili has contributed to numerous edited volumes and shared her findings at key scientific gatherings in Morocco, France, and beyond. Lately, she's been exploring how blockchain technology, sustainable finance, and post-COVID economic recovery intersect with consumer behavior in fintech. She also lends her expertise as an associate editor for The Journal of Contemporary Issues in Business and Government and regularly reviews submissions for academic journals and conferences. She's deeply engaged in educational innovation—championing tools like virtual reality, stock market simulation, and hands-on learning. Dr. Ismaili is affiliated with several professional organizations such as the Société Française de Statistique, the Moroccan Association of Financial Consolidators, and the Women Leaders Association of Fès. Beyond academia, she leads a school-focused nonprofit and mentors students through the JADARA Foundation. Always open to fresh ideas and collaborations, she welcomes opportunities involving research partnerships, cross-disciplinary projects, institutional connections, and developing creative educational programs.

Ramratan Guru, Assistant Professor Level III, School of Design, Mody University of Science and Technology, Lakshmangarh- 332311, Rajasthan,India. Research and Academic Experience: He has more than 10 Years of experience in academics and research. Research Area: His areas of interest include nonwovens, clothing comfort, medical textile, sewing thread/garment, biodegradables, plastic recycling, nanotechnology, sustainable materials and high-performance fibers and Fashion Merchandising. Number of Published papers: He has contributed more than 100 Research papers in referred journals and 51 research papers in International Conferences of repute. He has contributed 15 book chapters published by Intech UK, B P International UK, and Woodhead Publications. He has applied for more than 30 Indian/ International Patents and also 06 books published. Appreciate his research work to U.K., Canada, Australia and U.S.A. Government, Europe, Brazil etc.

Rahul Madhavan is a passionate finance student.

Arjun J Nair is working as a Professor with St. Lawrance College, Ontario, Canada. He has completed a Master of Science degree in Hospitality and Tourism Management from Madurai Kamaraj University, an MBA in Human Resources and Finance Management from the National Institute of Business Management in India, a Bachelor's Degree in Hotel Management and a Diploma in Hospitality Management from the American Hotel and Lodging Association in the United States. He holds professional memberships in several organizations, including the International Management Research and Technology Consortium in New York, the International Association of Innovation Professionals, the American Management Association, the National Human Resources Association and the Institute of Research Engineers and Doctors (Senior Member of the Universal Association of Arts and Management Professionals). With over 15 years of practical work experience in a variety of industries, such as education, exporting, hotel food and beverage, restaurant management and management training, he offers expertise in curriculum development, project management, lecturing, tutoring, general management, business administration, business development, staff management and public relations. He is a strategic thinker who has made significant contributions to training and facilitation, business development and the operations and management aspects of various organizations.

Jyoti Rani, Assistant professor, school of fashion design and technology. Research and Academic experience. 2 year experience in academics and research. Research area: fashion, textile, natural dyeing, consumer behaviour, AI, merchandising. she has published 28 research paper in refered journal and 5 book chapters.

Satish Rao A.B. is an Assistant Professor at the Welcomgroup Graduate School of Hotel Administration (WGSHA) at Manipal Academy of Higher Education. Specializes in Food and Beverage Service and handles practical sessions for first-year students in the Bachelor of Hotel Management (BHM) and Bachelor of Arts (Honours) programs. Holds a PhD in Tourism Management from Madurai Kamaraj University and has several years of teaching and management experience in various educational institutions. Research interests lie in service marketing & Tourism Management.

Preeti Sharma, an Associate Professor, having a rich and varied background in the field of education, spanning over 15 years. Throughout her career, she has served as a faculty member for management in several renowned institutions, including Amity University in Noida, Uttar Pradesh. Presently, she holds a position at Sharda School of Business Studies, Sharda University, located in Greater Noida. Driven by her expertise and specialization in Economics and Finance, she successfully completed her doctoral studies in Applied Business Economics in 2012. She has contributed to the academic community through publications in esteemed journals indexed in Scopus and ABDC. Moreover, she has actively participated in numerous international and national conferences, presenting valuable research papers. Dr. Preeti Sharma also serves as an editorial board member for two prestigious international journals and acts as a reviewer for three journals.

Partap Singh Professor is committed to teaching and research in Finance and Investment domain since last 18 years+. His qualification is PhD (Commerce), M. Com (Finance& Accounting), and MBA(Finance). He has rich work experience in the field of Teaching, administration and research as well. He held various responsibilities like Editor, Co-editor, and Editorial Board member, Associate Editor in number of national and international journals. He has regularly been receiving offers for writing books from the top publishing houses of India and received many letters of thanks& compliments for giving valuable suggestions and commendable views concerning improvement of many leading Publications/Books. He has written and published 5 books namely Financial Management, Risk Management, working capital Management, Management Accounting and Analysis of Financial Statements. Further, he has published more than 60 papers and book chapters in good reputed journals and he has also contributed numerous research papers in national and international conferences or seminars. He has good participation in MDPs. FDPs and STCs as well as Life Membership of reputed academic bodies. His future interest area of research is Financial Market, Financial Derivatives, Technological innovations in Finance& Investment, Artificial Intelligence and Its Impact on Finance and Investment. " Dr Partap Singh is currently working as Professor, Maharishi Markandeshwar Institute of Management, Maharishi Markandeshwar (Deemed to be University) University, Mullana, Haryana, India."

Index

T

U

V

www.ingramcontent.com/pod-product-compliance
Lightning Source LLC
LaVergne TN
LVHW060003031026
849161LV00025B/1350